Marxism and Alienation

Marxism and Alienation

Nicholas Churchich

Rutherford ● Madison ● Teaneck
Fairleigh Dickinson University Press
London and Toronto: Associated University Presses

Associated University Presses
440 Forsgate Drive
Cranbury, NJ 08512

Associated University Presses
25 Sicilian Avenue
London WC1A 2QH, England

Associated University Presses
P.O. Box 488, Port Credit
Mississauga, Ontario
Canada L5G 4M2

The paper used in this publication meets the requirements of the American National Standard for Permanence of Paper for Printed Library Materials Z39.48-1984.

Library of Congress Cataloging-in-Publication Data

Churchich, Nicholas, date.
   Marxism and alienation/Nicholas Churchich.
     p. cm.
   Includes bibliographical references.
   ISBN 0-8386-3372-2 (alk. paper)
   1. Alienation (Philosophy)—History. 2. Philosophy, Marxist.
I. Title.
B808.2.C48   1990
302.5′44—dc20   88-46151
                                     CIP

To Milan and Helena, my parents

Contents

Acknowledgments

I wish to thank the University of London library staff for allowing me to use the books for research connected with this work. Special acknowledgments are due to Veronica Boyle, who kindly read the manuscript and gave valuable advice, and to E. M. Simpson for typing it so painstakingly and making useful corrections.

Marxism and Alienation

Introduction

The problem of alienation is as old as the problem of evil itself. Being related to the metaphysical realm, it inevitably involves speculation and thus resists any satisfactory solution. In the absence of concrete data, no epistemological method of inquiry is adequate in finding the way out of gnoseological difficulties. Not surprisingly, disagreements here are unavoidable. From the non-Marxist point of view, alienation is a psychological as well as a physical phenomenon, involving the whole man as a created being. The conflict between spirit and nature, according to psychologists and theologians, is itself a reflection of the paradox of psychic life. In Jung's view, the conflict between the spiritual and the physical aspects of human existence manifestly indicates that in the last analysis psychic life "is an incomprehensible something."[1] In Hegel's *Phenomenology of Spirit*, alienation is presented as an ontological fact that is deeply rooted in human nature.[2] As a protagonist of Christian religion, Hegel maintains that the process of alienation is an inherent feature of human existence and that the Absolute or Spirit, which in this process "has separated itself from itself," will ultimately "return to its true state."[3] Rejecting Hegel's conception of alienation, Karl Marx (1818–83) gives special prominence to economic alienation, arguing that man in class society not only alienates his "essential being" but also the products of his spiritual and economic activity. In Marx's mature works, there is always an assumption that alienation is the product of private property and division of labor. Here the division of labor and private ownership are regarded as the sign of dehumanization and the source of all evil. Both Hegel and Marx stress that everything short of the whole or totality is imperfect and fragmentary. Individualism is rejected as a negative phenomenon. They argue that particular moments of the whole can never be absolutely true.

The subject of this work, written primarily from the point of view of philosophy, theology, and science, is an exposition and critique of the views of Marx and Marxists on alienation. Following an introduction, I examine in successive chapters theories of alienation; its causes; economic alienation; self-alienation and self-realization; religious, philosophic, scientific, social, and political forms of alienation; and the transcendence of alienation. Marx's views on alienation are contrasted with other views expressed in the Judeo-Christian tradition, psychology, and philosophy. The discussion in the work focuses on the expositions of Marx and Engels as expressed in their versions of Marxism. Occasional references are made to Lenin and other Marxists whose views have some relevant bearing on the subject of alienation. It is, of course, arguable whether Marx would have gone as far as Lenin or Stalin in the exposition and practice of Marxist ideology. One must remember, however, that Lenin, Bukharin, and Trotsky applied Marx's conceptual framework to very complex situations in Russia that Marx himself never considered. Although Lenin's Marxism is considered to be in sharp contrast with the main line of Marxian tradition, he is the principal interpreter of this tradition in the mainstream of twentieth-century communism.

Cogitating on the large range of commentaries—pro-Marxist and anti-Marxist—I have failed to detect anything but disagreements among the commentators. In the domain of Marxist philosophy, as in the domain of religion and politics, disagreements seem to be inevitable. Here there is no measure that would prove in an empirical way where "absolute truth" lies. Not surprisingly, as L. Kolakowski remarks, there is hardly any question relating to the exegesis of Marxism that is not a matter of dispute.[4]

Marx was writing within a particular intellectual milieu and within a time when his position on the subject of alienation was entirely new. Both he and Engels see classical Marxism as a point of no return to the philosophy that has insisted on the primacy of the mind or spirit. While accepting the essential tenets of dialectical materialism, their followers remain noticeably divided over the significance of alienation and dealienation in the history of man. Even in Marx's time, Marxist ideology began to acquire so many different meanings that Marx himself surprisingly enough declared: "All I know is that I am not a Marxist." It is unfortunate that among the many things Marx said about his own ideology, he failed to clarify the meaning of the term Marxism in this ideology. It is Engels who ultimately sanctioned the usage of the terms Marxist and Marxism. Today, as M. Rubel indicates, the term Marxism has been so abused that it is merely a "mystifying catchword."[5] Although in the strict sense Marxism is a body of ideas and theories elaborated by Marx and Engels, it is possible to argue that Marxism in fact is merely the opium of the Marxists whatever brand of Marxism they may represent—Leninism, Stalinism, Maoism, Titoism, or similar forms.[6] Stalinism is, as A. W. Gouldner remarks, a "logical result" of Marxism and Leninism.[7] It is wrong to believe that Stalinism is simply a myth invented to denigrate the Marxism of Marx. This Marxism, like Stalinism, is also permeated by utopian myths. No ideology can exist without myths, and Marxism is not an exception. Myths inspire, unite, and reduce to submission.[8]

For Sartre, Marxism is "the philosophy of our time." This statement is false and very misleading. The point is that today Marxism is interpreted in many different ways, and with the rise of communist states in the twentieth century the divisions and proliferations of different versions of Marxism, all claiming to be "true," have become even greater than in Marx's own time. Some modern political philosophers and sociologists divide Marxism into "critical" and "scientific" Marxism. Critical and scientific Marxists, they maintain, differ among themselves in their epistemology, their politics, and especially in their ideas of alienation and dealienation. While scientific Marxists link Marxism with science and technology, critical Marxists associate Marxism with Marx's early humanism and give more prominence to his essentialist theory of alienation. In scientific Marxism the concept of alienation is replaced by such concepts as exploitation and dehumanization. The so-called Western Marxists prefer to regard Marxism as a critique rather than a science. The Soviet and some other Marxists, on the other hand, treat Marxism as a science, "a theory based on a consistently scientific philosophy and political economy."[9] While the so-called critical Marxists focus their attention on the continuity between Hegel and Marx, the so-called scientific Marxists tend to reject the continuity between the young and the mature Marx.[10]

Although the relationship between the Marxism of Marx and that of the Marxists is important in the history of Marxism and communism, I have no intention of deciding which Marxists deviate and which adhere to the thought of Marx. I argue in the work as a whole that Marx's thought itself is far from being unified and coherent. It is impossible, therefore, to decide who are "the true Marxists." Like Lenin, all Marxists—orthodox and unorthodox—start from the premise that "the Marxist doctrine is true" and claim to be the stalwart defenders of Marxist "truth." Science begins with the belief that the world can be made orderly by human arrangement. The scientifically orientated people accepted the scientific account of the world as the best presently available, not as certainly true. The basic error of every Marxist ideological orientation is its claim that it always represents an objectively valid truth. This attitude is reflected in the institutionalized form of Marxism or communism. In spite of the fact that Marxism is supposed to be an international movement, it is clear that within each communist state a very vigorous national orthodoxy is normally imposed. It is impossible to determine which of these "orthodoxies" truly represent the Marxism of Marx. Lenin and his successors have elaborated a form of Marxism that, as M. Polanyi remarks, doubts the reality of almost everything that Russell and other positive thinkers teach us to respect.[11] Surely, the same is the case with other forms of Marxism. Engels and Lenin treat Marxism as "truth" demonstrated by Marx. Yet nowhere in Marx's writings can that demonstration be found.[12]

The purpose of this work is to present a full exposition of Marx's and Marxist ideas about alienation and to indicate some of their weaknesses and errors. What distinguishes this work from others in the same field is its analysis of all major forms of alienation. There are many original points, and some themes—including self-alienation and self-realization, causes and the transcendence of alienation and scientific alienation—are discussed in some detail for the first time. Marx's ideas are compared with relevant Hegelian concepts in every chapter. It is indicated that Hegel and Marx's accounts of alienation represent different points of view and that their views are necessarily subjective. Marx's claim to "absolute truth," indeed, his "truth view" as a whole, has been rejected. In modern interpretative literature, some aspects of Marxism are sometimes discussed without a single quotation from Marx's text. Because the main purpose of this work is a critical evaluation of Marx's theory of alienation, all statements here relating to the views of Marx and Engels are supported by quotations from their own writings. The views of other Marxists—orthodox and unorthodox—referred to in the text are not only carefully distinguished from those of Marx and Engels but are also supported by quotations from their works. Most of these quotations come from the works of Lenin which, it must be stressed, do not necessarily reflect Marx's own views.

Like any other philosophical system, Marxism has its own contradictions. This occurs mainly because Marx has made many statements about humans and human nature, religion, society, economics, science, and politics that are frequently ambiguous and inconsistent. This is particularly true of his theory of alienation. He has never made it clear whether the process of alienation should be conceived as an eternal and universal human phenomenon or simply as a historical human condition rooted in the movement of private property. Clearly Marx's postulates about humans and human nature lack comparative empirical dimensions that have always characterized experimental psychology and anthropology in general. In spite of his appeal to empirical facts and "the concrete," in spite of his insistence on the need of historical and materialist dimensions in the interpretations of socioeconomic conditions of "existing real men," it is impossible to deny that Marx's fundamental assumptions about humans and their alienation are strikingly speculative and inferential. In his view, labor power, that living source of value that creates capital, is the essential and most important defining character of "real historical man." Yet, his basic postulates about humans and alienation are not based on any real anthropological research. They are rather based, to use his own phraseology, "on arbitrary constructions" and are largely derived from his analysis of capitalist society.[13]

As a dialectical materialist, Marx has no room in his philosophical system for objective psychology. He derived the system of dialectical logic from Hegel and believes that the driving forces of history are material and economic. Although he maintains that man is a "self-creative" being liable to alienation, he rejects the idea that mind or spirit can be a self-sufficient cause of action. The essential forces at work in human development are sought in material conditions and social processes. In Marx's view, base and superstructure are different functions of one and the same *praxis*. This praxis is always linked with the materialist concept of history and dialectical materialism. The self-activating principle, according to this materialism, must be discovered within the historical process, and this process is essentially material. Marx, however, has never clarified the distinction between the base and the superstructure. In spite of his claim that consciousness is the superstructure of a material basis and "must be explained from the contradictions of material life," the role of consciousness is seen as dualistic, vacillating from passivity to activity and, *vice versa*, from activity to passivity.[2] Marx's own reality, it must be emphasized, is not an empirically verifiable entity. Marxist materialism is necessarily dualistic. Although the essence of reality is seen in material production, there is always an assumption that "something" lies beyond the realm of actual material production. As a result, Marx's ideas of alienation are also dualistic, although, of course, they are focused primarily on its material causes and are related to "real existing men," not to the state of consciousness as in Hegel's conception of alienation. In opposition to ideological or psychological alienation, Marx speaks of "real" alienation, alienation that involves socioeconomic relations rather than the human soul or mind. His original theory of self-alienation, however, contains psychological elements.

Marx has failed to formulate a consistent and unambiguous theory of alienation simply because he has failed to produce a coherent view of man and human nature. The idea that man is a conscious, spiritual, self-creative, and self-active being has never been harmonized consistently with the idea that man is merely a sensuous part of nature and a product of socioeconomic relations. The dualism that man is both physical and spiritual is reflected in Marx's theory of alienation. In his early writings, notably in the *Manuscripts of 1844*, he argues in favor of the essentialist theory of alienation. Later, however, he rejects this theory and replaces it with the economic theory in which alienation is identified with such concepts as dehumanization and exploitation. The tension between Marx's essentialist and economic theories, like the tension between voluntarism and determinism in his philosophical system as a whole, has led, not surprisingly, to bitter arguments among Marxists themselves about the relevance of these theories in the theoretical and practical life of man.

Accepting the continuity between original and mature marxism, the so-called critical Marxists are more inclined to treat alienation as an inherent phenomenon of human existence than as a purely socioeconomic product. Their opponents, the so-called scientific Marxists, maintain that the idea of alienation as a whole, let alone in its metaphysical dress, hardly plays any significant role in Marx's mature writings. The idea of alienation is therefore either abandoned altogether or substituted by similar economic categories which, in their view, dominate *Capital*. A special version of this development appears in anti-Hegelian fundamentalism expounded by Louis Althusser. Why, he asks, do so many Marxist philosophers find it necessary to appeal to the metaphysical and ideological concept of alienation to resove "concrete historical problems"?[15] These problems, he believes, can be resolved historically and scientifically without invoking such ideological and metaphysical concepts as alienation, which have no definite or concrete status. Unfortunately, Althusser's structuralist system is so abstract, ambiguous, and permeated with ideological concepts that it has rightly been characterized as a classic example of structuralist metaphysics and idealism. Like other "scientific" Marxists, he claims a complete objectivity for his philosophical system, but he fails to clarify the connections between "ideological and theoretical practice."[16] Like Marx, he frequently confuses philosophy with science. Believing that historical materialism is "the science of history," he argues that Marx's philosophy or dialectical materialism is "the theory of scientific practice."

On the whole, representatives of Western Marxism, especially those of the Frankfurt school, admit willingly that much of Marx's theory of alienation, as well as much of his other theories, in the literal form is essentially a nineteenth-century product and thus irrelevant to modern historical development. They indicate the need for a systematic clarification and reconstruction of historical materialism as a theory of practice. Critical Marxists are well aware that Marxism has become a dogmatic and *a priori* philosophy that in many cases conceptualizes facts and events before analyzing them empirically. The problem of identifying the source of contradictions and ambiguities in Marxism, however, remains as unsolvable as ever. Marx himself must be blamed for most of these contradictions and ambiguities, partly because he underrates the importance of empirical evidence and partly because he never clearly defines his epistemological conception of philosophy as a humanist emancipatory philosophy of *praxis*. This is reflected in his conception of communist society. Vacillating between philosophical and proletarian or crude communism, between the ideal and the real social movement, he has failed to make it sufficiently clear whether socialism and communism are equivalent or different economic systems. Many of his followers are still divided on this issue. Only the Soviet Marxists, following Lenin, have no doubt that "despite all the differences between socialism and full-scale communism, they constitute the two phases of the same system."[17]

Marx himself has treated his work as being primarily critical in character. This is evident from the titles and subtitles of all his major writings. His use of criticism as a weapon against his ideological opponents is not a novelty for the historical period during which Germany was marked by verbal wrangles about freedom, God, the self, reality, progress, dialectical laws, self-consciousness, alienation, dealienation, and similar abstractions. Even before the Young Hegelians opened their campaign "with a burst of artillery fire" against each other and focused their intellectual powers on criticism which, in Marx's view, has always been confined to religious and philosophical conceptions, Kant, the founder of German idealism, argued that "nothing but a sober, strict and just criticism can free" the German writers and philosophers from their "dogmatic illusions which, through theories and systems, have deceived so many by an imaginary happiness." It is only by criticism he says, that "metaphysicians and theologians can be saved from the consequent perversion of their doctrines."[18] Marx does not seem to be much worried about Kant's remark that 'criticism alone can strike a blow at the root of materialism, fatalism, atheism, free-thinking, fanaticism and superstition which are

universally injurious."[19] Like his opponents in the Young Hegelian movement, Marx is interested primarily in criticism that is directed against
religion.[20]

Marx's own theories, including the theory of alienation, have no special
claim to be treated as scientific. The many disagreements among the Marxists,
and the lack of any indication that they will ever disappear strongly indicate
that Marxism is not a science in the English sense of the term *science*, i.e., a
system of knowledge based mainly on observation and experiment, whatever
the German term *Wissenschaft* may have meant to Marx. Some commentators rightly point out that the English translation of Marx's terms *wirkliche
Wissenschaft* as real or true science is very misleading because the word
Wissenschaft, like the Slavonic term *nauka*, refers to any branch of human
knowledge. Disagreements do exist among scientists, of course, but they are
normally on a much smaller scale and are usually resolved without much
wrangling. The disagreements among Marxists are entirely different and
are normally resolved using revolutionary weapons, whatever form these
may take. Marx's science of history or, as Lenin calls it, "the science of communism," is a typical ideological entity, an imaginary substance that resists
any meaningful definition. As a result, "scientific Marxism or scientific
socialism" can only be treated, as John Plamenatz rightly remarks, as a logical absurdity, a myth, and a revolutionary slogan. Being the ideology of the
working class, "scientific communism" is nothing but a theory based on
Marx's conception of history and his one-sided political ideas.[21]

Because of a considerable metaphysical content in Marx's philosophical
system and the presence in it of polymorphous but incoherent diversity of his
thought, Marxism has been torn between revisionism and orthodoxy, between critical and scientific Marxism, between pro-Hegelianism and anti-
Hegelianism, between voluntarism and determinism, between relatively
liberal Western Marxism and Soviet dogmatism that shows no sign of abandoning the dictatorship of the proletariat as a form of government. The Soviet
theorists of Marxism, as Tucker indicates, do not foresee a stage beyond the
ownership principle and deliberately distort Marx's idea of communism as
merely being "the dynamic principle of the immediate future" rather than
"the goal of human development."[22] Unlike Marx, Lenin maintains that even
crude or thoughtless communism is acceptable. He also refers to "complete
communism" without defining its true meaning.[23]

Modern Marxism tends to detach Marxian ideology from Engels. Almost
everything positive and constructive is attributed to Marx and everything
negative and divisive to Engels. Yet, Marx has never publicly condemned any
part of Engels's ideology. Engels's philosophy of nature, especially as expounded in his *Dialectics of Nature*, may be interpreted as his uncritical following of Hegel's philosophy of nature, but Marx has at least tacitly approved
of this philosophy.[24] In his analysis of Marxism, Lenin indicates that "Hegelian dialectics was considered by Marx and Engels as the greatest achievement

of classical German philosophy" and that as such is very relevant to the actual course of all development, social and natural alike.[25] From the anti-Hegelian point of view, the worst thing that could happen to original Marxism would be a rehabilitation of Engels and his dialectical views. It should be stressed that it is definitely wrong to ascribe to Engels the sins and errors that he has not committed and immoral and tendentious to blame him for the inconsistencies and constradictions in Marxism, for most of which Marx himself is responsible. Most of modern sociological and anthropological criticism and coolness toward Marx's views derives from the influence of non-revolutionary sociology expounded by such writers as Auguste Comte, Émile Durkheim, Max Weber, Ernst Mach, and Nicholas Berdyaev.[26] Marx is a well-known advocate of a revolutionary theory of social change and, as a result, his concept of class conflict is now believed in the non-communist world to be obsolete for analyzing post-capitalist development and the phenomenon of alienation.

The epoch in which Marx has written his "Critiques" is characterized by the revolt against the oppressive forces of society in the interest of a freedom that, unfortunately, has always remained an abstract and empty category. As a whole, the nineteenth century is marked by the development of the capitalist market society with its emphasis on the concept of man as an appropriator and consumer of material things. In all utilitarian theories of the century, the centrality of the concept of man as a self-seeker and consumer is always evident. Inspired by the utilitarian ideas of happiness and wealth, the political economists have maintained that the maximization of wealth also is the maximization of happiness. In their view, man is essentially a bundle of appetites demanding immediate satisfaction. The accumulation of wealth for purely private ends and, sadly, the total disregard of any economic equality are the striking features of their socioeconomic theories. The reason for ignoring the claims of this equality is the belief that any regime of economic egalitarianism would destory incentives to the accumulation of capital and, as Jeremy Bentham indicates hypocritically, prevent the increase "in the aggregate of material goods for the satisfaction of the whole society." Following Adam Smith, Bentham argues that "self-regarding interest is always predominant over social interst." "For of what stuff," he says, "is public advantage composed but of private and personal advantage." (See Bentham's *Handbook of Political Fallacies*, edited by H. A. Larrabee [Baltimore: The Johns Hopkins Press, 1952], pp. 87 and 248.) The same idea is expressed in Bentham's *Deontology* (edited by Amnon Goldworth [Oxford: Clarendon Press, 1983], pp. 192–93). Even egoistic utilitarian philosophers and economists believed that the private and public interests always coincide eventually. In all his writings, Marx condemns the alienating ideas of capitalist accumulation and predicts that in the communist society there will be no greed, exploitation, or alienation.

Marx is not the first thinker of the nineteenth century who has claimed that a new epoch will realize man's goal in a form of society in which self-alienation will be followed by self-realization and that "freedom" will be extended to all men and women. Saint-Simon, Charles Fourier, Robert Owen, Auguste Comte; aristocrats like Shaftesbury; writers like Thomas Carlyle, Matthew Arnold, and John Ruskin; philosophers like John S. Mill and Thomas H. Green—each in his own way protested against the iniquities and abuses of society and strongly voiced their anger against pauperization, animal gratification, mammonism, social alienation, egoism, and "cash payment." Unfortunately, Marx has never shown any interest in their ideas, arguing that by advocating the improvement in the condition of "every member of society by peaceful means rather than by revolutionary action," these would-be reformers merely dream of experimental realization of their social utopias without having any chance to change the alienated social structure. Believing that revolutionary action is the only decisive method in the struggle against capitalist alienation and exploitation, Marx believes that only the revolutionary proletariat, "being the most advanced and resolute section of the working class," can generate a truly emancipatory socialism.[27]

Hating capitalism as an alien and inhuman force, Marx has devoted his life to the struggle against egoism and "naked self-interest" of the capitalist system that he believes has "reduced all human relations to a mere money relation." Although Marx's economic theory is not always without ambiguities, his account of the alienating capitalist economy is reasonably convincing and objective. His description in *Capital* of capitalist insensitivity and indifference to the suffering of poor and disadvantaged human beings is very impressive. It is not surprising that Marx's impact on European thought has been largely through *Capital*. The principal reason for this impact must be sought in his moral appeal, not in his mystifying dialectical laws which, from a scientific view, can play no meaningful role in the process of dealienation. The assumption that these laws are relevant to the development of society must be discarded as metaphysical nonsense. There is no scientific justification for the belief, expressed in the writings of some Soviet Marxists, that materialist dialectics will change man, society, and nature in such a way to lead to "qualitatively new dialectical laws" and thus perpetuate the dialectical process in favor of Marxist communism.[28] Some Western Marxists, including Antonio Gramsci, argued strongly against the conviction that there are any objective laws of historical development similar to natural laws. It is in the moral force of immorality, as Michael Polanyi sarcastically puts it, that the propagandist appeal of Marx's ideology lies, not in "the science of dialectics."[29]

Like other enlightened men of the nineteenth century, Marx has indulged in the belief that technical progress will facilitate the betterment of man's condition. Associated with the postulate that nothing could ever stop man's technology in its "inevitable" march forward, such optimistic beliefs have comprised much of the so-called theory of necessary progress. Many materialistically oriented men, including Marx and Engels, have maintained that the pathway to rapid progress can only be found in the control of physical nature. The Saint-Simonists have voiced the great hope of their epoch that domination over external nature would ultimately supersede the domination of man over man and that the rational exploitation of natural resources would terminate the exploitation of man by man. Marx and Engels have apparently shared the belief that the lust for political power is essentially an instrument of the lust for wealth and that such social evils as war, conquest, enslavement, alienation, dehumanization, and, generally, domination of man over his fellow human beings originate in the lust for accumulation and wealth. Similar deceitfully crude psychology has led Marx to maintain that greed, as "the urge of all," is not a natural phenomenon of human nature but rather a social phenomenon "created by general wealth."[30] The complete subordination of the lust for power to the lust for wealth and of greed to "individualized wealth," however, is far from being a realistic analysis of man's egoistic drives. In many respects, this subordination reflects pseudo-psychology and inverted anthropology. On the whole, Marx and Engels believe that progress can be guided by purely material forces, whatever these may be, rather than by mental powers.

It is clear to us today that many of Marx's predictions have never materialized. Many of the problems that beset the capitalist society of Marx's epoch are still with us. Class distinctions still exist in both capitalist and communist countries. Alienation and exploitation have not been transcended. Man is still "under the dominion of alien beings and egoistic needs."[31] In capitalist society, the number of unemployed men and women is ever increasing, and in many cases they are practically "left to die of hunger." In communist societies, however, the right to work does exist, at least in principle, although the worker remains alienated and, to use Sartre's vocabulary, is frequently "reduced to his own body, to the gloomy everyday awareness of his exhaustion." In many respects modern society, capitalist and communist alike, has not developed as Marx predicted. In fact, many fundamental expectations of his theoretical assertions have been falsified by history. In spite of Marx's preaching that religion is "the spirit of spiritless conditions" and that it must be eliminated, religion in communist societies has survived all persistent persecutions, and "the religious reflex of the real world" shows no sign of vanishing. Undoubtedly Marx and Engels have underrated the significance of religion in man's life. While Hegel treats religion as an essential part of human nature—above all of "intelligence"—Marx and Engels, following Ludwig Feuerbach, regard it as "the fantastic reflection" in man's mind of his own properties.[32] It must be stressed that Marxism is not a religion in any meaningful sense; like Nazism, it has nothing to do with spiritual values. Its claim to be capable of promoting spiritual life in any teleological order cannot be granted. Its sole interest is in material and economic life. Spinoza, Leibniz, Feuerbach, Kierkegaard, Berdyaev, and Eric Fromm—to mention only a few thinkers—stress the importance of love in human relations. Marx, on the other hand, is frequently scornful about love in any spiritual sense.

Like other determinists writing on alienation, I believe Marx has failed to elaborate a consistent and unified theory. Some commentators, including L. Kolakowski, D. McLellan, and Shlomo Avineri, maintain that it is a mistake to see a switch from the youthful humanist Marx to the mature, scientifically orientated Marx.[33] Although the analysis of truth of any particular view in this respect must be speculative and is beyond the scope of this work, I believe, like D. Bell, S. Hook, and N. Berdyaev, that there is a definite break in the development of Marx's ideas and that the *Communist Manifesto* and *Capital* differ considerably from the *Economic and Philosophical Manuscripts of 1844* not only in scope but also in substance. Among other things, Marx's emphasis on exploitation and class struggle rather than on self-alienation in his later writings strikingly demonstrates that mature Marxism is different from original Marxism. Actually, Marx's all-inclusive view of man and the world is not always either objective or historical. Like Feuerbach, he also sometimes "abstracts from the historical process," and his thought is not always free from the metaphysics of "abstract materialism." For this reason, his theory of alienation is ambivalent and obscure. The social and economic aspects of Marx's thought, however, contain elements of truth and thus are valuable even today. His critical account of alienation in his early writings and his strong and uncompromising condemnation of exploitation of man by man in his later writings should not be underestimated. The future of Marxism is impossible to predict—one can only speculate. Judging by the history of ideological movements, it is almost certain that its present structure will not survive for very long and that, as many philosophers and commentators remark, Marxism as a separate school of thought will ultimately vanish completely.

1
Theory of Alienation

Anyone coming across the term *alienation* in theology, philosophy, psychology, and sociology can easily see that it has a different meaning in each field. In classical antiquity the concept of alienation was primarily religious in nature, and its proper meaning was psychological, closely related to the realm of the soul. Virtually all religions have had and still do have a belief in something called a soul or spirit. In primitive religious consciousness, the soul was conceived to be an immaterial entity that had an independent existence within the body of man. Human life was viewed as a struggle of the soul against enslaving passions and bodily limitations. It was generally believed that final salvation from the alienated world would be achieved only when this material world was renounced in favor of the soul's search for rest and harmony in the unity with God. The principal goal in all religions, as Emile Durkheim indicates, was "to liberate the mind from its enslavement to tangible appearances" and to teach it how to dominate them.[1] In tribal religion, considerable emphasis was laid on the importance of sacrifice as a communion between the worshippers and the god. The totem or sacred animal, eaten by the god and his people at a common meal, was supposed to strengthen the bond of union between them. The sacrifice had a purely soteriological significance.

The roots of the idea of alienation can be detected in all religions. Although in polytheistic and pantheistic religions this idea is never stated explicitly, it is still always assumed. Whatever form of religion was involved, the believer always felt, as Durkheim remarks, that he was participating in a divine force that dominated him, raised him above himself, and gave him strength to face the trials of existence.[2] With the growth of ethical consciousness, prayer became the expression of a desire for higher values, and men were beginning to realize that without divine assistance they would remain helpless and powerless in all their earthly strivings. The feeling of human inadequacy is associated with an intense perception of the all-powerful and eternal deity. Confucian thought, with its preoccupation with human relationships, is less conscious of sin than the thought of India. Yet, even Confucius indicates that man's salvation can only come through the achievement of absolute conformity to the transcendent nature of the universal moral and divine law. "He who offends against Heaven," he says, "has none to whom he can pray." In the Vedic hymns, the external elements of physical nature are absolute and meaningful only when deified or "dealienated." The world of the sense is filled with confusion, error, and imperfection, and as such represents enslavement. The ethical ideal of Upanishadic ethics is self-realization through oneness with the deity. The soul is never content with the satisfaction of finite achievement. Fame, material goods, and wealth count for nothing when compared with the riches of unity with the divine being. Gratification of the flesh, being alienating and frustrating, is condemned. Hedonism, it is stressed, leads to misery, unrest, and enslavement. The life of the spirit is man's perfect freedom. All illusions of temporal success generate bondage, separation, and the feeling of being estranged from the "Great Self."

The Indian Vedas indicate that the soul, which pervades all things, is the highest limitless reality. Already in the Vedic period, the Hindu mind begins to realize that the "many change and pass" and that only the "One, Ātman or the great unborn soul" remains forever. Because the sensible world is illusory and unreal, the enlightened person should transfer all his interests to the eternal and make temporal things sublimely unimportant. It is in the conquest of the finite self with its vanities and in meditation on the "Great Self" that the highest blessedness lies. To turn merely to the things of this alienated world is to deny the possibility of redemption that only can come when man identifies himself with the Great Self. Similar ideas of human frustration, confusion, and imperfection, resulting from the disharmony between the finite and infinite self, can be found in the ancient religions of Babylon, Egypt, China, and Greece. They play a significant role in Platonism and Neo-Platonism as well. Both Plato and Plotinus, the founder of Neo-Platonism, believed in the supremacy of the soul. While they believe the soul, in their view, is divine, matter is evil and has no independent reality. Being the essence of all things, the soul or spirit represents varying degrees of divine perfection, goodness, and truth. The soul, Plato says, is like an eye. When resting upon that on which truth and being shine, the soul perceives and understands and is radiant with intelligence. It is only the "seeing of the things with the upward journey of the soul" that will "turn man away from darkness to light" and keep him away from evil-doing.[3]

The supersensible world alone, in Plato's view, is truly real. The physical world, on the other hand, is more than half illusion, and it exists only as it manifests the Form of Good or God. To the empiricist, the body is the medium through which man makes contact with the world of external reality, but to Plato and Plotinus the body is evil. The whole sensible world, in their philosophical system, is conceived as being imperfect and alien to spiritual life. The supreme realization of human reason, according to Plotinus, lies in its absorption into the divine realm through mystic ecstasy and knowledge. Plato represents knowledge as a conversion of the soul from darkness to light. Most men, he remarks, live their entire lives in darkness and estrangement, seeing nothing but shadows and hearing nothing but echoes.[4] Those men who enslave the divine element of their nature to the "wild part are disgraceful."[5] Both Plato and Plotinus refer to sin as an "evil principle" in man, although

Plotinus more specifically attributes it to free will. Maintaining that man's ignorance of his true good is the source of his wrong-doing and misery, Plato indicates that "sin cannot be healed by charms and sacrifices performed to the accompaniment of feasting and pleasure." Knowledge alone can make man free and divine-like.[6]

Neo-Platonism is essentially a religious philosophy that is closely associated with man's consciousness of the existence of evil and the felt need for redemption. In many respects, Plotinus's treatment of evil and alienation anticipates practically all theodicies since his time and has left considerable traces on Christianity. Christianity shares his belief that God is the ultimate unity of all human beings and that the love of God must entail the surrender of all earthly loves. Both Christianity and Neo-Platonism are concerned with God and his relation to the world; with the nature of sin, evil, and alienation; and with the way of man's redemption. However, the Christian consciousness refuses to regard the material world as independently and eternally real, denying at the same time that it is either a part of divine essence or an emanation from God's being. In Christianity, the world is seen to be entirely dependent on divine power, and its identity with God is rejected. Because all men are endowed with the free will, evil is the fault of man, not of his Creator. Man also is responsible for the whole process of his alienated condition.

The basic theme of Hebrew and Christian tradition is the estrangement between man and God expressed in the radical separation of the sacred from the profane. Men, it is believed, have sinned, and therefore they have alienated their essential powers and estranged themselves from divine goodness and love. This tradition asserts that mutual estrangement among men is itself the result of man's estrangement from God. Judaism and Christianity, therefore, contain a common metaphysical theme. It emphasizes that the divine order has been violated by the disobedience of man; and by alienating himself from the ways of God, man has lost his freedom and found himself in the external realm in which all his activity is determined from without. Many passages in the Old Testament indicate the universal sense of man's sinfulness and his alienation from God.[7] In the New Testament, Christ himself assumes the universal sinfulness of man.[8] In fact, the whole religious experience of both the Jew and the Christian bears witness to the estrangement and sinfulness of man. The belief in the universality of sin has shaped the story of Genesis: here sin is represented as personal hostility to the will of God and as lawlessness. Man's disobedience is seen as being motivated by the desire for personal or private gain. The effect of the Fall of Adam is reflected in the history of all his posterity. The book of Genesis, containing the story of the Fall, does not give a historical account of the origin of sin, but only a metaphysical analysis of its meaning.

The Fall as depicted in the Old Testament is expressed in a dislocation of man's inner and outer life and in a destruction of the harmony and unity of the human self as a whole. Clearly, sin issues in a divided and alienated self, and man becomes a stranger in the world. In the Judeo-Christian tradition, sin often is depicted as a stain, defect, burden, or disease, or again as an enemy attacking all human individuals. As a result of the Fall, the objectified world contains things that are strange to man. Man struggles against the estranged world, but without God his redemption is impossible. To have the human image, man must possess the divine image. Without unity with God, man necessarily feels a stranger in this world; thus in his separation from the divine source, he feels helpless and powerless, and his acts generate suffering and misery. The social life in which man moves without God becomes alien and hostile. Whatever its symbolism may be, the Fall is represented as enmity, hatred, violence, rejection, isolation, suffering, and determinism. In the New Testament, man's estrangement appears frequently in ethical forms. As a consequence of original sin, both man and nature have been alienated and reduced to objects. In the words of St. Paul, "The whole creation groans with pain."[9] In his conception of alienation, the emphasis is often on moral and social consequences of the "first sin," including "enmity, strife, jealousy, anger, selfishness, dissension, party spirit and envy."[10] Only unity with God and Christ is capable of generating such virtues as "love, joy, peace, patience, kindness, goodness, faithfulness, gentleness and self-control."[11]

The distinguishing characteristic of Christian and Hebrew theology is the assertion that all men share in the same universal estrangement from God. Alienation or estrangement is conceived as an experience in which the human individual feels isolated and powerless as a result of infidelity and disobedience to his divine creator. It is stressed that sin has not been sent to earth but "man of himself has created it." The Christian understanding of man implies that "all men are sinners,"[12] equally prone to pride and self-centeredness. This also is implied by the Psalmist when he says "my sin is ever before me" and "in sin my mother conceived me."[13] Common to both Judaism and Christianity is the Messianic mission of redemption or reconciliation that follows estrangement. There is an assumption that, although man is self-divided and his own enemy in alienation, he will be reconciled to God if he abandons his sinful ways. This requires repentance. Harmony, order, peace, happiness, and justice in the sensible world will be restored only if men are prepared to renounce certain alien powers and place their lives side by side with God. In return, according to Hebrew and Christian belief, men would receive divine powers and a new divine-like life.

To overcome destructive powers of estrangement, men must change their "evil hearts," and by changing themselves they will be able to change the whole world. In the Judeo-Christian tradition, this means obedience and fidelity to the divine will as well as the rejection of all forms of divination and idolatry. These were well-known phenomena in all ancient religions. They were forbidden in Judaism but never entirely stamped out. Practically all prophets taught that the worship of heathen gods was sinful. The core of Israel's covenant was fidelity to Yahweh. From the days of Solomon, the Jews realized that foreign alliances opened the door to "strange gods" and idolatrous practices. Believing that the favor of Yahweh was essential in any war, the idolatrous practices were condemned strongly by Jeremiah and Ezekiel. The prophet Jeremiah tells the Jewish refugees in Egypt that Yahweh will destroy them because their wives have burnt incense to other gods,[14] and Ezekiel is equally opposed to the idolatrous practices of the Jews. Because of "pride," wickedness, and idolatry, he says, the Lord will punish all worshippers of "abominable images."[15] To these prophets, idolatry is the same as estrangement, because both involve disobedience and infidelity to the will of God and have similar results.

Israel's idolatry and the sin of infidelity, according to Hosea, led to the "loss of divine favour" and to the end of convenant. He says that the madness of idolatry, reflected in isolation and estrangement, has brought material and moral ruin on Israel.[16] Idols are of human origin and lead to such evils as vanity, tyranny, war, grief, isolation, misery, and alienation. For this reason the concept of alienation and the idea of idolatry in the Jewish religion are almost identical in their denotation.[17] To the Jew of the Old Testament, the sin of idolatry, entailing the apotheosis of things, is tantamount to estrangement from Yahweh. Both are evil phenomena and indicative of man's loss of divine protection, of bondage, and of his subjection to an alien and hostile power. This is well expressed in the book of Judges in whcih idolatry is clearly seen as the cause of man's estrangement, enslavement, and the loss of control over himself. As a result of idolatry, it says, the "anger of the Lord was kindled against Israel and he gave them over to plunderers who plundered them; and he sold them into the power of their enemies so that they could no longer withstand their enemies."[18] What is characteristic in the conception of alienation in the Old Testament is the emphasis that excessive devotion to secular objects and interests always ends in powerlessness, disappointment, slavery, tyranny, vanity, and isolation. Man cannot live a harmonious happy life without specific direction from God. The need to avoid "strange gods," "vain things," and "alien powers" is a constant warning of the writers of the Old Testament.

The striking aspect of the Judeo-Christian approach to alienation or estrangement is the lament about being separated from the all-powerful deity and feeling powerless. After alienating himself from the "ways of God," man finds himself being opposed by a hostile and alien power of his own making. Infidelity to God led to the loss of freedom, degradation, a confused mind, and helplessness; thus man became the object rather than remaining the free subject of history. Awareness of his helplessness and isolation made his alienated and divided existence unbearable. The experience of alienation aroused anxiety, dissatisfaction, vanity, shame, and guilt. Estranged, man became aware of a split within himself involving the dislocation of his inner life. There is a general assumption that man can only live a meaningful life if he submits to the will of God. In maintaining right relations with his Creator, man can find a new harmony and security that have been so much a part of his religious striving after the Fall. After losing his paradisal harmony, he must realize his personal insufficiency and seek help in union with God. It is through the energics of the practical self directed toward this unity that man will be able to realize his immortal essence.

In the Christian consciousness, there is always an awareness of one's own imperfections and weaknesses. These can be transcended only when man relates his life to the Eternal. The temporal order, as Kierkegaard indicates, cannot be the transparent medium of the Eternal. In the conflict between the "temporal and the Eternal," man should always be on the side of the Eternal.[19] Accepting the reality of universal alienation, St. Augustine, like St. Paul, insists that man should dissociate himself from his own imperfections and weaknesses and submerge his whole life in the divine realm. "We are weak," he says, and must "keep ourselves intact from the savage monster pride, from the sloth and the sensual pleasures of lust and from quibbing knowledge that is knowledge only in name."[20] The words "seek God and your soul shall have life" are not mere sounds that strike men's ears. "They are a call to action so that the earth may produce a living soul." In opposition to the Manichaeans, who were dualists, St. Augustine maintains that evil originates from perverseness of will, not from some "ambiguous substance." Unlike Pelagius who denied any corruption of human nature as a result of the Fall, he speaks of a loss of higher goodness, a "*privatio naturae*" that amounts to a "*depravatio naturae*." Men inherit a nature that is not entirely corrupt and yet has a positive inclination towards evil. Calvinists and many Lutherans pushed St. Augustine's conception of the Fall as far as to assert the total corruption of human nature. Calvin himself maintains that man in himself is wholly corrupt and possesses no mroal freedom. Exaggerating the consequences of the Fall, Calvinism has generated a gloom over the whole of human life. Because they were treated as corrupt, men tended to become corrupt and do nothing about overcoming their own alienation.

The ultimate ideal of the thinkers and writers of the Middle Ages was an all-embracing unity—unity in belief, spirit, and thought. Dante expresses this ideal when he says that the "human race is most like to God when it enjoys the highest degree of unity ," for the principle of unity dwells in God alone.[21] The human nature in Adam, which was sinless, was endowed with free will. On its own accord, he says, "it exiled itself from Paradise and deprived itself of life."[22] The estrangement of man, in his view, is man's own creation. Dante studied closely the works of Thomas Aquinas, and the theological structure of the *Divine Comedy* owes more to him than to any other single theologian, so much that he places St. Thomas in Paradise among the Doctors of the Church. To Dante, he "is a flame of heavenly wisdom," even wiser than Aristotle. The central point in St. Thomas's theology is the belief that "God is supremely perfect" and that all created things are "imperfect."[23] In God, essence and existence are identical, and God's nature is only known through what it is not. God knows evil things because His knowledge of good involves knowing the opposite evil. Man possesses free will and is responsible for his estrangement from God. In *Summa Theologica*, he explicitly states that this estrangement is a result of sin.[24] No man can be freed from sin except by grace. Man, he says, "may be preserved in a state of grace by ever clinging to God, wherein his peace and salvation consist."[25] "Sin is more in the will than in the intellect." Thus love of God is greater than the knowledge of Him. Divine law directs men to love God and, to a lesser degree, our neighbour. Love of God, he stresses, should be the "end of all human actions." "Charity removes our estrangement from God that sin has brought about and not knowledge alone. Thus it is charity which joins the soul directly to God in love by the bond of a spiritual union."[26]

Rationalist thinkers of the eighteenth century dissociated themselves from the Judeo-Christian approach to man's alienation and rejected the view that estrangement from God through original sin is the origin of human misery and social unrest. On the contrary, they believed, man's happiness and progress had been thwarted by the impostures of religious superstitions and ignorance. Most eighteenth-century writers in Western Europe were preoccupied with the problem of man and nature. As one who shared the views of the Encyclopaedists, Voltaire rejected both "optimistic theology and pessimistic atheism." It is evident, he says in his *Philosophical Dictionary*, that in morals it is most important to recognize a deity. It is "certainly for the interest of all men that there should be a divinity who punishes what human justice cannot repress. But it is also clear that it is better not to recognize a God than to adore a barbarous deity to whom human beings are sacrificed."[27] Voltaire denounces Leibniz's metaphysical explanation of evil. There are no indications, he says, that "particular and relatively small evils make up the general good. A strange general good!—composed of all diseases, all crimes, all suffering, death and perdition."[28] The doctrine that makes evil an element of good is illogical. "The question of good and evil," he indicates in his *Philosophical Dictionary*, "remains a hopeless chaos for those who examine it in good faith and for disputants it is merely an intellectual game—they are galley slaves who sport with their chains."

All Encyclopaedists except Turgot were free-thinkers and argued that the policy of the ecclesiastical circles in France was the great obstacle to the enlightenment of men. They tended to emphasize that religious alienation is the principal cause of all forms of estrangement and misery, both individual and social. Diderot, one of the most eminent Encyclopaedists, pointed out that once man had succeeded in his critique of the "majesty of heaven"—a phrase that deeply impressed Marx—he will not hesitate for long to attack the "other oppressors of mankind."[29] His contemporary Rousseau, father of the romantic movement and a deist, denounced alienation in many of its manifestations. The central theme of his thought, however, is man's alienation from nature and society. At the beginning of *Émile*, he writes: "God makes all things good; man meddles with them and they become evil." It is man himself, not God, who is blamed for creating his own misery and alienation. Rousseau believes that science and philosophy are the worst enemies of morals, and that by creating wants, they are the sources of slavery. "By nature," he says, "a man bears pain bravely and dies in peace. It is the doctors with their rules, the philosophers with their precepts, the priests with their exhortations who debase the heart and make us afraid to die."[30] In some respects his idea of alienation is similar to those expressed in Judaism, Christianity, and Marxism. The whole blame for alienation is attributed to man, not God or nature. "Man destroys and defaces all things; he loves all that is deformed and monstrous; he will have nothing as nature made it, not even man himself who must learn his paces like a saddle-horse and be shaped to his master's taste like the trees in his garden."[31]

For Rousseau, alienation is the result of man's own activity. It entails the loss of personal freedom and the experience of powerlessness. "To alienate," he says, "is to give or sell. But a man who becomes the slave of another cannot give but must sell himself, at least for a subsistence."[32] Rousseau's critique of alienation, although brief, is probably the most emphatic before Marx. Holbach, a prominent French materialist philosopher, does not refer to alienation as such but merely speaks of natural evils that easily affect the life of man unless checked. Maintaining that all phenomena in nature are determined by natural forces, he and La Mettrie argued that the social world will never be happy and harmonious as long as it remains enslaved by theological dogmatism and superstitious beliefs,[33] The whole emphasis of the Encyclopaedists is placed on man's need to understand that his deliverance from all alienated life requires enlightenment and passive submission to his environmental conditions that are the work of nature. "What especially characterises the period of Encyclopaedists," Engels writes, "is the elaboration of a peculiar general outlook, the central point of which is the view of the absolute immutability of nature. All change, all development in nature, was denied."[34] In his opinion, "abstract materialism" of the Age of Reason did not contradict the Christian view of man and "merely posited Nature in place of the Christian God as the Absolute facing man."[35] He believes that the anthropology and social theories of the Encylopaedists are as wrong as those of Judaism and Christianity and must be rejected.

While the Encyclopaedists showed very little interest in alienation and merely spoke of "human ills and miseries" without finding any permanent solution except in enlightenment, idealist writers in nineteenth-century Germany became well aware of both the existence of alienation and the need for its elimination. Their views, however, differed considerably and were frequently incongruous with those expounded in the past centuries. The distinguishing mark of the concept of alienation in German idealism is the emphasis on the estrangement of the spirit. Here, alienation is analyzed in purely metaphysical terms. The classical concept of alienation, based on original sin and idolatry, has been abandoned in favor of a speculative approach to its meaning and significance. Although it is Fichte, an early representative of German idealism, who uses the term alienation in the sense of *Entäusserung*, the terms *Entäusserung* (alienation) and *Entfremdung* (estrangement) received their first significant philosophical treatment in Hegel's *Phenomenology of Spirit*. Here the concepts of alienation and estrangement are used in several senses, and their meanings are not always clarified sufficiently. Broadly speaking, by alienation he means "giving up" or transferring something that is one's own to somebody else. Some philosophers refer to this renunciation of one's own possession as "exteriorisation or externalisation."[36] In Hegel's view, estrangement is alienation that comes after the renunciation and transfer of one's own possession to somebody else. During the process of estrangement, men become strangers and enemies to one another. All their individual and social strivings are motivated by self-interest and pride. This is reflected, for example, in the relationship between subjects and rulers, slaves and masters.

In his analysis of alienation, Hegel pays specific attention to the alienation of Spirit and self-consciousness. The subject of the process of estrangement is not primarily the individual human being but world Spirit or pure self-consciousness. During the process of development, this "self-consciousness ceases to be the consciousness of any particular individual and becomes a consciousness shared by all individuals."[37] This "consciousness shared by all individuals" is the consciousness of the self-conscious Spirit or of the "universal individual." In its essential existence, the Absolute or Spirit is "before the creation of the world and outside of it."[38] The spiritual alone is the actual. "It is essence or that which has being in itself. It is also other-being and being-for-self."[39] Absolute Spirit or God or the Eternal is expressed not only as Substance but also as Subject.[40] Such Substance, Hegel believes, can only be found in the Spirit that unfolds itself in human history. This implies the idea of an Absolute that manifests itself by means of a non-absolute, finite reality.

Nature, in Hegel's view, is only a self-estranged form of Absolute Idea, and man is the Absolute in the process of dealienation. Being a partial expression of the Absolute, nature contains the principle of unity concealed. This unity strives to assert itself in animate and inanimate creatures in nature and is ultimately successful in finite spirits or men who are the highest product of God's creation. Like the Idea or Spirit, nature is subject to the process of alienation but for the sake of Spirit, which in the movement of becoming historical, regains itself, "brings itself back to its true state" and finds itself again in unity with itself."[41] Positing itself as a unity of thought and reality, of being in itself and being for itself, the Idea is "absorbed into the immediacy of Being" and becomes nature without ever ceasing to be itself. Nature neither thinks nor knows itself. The process of alienation and dealienation consists in self-knowledge, in bringing mind "to know what it is integrally." The goal of absolute knowledge must lead to the recollection of spiritual forms as they are in themselves. The spiritual, being the essence of all things, is distinguished from the natural in that only the spiritual has "being in itself," is able to know itself and can realize itself. Once the objects of thought are cognized by mind as subjects, they cease to represent "alien something other" or "otherness" outside of Spirit. Hegel believes the understanding of an "other or other-being" is the realization that the finite self is non-absolute. The finite self always has its limitations, which are expressed "in the unhappy con-sciousness."[42] Although yearning toward Spirit, the unhappy consciousness can never succeed in recognizing Absolute Spirit as itself.

The actual world of which man is a part appears to "self-consciousness as an alienated world which has the form of a fixed and solid reality over against it."[43] At the center of Hegel's *Phenomenology* is the dialectic of subject and object, of spirit and nature. Everything in the universe has an opposing tendency. Both unities and contradictions are relative to the assertion and quality of being or to the moment of its development. Being historical, unity and contradiction pass through the phases of historical development, which are dialectical and antithetical. "The present actual world has its antithesis directly in its beyond which is both the thinking of it and its thought-form, just as the beyond has in the present world its actuality, but an actuality alienated from it."[44] Spirit creates for itself "not only a world but a world that is double, divided and self-opposed."[45] The alienation process involves both the infinite and finite selves. "The alienation of the divine Being consists in the moments going apart from one another and in one of them having an unequal value compared with the other."[46] In his essence man is a free being but in his alienation he loses his freedom. In Hegel's view, man is unavoidably alienated in object-making—every objectification is an instance of estrangement.

Hegel's objective idealism has the inseparable connection between the divine and the human, man and nature, subject and object. In this connection he, like Fichte and Schelling, sees the origin of alienation. To them, nature is externalized Spirit that is unconscious of itself as Spirit. Some representatives of the Young Hegelians, notably Bruno Bauer and Max Stirner, were fasci-nated by this idealist subject-object philosophizing. Marx, not surprisingly, accuses them of "replacing the natural and human connection between the world system and world events by a fantastic connection, a mystical Subject-Object, just as Hegel replaces the real connection between man and nature by an absolute Subject-Object which is at one and the same time the whole of nature and the whole of humanity, the Absolute spirit."[47] Feuerbach shares Hegel's view that man can be alienated from himself but rejects his idea ex-pounded in *Phenomenology of Spirit* that nature is merely a self-alienated form of the Absolute. Anxious to liberate man from religious alienation, he argues that God is nothing but alienated man himself. All the attributes of the divine nature, he belives, are essentially human attributes—the attributes of human nature. Man, he says, "is a real being, the true *Ens realissimum*," not a reflection of Hegel's Absolute Mind.[48] Feuerbach's principal aim in *Essence of Christianity* is to represent man as a "sensuous being" and, uncharacteristic from a Protestant theologian, to replace God by man. Man, he maintains, is alienated from himself when he creates and projects above himself an imagined higher being and then kneels before it and worships it. Thus images of divine power, according to him, are merely the means through which man projects externally his own attributes. The separation of essence from existence in objective idealism confuses the "abstract and concrete" and fails to explain the origin of alienation.[49]

Unfortunately, Feuerbach's own theory of alienation has failed to convince his contemporaries that it is an adequate mechanism for explaining the process of alienation in human life. Not only was it rejected by Marx and Engels, but also by Arnold Ruge, Moses Hess, and Young Hegelians who wanted to eliminate totally the concept of alienation in favor of humanist ideology. According to Marx, Feuerbach has never completely secularized the idea of alienation. Although he boasts of transcending theological dogmatism, he could not grasp the alienation of real, existing men.[50] By remaining in the realm of theory and contemplation, Marx indicates that Feuerbach "gets no further than recognising the corporeal man emotionally."[51] His ideas of alienation are not very different from those of Bruno Bauer, whose humanism consists merely of "thinking and of building a spiritual world."[53] Criticizing the representatives of German idealism and "true socialists," Marx accuses them of "judging everything *sub specie aeternitatis* (in terms of the essence of man)" rather than "viewing everything practically in terms of actually existing men and circumstances."[53] The real clue to history only can be found in man's economic life, and it is in this life that the origin of alienation must be traced.

Hegel's conception of history is strongly teleological, a march of the temporal heading toward a predetermined goal. Man is God's image because of the divine purpose that is operative in him. For Hegel, alienation is an ontological fact, rooted in the nature of human existence. In Marx's view, the Hegelian universe and his teleological anthropology are creatures of his own making. He criticizes Hegel for reducing history to the act of thinking and seeing concrete events and things only as manifestations of Spirit. All human history has its earthly basis that is linked closely with the material production of life. Human needs and their satisfaction cannot be measured without being related to the modes of production. The main difference between human and animal needs is that animal needs are essentially purely natural and determined by nature, whereas human needs are basically social and historical, determined ultimately by man himself. Man's awareness of his needs is a product of his historical development. Unlike Hegel, Marx argues that man's consciousness of the need for particular objects is itself a product of concrete historical situations and never can be determined by pure thinking.

In the Hegelian metaphysical system, alienation in regarded as a state of consciousness that can be overcome only by another state of consciousness.

Yet alienation involves both conscious beings and non-human entities, including Absolute Idea and nature. There is very little distinction, if any, between the alienation of selves and things. In Marx's philosophy, alienation is related to "real existing men" and the objects they produce.[54] Both man and objects, he maintains, presuppose a material basis, a distinctly "natural and physical substratum" that must not be identified with the spiritual principle and pure consciousness. Idealist metaphysics, including Hegel's, objectifies the ego and spirit, the subject and concept. Hegel sees subject and object as correlatives: "The transition from the subject to the object appears strange" but cannot be denied.[55] Man is a subject-object being with his body as the object and his mind as the subject. God himself is not only the absolute Subject but also the "absolute Object." "As absolute Object, however, God does not take up the position of a dark and hostile power over against subjectivity."[56] Marx does not deny that man is both subject and object, but he rejects Hegel's conversion of "real man" into a "creature of abstraction."[57]

For Marx, alienation is a historical, not a mental, process, and he insists it is brought about by historical and socioeconomic conditions. Maintaining that human nature is historically conditioned, he categorically rejects the view that human consciousness or thought is the basis of man's real life. "It is not consciousness that determines life but life that determines consciousness.[58] When divorced from real life of human individuals, ideas and consciousness are valueless. Abstractions and ideas "can only facilitate the arrangement of historical material but they cannot give us a recipe or schema for any realistic approach to history."[59] Marx criticizes Hegel for turning the whole material world into a world of ideas as well as for reducing the whole human history into a history of ideas. Hegel's view that the history of man is nothing but the history of the Absolute Spirit is rejected. "History," he says, must be seen as the "true natural history of man."[60] Only in the light of this history does the concept of alienation become intelligible and meaningful. Yet, the fact is that Helgel's theory of alienation is not only a target of his criticism in the *Manuscripts of 1844* but also the principal source of his own analysis of man's estrangement. In spite of Marx's denunciation of Hegel's *Phenomenology of Spirit*, he cannot always avoid presenting the real in terms of the ideal and abstract. This is obvious in the *Manuscripts* where Marx's theory of alienation is frequently described in purely metaphysical terms. Here he borrows anthropological models from Feuerbach's writings and presents them in Hegelian form. The result is synthesis in which the terminology and arguments are largely Hegelian whereas their metaphysical content originates mainly from Feuerbach.

Such Feuerbachian concepts as "man," "human essence," and "man's species being" appearing in Marx's early writings and his continuous use of the Hegelian vocabulary indicate the strong influence of Hegel and Feuerbach on his theory of alienation. There are, of course, other influences, including those of the British political economists and French socialists, that helped him shape his ideas of the "devaluation of the world of men," but Hegel's theory of alienation and Feuerbach's anthropology are the most important. In *Manuscripts*, Marx's critique focuses on the Hegelian treatment of the alienation of self-consciousness and its relevance to objectification. Hegel, believes objectification or externalization is a process in which Spirit externalizes itself and in it ultimately realizes its potentialities. In externalizing itself in all its diversity, Spirit, unaware initially of its objectification, rises to self-consciousness in men. The whole process of this externalization or objectification also is expressed in man and entails his alienation. Alienation, in Hegel's view, is only possible because externalization of the Idea or Spirit involves unconsciousness during some phase of its development. It is "through its externalization" that "actual self-consciousness passes over into the actual world" or the world of the unconscious. This is followed by its "return to actual self-consciousness."[61]

Strictly speaking, in Hegel's conception of objectification or externalization, alienation is rooted in the unconscious, an idea that plays a significant role in Freud's psychology and especially in his theory of psychosis and neurosis. Marx agrees with Hegel that alienation entails man's absence of control over himself. To be a subject in any real sense, man must have power and control over his own activity. He disagrees with Hegel, however, that all objectification is alienation. Both Marx and Hegel maintain that man develops his powers through work or object-making. Unlike Hegel, Marx gives much prominence to the negative side of work, believing it has been neglected in the Hegelian theory of alienation. Marx asserts that the specific conditions of objectification or object-making that exist in the world of capitalist greed, and not the nature of objectification itself, make man's creative activity alien, frustrating, and dehumanizing. In capitalism with its emphasis on private exchange and market economy, alienation inverts the subject-object relationship and as a result, man is ruled by the objects he produces. Instead of leading man to self-realization, objectification in a capital-dominated society causes alienation.

Objectification, as conceived in Hegelianism, is above all externalization. According to the existentialist philosophy of N Berdyaev, it is the "ejection of man into the external," into the world of objects, necessity, and determination from outside. Like Hegel, he believes that objectification is the alienation of spirit from itself.[62] Man is, above all, a subject. Sartre expresses similar view. There is no universe, he says, other than a human universe, the universe of human subjectivity. Unlike materialism, which treats men merely as objects, he views existentialism as the only theory that gives man dignity and does not reduce him to an object.[63] Like Berdyaev but unlike Marx, Sartre connects man's alienation or "losing himself outside of himself" with his pursuit of "transcendental goals."[64] Marx's own analysis of the relationship between alienation and objectification in *Manuscripts* is far from being clear. Here he definitely praises Hegel for "grasping the self-creation of

man as a process, objectification as loss of the object, and the alienation of
man's essence."[65] This could be interpreted to mean that he agrees with
Hegel that objectification entails alienation. Although many commentators
deny this interpretation, Nicolaus's view that Marx is strikingly ambiguous
about his concept of alienation and its relation to objectification is probably
correct.[66] Marx certainly does not say anything about the universality or tran-
sitoriness of alienation.

Even in *Grundrisse*, in which Marx distinguishes more intelligibly between
alienation and objectification, it is not clear whether alienation is to be
thought of as a universal and permanent phenomenon or as something transitory. Here he argues that objectification is esssential to man's life if he is to
transform nature into the expression of himself. Alienation, on the other
hand, is related to an inverted from of man's activity. "But with the suspension of the immediate character of living labour, as merely individual," and
"with the positing of the activity of individuals as immediately general or
social activity, the objective moments of production are stripped of this form
of alienation."[67] Marx does not say that the "positing of man's activity as
social activity" will eliminate all forms of alienation. He merely assumes that
in communist society the process of objectification or object-making will not
necessarily result in the alienation of human labor. His assumption, like
Hegel's assumption that the "being of the estranged world will ultimately
return to its divine source," is purely speculative and alien to empirical
facts.[68] The claim by some modern Marxists that in communist countries
alienation has already "in principle" been eliminated must be rejected.

In *Manuscripts of 1844*, Marx really expounds two theories of alienation—
the essentialist and the economico-sociological—that never have been
harmonized. Starting, like Hegel, with the analysis of alienation as a psychological phenomenon, he then discusses the alienation of the worker from his
labor. Orthodox Marxists overlook this dualism and concentrate their attention on the alienation of the laborer.[69] They fail to see that in his early works
Marx really uses the concept of alienation in both psychological and
economico-sociological contexts. The key problem in Marx's theory of alienation, they indicate, is alienated labor under capitalism in which work is compelled rather than spontaneous. Although this is true, it is not the whole
truth. It is impossible to deny that in *Manuscripts* Marx is almost as much
interested in man's inner conflict, in his alienation from his essence, as he is
interested in socioeconomic conflicts, in the inability of man to realize himself
in work.[70] One must not forget that in this work Hegel's influence is still very
impressive. As Althusser remarks, one thinks immediately of Hegel when
one reads *Manuscripts of 1844*.[71] The ideas taken from Hegelian idealism and
those taken from materialism have never been unified in an organically complete whole. Marx himself must have felt this incoherence, and this work was
never been published in his lifetime.

In spite of Marx's emphasis on alienation as a material, phenomenal, and historical evil, he also believes that alienation can be described in a psycho-logical and superstructural manner as a "mistake, a defect which ought not to be."[72] This suggests that his theory of alienation, at least in its essentialist form, is not deprived entirely of psychological or psychiatric connotation. In this sense, man always has been alienated from his "true, essential nature." The beginning of man's alienation remains in the realm of speculation, of course, and no thinker has penetrated into themystery of its origin. Marx himself leaves the same question unanswered. Some modern Marxists main-tain that a "psycho-sociology of alienation" is not contradictory to Marx's concept of alienated labor.[73] This is partly true and partly false. Marx certain-ly refers to both spiritual and physical aspects of man's alienated life, but his main emphasis is on the alienation of "corporeal man," man without a soul. He argues strongly against Hegel's transcendental and abstract conception of alienation and equally denounces Christianity "with its cult of the abstract human being."[74] Marx argues that man is not a "non-objective, spiritual being" but a "corporeal, sensuous, objective being" and it is this corporeal being that has been alienated.[75]

Much confusion about Marx's theory of alienation arises because he never defines the term *alienation*, merely describing it as it occurs in man's socioeco-nomic life. In this description his thought is a synthesis of the phenomenal and superstructual, the historical and the spiritual, although the socioeconomic elements predominate. Unfortunately, in this respect his thought is far from being a unitary process. In his early works, including *Manuscripts*, he vacil-lates from Hegel to Feuerbach and back to Hegel, without formulating a coherent theory of alienation. Finally, he denounces both of them on the ground that they have failed to explain alienation historically. Instead of start-ing from the abstractions, he says, they should have started from the concrete life of the human species, from man's factual socioeconomic relations. With-out considering these relations, the concept of alienation becomes illusory and meaningless. For this reason, the mature Marx rejects the Hegelian analysis of alienation in its abstract form and moves to its analysis in terms of socioeconomic relations. Both Marx and Hegel believe that alienation can be transcended. However, their difference in the meaning of the terms *alienation* and *transcendence* is unbridgeable.

The mature Marx sees alienation as a feature of a particular mode of pro-duction. In this sense, alienation is associated with the division of labor and private property or, in short, with the labor process itself. The concept of the labor process is now of primary importance to Marx's theory of alienation because it is primarily in the light of this process that man's life becomes intelligible. He agrees with the Young Hegelians that alienation cannot be confined to the merely religious life of man. In *German Ideology*, he argues that religious and idealistic concepts of alienation are incompatible with the ideas of historical materialism. In religion, the material world is either ignored or distorted. Both theology and idealism, he believes, are only interested in the alienation of the spirit or self-consciousness.[76] This, or course, is an exaggeration. The fact is that in religious and non-Marxist thinking, the roots of estrangement are located within man himself, but theology and idealism do not confine this estrangement to the spiritual alone.[77] Egoism, greed, and avarice are regarded as manifestations of man's self- centeredness, and his alienation is seen as an inherent quality of all human life.

Any serious theory of alienation must begin with a theory of man and human existence. What is essential in the existence of man is the fact that he is a part of nature, yet he somehow and in some ways transcends nature. Man is aware of himself, of a core of his personality that persists throughout his whole life in spite of varying external circumstances. Without belief in this persistence of self, man's personal identity disappears in the realm of impersonalism and his life becomes meaningless. Marx's conception of human nature, like his theory of alienation, is frequently ambiguous and contradictory. Sometimes he speaks of human nature in terms of essentialism and sometimes he denies the existence of human nature altogether. The idea that there is no human nature was accepted later by Sartre. Yet, like Marx, he speaks of human reality without ever explaining the difference between this reality and what is commonly called human nature.[78] To say that man is nothing except what he makes of himself, as Marx and Sartre maintain, is meaningless unless there is human nature. It is this nature, as Marx indicates correctly in *Manuscripts of 1844*, that has been alienated, not the "unconscious something thrusting itself towards existence." In his later works, he has changed this view, assuming wrongly that man is social before being human.[79] In trying to discredit Hegel's conception of abstract man, he fails to formulate a theory of human nature that is simultaneously consistent and unambiguous.

According to the Judeo-Christian conception of human nature, man is composed of spirit and body, with prominence given to the primacy of the spirit. This dualism, which also characterizes Plato and Aristotle's philosophy, dominates the minds of rationalist philosophers and is evident in empiricist theories of man. Hegel and his followers emphasize the spiritual principle as being the characteristic part of human nature. It is by this principle that man knows himself to be different from the world of nature and by which he is self-conscious. Even Charles Darwin, in *Descent of Man*, could not ignore the spiritual or psychic characteristics of human nature. The great majority of non-Marxist thinkers maintain that man is the only animal who does not feel at home if confined to the merely natural. Being aware of himself, he also is aware of his powerlessness and the spiritual need for meaningful life in the realm that somehow transcends the merely natural. If human life consisted only of self-evident factual matters, then men could content themselves with what Jung calls a "sturdy empiricism."[80] Jung believes the psychic alone has "immediate reality," and the conflict between spirit and nature is itself a reflection of the paradox of psychic life.[81] Jung, of course, does not ignore the physical aspects of human nature. He merely stresses that, if he recognized only "naturalistic values" and "explained everything in physical terms," he would hinder or even destroy the chances of his patients' recovery.[82] Hegel's view of human nature is essentially psychocentric. Believing that man is "finite self-conscious spirit," he denies that he is "merely pure thought."[83] In contrast to Hegel, Feuerbach maintains that the opposition between the "noumenal or invisible divine nature and the phenomenal or visible nature" is actually the opposition between the "nature of abstraction and the nature of perception." Only the nature of perception is real nature. Feuerbach, however, overlooks the fact that his own idea of "man as a species being" is far from the realm of perception. His criticism of the noumenal nature is inconsistent, hypocritical, and superficial.

Marx believes Feuerbach lacks Hegel's sense of history and only very generally holds that man is essentially natural, sensuous, and progressive.[84] He criticizes Feuerbach for remaining in the realm of theory. "Apart from the fact that he only conceives man as an object of senses," Feuerbach fails to see men "in their given social connections which have made them what they are. He never arrives at the actually existing, active man, but stops at the abstraction man and gets no further than recognising the actual, individual, corporeal man emotionally."[85] Both Marx and Engels recognize that Hegel's conception of man as a social being is considerably superior to that of Feuerbach's. Not surprisingly, perhaps, Marx compares Feuerbach unfavorably with Hegel,[86] indicating that Feuerbach adds little of his own to what Hegel says about man, human nature, and alienation. Secularizing the idea of estrangement, Feuerbach merely takes over some of Hegel's ideas of man and alienation that are contained in his *Phenomenology*. Marx reproaches Feuerbach for giving too much prominence to the Hegelian idea of "human essence," to the "concept of man, man as conceived, the essence of man, Man."[87] Contradicting his own essentialist view of human nature expounded in *Manuscripts*, Marx argues against essentialism in the *German Ideology*. Here both Hegel and Feuerbach are criticized for perpetuating this essentialism in their theories of man's nature and of alienation.

Feuernach is wrong, Marx writes, not merely because he "posits Man instead of real historical man" but also because he fails to see that the "sensuous world around him is not a thing given direct from all eternity, remaining always the same, but the product of industry and of the state of society."[88] Feuerbach's conception of man and alienation is confined to mere contemplation and sentiment. Marx and Engels are equally opposed to Feuerbach's contemplative theory of human nature. According to Engels, the cult of abstract man, which "formed the kernel of Feuerbach's new religion, had to be replaced by the science of real men and of their historical development." The further development of Feuerbach's anthropology, he says, "was inaugurated by Marx in 1845 in the *Holy Family*."[89] Feuerbach's man is not a real man but the "quintessence of the numerous real men, man in the abstract, therefore himself a mental image."[90] It is true, Engels remarks, that Feuerbach starts from man, "but there is absolutely no mention of the world in which this man lives." In Feuerbach's conception of human nature, "man remains always the same abstract man. For this man," Engels writes, "is not born of woman. He therefore does not live in a real world which has historically come into being and is historically determined."[91]

Marx's anthropology, like his idea of alienation, has been shaped considerably by Feuerbachian concepts of the "true nature of man," in spite of his sharp criticism of Feuerbach. Feuerbach's conception of "sensuous consciousness and of sensuous needs" is reflected in Marx's picture of the "real, corporeal man, man with his feet firmly on the solid ground, man exhaling and inhaling all the forces of nature."[92] Following Feuerbach, he argues in *Manuscripts* that the Hegelian conception of the essence of man, entailing the estrangement of abstract man, is a distortion of man's essence. Just as man's alienation canot be reduced to a purely mental entity existing only in self-consciousness, so the real essence of man cannot be reduced to mind. As long as man refuses to recognize himself as a real, sensuous, and social being and is incapable of organizing the social world in a natural, human way, he will remain alienated from himself, and the whole society in which he lives will appear as estrangement. "To be sensuous, that is, to be an object of sense, to be a sensuous object, and thus to have sensuous objects outside oneself—objects of one's sensuousness" means, in reality, to be truly human and to have real human nature.[93]

In his own conception of human nature that is central to his theory of alienation in *Manuscripts*, Marx rejects both Hegel and Feuerbach's anthropology on the ground that man in it is merely an abstraction, an estranged essence, a being conceived unhistorically and metaphysically. In this work, however, Marx's ideas of man and human nature are far from being free from abstractions and essentialism. When criticizing Hegel's conception of man's essence, he is not trying to eliminate the concept of "man's essence" but only the representation of "human essence" as an "abstract, thinking essence."[94] He does not elaborate on the difference between his concept of man's essence and that of Hegel. The fact is that essentialism remains, and it is only in his later writings that he abandons it altogehter. Some commentators maintain that the concept of man, not just the concept of man's essence, is already absent in *German Ideology* and that, as a result, the whole idea of alienatiion has been repudiated by the mature Marx.[95] Unlike Daniel Bell who clearly and unambiguously speaks of a break between original and mature Marxism, Tucker speaks of "continuity in change" without seeing a contradiction between the terms *continuity* and *change* or alteration.[96] Although it is arguable whether the concept of man continues to play any significant role in Marx's later works or not, the fact is that in these works he is much less interested in human nature. In the *Communist Manifesto*, it is true, Marx still refers to human nature, but this nature is related neither to "human essence" nor to man as a "spiritual and physical being" but to man as a "class entity."[97]

Here the conception of "human nature, of Man in general who belongs to no class and exists only in the misty realm of philosophical fantasy" is rejected categorically.[98] A similar idea is expressed in the sixth thesis on Feuerbach. "The essence of man," he says here, "is no abstraction inherent in each single individual. In its reality it is the ensemble of the social relations."

Marx believes the socioeconomic relations that unite men with nature and society are the real relations, and it is these relations that have been alienated. Man's alienation cannot be explained unless it is related to the totality of socioeconomic relation. Real man cannot be understood unless he is related to his social milieu and nature. The human essence of nature exists primarily for social man. The central point in Marx's anthropology is the belief that human beings have roots that are both social and natural. "The nature which comes to be in human history—the genesis of human society—is man's real nature; hence nature as it comes to be through industry, even though in an estranged form, is true anthropological nature."[99] In *Manuscripts of 1844*, Marx tends to identify the essence of man with nature or, more precisely, with the part of nature that man appropriates in his social environment. Some of his comments suggest that this essence is really man's activity and that it is this activity that has been alienated.

On the whole, Marx distinguishes between "human and social mode of existence." Sometimes, however, this distinction is ignored and man is seen merely as the "aggregate of social relations." Thus Marx's theory of alienation is not a coherent and unified system. The ideas expressed in it indicate the lack of clarity in his thinking about man, human nature, and estrangement. Although he has tried to unify the incoherent ideas of man that originate from the incongruous philosophical systems of Hegelian idealism and Feuerbachian and French abstract materialism, he has obviously failed, and as a result, has produced an ambiguous dichotomy of being and consciousness, reality and utopianism. Like Hegel, Marx believes that man's image of himself is bound up with his image of the world and that man's ways of thinking about nature inevitably affects his ways of thinking about society. For both, a fully realized human essence and the fully realized essence of human society are, in the light of historical development, the same process. Man makes history, but this history becomes intelligible only when seen as a social process. The realized human society, in their view, is a society of realized human beings. Marx praises Hegel for "conceiving the self-creation of man as a process" that takes place in history through the development of human society.[100] However, he criticizes Hegel for believing that this process originates from ontological contradictions of the Absolute that in its externalization is "at war with itself" rather than from man's interaction with his social and external environment. Thus Hegel's account of history, based on metaphysical speculations, is rejected because of its transcendental implications.

The mature Marx moves away from essentialism and, as Althusser indicates, breaks radically with every theory that bases human history on the essentialist conception of man.[101] By rejecting the concept of the essence of man as his theoretical basis, he has, rejected the essentialist theory of alienation. Marx's new emphasis is on the historically guided influence of socioeconomic relations on man's needs and their satisfaction. Man's basic needs are primarily biological and physiological. In this respect, man is not different from an animal. Yet, unlike an animal, man also has spiritual needs and is aware of his existence. Men involved in real alienation, Marx argues, are not abstract but real and existing individuals. "In the objective world man is affirmed not only in the act of thinking but also with all his senses."[102] Man's constitution impels him to express himself through all his senses, including the "so-called mental senses," and in that way realize his "essential powers."[103] The historicization of man's nature is a continuous process. Possessing consciousness, man feels an intrinsic drive for creative and truly human activity. His most impelling needs, rooted in his unique nature, include the need for creativity and self-expression. "Man is not merely a natural being; he is a human natural being. That is to say," Marx stresses, "he is a being for himself."[104]

There is nothing new in this statement except perhaps that it implies the exclusion of supernatural elements that are so important to idealist anthropology. While Hegel and his followers consider man as a psychosomatic being incorporating many levels of mental and physical activities, Marx sees man as being primarily a subject of sensibility. Regarding man as a "being for himself," he believes that man alone in the animal world is able to produce his means of life and can shape nature to his own requirements. The uniqueness of the being for himself in the human individual lies in his awareness of himself as a person who can understand the limitations of his existence, his powerlessness, as well as the importance of his productive activity in society. Possessing mind and imagination, man, unlike an animal, is aware of the necessity of solidarity and co-operation with other living human beings.[105] The bond between society and particular human individuals reflects man's relationship to "natural and human natural reality." This relationship, in Marx's opinion, is experienced by social man at the existential and natural level. Only a human natural being can create refined needs and confirm his existence through thinking and knowing.[106]

Everything in human history is the product of real, corporeal men, of their labor and creativity. The historical modification of man's natural powers is possible only in "objects outside his own body" and is always in harmony with the development of productive forces. These forces, Marx maintains, develop historically in ever-increasing complexity and, as a result, express different degrees of alienation at different stages. Because the productive forces are themselves of human origin, their effects on man's life are ultimately his own acts. "In production, men not only act on nature but also on one another. They produce only by co-operating in a certain way and mutually exchanging their activities."[107] The entire theoretical structure of Marx's materialist anthropology rests on the premise of man's social and natural relationship. Without being social, natural, and objective, man would simply become an absurdity. In *Manuscripts*, he says that man is neither human nor natural alone but both at the same time—"humanly natural and naturally human." There is no novelty in his statement that "man lives on nature" and "appropriates his total essence in a total manner, that is to say, as a whole man."[108] No sensible person has ever denied that "man lives on nature" and "must remain in continuous intercourse with nature if he is not to die."[109] Man's physical life is certainly linked to nature simply because, as Marx rightly indicates, man is a being of nature. He is obscure, however, when he speaks of "nature being humanised."[110] This obscurity is partly the result of his inability to decide whether primacy should belong to man or nature. He sometimes gives the impression that there is no difference between nature and human nature.

In *Manuscripts*, Marx speaks of the "human essence of nature" and the "natural essence of man" in a confused manner, suggesting the total identity of man and nature.[111] As he does not explain the difference between these expressions, it is possible to argue that he entirely reduces man to nature, thus depriving him of the qualities that are supposed to differentiate him from plants and animals. Marx's total reduction of the human to the natural is implicit in his statement that the "meaning of the bond between man's physical and spiritual life and nature is simply that nature is linked to itself."[112] The assertion that the distinguishing mark of man is his awareness of his "spiritual inorganic nature" is meaningless unless this spiritual inorganic nature is different from the "goddess nature."[113] Without this differentiation, the concept of alienation would denote, as in Hegel's system, similar estranged phenomena in man and nature. On the whole, Marx differentiates between man and nature, but such phrases as the "humaness of nature," "at bottom man is nature," "nature linked to man is nature linked to itself," and "the intimate ties of man to the earth" are bound to lead to confusion and expose his theory of alienation to the charge that objectification and alienation are, as in Hegelianism, essentially analogous and correlative processes involving both man and nature.[114] The crucial difference between Hegel and Marx is expressed in the difference between dialectical idealism and dialectical materialism. Although Marx agrees with Hegel that the dialectical movement is the "life and soul of scientific progress," he rejects categorically "the mystifying aspect of the idealist dialectic," maintaining that only materialist dialectic can explain the alienation of real, corporeal man.[115]

Broadly speaking, both Marx and Hegel believe human nature is not a fixed, immutable entity. The conception of a static human nature is alien to their theories of alienation, just as it is to the Christian conception of estrangement. In Christianity, the emphasis is on a change of heart and a search for perfection. St. Paul speaks of the need for "putting off the old nature and putting on the new nature." Although "our outer nature is wasting away, our inner nature is being renewed every day."[116] The idea of the need for change within man is much older than Christianity and it is assumed in all religions. The metaphysics of Heraclitus gives much prominence to perpetual change. "Everything," in his view, "is in a state of flux." The conservative Parmenides believes, on the contrary, that "nothing changes." Hegel contrasts historical with natural change. Change in nature shows only a "constant cycle of repetition." There is nothing new in this change. Only changes in the realm of Spirit create new things and new ideas. Although natural development, in Hegel's view, reproduces the same unchanged natures rhythmically, historical development does not. This contrast between natural and historical change reflects the difference in the natures of the two developments. In its natural and ontological form, man's essential nature is eternal and immutable.[117] Yet, unlike the "stones and beams" that merely "obey the law of gravity" and are unconscious of any change around them, "men develop themselves and their aims in accordance with their natural tendencies and build the edifice of human society."[118]

In his comments on human nature, Marx maintains that human nature not only can be changed but needs to be changed. "By acting on the external world and changing it, man at the same time changes his own nature."[119] Inspired by the idea of progress and the optimism of the eighteenth century, he insists that change is more important than philosophical speculation.[120] He does not explain, however, how change can evolve without thought. Surely, man cannot "act on the external world and change it" without careful deliberation. The fact is that Marx's references to change in human nature are far from being clear. He says much about man's power in transforming nature and his own nature. There is an assumption in his theory of alienation that man's conquest of nature will result in the termination of all forms of estrangement. In *Poverty of Philosophy*, he reproaches Proudhon for failing to realize that "all history is nothing but a continuous transformation of human nature."[121] What this continuous transformation really means in practice, however, he does not say. If the essence of man is nothing but the "ensemble of social relations," as Marx thinks, then man can hardly be anything but an animal alone, deprived totally of his inherently human qualities. The problem is that he rarely refers to permanent elements within human nature except in the early works.[122] Even in *Manuscripts*, personal identity is enveloped in the "species being" that alone can survive death.[123] Some commentators wrongly maintain that Marx neither rejects the concept of human nature nor deprives man of his genuinely human properties.[124] Attempts to define self-identity in terms of social relations are bound to be unsatisfactory, just as Hume's attempts to define it in terms of "perceptions" are unsatisfactory. The relation between different experiences of the same self is radically-different from the relation between members of a mere aggregate like a heap of bricks.

Engels and Plekhanov merely repeat Marx's assertions about change in man and nature. In Plekhanov's view, the concept of the immutability of nature and human nature "was inherited in its entirety by the writers of the nineteenth century from the writers of the Enlightenment." Marx's contribution, he says, "lies in the fact that he approached the question from the diametrically opposite side and that he regarded man's nature itself as the eternally changing result of historical progress, the cause of which lies outside man."[125] Fascinated by the idea expressed in the sixth thesis on Feuerbach, he reiterates Marx's belief that the historical development of man can only be explained "by the characteristics of those social relations between men which arise when social man acts on external nature, not by man's nature."[126] As in Marx, there is an assumption that change involved in the process of historicization must be planned. Although man develops by appropriating the forces of nature, his development is "determined at every given time by the degree of development of productive forces."[127]

In his theory of alienation, Marx argues that man's fundamental alienation takes place in the elementary productive attitudes of society, in historical development, not, as Hegel and his followers believe, in subjective states of consciousness. Philosophers, theologians, and abstract materialists, he indicates, have failed to realize that the ideas of the essence of man and metaphysical substance are irrelevant to the understanding of history. "They believe in all seriousness that chimeras like the God-Man, Man, etc. have presided over individual epochs of history."[128] Being merely theoriests, they believe wrongly that "all the relations of men can be derived from the concept of man in general" rather than from the existing social relations molded by the mode of production.[129] Marx's new reality describes in *German Ideology* and in his mature works is human society, not man in general. As a result, his concept of the inner conflict of alienated man, like his idea of the essence of human nature, almost disappears completely and is substituted by the concept of "alienated masses," of man in class war against the alien forces of capitalism. Analyzing Marx's essentialist ideas of human nature, Althusser is led to the conclusion that the mature Marx has thus substituted the essentialist concept of man by the concept of "masses."[130] This seems to suggest that the mature Marx lost his interest in both man's essential mature and self-alienation, thus moving, as Tucker and Bell indicate, from the psychological to the sociological analysis of dehumanization and estrangement.

Analyzing the estrangement of the worker in capitalist society, Marx uses his theory of alienation to clarify his approach to both the individual man and capitalism. This analysis has led him to the conclusion that capitalism is the "denial of man" and that in subordination to alienated products man degrades and distorts his "true anthropological nature." It is in the light of the alienating aspects of capitalism that the so-called mature Marx formulates his materialistic theory of alienation. In *Manuscripts*, he reproaches Hegel for equating real man with self-consciousness and real estrangement with the estrangement of self-consciousness. He also criticizes politicial economists for basing their theories on fallacious reasoning, rendering them unable to explain anything. Rejecting their approach to man's socioeconomic relations as "nebulous and unrealistic," Marx believes he has found the riddle of historical alienation in alienated labor, in dehumanized man subjected to the alien forces of private ownership and market economy. There is, he says, a close connection between private property and alienation.[131] Motivated by his own moral values, he focuses his criticism on capitalist greed, avarice, and devaluation of men.[132] Real alienation begins with the appearance of private property, division of labor, and labor markets in which men sell their labor power. In capitalism the "relation of exchange between labor and capital is a mere semblance."[133] During the exchange of pseudo-equivalents, the worker is always cheated and alienated.[134] In *Manuscripts*, Marx also speaks of the non-worker or capitalist as being in "a state of alienation."[135] In capitalism everyone is alienated, although labor is most alienated.

The term *alienation* is always used in an ambiguous and obscure manner in Marx's theory of alienation. In his mature works, however, the term is used sporadically, and when it does appear in the text, Althusser remarks, it is used either ironically or as an equivalent to exploitation, dehumanization, and enslavement.[136] In *Communist Manifesto*, Marx mocks those socialists who give too much prominence to the idea of alienation, although here he does not condemn the word outright.[137] There are several reasons for his rejection of the original essentialist theory of alienation, but perhaps the most important one is his awareness that essentialism is incompatible with dialectical materialism. Challenging the view that the laws of human development can be explained in terms of human nature, he had been led to the conclusion that it is only the material life of men, expressed in their social relations, that can realistically explain their history and "real alienation." The fact that the term *alienation* had already re-established its idealistic connotations among his socialistically-minded opponents during his lifetime was probably another reason for forsaking both the concept of "human nature in general" and the concept of alienation as used in classical sociological works of the nineteenth century. By transforming his theory of alienation into the theory of exploitation, Marx believes he has rescued the "world of man" from the "inverted world of idealism."[138]

Marx's theory of alienation differs considerably from the theories expounded in Hegelian idealism, Feuerbachian pseudo-materialism, existentialism, and psychoanalysis. All these theories, like Marx's, see man as subject to irrational, alien forces that thwart, dominate, and impoverish his life. They all stress the undeniable fact that man is a suffering being who, instead of living a meaningful and happy life, can easily "regress to natural simplicity" and, more importantly, to fetishistic and alienating practices.[139] The existentialists, like Kierkegaard and Berdyaev, retain the existential emphasis of Hegelian idealism, indicating that "man's inclination to self-alienation" is inherent. In Freudian psychology, a central position is occupied by unconscious processes summarized in the phrase "the unconscious mind." Freud, Jung, and their followers regard self-alienation as a psychic or mental phenomenon, originating from the split between conscious and unconscious forces within man. The distinguishing feature of Marx's theory of estrangement is the rejection of any separate ontological status of mind. He believers in an ontology of elementary building blocks of the universe that are essentially material. Everything in the universe is reducible to them and, in his view, there is no soul. Even social relations are ultimately reducible to bits of "thinking matter."

In Marx's materialist system, man stands alone in a predominantly hostile nature. Man is comforted, however, by the thought that he can change nature and subdue its wild forces for his own benefits.[140] The laws of human actions that determine *praxis* are to be deduced from the principle that the mind is a collection of sensations caused by physical impressions on the organ of sense. Admittedly, men have history that includes their spiritual strivings as well, but Marx believes "they have history only because they produce their life" and the way in which this is done "is determined by their physical organisation."[141] The principal weakness in Marx's theory of alienation is the assumption that man and his spiritual goals are only a product of material and external forces and that the effects of social relations on human life are progressively positive. His dogma that socioeconomic conditions alone are at the roots of all alienation must be discarded. The great majority of modern psychologists and psychoanalysts, including Freud and Jung, find this dogma entirely unacceptable. If men are to be the masters of their destiny as Marx wanted them to be, then surely this could only be through their ideas, reflecting their spiritual goals, not through mere satisfaction of their "bodily needs." Unfortunately, in Marx's ideology these ideas belong to the derivative realm of "phantoms" and the form they take is determined by economic forces.[142]

In *German Ideology*, Marx speaks of "liberating men from the chimeras, the ideas, dogmas, imaginary things under the yoke of which they are pining away,"[143] without realizing that constructive ideas are more fundamental and more powerful in changing men and their social relations than the more complex material means of production. The naturalistic method used in Marx's theory of alienation is essentially descriptive. Not surprisingly, intellectual production has been identified with material production, and as a result, spiritual alienation has been reduced to economic alienation. This does not mean that his theory of alienation should be rejected as a figment of imagination. His analysis of "alienated labour" in capitalist society is a great contribution to the understanding of human relations between labor and capital, "the worker and the non-worker." Marx has shown much interest in the problem of exploitation and alienation of existing men. Yet, his preoccupation with the socioeconomic determinant of human history and his overemphasis on man's material conditions shaping this history make his conception of alienation narrow and unrealistic. Among other things, his theory of alienation seems to imply that man is somehow social before being human. For non-

Marxist analysts of the human world, the ultimate determinant of the course of history is the combination of psychological and biological, spiritual and material factors, interacting and strengthening one another. For Marx, however, this determinant is "corporeal man with his feet on the solid ground," always determined, like plants and animals, by external material forces.[144]

Marx overlooks the ontological fact that alienation is a universal, pre-eminently psychological phenomenon and that to be human means to be alienated. Orthodox Marxists share his view that labor is the condition of "all spiritual human activity" and that the phenomenon of alienation is merely the product of "alienated labour." Unfortunately, some commentators ignore the difference between psychological and socioeconomic aspects of alienation and concentrate entirely on the latter. Confusing the terms *alienation* and *exploitation*, *psychology* and *economics*, I believe Kolakowski wrongly maintains that "commodity fetishism" referred to in *Capital* is nothing "but a particularisation" of alienation. The passage he quotes from *German Ideology* is far from being "evidence" in support of his claim that Marx has never abandoned the "category of alienation."[145] His suggestion that self-alienation and exploitation, psychological and economic phenomena are identical processes is ideological nonsense and cannot be defended by any rational argument. On the whole, the view that "the deformation of consciousness" is a consequence of alienated labor is rejected by psychologists, theologians, and philosophers. Similar confusion can be detected in Mészáros's exposition of Marx's theory of alienation.[146] Marx, he says, has never "turned his back" on the concept of alienation as this concept plays a similar role in *Manuscripts* and *Capital*. Without any convincing evidence, he jumps impetuously to the conclusion that *Manuscripts* "begin as full-blooded mature Marx."[147] The persistence of alienation in all social structures, as even some modern Marxists admit, indicates clearly that alientation in the strict sense has little to do with class antagonisms. The mature Marx seems to have realized the ambiguity of the term *alienation* and has rightly transformed his theory of alienation into the theory of exploitation.

2
Causes of Alienation

It must be stressed at the outset that Marx has written considerably less on causality than Hegel, Feuerbach, Engels, or Lenin. Surprisingly enough, we can learn more about the Marxian conception of causality from the writings of Engels and Lenin than from those of Marx himself. His account of the causes of alienation is brief, ambiguous, and obscure. The main source of ideas in this account is the Hegelian belief in reciprocity as the "proximate truth of the relation of cause and effect" expounded in *Logic*.[1] Marx seems to share Hegel's belief that "reciprocal action alone can, in the long run, explain and realise the causal relation in its complete development." In reciprocity, Hegel explains, the "rectilinear movement out from causes to effects, and from effects to causes, is bent round and back into itself, and thus the progress *ad infinitum* of causes and effects is, as a progress, really and truly suspended."[2] The whole "rectilinear movement" from causes to effects and *vice versa* becomes intelligible in the light of necessity. Actually, neither Hegel nor Marx discovered the concept of "reciprocal causality"—it appears in Kant's "exposition of the cosmological idea of freedom in harmony with the universal law of natural necessity."[3] Kant distinguishes between "empirical causality" and the "causality of reason." The causality of phenomena is subject to conditions of time. "No phenomenal cause can absolutely and of itself begin a series." In Kant's view, a primal action—one that forms an absolute beginning—is beyond the causal power of phenomena. "The causality of reason in its intelligible character does not begin to be; it does not make its appearance at a certain time for the purpose of producing an effect."[4] When presenting the natural conditions of natural events and analyzing their causes, a "belief in the reciprocal causality of phenomena is certainly necessary."[5]

The Hegelian conception of causality and necessity that left an indelible mark on Marx's mind is, like that of Aristotle, Descartes, Kant, and even of Newton, essentialist and transcendental. The problem of motion and change is explained by reference to the invisible structure of things or to their hidden, unobservable elementary constituents. Motion, as Descartes puts it, is known empirically to us only as passage from one location to another. Like existence itself, it is explicable only in a metaphysical, theistic manner. In his view, causal relation is a relation of dependence without time sequence. All changes, *quâ* causal, are instantaneous; effects are not temporally sequent to their causes. Finite bodies are incapable of causing changes in one another, and the changes discernible empirically in them are caused directly by God's creative action.[6] Being a finite being, man himself is the source of evil propensities and corruption. Marx, of course, rejects all transcendental concepts of causality as being irrelevant to the "connection of money relations with production in general and intercourse."[7] For him, only the material causes taken in a dialectical sense are significant and real in determining man's historical development. Philosophers, in his view, always have in mind the imaginary relationship of men to their real conditions of existence and merely speculate about their causes instead of explaining these conditions.

One distinguishing aspect of Marx's causal theory of alienation is the refusal to be involved in "distant and nebulous causes." Analyzing the phenomenon of alienation in *Manuscripts of 1844*, he criticizes theology and political economy for pushing the question of the origin of alienation into a nebulous distance. "Do not let us go back," he writes, "to a fictitious primordial condition as the political economist does when he tries to explain. Such a primordial condition explains nothing." Theology "in the same way explains the origin of evil by the fall of man: that is, it assumes as a fact, in historical form, what has to be explained."[8] Rejecting all speculation about causality, Marx insists on the relevance of "actual economic facts" because these alone can help men to discover the "hidden substratum" in the relationship between their productive activity and alienation. He has, of course, failed to conform his causal theory of alienation to "empirical facts," and, as Althusser remarks, in his early works Marx seeks and finds causes for alienation in the imaginary realm, in essentialism.[9] In his later works, Marx has rejected essentialism and with it, it seems, Hegel's concept of "reciprocal causality."

As a schoolboy Marx was well aware of the existence of evil and egoism, but later the Hegelian and Feuerbachian analysis of the capitalist social order led him to the belief that human avarice, wickedness, and alienation are the products of a definite social development rather than natural or inherent phenomena. His mature writings emphasize what Althusser calls "structural causality" and material alienation. Instead of dwelling on the ideological myth of a philosophy of origins and its related concepts, Marx has paid special attention to recognizing the "givenness of the complex structure of concrete objects" that regulate the development of these objects and theoretical practice.[10] Thus relations of production as a totality constitute the crucial economic structure that is at the center of Marx's conception of causality and alienation. He sees this structure as the ruling class pattern of the totality of productive relations involving contradictions and conflicts between those who own most of the means of production and the minority who own few or none of the means of production. In Marx's view, effective ownership of productive forces by some individuals always implies corresponding alienation of all members of society.

Marx's causal theory of alienation is based on the belief that the estrangement of man cannot be dissociated from material production. Resisting metaphysical implications and confining himself to the "earthly basis of history" as much as possible, he strongly criticizes the view that social evils, including alienation, result from any mental or spiritual imbalance. Marx categorically rejects the causal analysis of alienation in terms of "divine laws" or any psychological and philosophico-existentialist concepts. From the non-Marxist view point, alienation is a psychological as well as a physical phenomenon, involving the whole man. This psychological approach to the causes of man's loss, or what Fromm calls insanity, is well reflected not only in theological theories of estrangement but also in psychoanalysis. Freud's discovery of the unconscious, Jung's theory of the inherent tendency of the "psyche to split," and Fromm's conception of the "existential split in man" expressed in his feelings of powerlessness, isolation, frustration, and alienation have enlarged considerably the horizon of conditions and sources of alienation, especially emphasizing the relevance of internal factors in the process of man's self-alienation.[11] The existentialist theories of Kierkegaard, Berdyaev, and Sartre have concentrated equally on the importance of subjective experience and internal or spiritual factors in the etiology of the estrangement of man.[12] They all believe that a purely economic or material explanation of the origin of alienation is inadequate. Indeed, even some liberally minded Marxists, like Roger Garaudy, point out that the origin of alienation cannot be traced "simply to its economic causes."[13]

Deeply concerned with the etiological issue of evil tendencies in human nature and society, Freud maintains that alienation expressed as frustration, hostility, and aggression has its roots within man himself. In *Civilisation and Its Discontent*, Freud starts from the premise that human nature is common to the human race throughout all ages and cultures. All of man's frustration and alienation are caused by conflicting demands that are part of human nature.[14] However, Freud's causal theory, tracing all important psychic phenomena to the physiological substratum of human passion in the libido, has been rejected by many modern psychologists and psychoanalysts, including Jung and Fromm. Indicating that Freud's causal theory has been motivated solely by intellectual imagination rather than by experimental facts and scientific evidence, Fromm has tried to free Freudian theory from instinct, replacing explanation in terms of libidinal drives by those of cultural conditions.[15] He believes man's most intensive passions and needs are not those rooted in his body—they are not primarily material or physical. Instead they are those passions and needs that are rooted in the very peculiarity of human existence.

Jung's criticism of Freud's mechanistic libidinal causality is much stronger than Fromm's. He accuses Freud of confining himself to sexuality and its ramifications in the psyche, overlooking the fact that sexual dynamics is only one particular element in the total human self.[16] The defect of the Freudian view of causal connections lies in the one-sidedness and tendentious subjectivity expressed in the assumption that causes remain immutable substances that operate continuously in the psyche. Freud's assumption that the sexual component plays the decisive role in the cause-effect chain is rejected.[17] In Jung's view, the nature of the psyche reaches into obscurities far beyond human understanding, containing as many riddles as the universe itself. Alienation is associated with inherent powerlessness and limitation reflected in man's natural restlessness and lack of meaning in life.[18] Jung, unlike Marx and Engels, resists the belief that causality can explain all human and social evils. He indicates that men should make allowance for absolute irrationality in certain cases of psychic phenomena, remembering that in the last analysis causality is no more than a statistical truth.[19]

Science, as Jung understands it, has never grasped the riddle of life either in organic matter or in the mysterious trains of mental imagery. Stressing, unlike Marx, in his concept of man, that the source of all life must somehow transcend experience, Jung is strongly anti-materialistic. Modern men, like primitives, he says, still tend to live in the world of images or mental fabrictions, deluding themselves that they know much more about matter than about mind or spirit. Materialists overestimate material causation and maintain that it alone can afford a true explanation of life. "They forget that matter is just as inscrutable as mind."[20] The dogma that mental diseases are the result of the pathological condition of the brain is, in Jung's view, a hangover from the materialism of the 1870s. Life as a function of matter postulates sponstaneous generation that can never be made intelligible in the light of purely materialistic dogmas. Materialism and idealism are psychological opposites, just like atheism and theism. They represent two different methods of dealing with the alienating effects of the unconscious, one by denying totally the internal factors in the process of causation and the other by recognizing them.[21] Unlike Marx, Jung insists that life has a specific law of its own that cannot be explained in terms of chemistry or economics. For Marx, the conception of internal laws issuing in alienation is entirely illusory. The only law that is relevant to the alienation of "real, corporal man" must be expressed in terms of dialectical materialism.

Discoveries of modern science have made a significant change in man's scientific picture of the universe. They have shattered the absolute validity of natural law and thus have made it relative. To the physicist, natural laws are primarily statistical truths and causally significant only in the domain of macrophysical quantities. In very minute quantities, prediction, as Heisenberg has found out, becomes uncertain if not impossible, because minute quantities of matter refuse to behave according to known natural laws. Heisenberg seems to have proved that belief in a complete deterministic account of the universe is untenable in principle and must be rejected. Yet, it is on this belief that Marx's causal theory of alienation is based. Modern Marxists are aware of physical complexities involved in any form of statistical determinism, indicating that the multiplicity of determinisms inevitably poses the problem of their unity. Without any scientific evidence, they take for granted that any apparent contradiction in causal laws disappears as soon as they are analyzed in a dialectical manner. This, of course, is the Hegelian assumption only in its "inverted" form. In the Marxian view, the physical determinism of human activity is always linked with the concept of "man in nature."[22] Marx and Engels assume that the causal patterns embodied in dialectical laws are universal. Law and necessity are categories that are at the heart of the Marxian theory of causation, regulating the origin, existence, development, and death of all living organisms.

In science great care is needed in investigating causal relations between antecedents and consequents that are not always necessarily causes and effects. The identification of any mere antecedent with the cause may lead to absurd conclusions. Science seeks the immediate cause of things; the immediate cause reaches full action only when the effect begins to be observed, and this is normally open to empirical evidence. Marx insists that his causal theory of alienation is based on empirical facts without realizing that empirical observations are never certain and that as Hume remarks, mere temporal sequence of events is not the same as causation. *Post hoc* is not the same as *propter hoc*. In Marx's causal theory of alienation, involving "man with feet on the solid ground," it is assumed that the relation between a cause and its effect is an observable fact.[23] One could argue that his theory is not intended to defeat the skepticist argument that causation is not an object of demonstrative reasoning and that the inherence of an effect in its cause is a nebulous entity that can never be discovered either in nature or in human relations. Yet Marx's total disregard of the phenomenalist analysis of causation, especially in the light of growing positivism, can only be indicative of his great interest in the destruction of skepticism, the "confessed inability to solve the contradictions with which one is ultimately faced."[24]

Like Hegel, Marx and Engels have consistently combated the skepticist view that the conflict between reason and sense, conception and perception, is irreconcilable, and consequently the nature of causal reality is essentially unknowable. Considering their claim that the Marxian causal theory of alienation is based on "empirical facts," it is difficult to understand their rejection of the Humean conception of causal relations. Hume's analysis of causation has been influenced significantly by his epistemological ideas, especially his general empiricist view that all meaningful statements can be analyzed in terms of the sensory impressions from which all ideas are derived. In Hume's view, the impression of "force or motion" that may be associated with causality does not exemplify the "idea of necessary connection." "There is no object which implies the existence of any other," he says, "if we consider these objects in themselves and never look beyond the ideas which we from of them."[25] The effect is totally different from the cause and consequently never can be discovered in it. Unlike Marx, Hume argues that all empirical statements are contingent and that even when true they can be denied without self-contradiction. Nothing in the realm of empirical facts is certain and immune from doubt. The experience of constant conjunction between some events, whether in history or nature, does not provide a logical link that enables us to make causal inferences by demonstrative reasoning.

Without an appeal to the uniformity of nature, which Hume has rejected as non-rational, the empiricist never can prove that the same power must continue in the same object or collection of sensible qualities, let alone that "a like power is always conjoined with like sensible qualities." In his reaction to Hume's causal theory, Kant admits that the notion of cause contains a strong empirical component. In the empirical world the cause is necessarily "phenomenised in perfect accordance with the laws of empirical causality and the acting subject, as a causal phenomenon, continues ro preserve a complete connection with nature and natural conditions."[26] Yet the perception of objects always implies the principles of objective determination in space and time. This objective determination is not just perceived. Scientific thinking entails an experience in which the distinction between objective and subjective elements is always made, although admittedly the principles of scientific reasoning have no application beyond the limits of experience. Kant argues that causation is involved in both thinking and objective perception and that it can be a principle used in objective thinking without involving the conclusion that the nature of reality must be an order of events causally determined in time. "Pure reason, as a purely intelligible faculty, is not subject to the conditions of time."[27] Because reason is the permanent condition of all sections of the human will, the "sensuous condition of an empirical series of effects which resides in reason is non-sensuous and thus cannot be originated."[28]

Criticizing the Humean and Kantian conception of causality, Lenin following Engels, rejects entirely the "standpoint of Kantian and Humean school wisdom" reflected in their causal theories. "The distinction between the Humean and the Kantian theories of causality," he writes, "is only a secondary difference of opinion between agnostics who are basically at one, viz., in their denial of objective law in nature, and who thus inevitably condemn themselves to idealist conclusions of one kind or another."[29] Lenin is very hostile to the agnostics Mach and Avenarius for their belief that "apart from logical necessity no other necessity exists." This view, he points out, "has been so vigorously combated by Feuerbach. It never even occurs to Mach to deny his kinship with Hume." Like Hume, Mach denies the existence of causes and effects in nature, falsely maintaining that "all forms of the law of causality spring from subjective motives and that there is no necessity for nature to correspond with them."[30] In Lenin's view, Hume and Mach's scepticism about necessary connections in nature amounts to "solipsism and pure Kantian idealism." Using his sarcastic sense of humor, he points out that the "poor mystics, Feuerbach, Marx and Engels have been talking all the time of necessity in nature and have even been calling those who hold the Humean position theoretical reactionaries."[31]

Lenin praises Feuerbach and Engels for their consistent recognition of objective law in nature and objective causality. The connection between natural phenomena is obviously causal, objective, and dialectical. The recognition of objective causal law in nature, he says, is materialism. "All other views, or rather any other philosophical line on the question of causality, the denial of causality and necessity in nature, are justly regarded by Feuerbach as belonging to the fideist trend." "The subjectivist line on the question of causality is philosophical idealism (the varieties of which are the theories of causality of both Hume and Kant) and fideism."[32] In support of the dialectical view of causality, Lenin relies mainly on Engels, and somewhat surprisingly on Feuerbach. Although Marx has rejected Feuerbach's abstract materialism," Lenin says that Feuerbach's views "are consistently materialist," implying that Feuerbach's conception of causality is entirely in line with dialectical materialism. Actually, Feuerbach says very little about causal connections. In *Essence of Christianity*, he merely asserts that "existence is the absolute necessity and the cause of conscious existence is the need of life." The world originates from its own "inherent necessity."[33] The emphasis on objective law and necessity as expressed in the connection between natural phenomena is obviously, in Lenin's view, a positive feature of Feuerbach's materialism and his theory of causality.

Lenin believes that Engels more than anybody else has produced authoritative and convincing arguments in defense of dialectical materialism and, of course, against the theories of causality expounded by Hume and Kant. After all, it is Engels who has entirely dissociated himself from the agnostics on such fundamental problems as necessity and causality.[34] Lenin in this respect is very uninformative and seems to hide the fact that Engels's "dialectical view of cause and effect" originates from Hegel's metaphysics. Engels himself acknowledges his debt to the "genius of Hegel," indicating that natural science has confirmed Hegel's thesis that "reciprocal action is the true *causa finalis* of things."[35] He obviously exaggerates the scientific value of the Hegelian conception of reciprocal action, and unsurprisingly praises Marx for accepting Hegel's idea of reciprocal causation in his own theory of alienation.[36] Arguing against Hume's skepticism in a manner similar to that of Hegel, Engels accepts the view that our senses as well as our reason may sometimes deceive us. "But it is precisely the possibility of deception that proves causality instead of refuting it because we can find out the cause of all deviations from the rule by approximate investigation.[37] Indicating that the "activity of human begins forms the test of causality," Engels seems to suggest that the distinction between the cause-factors and the effect-factors rests essentially on the distinction between things done and acts, events and things realized through human actions. This could be interpreted to mean that the concept of causation becomes more intelligible when connected with a man's manipulative ability to produce desired effects. To think of a relation between acts and events as causal is, in fact, not much different from thinking of it in terms of possible human action.

In *Dialectics of Nature*, Engels holds that it is "by the activity of human beings that the idea of causality" can finally be established.[38] Any "test of causality" must be based on this activity. "If we bring the sun's rays to a focus by means of a concave mirror and make them act like the rays of an ordinary fire, we thereby prove that heat comes from the sun." Here Engels is considering only particular causal occurrences that are testable by any normal human individual. In science, however, causes are frequently sought to explain such general phenomena as planetary motions, magneticism, light, tides, and earthquakes rather than particular occurrences or their opposites. Scientists maintain that events can be explained and predicted only in so far as they have repeatable characteristics but not in so far as they are particulars. Metaphysicians, Engels indicates, tend to analyze causal relations in terms of individual events.[39] The general picture of appearances is inadequate in explaining the "details of which this picture is made up and so long as we do not understand these, we have not a clear idea of the whole picture."[40]

Following Hegel's analysis of causal relations in the world, Engels maintains that in the ordinary or narrow sense, "cause and effect are conceptions which only hold good in their application to individual cases." "As soon as we consider the individual cases in their general connection with the universe as a whole, they run into each other, and they become confounded when we contemplate that universal action and reaction in which causes and effects are eternally changing places, so that what is effect here and now will be cause there and then, and *vice versa*."[41] This Hegelian conception of reciprocity is re-emphasized by Engels in *Dialectics of Nature* in which the forms of motion are seen as passing into one another and "being in place cause and in another effect."[42] Hegel, like Kant before him, gives considerable prominence to the conception of the reciprocal action of phenomena in *Logic*. As primary fact, he writes, the cause is qualified as having absolute independence in face of the effect. "But in the necessity, whose identity constitutes that primariness itself, it is wholly passed into the effect. The primariness of the cause is suspended in the effect in which the cause makes itself a dependent entity. The cause, however, does not for that reason vanish and leave the effect to be alone actual."[43]

Even in finite cause and its conception, Hegel indicates, it is possible to observe the identity between cause and effect in their common content. "The rain (as cause) and the wetness (as effect) are the self-same existing water. In point of form the cause (rain) is dissipated or lost in the effect (wetness), but in that case the result can no longer be described as effect, for without the cause it is nothing."[44] Hegel warns us not to rely entirely on the concept of reciprocal action and its "deceptive moments." In historical research, reciprocity is undoubtedly the proximate truth of the relation between cause and effect and stands, as he says "on the threshold of the notion." But on that ground, he points out, we should not be content with applying this relation. If we get no further than studying a given content under the point of view of reciprocity, he says, "we are taking up an attitude which leaves matters utterly incomprehensible." We are left with a mere dry fact and the "call for mediation, which is the chief motive in applying the relation of causality, is still unanswered."[45] Like Kant, Hegel assumes that "a primal action" that initiates an absolute beginning is beyond the causal power of phenomena in nature and history. Although the teleology of history and its efficient causation are linked necessarily with actions of human beings, it is, in Hegel view, the Absolute or world Spirit that makes its saving appearance and an absolute beginning. The world of spirit and the world of nature, according to Hegelian idealism, "continue to have this distinction that the latter moves only in a recurring cycle while the former also makes progress."[46]

Marx strongly rejects Hegel's idealist analysis of causal connections whether these connections are assumed or observed in nature or in human history. However, he retains Hegel's belief that events and ends of human activity occur as the result of the conflict of opposing tendencies. The Hegelian idealist philosophy, in Marx's view, is pervaded by the concept of "otherness" that makes the dialectical nature of thought rather than the dialectical interaction between causes and effects in the process of alienation. Marx does not object to Hegel's belief that causes strictly belong to the sphere of necessity and that the nature of parts is determined by the whole. There is nothing new in this belief, because even the primitive mentality has indicated a keen awareness of this whole. Whenever picturing objects, events, or causal series in the world, man has always felt the need to reintegrate these phenomena into a unity of totality. Marx, like Hegel, maintains that all particular causal series in history are affected profoundly by their interrelations as well as their relations to the whole. When a part is viewed in relation to the totality of things or events, it is seen immediately as being dependent for its existence on the whole that alone is truly real. Stressing the logical priority of the whole or totality to the parts, Marx believes that the only structure that is antecedent and factual pertains to the concrete, material, and economic processes as expressed in human history.[47]

Marx views the Hegelian totality as spiritual, expressing merely the alienated development of a mystical unity that is only a moment of the development of the Absolute. Rejecting Hegel's conception of the alienation of self-consciousness, he also rejects Hegel's spiritual principle that constitutes the internal unity of the "end or final cause and the mere efficient cause." In Hegel's causal theory, the end or final cause is "never free from otherness." Yet even in its causal chain, this cause "retains itself and is at the end what it was in the beginning or primordial state."[48] The teleology of historical development and its efficient causation interact necessarily in the dialectical production of the "unity or actuality of essence with existence or of the inward with the outward."[49] Marx criticizes Hegel's idea of efficient causation as a mere tool for realizing non-human, abstract, and divine teleology. "For Hegel, the whole of nature merely repeats the logical abstractions in a sensuous, external form."[50] Hegel almost identifies teleology with occultism, in which the future acts causally on the present. In the Hegelian theory of causation, everything is reduced to "spiritual causes."[51] The "formal cause means nothing more than eternal design and things are supposed to be merely means employed and spent in realising a purpose which lies outside of them."[52]

Having rejected Hegel's divine dialectic of "pure thought" and his conception of alienation as a divine process, Marx reverses his emphais on spiritual efficient causation, indicating the priority of material and economic causation in the etiology of alienation.[53] Hegel's belief in the spiritual origin of alienation, according to Marx, is an inescapable consequence of his idealism and "false positivism."[54] He reproaches Hegel for overlooking the causal explanation of the nature and real structure·of the sociohistorical relations at different stages of human development. Hegel's interest in these relations is only to reveal them as the "form of the Idea's other being" and to indicate that alienation of these relations is inherent in their dialectical movement.[55] Although Marx has never departed from the relational conception of alienation that is implicit in Hegel's causal theory, he rejects entirely his belief that the logical movement of the Absolute can be found in every domain of human life and that every contradiction can be transcended in a progressive movement of reason.

Marx's materialist theory of alienation and its causes is an inversion of Hegel's essentialist and idealist theory that treats alienation, error, and evil merely as evidence of the existence of the Absolute. Both Marx and Hegel stress that the ills of human society are inevitable rather than accidental. Hegel's principal thesis is that everything short of the whole is imperfect and fragmentary. This incompleteness or imperfection is a phenomenon that appears equally in the realm of spirit and in the material world. Only the Absolute Idea is complete, has no opposite and no discord, and being wholly spiritual and rational, it is free from evil. In *Philosophy of Religion*, Hegel strives to prove that sin and evil have a rightful place in a universe that is essentially good. Like Leibniz, he maintains that such phenomena as alienation and evil necessarily belong to the nature of finite beings. There is nothing in these phenomena that cannot be absorbed in the Absolute and contribute to the harmony and perfection of the whole. In *Phenomenology of Spirit*, he clearly incorporates alienation and evil into the Absolute. Self-centeredness, which is the root of alienation and evil, is an essential moment in the life of the Absolute. According to Hegel, "good enters into actuality and appears as an existent self-consciousness." Alienation and evil, however, are "nothing other than the externalisation and self-centeredness of the natural existence of Spirit."[56]

While Hegel is preoccupied with alienation of the divine Being and its teleological externalization in "otherness," Marx argues that the Hegelian conception of self-objectification as self-alienation has absolutely nothing to do with real anthropology. Alienation and its causal connections only can be grasped when man is seen as an active natural being related historically to other men and when human history is conceived as a collection of socioeconomic facts rather than an "imagined activity of an imagined subject."[57] Instead of searching for any specific causal relations between antecedents and consequents in complex social structures, Marx argues against the political economist that one must begin in this respect by accepting the existence of the interaction and then try to "grasp and explain the essential connection" between alienation and the socioeconomic and historical factors that reflect man's real life.[58] To suit his materialist teleology, he manipulates the significance and priority of various factors involved in the appearance of alienating effects. He is convinced that these effects are not accidental but rather the result of dialectical necessity. Marx contends that natural necessity binds man to other men. The communist materialist, he says, "sees the necessity as the condition which plays the primary role in any transformation of the social structure."[59] In the Marxian system of reciprocal relations, everything depends on the existing conditions. These conditions, Althusser indicates, are the very existence of the whole in a determinate position.[60] The existing conditions are believed to reflect the contradictions that constitute the entire historical process.

Marx's conception of internal relations is similar to that of Spinoza and Hegel. According to Spinoza, all components of "divine substance," whether thoughts or material things, merely express the totality of interrelations that determines their individual characteristics. "In the nature of things nothing is contingent and all things are determined by the necessity of divine nature for existing and working in a certain way.[61] In Hegel's philosophical system, the "process of necessity begins with the existence of scattered circumstances which appear to have no interconnection and no concern with one another."[62] He distinguishes between a merely external necessity that means determination from without and the real inward necessity that is identical with freedom.[63] The real internal necessity is the distinguishing feature of the Absolute or of the context of the whole. "The contingent, roughly speaking, is what has the gound of its being not in itself but in something else."[64] A similar idea is expressed by Sartre when he says that totality can come to particular events and beings only by a being that has to be its own totality in their presence, and that totalities always reflect the internal relations between the constituent elements of the whole and the whole itself.[65] Marx criticizes Hegel for treating the internal relations of men as "alienated thinking," but it is interesting to notice that he does not reject the relational status of his particular things or events and their dependence on the totality or whole. His theory of causal connections in the socioeconomic realm, like his theory of alienation, is beyond empirical evidence. Some modern Marxists, like Althusser, believe that "theoretical" concepts of the complex relation of reciprocal conditions involved in the genesis of alienation are essential to Marx's understanding of the contradictions within the historical development of the whole.[66]

Like Hegel and Feuerbach, Marx tends to analyze physical and spiritual phenomena in terms of relations. Hegel thinks of causality as a relation between action and reaction.[67] Feuerbach defines physical life as the "perpetual interchange of the objective and subjective relation."[68] Indeed, most philosophers, including Hume and Kant, view the world *sub specie relationis*, and Marx is no exception. "Only the animal," he says, "does not relate itself to anything, it does not relate itself at all."[69] Agreeing with Hegel, he believes that the internal structure and meaning of particular elements of reality can only be intelligible when analyzed in their interrelationship inside the totality that alone can reflect their unity. However, Marx reproaches Hegel for ignoring the specific qualities of the material and economic relations that constitute this totality. Because Marx regards Hegel's totality as the abstract aggregate of particular forms of spiritual reality, the Hegelian conception of the relation between the particular and the universal is rejected. Marx's totality is primarily socioeconomic, and it is in the light of this totality that he analyzes the origin and effects of alienation. This analysis, according to many of his followers, represents "absolute truth." It is unfortunate that Marx took no warning from such distinguished empiricists as Berkeley, indicating that the "obscure ambiguous term *relation* frequently confounds and deceives us." Berkeley denies the existence of "corporeal causes" and believes that "God alone is the immediate efficient cause of all things."[70] His causal theory, which reappears in a different form in Hegel and Max Stirner, aims at refuting materialism, the very system Marx defends. The only thing they have in common is the claim that all their philosophical assertions are realistic and can be tested by experience.

Marx shows no interest in metaphysical theories of causation. His objective is not to interpret the world but rather to change it. Yet he does not altogether rule out the relevance of explanation, especially when the origin of the movement of private property and its relation to alienation are concerned. Political economy is criticized because he thinks it has failed to explain the existence of such obvious antagonisms as the class war between workers and non-workers. Political economists, maintaining their ahistorical and obsolete theories, he says, have never sought to explain realistically the causes of alienation and the development of socioeconomic relations that have engendered the capitalist mode of production. Marx is unequivocal in arguing that the estrangement of man is a consequence of production. He accuses the political economists of concealing this estrangement by disregarding the fact that private ownership and capitalist exchange manipulate production for human use in favor of profit making. "Under the semblance of recognising man, the political economy is really no more than consistent implementation of the denial of man, since man himself no longer stands in an external relation of tension to the external substance of private property but has himself become this tensed essence of private property."[71]

Analyzing the causal relationship between labor and capital in the genesis

of alienation, Marx is concerned primarily with private ownership of productive forces that entail the power to subjugate and alienate the labor of others.
According to Marx, the form of property always corresponds to the form of
the social division of labor, and the form of the division of labor, which also
plays a significant role in the etiology of alienation, is determined by the mode
of production. Changes in the mode of production necessarily lead to changes
in property relations. The distinguishing feature of Marx's analysis of alienation is his emphasis on the changes in socioeconomic relations that result from
man's industrial and commercial pursuits. He always connects the appearance
of the estrangement of man with a socioeconomic basis. The degree of this
estrangement depends ultimately on the way material goods are socially produced and owned. Bourgeois economists, he says, "obliterate all historical
differences and see in all social phenomena only bourgeois phenomena."[72]

Criticizing bourgeois economists for their inability to see the connections
between alienation and competition or the "war among the avaricious," Marx
argues that economy is the backbone of historical becoming and that political
economy is a product of real economic movement. The deficiences of human
existence have their roots in circumstances outside man himself, in societies
based on exploitation and market economy. "The being of men and their
actual life process are conditioned by a definite development of their productive forces."[73] In the process of production "man can only work as nature
works by changing the forms of matter."[74] The necessity for economic change
is of paramount importance whenever there is a need for eliminating the
alienating conditions of human life. Marx always assumes that publicly owned
means of production will not only humanize and dealienate the production
process, but that it also will sustain the moral climate and endeavor necessary
for socioeconomic change. He believes that men enter into the relations of
production that are dialectically indispensable and independent of human
will. The productive relations correspond to a definite state of development of
productive forces. The totality of productive relations constitute society's economic structure, the basis of human existence.[75]

Marx attributes all forms of alienation and all social evils to the "god of
practical need and self-interest" and to the capitalist social order that "degrades all the gods of man and turns them into commodities."[76] The passion
of greed and avarice described in *Manuscripts of 1844* and *Grundrisse* is an
alienating inhuman force. The origin of this force, Marx says, is in the property and money system of bourgeois society. Therefore, it is essential to grasp
the causal relationship between "private property, avarice and the separation
of labour and capital, the connection between alienation and the money
system."[77] Both Marx and Engels maintain that the emergence of private
property is conditioned historically and that the system of private ownership
"exists only where the means of labour and the external conditions of labour
belong to private individuals."[78] Engels sees in this system a "spiritless principle opposed to the human and spiritual principle." Alienation is at its worst

when "money—the alienated, empty abstraction of property—is made master of the world."[79] Human individuals living under the alienating conditions of bourgeois society cease to be the slaves of man and become the slaves of dead objects.

The most fundamental implication of Marx's causal theory of alienation is that the alienating process in society entails the loss of man's autonomy and the failure to realize his potential. As long as human society has class divisions, man cannot realize himself by objectifying himself. Capitalist society sanctions the exploitation of man by man, making it impossible for most men and women living in the same system to develop their capacities and satisfy their spiritual and physical needs. The alienating process of capitalist economy follows directly from dehumanizing conditions manipulated by those who own the means of production. What is striking in Marx's causal theory of alienation is his belief that, because of its disadvantageous position, labor power involved in the process of alienation depends entirely on the "domination of property and filthy self-interest."[80] He reproaches bourgeois writers for overlooking the fact that in commodity production labor power is treated merely as a commodity on the same level with other non-human commodities.[81] The appearance of labor markets in capitalist society in which the working men sell their labor power is a condition that Marx believes must be linked with alienation.

Having convinced himself that every movement in human history must have an economic cause, Marx searches for any economic cause that may explain the estrangement of man and his loss of freedom. On the whole, his analysis of the economic causes of alienation lacks clarity and consistency. He sees too many connections between alienation and socioeconomic factors to be able to discover any definite circumstance that clearly associates alienation with its real cause. In his accounts of the causes of the estrangement of man, Marx usually recalls three possible socioeconomic factors that must be responsible for the genesis of all alienation. Sometimes he says that alienation is the result of the system of private property, and other times he maintains that it is the product of a historical, special division of labor. He also argues that the source of alienation must be traced to the commodity mode of production or exchange. In *Manuscripts*, Marx makes his causal theory of alienation entirely unintelligible and ridiculously confused when he tries to convince his readers that alienation is so closely related to private ownership that the "movement of private property" could really be seen as the principal source of alienation. "The concept of alienated labour," he says, "is derived from the analysis of the movement of private property."[82] This suggests that there is no alienation and no alienated labor unless the system of private ownership already exists. Alienated labor only can arise if and when some people in society are already treating the conditions of their existence as private property. Yet, paradoxically, Marx is so confused that he also argues on the same page that alienation may not be the result of private property. "It becomes clear," he says, "that although private property appears to be the source, the cause of alienated labour, it is really its consequence."[83]

The "secret of private property" is so unfathomable in Marx's search for the causes of alienation that he cannot decide whether the "movement of private property" precedes alienated labor or is subsequent to it. Only after a very painstaking examination of the appearance and reality of private property does he conclude that the movement of private property really follows rather than precedes alienation. The apparent priority of private property is false, and what appears to be the cause is in reality an effect. Alienation, therefore, is the prior fact, generating the movement of private property as its product. There is no explanation, however, why alienation precedes private property. Marx makes this assumption without elaborating on the assertion that private property is "really an effect, a consequence" rather than the cause of alienated labor. "Private property thus results by analysis from the concept of alienated labour, i.e., of alienated man, of estranged labour, of estranged life, of estranged man."[84] The appearance of private property in socioeconomic relations is misleading, and Marx's analysis suggests that private property can only be the "product, the result, the necessary consequence of alienated labour, of the external relation of the worker to nature and to himself."[85]

Obviously Marx's analysis of the causal relationship between alienation and private property is far from being consistent and logical. He is so confused by the "secret of private property" that its role in the genesis of alienation for him becomes unavoidably ambivalent. He criticizes bourgeois economists for their inability to go "beyond abstract formulae" and to reach the real cause of alienation without realizing that he himself is equally unable to discover the priority in the causal relationship between alienation and private property. His appeal to "actual economic facts" ends in the failure to establish any manifest historical primacy in this respect. The prevalent view in *Manuscripts of 1844* is that private property follows rather than precedes alienation. The institution of private property, he says, can only be seen as a "result of estranged labour" or "the material sensuous expression of estranged human life."[86] This is reinstated in the sentence that private property becomes intelligible only when conceived "as the material, summary expression of alienated labour."[87] This corresponds to Engels's view that private property is essentially" the basic form of alienation."[88]

Following Hegel's theory of reciprocity and his belief that "reciprocal action alone can realise the causal relation in its complete development," both Marx and Engels maintain that causal relations are so complex that they can be intelligible only in terms of reciprocity. Unlike Marx, however, Engels refuses to be involved in the causal analysis of alienation, assuming that private property is an aspect of alienation. His brief discussion of reciprocity is related to causality in the field of natural science.[89] Marx's reference to reciprocity, however, is obviously linked to the relationship between alienation and private property. Unlike Hegel, he assumes that reciprocity is applicable to all causal relations, including those based on "empirical facts." He ignores Hegel's warning that reciprocity is only the "proximate truth of the relation of cause and effect" and that in complex relations that transcend direct observation, "one should not rest content with applying this relation."[90]

Hegel explains his conception of reciprocity or action and reaction in causal chains in terms of the movement of the Absolute just as he does the appearance of alienation and evil. Marx rejects this metaphysical explanation without offering any convincing explanation of his own. Because he is unable to trace the origin of private property, it is not surprising that he finds it impossible to explain clearly and consistently the causal relationship between alienation and private property. He is well aware of Feuerbach's failure to offer a satisfactory explanation for the phenomenon of religious alienation. In extending Feuerbach's causal explanation from anthropology to economic life, Marx searches for some "concrete socio-economic facts" that could help him demonstrate how alienation is connected with the movement of private property. He rejects Feuerbach's anthropological explanation of the origin of alienation and Hegel's belief that alienation is the inherent and inescapable fate of all human beings, but he fails to find any coherent and unambiguous alternative. Not surprisingly, he is involved in unsurmountable contradictions. The most glaring example is his statement that the "concept of alienated labour is obtained from an analysis of the property system," suggesting that alienation follows private property, and arguing concomitantly that "estranged labour is the direct cause of private property."[91]

Marx takes for granted that the causal relation is a relation of necessary connection. Unlike Hume, he seems to maintain that causation is an object of demonstrative reasoning. Alienation, in his view, only can be linked to material causes and these causes can be demonstrated.[92] The causal dependence of consequents on antecedents is contained in the things and events themselves. Basing his causal theory of alienation on the dialectical interaction between antecedents and consequents, Marx never doubts that there are natural, material, and objective interconnections between the phenomena of the socioeconomic world and that these interconnections can be demonstrated as dialectical and reciprocal action. He ignores entirely Hume's account of causation, and this must be interpreted to mean nothing less than his total rejection of Hume's scepticism in this respect and of Hume's attempted reduction of the objective content of causal relations to constant conjunctions. Hume denies that there is any direct relation between certain objects and events and that necessity assumed to be involved in the causal relation lies in the objects and events at all. Necessity, he says, is not found "either in superior or inferior natures, either in body or in spirit." "Necessity is something that exists in the mind, not in objects."[93] Unlike Hume, Marx assumes that causation is analyzable and distinguishable from coincidental sequences without essential reference to the regularity of sequence. Relations in the socioeconomic world are not causal simply because they are regular, constant, and uniform. On the contrary, these relations are regular because they are causally and dialectically linked.

Analyzing the causal links between alienation and private property, Marx definitely uses Hegel's idea of reciprocity, which entails dialectical action and reaction of opposites. Although his dialectical method is different fundamentally from Hegel's, Marx never departs from Hegel's belief that "everything that surrounds us may be viewed as an instance of dialectic" and that "dialectic is the very nature and essence of everything predicated by mere understanding—the law of things and of the finite as a whole."[94] It is in terms of dialectical movement rather than in terms of "regular sequence" or "constant conjunctions" that, in Marx's view, the objective content of causal relations between alienation and private property can be demonstrated. The result of his analysis, however, is far from convincing. He does not seem to be aware that if private property is an effect or a "necessary consequence" rather than the cause of alienation, then it is difficult to see how the elimination of private property can lead to the transcendence of alienation. Marx's assertion that "the positive transcendence of private property as the appropriation of human life is the positive transcendence of all estrangement" certainly implies that private property is the cause of alienation.[95]

In Marx's mind there is always a close connection between private property and the division of labor, although he never explains their real connection. He merely says that they are identical phenomena equally involved in the genesis of alienation. "Division of labour and private property," he writes, "are identical expressions: in the one the same thing is affirmed with reference to activity as is affirmed in the other with reference to the product of the activity."[96] A similar idea is emphasized in *Manuscripts*, although here Marx gives more prominence to the movement of private property than to division of labor in his causal theory of alienation.[97] In *German Ideology*, he seems to suggest that the division of labor somehow precedes all other socioeconomic contradictions, including private property. Thus, although division of labor and private property are "identical expressions," it is the division of labor that "offers us the first example of a cleavage between the particular and the common interest."[98] As soon as the division of labor comes into being, each man assumes a "particular, exclusive sphere of activity which is forced on him and from which he cannot escape."[99] Like private property, division of labor, in Marx's view, is connected inevitably with alienation. In *Capital*, Marx analyzes the role of division of labor in the small ancient Indian communities and says nothing about alienation. Although the mechanism of the economic structure of these communities could be characterized by what he calls the "purposive division of labour," he cannot deny the existence of a rigid division between mental and physical work even in them. It is probably true to say that the position of the manual worker in these communities was less liable to be alienated, but even Marx cannot say categorically that alienation here was absent entirely.

Analyzing the causal connections between alienation and economic factors, Marx fails to establish any direct connection between the division of labor and alienation as he does in the case of private property. His accounts of the division of labor in *Manuscripts* and *German Ideology* in this respect are sketchy and incoherent. In these works he merely assumes that the division of labor is somehow causally connected with alienation, but he never explains their real causal relationship. "Division of labour only becomes truly such," he writes, "from the moment when a division of material and mental labour appears."[100] By adding the qualification "truly such," he seems to have in mind only specific divisions of labor, but he does not state clearly what kinds are actually involved in the etiology of alienation. His mere suggestions do not amount to a clear and adequate account and his identification of division of labour with private property is far from being helpful. Identity, as Hegel remarks, is an ambiguous concept, and one "must guard against taking it as abstract identity to the exclusion of all difference."[101]

When Marx speaks of division of labor and private property as "identical expressions," he does not, of course, say that they designate absolute sameness; yet he does not say much about their difference either. Even if there is a correlation between division of labor and private property in the sense that they both affirm alienation, as he suggests, it is still undecided which one is the cause and which the effect. Marx does not seem to realize that "material and mental labour" can be sharply separate regardless of the movement of private property and market economy and that, as Plamenatz indicates, it is possible to have private ownership and even exchange economy without any rigid division between mental and physical labor.[102] Based on Marx's statements about alienation, it is impossible to discover whether the division of labor precedes or follows alienation. He also does not say that their relationship is reciprocal in any meaningful sense. While private property has its "secrets" that are bound to confuse the Marxian explanation of the origin of alienation, Marx's writings do not refer to any "secret" of division of labor. Yet, if division of labor and private property are at all "identical," then division of labor must also have "its secret" and somehow be involved in the reciprocal relationship with alienation.

Without clarifying the causal relationship between alienation and division of labor, Marx argues that as long as man's activity is divided he will be alienated and enslaved.[103] In *Capital* he points out that the division of labor "invades all the other spheres of social life in addition to the economic sphere and everywhere forms the basis for the growth of specialisation."[104] Distinguishing here between the social and manufacturing division of labor, he indicates that the social division of labor plays a major role in the genesis of alienation. While Adam Smith traces the origin of division of labor to trade and exchange and James Mill to commercial factors, Marx locates its roots in the contradiction between productive forces and productive relations. The division of labor in which these contradictions occur necessarily entail the unequal distribution of labor and its products, and this inequality leads to the estrangement of man. There is a general assumption that a more extensive division of labor, like a more extensive private ownership, brings more severe alienation.

Mutilation of the worker by the division of labor in capitalist society is a dominant theme of *Capital*. The social division of labor is brought about by the exchange of commodities. Because this exchange, in Marx's view, implies mutually exclusive and contradictory relations between employers and employees, market norms in capitalist production necessarily intensify both division of labor and alienation. Thus, in addition to blaming private property and division of labor for causing alienation, Marx also sometimes attributes the estrangement of man to market economy or exchange. The contradictory reality of the bourgeois mode of the production of capital reflects the relationship of exploitation and dehumanization, on the one hand, and the money system, on the other. "The relationship of exchange being presupposed, labour becomes directly labour to earn a living. This relationship of alienated labour," according to Marx, "reaches its highest point when labour power and the product of the worker are determined by social combination alien to the worker."[105] Contrary to the views of some commentators, he never says explicitly that exchange is the cause of alienation.[106] Indeed, in *Manuscripts of 1844* he indicates that division of labour and exchange are both "embodiments of private property."[107] These two entities are merely the "two phenomena in connection with which the political economist boasts of the social character of his science." They both, however, rest on private property.[108]

In Marx's view, the abolition of private ownership is of primary importance for the transcendence of alienation. He argues that "proletariat and wealth" are both the creation of the movement of private property. Private ownership produces the "proletariat *as* proletariat and poverty necessarily generates dehumanisation and alienation."[109] Ownership of the forces of production by some always involves the alienation of others who own nothing. The "antithesis of property and propertylessness" provokes the division of society into antagonistic classes. This antithesis between poverty and wealth is particularly a feature of capitalist society in which property functions as the "almighty being."[110] All forms of private ownership under capitalism entail alienation. In the relationship of the movement of private property to alienated labor, Marx sees the denial of any "human value of the worker" and mutilation of men's objective lives. Alienated labor in capitalist society appears in many forms and is easily transformed into capital and money. The downfall of estranged labor must lead necessarily to the downfall of private property. Marx warns his readers that "only when labour is grasped as the essence of private property can the economic process as such be penetrated in its actual concreteness."[111]

Both Marx and Engels maintain that the removal of economic and social contradictions in the capitalist system will produce socialism that will liberate man from his alienated position as a commodity. Human labor will then be a "free manifestation of life."[112] As long as competition is the governing power of production, it is impossible to consider the worker as a man, let alone a free man. Under capitalist conditions of production, labor becomes external to man and objectification itself becomes an alien power hostilely, confronting the worker.[113] Marx does not hide his contempt for the bourgeois conception of man and capitalist values. One the whole, his argument against capitalism is a moral one, charging that capitalist owners of the means of production are dishonest and corrupt hypocrites because they fail to practice their own principles of morality. Without the assumption that "callous cash payment" is morally bad, he would have no ground for condemning the bourgeois hypocrisy as morally vicious. Yet, despite his contempt for capitalist morality expressed in greedy self-indulgence, prostitution, cruelty, deception, and selfishness, Marx merely demands an end to alienation without offering an alternative.

Analyzing the causal relationship between alienation and the methods of production, Marx describes the capitalist system as the most enslaving and alienating in man's history. In fact, all classes, not only the working class, in this system suffer under the "sway of inhuman power."[114] It is true, the working men and women are the most alienated, but in capitalism everyone is somehow reduced to an alienable object.[115] Egoism or practical need, Marx believes, only appears in a pure form in a market economy in which everything, alienated man and alienated products, is "submerged in avarice."[116] Money, as the comprehensive representative of commodities, is seen as the "good among commodities." From its servile and alienating role, it easily changes into the object of greed. Originating "out of exchange of commodities," Marx claims that money "represents the divine existence of commodities, while they represent its earthly form."[117] In *Grundrisse*, he indicates that in capitalist society commodities are produced as exchange values rather than use values. "Money exists as the exchange value of all commodities alongside and outside them. It becomes the general denomination of exchange values, of commodities as exchange values."[118] Because exchange value forms the substance of money, exchange value in alienating capitalist society necessarily represents wealth. Beneath the surface of capitalist accumilation and profit making, Marx sees an inevitable class conflict expressing alienation of both the capitalist employer and employee.

In capitalist commodity production, "commodities are in love with money," although the process of this love is never smooth.[119] The essential content of economic laws governing the capitalist pattern of socioeconomic relations is, in Marx's view, the regular extraction of surplus labor and thus of profit by the owners of the means of productioin from the direct producers of wealth. The worker is forced into the labor market, and his choice of a job is very limited. In the market the "slave owner buys his workers as he buys his horses."[120] Capitalist commodity production and private ownership make the division of labor almost unbearable. Under capitalism, the production process becomes an alien power that enslaves and robs the "worker of rest, fixity, security of existence, simultaneously threatening to deprive him of the means of labour and of the means of life."[121] With the progressive fragmentation of the division of labor and the increasing alienating effects of private ownership and exchange in bourgeois commodity production, all men and women lose their independence and freedom.

The alien power of capital over the worker always reflects the crude barbarism of need and the "estranged, alienated positing of human activity." It is only in communism, Marx believes, that productive activity can develop powers capable of ultimate fulfillment. The alienating power of capital and money transform the "real essential powers of man and nature into tormenting chimeras."[122] Whatever the cause of alienation may be, Marx has no doubt that human estrangement reaches its peak in capitalist society, in which everyone and everything is reduced to a saleable commodity. "The motive of those who engage in exchange is not humanity but egoism."[123]

In his critical examination of alienation, Marx connects such phenomena as egoism, avarice, greed, and inhumanity with private interests and "huckstering." Men are alienated when they produce under the domination of "selfish needs."[124] Thus he sees the need for money as the only need modern capitalism produces. The capitalist economic order, based on private property and exchange, encourages an unnatural greed for capital and accumulated wealth. Hegel believes that "exclusive egoism or self-assertion is evil in its pure form" and that this "evil appears as the primary existence of the inwardly-turned consciousness," leading to misery, discord, and alienation.[125] The key to the Hegelian theory of alienation is the antagonism in the subject due to its finite-infinite nature. The solution of the contradiction is in the concept of spiritual development. The withdrawal of the existent consciousness into itself makes it self-discordant, self-centered, and egoistic. The idea of withdrawal is echoed in Marx's early writings in which he speaks of egoistic man as an "individual withdrawn into himself, into the confines of his private interests and private caprice and separated from the community."[126] While Hegel is concerned with the metaphysical explanation of such phenomena as egoism and alienation, Marx ignores this explanation and treats them as merely "unnatural" phenomena.

Both Marx and Engels speak frequently of greed and egoism as the self-centeredness of human individuals entirely indifferent to the welfare of others. Greed and egoism are seen as effects rather than causes of alienating relations in capitalist society. Competition, private ownership, division of labor, and exchange are regarded as the causes responsible for greed rather than vice versa. In *Grundrisse*, Marx makes his position in this respect perfectly clear when he says that "greed itself is the product of a definite social development, not *natural* as opposed to historical. Hence the wailing of the ancients about money as the source of all evil."[127] In the Judeo-Christian tradition, the "love of money" is regarded as the "root of all evil," but this does not preclude the belief that greed and egoism are natural and inherent phenomena in human life.[128] It is interesting that Marx quotes from a religious source to support his claim that money is the "fountainhead of greed" and, on the other hand, ascribes "practical need or egoism" to Judaism and Christianity. There is no awareness of contradiction when this suits his causal theory of alienation.[129]

Throughout human history, man's progress has been hampered by egoism and ineradicable selfishness. Human aggressiveness, enmity, violence, and war have revealed man's inability to govern himself. Neither religion nor science has ever suggested that humans are perfect in the sense of possessing great powers of intellect, will, and decision-making. Freud and Jung stress that aggressiveness, violence, and greed are the inherent characteristics of the "ego-instincts." The originally simple and unequivocal instinctival determinants, in Jung's view, can appear transformed into "pure greed" and into many aspects of "boundless desire or insatiability."[130] Like hunger, greed is a characteristic expression of self-preservation. Fromm, however, maintains that greed is merely one of the strongest non-instinctive passions in man, thus, to some extent, coming closer to Marx's conception. By associating greed with passions and sin, Fromm is far from being clear and consistent on this issue.[131] Sin and passions originate wholly in the inevitable conditions of human existence; therefore, they cannot be explained merely in terms of pathology or economics.

It may well be that greed is encouraged to a greater degree in capitalism, but it is impossible to deny that greed precedes rather than follows the capitalist economic order. Marxists, like Mészáros, who blindly follow Marx fail to realize that egoism and greed have their real source within human nature itself. To argue that egoism and greed are the effects of man's strivings for material wealth and merely products of a "definite social development" is putting the cart before the horse.[132] Humans, like animals, are born with greed. The nursing child knowing nothing about capitalism and dialectical materialism, will instinctively overfeed himself. Even workers, as Marx himself observes, have a mania for wealth. It is very unconvicing to maintain that greed and egoism are unnatural phenomena that will disappear in communist society. No mutual interaction of economic forces, including private ownership, division of labor, and exchange, can ever give rise to human greed, although this interaction can influence its intensity. Greed and selfishness are defects of human nature and not defects of socioeconomic relations. The primacy of greed and self-interest over other human passions has nothing to do with capitalist economy or, as Fromm seems to suggest, with neo-behaviorism and bourgeois ideology.[133]

Marx's belief that egoism and greed only operate in societies based on competition cannot be supported. As alienation itself, egoism, greed, avarice, and what Spinoza calls the immoderate desires of glory, honor and riches are not absent from communist society.[134] In spite of Marx's optimistic belief that "greed is impossible without money" and that human needs "will lose their egoistical nature" after the abolition of private ownership and exchange, the mania for greed and selfishness remains the ineradicable source of alienation under communism as well.[135] There are no signs that the transcendence of "capitalist private property" in communism is followed by the disappearance of alienation, greed, and egoism. Criticizing Stirner for his inability to see a close link between the methods of production and egoism, Marx states clearly that in a communist society based on "self-earned private property," there will be no room for alienation, greed, and egoism. "The individuals' consciousness of their mutual relations within communist society," he writes, "will change so completely that egoism and greed, like love or *dévouement*, will be entirely absent."[136]

Marx's analysis of "greed as such," like his analysis of the causal relationship between alienation and production, is unclear and inconsistent. In *Grundrisse* he argues that greed is an entirely artificial, economic, and unnatural drive, totally dependent on money.[137] "Greed as the urge of all," he says, "is only created by general wealth." Yet without explaining the difference between "greed as such" and the "mania for possessions," he admits that the "mania for possessions is possible without money," thus suggesting the instinctive, psychological, and inherent nature of greed. Distinguishing between the "craving for particular kinds of wealth like clothes and jewels" and "greed as such," Marx overlooks that the craving for wealth is psychologically and morally the same as "greed as such" and that, as Spinoza remarks, an "avaricious man may throw all his wealth into the sea to save his life and yet remain avaricious and greedy."[138] It is not money that is the source of greed: rather it is greed, the instinctive drive within man himself, that motivates him to strive for possessions and wealth. After all, "jewels and clothes" are not obtainable without money or its equivalent.

Having inverted Hegel's ideas of alienation and causation, Marx has turned for the explanation of egoism and greed to the French thinkers of the Age of Reason. According to them, wickedness, egoism, greed, and other social evils are merely unnatural states of the evil mind. Because these states are determined by a natural and social environment, they believe men must change their environment if they wish to combat these evils. Marx, however, only shares with the French materialists the belief that egoism, greed, and alienation are "unnatural and historical" phenomena. He reproaches them for failing to connect them with the methods of production and a definite social development rather than with "natural and social environment in general." Proudhon is criticized for failing to realize that egoism and greed originate in competition and private property.[139] In the real world, Marx says, property ownership, exchange, and division of labor are social relations, and outside these relations the bourgeois ideas of the origin of alienation, greed, and egoism are "metaphysical illusions."[140]

For Marx, alienation and egoism are neither metaphysical entities nor extra-economic phenomena—they are historical products generated by the desire to reduce all human relations to the relation of "independence and disregard for others." The key to the genesis of alienation must be sought in the mode of production, not in the "mystical, abstract and eternal categories" of idealism and "abstract materialism." The economic life of man and his psychology, Marx insists, represent two sides of the same phenomenon of the production of life. Because the psychology of society always corresponds to economic relations and is always determined by the current method of production, the new state of productive forces gives rise to a new economic structure that includes its corresponding superstructure. Ideas and opinions alone can never be causally efficacious. Instead of causing something, ideas, in Marx's view, are always caused by material causes.[141] He overlooks the fact that intellectual, mental, or spiritual causes underlie every change in the methods of production and that without these causes the changes in the methods of production could neither occur nor be explained. Marx merely states that changes in the methods of production cause new ideologies, stressing that the capitalist method of production is the most alienating, but he fails to realize that human progress can only be intelligible in terms of "mental or intellectual" causation. No reasonable person will deny that the invention and use of new tools and machinery are the primary product of the human mind rather than of fortuitous economic factors.

The nineteenth century in which Marx lived was dominated by the belief that all worldly phenomena could be described by their causes. This belief was not less scholastic than the belief of the earlier ages that everything is contained in the First Cause. Newton's method of scientific investigation, a marriage of the logical and empirical, remained the standard method for every science. While the Newtonian insistence on causal connections in the world showed satisfactory results in many investigative fields, including physics, geology, and chemistry, in non-empirical researches such as economics and sociology, the results were entirely negative. This is reflected in the researches of political economists and of Marx himself. Marx overlooks the fact that economics has never become an empirical science. No economist has discovered the causes of such complex phenomena as economic depression and alienated labour, which play significant roles in Marx's causal theory of alienation. The causation of alienation is much more intricate than assumed in his pseudo-empirical theory. Ignoring the relevance of internal and psychological factors in the genesis of alienation, his conception of cause-effect interaction is unsatisfactory. Because he insists on the existence of merely material and economic causation in human history and because of his categorical denial of any other form of causation, Marx is unable to uncover the network of cause and effect and their real relationship in the genesis of alienation.

3
Economic Alienation

Marx's economic ideas reflect a modified development of the labor theory of value formulated by John Locke and later elaborated in the writings of the classical economists of the early nineteenth century. These economists believed that the system of private ownership is the only way toward economic prosperity and that in a free market economy, every man receives the proper return for his labor. Basing their economic theories on natural laws, they maintained that, if left to work freely, these laws would inevitably produce the best possible results. They were unanimous in believing that labor creates property and gives value to most things. Accepting the traditional economic outlook of medievalism, Locke says that "labour puts the difference of value on everything" and that the "improvement of labour makes the far greater part of the value. Of the products of the earth useful to the life of man, nine-tenths are the effects of labour."[1] Locke believes the possession of private property is fundamental in human life and belongs to man in the state of nature. For Rousseau and Hegel, private property is the "sacred foundation of civil society." Defending the institution of private ownership, Adam Smith indicates that the division of labor is the necessary consequence of the propensity to exchange one product for another and that this propensity is "common to all men."[2] Marx criticizes the political economists for their hypocrisy and for "locating private property in man's own being."[3] The relations of man determined by property relations, in his opnion, have become fetters contradicting social and economic processes in historical development.

Contrary to the bourgeois economists, Marx analyzes the relationships of capitalist market economy in terms of alienation and exploitation. Where the bourgeois economists see merely a relation between things, he wants to show the existence of a concrete relation between individuals. "The classics, like Adam Smith and Ricardo, represent a bourgeoisie which, while still struggling with the relics of feudal society, works only to purge economic relations of feudal taints to increase the productive forces and to give a new upsurge to industry and commerce."[4] The apologists of bourgeois economic relation have frequently stressed that the institution of private property is essential to human freedom. Marx rejects this view and argues that the abolition of "bourgeois property" is the only way toward elimination of economic alienation.[5] Bourgeois property, he claims, is the source of slavery, exploitation, and alienation and must be abolished. Alienation of human labor will only cease when the means of production are transformed into common property. Private property, as the antithesis to social, collective property, Marx argues in *Capital*, exists only where the means of labor and the external conditions of labor belong to private individuals. The bourgeois economists forget that private property "can only grow upon the tomb of the producer's own labour."[6]

Marx maintains that alienation is the inevitable result of private ownership. It occurs in societies in which men and women are dehumanized into owners and non-owners, into non-workers and workers. Here the interests of the owners of the means of production are always antagonistic to the interests of the non-owners. The contradictory reality of the bourgeois mode of production reflects the relationship of alienation and exploitation. In this relationship between the worker's wealth-creating activity and the alienating capitalist exploiter, the mutual exchange of the activity itself gives rise to the undesirable division of labor, turning man into an empty alienated being. "Just as the mutual exchange of the products of human activity appears as barter, as trade," Marx says, "so the mutual completion and exchange of the activity itself appears as division of labour, which turns man as far as possible into an abstract being, a machine tool, etc., and transforms him into a spiritual and physical monster."[7]

Marx sees alienation as being related to man's real life. While religious estrangement "occurs only in the realm of consciousness, economic estrangement is that of real life."[8] Although the term *alienation* is not always used as explicitly as in *Manuscripts of 1844*, it is economic alienation that dominates most of Marx's writings. In *Manuscripts of 1844*, he addresses the problem of alienated labor and accuses political economy for concealing the estrangement inherent in labor by disregarding the direct relationship between the worker and production. Political economists, he says, merely explain how production is carried out in the relations existing in bourgeois market economy, but they do not explain how these relations themselves are generated. These relations do not express any fixed, immutable, or eternal economic categories as Adam Smith, Ricardo, and even Prodhon have maintained. They have a "historical background which gave them birth."[9] Arguing from the point of view of historical materialism, Marx stresses that the existing economic relations do not represent abstract, motionless metaphysical essences and thus cannot be transferred into some supersensible or ahistorical sphere that lies outside the actual relations of men. Under the influence of the productive forces, the actual socioeconomic relations of existing men are constantly changing and cannot be expressed in any abstract formulae.

Marx's approach to economic and social relations as expressed in his early writings is based on Hegel's analysis of civil society. Protesting against the identification of economic wants and biological needs, Hegel always insists that crude impulses should be subordinated to the ethical life of customary morality. Wants and desires, as states of reason, must be dependent not only on economic relations but also on moral evaluations. Even the idea of private property itself, in Hegel's view, can be transcended by the idea of morality. Rejecting the Hegelian idea that "private property as a thought can ever be transcended in the thought of morality," Marx argues that economic alienation is not an abstract category but rather the expression of man's real existence in the society based on greed, avarice, and economic inequality.[10] Alienation is a historical reality, originating in the movement of private property. Hegel leaves this reality unexplained and in his theory of alienation finds only the "abstract, logical, speculative expression for the movement of history."[11] Crediting Hegelian idealism with the awareness of creative activity, Marx indicates that "idealism does not know real, historical and sensuous activity as such."[12] In spite of the fact that Hegel sometimes expresses almost materialist views, he regards property relations as the realization of "civil rights" that develop by their own internal force. "Descending everywhere from his political spiritualism into the crassest materialism," Hegel fails to see that private ownership alienates man's real, sensuous activity and his relation to other men.[13] Elimination of the capitalist economic system that alienates and exploits its innocent victims is, in Marx's view, the only way to achieve a meaningful and fully human existence.

Marx's economic theory is embedded in the materialist conception of history and as such is opposed diametrically to all varieties of idealism. Hegel's dialectical idealism is no exception. Although Marx praises Hegel for grasping the essence of labor and comprehending objective man as the product of his own labor, Hegel's conception of *homo economicus* is similar to that of political economy. "The only labour which Hegel knows and recognises," Marx says, "is abstractly mental labour."[14] Hegel also is criticized for believing that "wealth and economic and political power as entities estranged from the human being" are merely alienated forms of abstract thinking. In opposition to Hegel who analyzes private property, wealth, and objectification in terms of human thinking, Marx claims to see all economic categories in the light of human production and real life. Unlike Hegel, Marx argues that property relations are determined by mutual socioeconomic relations into which men enter in the production of their life, not by any transcendental quality of the Idea. Whereas Hegel depicts all relations as relations of the objective Spirit, Marx maintains that all relations in human societies have their roots in the material conditions of life.

The key to any intelligible explanation of the property relations in capitalist society, according to Marx, lies in the institution of law. "One can imagine, an individual savage as possessing something. But in that case possession is not a juridical relation."[15] In the modern bourgeois form of private property, property that alienates and exploits wage labor, however, always presupposes "concrete juridical categories." In *German Ideology*, Marx indicates that "civil law develops simultaneously with private property" and that "law as such has just as little an independent history as religion."[16] "The modern

French, English and American writers," he remarks, "all express the opinion that the state exists only for the sake of private property so that this view has also been generally accepted by the average man."[17] Originally "property means no more than a human being's relation to his natural conditions of production as belonging to him, as his, as presupposed along with his own being."[18] Tribal property, Marx believes, evolved through various stages to modern capital, determined by large-scale industry and universal competition. This capitalist form of property he calls "pure private property."[19]

Marx believes men do not own any property until they have "exchange rights in it." Thus private property could be analyzed in terms of these rights. He argues that the economic structure of capitalism with private ownership of the means of production and profit as a motivating agency grossly inhibit the full use of productive forces and that this structure, therefore, needs changes in property relations. The capitalist economic system is alienating and inhuman because in it "every person tries to establish over the other an alien power so as thereby to find satisfaction of his own selfish need. The increase in the quantity of things obtained and privately owned is accompanied by an extension of the realm of the alien powers to which man is subjected, and every new product represents a new potency of mutual swindling and mutual plundering."[20] To allow constructive use of productive forces, it is essential to substitute "human needs" for "vulgar needs" and social benefits for private profit. Marx admits that capitalism has performed a significant historical task by "putting an end to all feudal, patriarchal, idyllic relations," but unfortunately it has done this by depriving most of society of any ownership in the means of production. The bourgeoisie, according to Marx and Engels, "has left remaining no other nexus between man and man than naked self-interest and cash payment." Above all, the bourgeois system has resolved personal worth of man into exchange value and has created the conditions for "naked, shameless, direct, brutal exploitation."[21]

In its modern capitalist form, property, in Marx's and Engels's view, is based on the antagonism between capital and wage labor. Capital and labor as antagonistic forces belong to the world of private property. Considered as independent forms of social life, they are relative and alien to each other. "The labour which stands opposite capital is alien labour, and the capital which stands opposite labour is alien capital. The extremes which stand opposite one another are specifically different."[22] When analyzing the exchange between capital and labor in *Grundrisse*, Marx elaborates on the significant differences in economic relations between the capitalist and the laborer. "The worker sells his commodity, labour, which has a use value, and, as commodity, also a price, like all other commodity, for a specific sum of exchange values, specific sum of money, which capital concedes to him."[23] The capitalist, on the other hand, "obtains labour itself, labour as value-positing activity, as productive labour which maintains and multiplies capital."[24] Marx remarks that within the capital and wage labor antithesis the owner of private property represents the conservative side and the wage laborer the destructive side of the forces of production. "From the former arises the action of preserving the antithesis, from the latter the action of annihilating it."

Having turned Hegel upside down, Marx still uses his dialectical mechanism in explaining the movement of private property and class relations in capitalist society. Hegel's analysis of the master-slave relationship has deeply impressed Marx's mind. Without the Hegelian conception of the conflict of opposing tendencies, Marx never could say so confidently that capitalism, by creating a class conscious proletariat as its opposite, is inevitably forging the instrument of its own destruction. He does not question the "general forms of dialectical movement" as expounded by Hegel. He agrees with him that the "dialectical principle constitutes the life and soul of scientific progress" and that "dialectic is at work wherever there is movement or life and wherever anything is carried into effect in the actual world." Marx is criticizing only the "mystifying aspect of the Hegelian dialectic."[25] As he sees it, this dialectic is linked primarily to a conceptual analysis, to the movement of thought. He ignores Hegel's claim that his dialectic has a universal application and that he is not confining the relevance of dialectic to mere consciousness.[26] Marx exaggerates the "mystifying aspect of Hegelian dialectic," overlooking that this dialectic "gives expression to a law which is felt not only in the domain of consciousness but also in general human experience as a whole."[27]

In the preface to *German Ideology*, Marx admits that "Hegel was not content with recording thought entities; he also sought to describe the act of creation."[28] Yet, in his "Critique of the Hegelian dialectic and philosophy as a whole," he says that Hegel's view of economic relations is "that of modern political economy." "Hegel grasps labour as the essence of man" but, Marx adds, "he sees only the positive, not the negative side of labour."[29] While Hegel sees labor as a process going on between man and spirit, Marx sees it as a process going on between man and nature. If man does not work, Marx says, he lives by the labor of others, and this is the case with the capitalist. Being the source of use value and exchange value, it is "labour which posits exchange value that causes the social relations of individuals to appear in the perverted form of a social relation between things."[30] Political economists, like Adam Smith, realize that labor is the real source of wealth, but they overlook that in capitalist society labor is treated merely as a commodity. Here, Marx argues, "labour produces not only commodities: it produces itself and the worker as a commodity—and does so in the proportion in which it produces commodities generally."[31]

Marx criticizes bourgeois economists for failing to see the intrinsic connection between money and labor that posits exchange value. All the illusions of the monetarists, "arise from the failure to perceive that money, though a physical object with distinct properties, represents a social relation of production."[32] In *Manuscripts*, Marx indicates that with the growing scale of bourgeois production and the ever-increasing division of labor, the worker's role is transformed from activity to passivity, from that of a human to that of a thing. "Even in the condition of society most favourable to the worker, the inevitable result for the worker is overwork and premature death, decline to a mere machine, a bond-servant of capital, which piles up dangerously over against him, more competition and for a section of the workers starvation or beggary."[33] In the labor process under capitalism, the capitalist and worker are inevitably in hostile confrontation and, strictly speaking, neither is fully human. Any technological progress under capitalism, according to Marx, entails increased alienation and dehumanization of the worker and increased alienation leads to increase in his misery and economic plight.

In capitalist society, Marx argues, workers are alienated at every level of production. They spend their working days in making things for the capitalist or non-worker rather than for the joy of labor, creativity, self-expression, and self-realization. The things they produce are not even for their own use, and their work is merely a means for satisfving crude bodily needs.[34] Marx streeses that bondage to bodily needs must end and that workers must have adequate time for creative activity and spiritual enjoyment. Because the political economy "knows the worker only as a working animal—as a beast reduced to the strictest bodily needs," Marx critically examines the relation of the worker to the product of his labor which he believes is merely an alien object exercising power over him.[35] The chief fault of political economy, according to Marx, is its failure to adequately explain capitalist economic life. Starting from the institution of private ownership, political economy does not disclose the origin of the division between capital and labor. The laws of production described by Adam Smith and Ricardo are "universal and natural" only within the historically restricted domain of capitalist production. Outside this domain they are false and parasitic on the social relations of production existing in bourgeois society.

Marx's criticism of political economy in *Manuscripts* represents his first attempt to explain the antisocial accumulation of wealth by one class and the persistent improverishment of another in an economic system based on market economy and private exchange. In this work he has already adopted the viewpoint that occupies him for the rest of his life. As he indicates, he begins his criticism of bourgeois economic theories from the presuppositions of political economy itself. He accuses political economy for its inability to grasp and explain the internal and structural dynamics of capitalist economics.[36] Bourgeois economists take for granted that the momentary results of human relations as they appear in greed-motivated societies reflect permanent categories and natural laws. They argue that everyone gains from the exchange of labor power and that wage workers voluntarily sell their labor power on the market. Competition, economic values, profits, wages, capital, labor, and even exchange itself are explained in terms of eternal or natural laws. In Marx's view, all these categories are the product of socioeconomic conditions that always express the mode of production.

Bourgeois economists, according to Marx, overlook that the bourgeois mode of production is contradictory and alienating because of its tendency toward the absolute development of productive forces and because this tendency always conflicts with the specific conditions of production in the system in which capital dominates. Although these economists proceed from labor as the essence of production, they give nothing to labor and everything to the owners of the means of production. Marx links the existence of the worker in the capitalist economic system with suffering, beggary, exploitation, and alienation. The worker has to struggle not only for material subsistence but also for a job. When the social or national wealth declines, the worker is the principal sufferer. Marx argues that under capitalism the worker is so dehumanized that he "sinks to the level of a commodity" and indeed, becomes the "most wretched of commodities."[37] The wretchedness of the worker is "in inverse proportion to the power and magnitude of his production."[38] The harder he works, the more alienated he becomes. "The more the worker spends himself, the more powerful is the alien objective world which he creates over against himself, the poorer he himself—his inner world—becomes, the less belongs to him as his own."[39] The alienated worker accepts his wage not because he is convinced that it is a fair and adequate wage or reward for his labor but simply because he must accept it or starve to death. Bourgeois economists have assumed wrongly that buyers and sellers of labor, capitalists and workers, operate on equal terms in a free market and each gets what he earns. Marx strongly rejects their view that the bargaining power of the two antagonistic sides is that of equality and that the institution of labor exchange is non-coercive.

In his analysis of bourgeois economic theories, Marx indicates correctly that wage laborers in his days were not receiving their fair share. Unfortunately, however, he could not see that there might be other ways than revolution for dealing with this problem. He contends that revolution is in the best interest of the proletariat, the suffering class representing the "interest of the immense majority." Because the capitalist economic system cannot satisfy the interests of the majority of society, proletarian revolution would simply be the "expropriation of a few usurpers by the mass of the people." To realize their aims, the working classes have to seize power via a revolution and thus bring the reign of capital to a close. Many writers and economists, well aware of the exploitation and alienation of the poor by the rich, reject Marx's revolutionary ideology altogether, maintaining that socialism would come, not by means of revolution and violence, but by gradual social and economic reforms. The argument against the rationality of revolution was, in fact, the theme of all non-Marxist socialists in the nineteenth century. The semi-revolutionary ideas of the trade unions of Robert Owen's time were not really inspired by communism but rather by humanitarian ideals. Marx's contemporary socialists in the western world were convinced that a fundamental change in the workers' environment and treatment could bring about a fundamental change in their economic condition.

Many employers realized that discontented laborers were bad laborers and improved the conditions of their employment where possible. This was inadequate, of course, and the worker remained alienated and dehumanized. In his foreword to the second edition of *The Condition of the Working Class in England* (1845), Engels admits that, in almost half a century, there had been a substantial improvement in the material and social state of British workers. In the article on "Progress of Social Reform on the Continent" (1843), he indicates that the "English socialists are a long way before us and have left very little to be done" in the fields of socioeconomic development.[40] Marx is not the only writer who has exposed the alienation and exploitation of the worker in the nineteenth century. Eugène Buret, a Christian and French economist, is one of many distinguished writers of the century who denounced political economy of bourgeois economists as an "ontology of wealth," a science of poverty that "considers labour in the abstract as a thing or a commodity" and regards the worker only as the seller of labor. Marx shares Buret's view that treating labor a mere commodity necessarily leads to alienation of the worker. "The capitalist is always free to use" or rather to abuse labour while the "worker is always forced to sell it." Any claim that human life is merely a commodity amounts to the defence of "slavery."[41]

Buret's writing on the "misery of the working classes in England and France" has undoubtedly influenced Marx and Engels. Buret's ideas of relative and absolute poverty and of labor as a commodity must have especially permanently impressed their searching and restless minds. Like Buret, they contend that capital is a power that commands and alienates labor. Based on capital's power, bourgeois economy inevitably engenders a relationship of mastery and slavery, of domination and servitude, of capitalist enjoyment and proletarian suffering. Unfortunately, Marx and Engels have tended to see in Buret, as they did in Proudhon, a petty bourgeois socialist and thus have disregarded the remedy he has offered in the economic field. Marx has equally ignored the remedy offered by the "piecemeal reformers who either want to raise wages and in this way to improve the situation of the working class or regard equality of wages (as Proudhon does) as the goal of social revolution."[42] Marx believes the alienation of the worker can only be eliminated when the capitalist economic structure is completely destroyed.

The science of bourgeois political economy, according to Marx, entails the affirmation of alienation. "It does not consider the worker as a human being when he is not working."[43] In this bourgeois science of poverty, "labour occurs only in the form of wage-earning activity." What is needed, Marx believes, is a radical critique that would annihilate the system that merely gives the appearance of objectivity and equality whereas it actually concentrates all its political, social, and economic means on obtaining wealth for the owners of property and producing poverty for most laborers. Although the bourgeois economists of the early nineteenth century have come close to penetrating the veil of commodities in their analysis of capitalism, Marx contends, they have remained wrapped in mysteries and are unable to follow their own theory of value to its logical conclusions. In the nebulous world and realm of appearance, the bourgeois economists find their "abstract formulae" for the solution of economic problems.[44] Marx argues that workers cannot merely appear to be giving the owners of capital their surplus labor, nor can their alienated labor merely appear to be forced and involutary. Alienated workers and alienated labor in capitalist society are realities generated by avarice and total disregard for the "world of men."[45]

In *Manuscripts*, Marx argues that the quest for an alien being above and outside man will cease with the abolition of alienated labor in communism. Representing the interest of the wage laborer, he stresses that the dignity of human labor is mocked when the parasitical elements in society are activated by appeals to the basest motives. In the society based on self-interest and greed, the wage laborer can hardly provide adequate means to satisfy his most elementary needs. The wage he receives is frequently so low that he cannot avoid starvation. Many workers allow themselves to be cheated, and to avoid starvation, they are compelled to sell their labor power at any alienating price on the exchange market. "The extremity of the worker's bondage," Marx indicates, "is that it is only as a worker that he continues to maintain himself as a physical subject, and that it is only as a physical subject that he is a worker."[46]

Economic alienation, in Marx's view, does not consist merely in separating the worker from the product of his labor but also in reducing him to an object. The worker is alienated from his product because the activity that produces the product has been dehumanized by the capitalist owner of the means of production. "If then the product of labour is alienation, production itself must be active alienation."[47] Whenever the worker is related to the "product of his labour as to an alien object," he becomes "a slave of this object" and all that remains of him is merely the "abstract individual."[48] Whatever the laws of political economy may be, they all express the estrangement of the worker in the objects he produces. "The more the worker produces, the less he has to consume; the more values he creates, the more valueless, the more unworthy he becomes; the better formed his product, the more deformed becomes the worker; the more civilised his object, the more barbarous becomes the worker; the more ingenious labour becomes, the duller becomes the worker and the more be becomes nature's bondsman."[49]

Alienation of the worker in his product, Marx points out, not only means that his living labor becomes an object, an external existence, but also that the object he produces exists outside as something alien, becoming a power on its own and confronting him as a hostile force.[50] Marx refers to the worker's product in this way to emphasize the worker's helplessness and powerlessness over his own products and also to stress the alienating effects of the worker's lack of control over his own activity. Although the bourgeois economists have been preoccupied with economic appearances and unwilling to consider the real causes of the alienation of workers, Marx argues that it is precisely the capitalist method of production that deprives the workers of their own products and of the very means of life. Under capitalism, the worker's product, representing a hostile force, alienates him and cuts him off from his livelihood. "So much does the appropriation of the object" by the non-producer "appear as estrangement that the more objects the worker produces the fewer can he possess and the more he falls under the dominion of his product, capital."[51] Labor's realization, in Marx's view, is its objectification. Objectification as such does not necessarily entail alienation. Rejecting the Hegelian conception of objectification as a merely illusory projection of consciousness, he contends that objectification, unlike alienation,is a perfectly normal and natural process through which man realizes his potentialities. In the capitalist economic structure, however, realization of labor "appears as loss of reality for the worker; objectification as loss of the object and object bondage; appropriation as estrangement or alienation."[52]

What makes the worker's objects alien and hostile to him is the fact that in the process of producing them he "objectifies himself inhumanly."[53] In this inhuman objectification, the worker is robbed of the objects that are essential not only for his life but also for his life activity. The tragedy of bourgeois economy lies in the fact that it turns men into things that become their own enemies. In his objectified from, the worker is his own enemy because the objects he produces belong to the capitalist who is always the incarnation of inhuman forces. Marx is perfectly intelligible when speaking about the devaluation of man increasing in direct relation with the increase in the value of things. However, his use of metaphor makes him less intelligible when he speaks of labor "turned into a physical thing and becoming its own product."[54] Saying that something embodies labor merely indicates that it is a product of labor. Marx surely realizes that labor cannot exist outside the worker or stand opposed to him as an autonomous power except in a figurative way. He contends that the product of labor dominates the worker and not vice versa. It exists independent of the producer, becoming a power on its own and alienating him.[55] The product sadly belongs to the capitalist because it is the result of a process involving the bargaining power of capital. As long as the socioeconomic relations are based on capitalist exchange, the things produced by the worker will become the property of the non-worker.

In all societies, man's productive activity is objectified in his products. No society could possibly survive without these products. Indicating that the "product of labour is but the summary of human activity or production," Marx is anxious to emphasize that the appropriation of the product by the capitalist or non-worker inevitably engenders the alienation of the worker. Because the worker's products serve the purpose of the non-worker, they become a blind force that ultimately alienates and dominates the worker. Once alienated, the worker functions as human only while he is producing objects for the capitalist. "The worker produces capital, capital produces the worker, and man as worker, as a commodity, is the product of this entire cycle."[56] In this antithesis of capital and labor, the worker has the misfortune to be a living capital, a capital with bodily needs, degraded, dehumanized, and alienated, facing the possibility of losing his wage at any time and endangering his livelihood whenever not working. Although the worker needs products, he is unable to possess them in the conditions of capitalist relations based on egoism and greed.

The power of capital, Marx argues, always reflects the power of the alien force that rules the powerless worker. Not surprisingly, in the antithesis of capital and labor, the capitalist-worker relations are always antagonistic and characterized by class struggles. The alien character of forced labor, he says, "emerges clearly in the fact that as soon as no physical or other complusion exists, labour is shunned like the plague."[57] Thus, "external labour, labour in which man alienates himself, is a labour of self-sacrifice, of mortification."[58] Alienated labor is the property of the capitalist. Because this labor does not belong to the worker, the worker himself involved in it must also belong to the owner of capital. Without capitalist involvement in production in which the productive force is alienated labor, Marx believes there would be no capitalists and therefore no alienation.

In *Manuscripts*, Marx emphasizes the alienation of the worker who sells his labor power to the master of capital. In capitalist society, he indicates, "everything is in itself something different from itself" and everything is "under the sway of inhuman power" that threatens the livelihood and dignity of the worker and may ultimately threaten the livelihood and dignity of the capitalist as well.[59] In capitalist production, the non-worker is not dominated by objects in the same way as the worker and the worker suffers more than the capitalist, but they both suffer. "The worker suffers in his very existence whereas the capitalist suffers in the profit on his dead mammon."[60] Analyzing the alienating effects of capitalism, Marx stresses that capitalist production not only produces man as a commodity or in the role of commodity, but also the conditions that lead inevitably to the dehumanization of both the worker and the capitalist. What distinguishes capitalist economy from others is the fact that in it the capitalist and the worker communicate only as commodity proprietors, as the buyer and seller of labor or as the owner and object of private ownership.

Marx maintains that capitalism is the most advanced form of commodity production. It is characterized, however, not only by technological progress but also by alienation, reification, inhuman objectification, and above all by indifference toward the suffering of the worker. The worker sells his labor in the market, and the product of this labor belongs to the non-worker. In all his writings, Marx regards the capitalist as the most ruthless and inhuman of exploiters, entirely heartless and indifferent to the plight of wage earners. The degree of alienation is correlated to the degree of capitalism. Alienation reaches its highest dimensions in capitalist society because here the products of labor are produced for exchange and monetary gain rather than for con-

sumption. Marx stresses that the motive of those engaged in exchange is egoism or self-interest, not humanity or philanthropy. Under capitalism, men
treat each other only as means. The capitalist treats the worker as a means to
surplus value and the worker treats the capitalist as a means to survival and
physical subsistence. The capitalist is the "ascetic but rapacious miser and the
worker is the ascetic but productive slave."[61]

In the capitalist system of production, relations are reduced to the relations
of commodity exchange. Here, capital is the "governing power over labour"
and the worker's products.[62] The capitalist possesses this power as the owner
of capital, not because of any human or personal distinction. The distinguishing quality of the capitalist is avarice. The capitalist's relation to the product of labor, Marx maintains, places him in a state of alienation. "It has to be
noticed that everything which appears in the worker as an activity of alienation, of estrangement, appears in the non-worker as a state of alienation, of
estrangement."[63] The capitalist's life is not without worries and problems
because he, like the worker, is also dominated by the socioeconomic conditions
in which alienated objects are produced and exchanged. Living under these
conditions, the capitalist easily becomes prey to his own cupidity, "behaving
as a mere ephemeral individual." Although in the antagonistic struggle between the capitalist employer and his workers "victory necessarily goes to the
capitalist and the capitalist can live longer without the worker than the worker
without the capitalist," with the increase in the concentration of capital the
"big capitalists ruin the small and a section of the one-time capitalists sinks
into the working class."[64]

Among other things, capitalist production is frequently associated with
chronic unemployment, and the process of competition that creates unemployment simultaneously increases poverty and decreases the number of capitalists. Marx believes there is a correlation between the increase in capital and
the reduction in the number of capitalists. Under capitalism, competition between the owners of capital plays an important role in the economic structure
of society. "Competition is only possible if capitals multiply and are held in
many hands."[65] Because capital evolves only by accumulation, its maximization can only be the result of multilateral accumulation of wealth. Competition increases the accumulation of capitals, and the first to suffer in this competition is the small capitalist. In this state of alienation, the "big capitalist has
all the advantages over the smaller capitalist" just as he does "over the
worker."[66] Stressing that competition is always motivated by egoism, Engels,
following Marx, maintains that the "contradiction of competition is exactly
the same as that of private property." In both cases the "general and the
individual interest are diametrically opposed to each other."[67] Considering
the "avarice of the calculating and gambling speculators," he adds that "no
one at all who becomes involved in the struggle of competition can stand the
strain without the utmost exertion of his powers, without renouncing every
truly human purpose."[68]

Marx argues that the worker is alienated in his real life whether he works or not. The capitalist's alienation is the result of his treatment of workers as mere objects of exploitation. The capitalist is also alienated because his life lacks any "real, practical activity." Under capitalism, both the worker and the non-worker become "spiritually and physically" reified, dehumanized individuals. Criticizing political economy, Marx points out that its scientific aim is a contradiction. On the one hand, political economy is the "science of wealth, of denial, of want, of thrift and of saving." On the other, it is the science of poverty, exploitation, and enslavement of erso. Its cardinal doctrine is the denial of life and human needs. "The less you eat, drink and read books; the less you go to the theatre, the dance hall, the public house; the less you think, love, theorise, sing, paint, fence, etc., the more you *save*—the greater becomes your treasure which neither moths nor dust will devour—your capital. The less you *are*, the more you *have*; the less you express your own life, the greater is your *alienated* life—the greater is the store of your estranged being."[69] The source of this criticism of the rich can be traced to Judaism and Christianity, although Marx does not indicate it. Part of this criticism appears in the Sermon on the Mount, and Marx obviously uses Christ's admonition of the rich for his own purpose.[70] What is needed, in Marx's view, is a radical critique that would destroy all illusions about free competition and laissez-faire economic policy.

Marx's denunciation of capitalist economy as a source of alienation is always bitter and contemptuous. Denouncing the worship of material wealth and its effects with the bitterness of the prophet Amos, he indicates that there is nothing inherently human about the accumulation of material wealth.[71] Humans should never surrender their "inner wealth to the outer world."[72] The capitalist does not care much about his "inner wealth," his principal concern is the accumulation of capital, that wealth which in *Manuscripts* is defined as the governing power over labor. Capital and money, the distinguishing characteristics of capitalist society, are the themes that run through Marx's early and later writings, although in *Grundrisse* and *Capital* they are given special treatment. In the introduction to *Grundrisse*, he reiterates that capital is the governing and alienating power over labor, adding that as such it is exclusively the "all-dominating economic power of bourgeois society."[73] In the system of bourgeois society, he says, "capital follows immediately after money."[74] In *Capital*, Marx defines the "accumulation of capital" in terms of surplus value or profit. The capitalist as the accumulator of capital is described as a vampire feeding on the innocent blood of the alienated worker. As a capitalist he is merely capital personified. Totally lacking inner wealth, the capitalist's only aim is self-expansion. "Capital," Marx points out, "is dead labour and, like a vampire, can only keep itself alive by sucking the blood of living labour. The more blood it sucks, the more vigorously it lives."[75]

Marx speaks of the alienated worker as "variable capital," indicating that the capitalist is contained in the category of capital. Bourgeois economists

treat capital as a natural rather than a historical product and, more importantly, they treat it as a thing rather than a relation. The result of this conception,
in Marx's view, is abstraction. It is entirely wrong, he believes, to regard
capital as an ahistorical product or a thing that is necessary for all forms of
production.[76] Failing to realize that capital cannot be dissociated from social
and historical relations, political economists assume wrongly that capital relations of production based on capital and private accumulation are independent of history. "If the specific form of capital," Marx says, could be "abstracted away and only the content emphasised, then it would be easy to
demonstrate that capital is a necessary condition for all human production."[77]
The catch is that if all capital is objectified labor that serves as means for new
production, it does not follow that all objectified labor that serves as means
for new production is capital."[78] In opposition to the bourgeois ecomists,
Marx contends that capital is essentially a historical system of social relations.
     Marx's analysis of capital begins with his examination of its concept. "The
exact development of the concept of capital," he writes in *Gundrisse*, "is
necessary, since it is the fundamental concept of modern economics, just as
capital itself, whose abstract reflected image is its concept, is the foundation
of bourgeois society."[79] To Adam Smith, capital appears merely as "human
natural force in general."[80] To Marx, all bourgeois appearances, including the
appearance of capital, are "empty abstractions" because they overlook that
capital has alienating effects on labor. Being empty abstractions, they inevitably obstruct any realistic approach to the analysis of the conept of capital. In
Marx's view, the analysis of such economic categories as capital, money, and
production can only be realistic when it takes into consideration the concrete
relations of men. "The labour of the individual is posited from the outset as
social labour."[81] The concrete analyzed in *Grundrisse* is simply capitalist production as reflected in the totality of human relations. Unlike the bourgeois
economists, Marx differentiates between "production in general" and "particular production" only to emphasize the difference between the historical
and unhistorical analysis of production. "Production in general" is treated "as
an abstraction." In his view, "production is always a particular branch of
production."[82]
     Believing that production is based on external, natural, and unhistorical
relations, bourgeois economists like Smith, Ricardo, and Mill regard
bourgeois relations as the "inviolable natural laws on which society in the
abstract is founded."[83] Marx criticizes these economists for separating production from distribution and consumption, stressing that they are "all members of a totality, distinctions within a unity." Bourgeois economists distinguish between production "as encased in eternal natural laws independent of
history" and distribution as being subject to arbitrary social arrangements."[84]
In the introduction to *Grundrisse* Marx contends that "production, distribution, exchange and consumption" are moments of the same economic process
in which "production predominates not only over itself, in the antithetical

definition, but over the other moments as well."[85] Because bourgeois economists treat capitalist production as essentially the same as all other forms of
production, he believes this treatment "extinguishes all historical differences"
and removes capitalist relations from "human history and the concrete."[86]

Like other nineteenth-century socialist thinkers, Marx argues that in the
capitalist system of production "all the methods for increasing the social productivity of labour are carried out at the cost of the individual worker." In
Capital he stresses that capitalist production is alienating not merely because
it is the production of commodities for exchange but also because "it is essentially the production of surplus value. The worker does not produce for himself but for capital."[87] Capitalist production maintains alienation because it
"reproduces and eternalises" the conditions for exploiting the worker. The
whole system of capitalist production, "is based on the fact that the alienated
worker is forced to sell his labour power as a commodity."[88] The capitalist
methods of production are so crude and inhuman that "they mutilate the
worker into a fragment of a human being, degrade him to become a mere
appurtenance of the machine, make his work such a torment that its essential
meaning is destroyed and estrange from him the intellectual potentialities of
the labour process in very proportion to the extent to which science is incorporated into it as an independent power."[89]

In an advanced capitalist society, according to Marx, the condition of the
manual laborer is deplorable. What is common to all types of capitalist production, "in so far as they are processes for promoting the self-expansion of
capital," is the fact that in them the "worker does not use the instruments of
labour but the instruments of labour use the worker."[90] The factory transforms the worker into a crippled, dehumanized being whenever the possibility
of creative work is denied to him and when the product of labor is expropriated by non-workers only to be used against him as the producer. Expropriation of the product of labor by the capitalist always engenders and maintains
alienation. Alienation of the worker is the result of production for exchange
that necessarily entails "contradictory and mutually exclusive relations."[91]

According to Marx and Engels, all exchange or production for sale is private. In capitalist society, commodities are always produced for exchange, for
profit-making rather than for mere use, or for satisfying human needs. Marx's
particular interest is in the exchange between capital and labor because in this
exchange the worker is cheated, degraded, and alienated. By selling his labor
to the capitalist employer, the worker only obtains a right to the price of his
labor, not to its product or to the value that his labor has added to it.[92] In
Grundrisse, Marx says that the exchange between capital and labor is composed of two parts that are "qualitatively different and even contradictory."[93]
He refers somewhat confusedly to these two composite parts of the exchange
as "processes." In the first process the worker sells his labor power to the
capitalist for wages and the capitalist buyer gives the seller the monetary
equivalent of the commodity's exchange value to obtain its use value. The

consumption of labor bought by the capitalist or, as Marx puts it, the "appropriation of labour by capital," makes up the second process, which is "qualitatively different from simple exchange and only by misuse could it be called any sort of exchange at all."[94]

Marx maintains that the worker sells to his employer the living power with its productive value exceeding the exchange value. The use value obtained by the capitalist in this exchange necessarily leads to the creation of exchange values, profit-making, and thus alienation of the worker. The worker only gets a means of subsistence from this exchange. He obtains money, but "only as a self-suspending and vanishing mediation"; he does not obtain exchange value or wealth. These belong to the capitalist. The most alienating element in the exchange between capital and labor is the sale of the worker's control over his labor to the capitalist. In Marx's view, labor in this exchange is always treated as exchange value. The worker as exchange value represents merely an objective condition for the reproduction of capital. He has no power over his own products because they are the property of the capitalist. Thus labor is a living power that entails a living contradiction. "It is clear, therefore, that the worker cannot become rich in the exchange," Marx writes, "since in exchange for his labour capacity as a fixed, available magnitude, he surrenders its creative power, like Esau his birthright for a mess of pottage."[95] He rather impoverishes himself "because the creative power of his labour establishes itself as the power of capital, as an alien power confronting him."[96]

Distinguishing between labor and labor power or labor capacity, Marx assumes that in this way he can explain the "inherent contradiction" of the classical theory of value and thus resolve the mystery of capitalist accumulation. In *Capital* he defines labor power as the "aggregate of those bodily and mental capacities existing in a human being which he exercises whenever he produces a use value of any kind."[97] The real value of the worker's labor power is equal to the working time needed for producing the means of his subsistence. Labor by which the laborer produces commodities with value equivalent to the value of objects required for his subsistence Marx calls "necessary wage labour" as opposed to "surplus wage labour," which produces the value in excess of the cost of the worker's subsistence. This value, in Marx's view, is roughly identical with profit. Analyzing the rate of surplus value and the exploitation of labor power by capital as important aspects of alienation, he also distinguishes between "necessary labour time," the labor time necessary socially for the production of commodities in general, and "surplus labour time," which "serves to create surplus value, smiling on the capitalist with all the charms of an entity created out of nothing."[98]

According to Marx's economic theory, surplus labor, surplus labor time, and surplus value are the evidence and measure of the exploitation of the worker by his employer. They reflect most evidently the worker's alienation. Marx takes for granted that whenever the laborer works longer hours, he produces surplus value as profit that belongs automatically to the buyer of his labor power. The objects produced by this power assume an independent existence and "confront the worker as something alien to him." The labor process in which the alienated worker has "overstepped the limits of necessary labour time, costs him labour, calls upon him for the expenditure of labour power but it does not serve to create any value for him."[99] It creates surplus value for the buyer of labor capacity. When selling products or commodities in the market produced by alienated labor, the capitalist is not as interested in satisfying human needs as he is in profit making. The principal aim of the capitalist in any labor process, in Marx's view, is the "increase of his capital, the production of commodities which contain more labour than he pays for, which contain a portion of value that costs him nothing and can nevertheless be realised by the sale of these commodities."[100] The production of surplus value is an "absolutely necessary law" of the capitalist method of production. The greater the labor productivity, the fewer working hours will be needed for producing the means of the worker's subsistence, thus more hours will remain for his exploitation.

The principle of high productivity of labor, Marx points out, is the basis of capitalist exploitation that produces and maintains alienation. High productivity of labor is manifestly alienated labor, and this labor transforms all human relations into the relations of things. "Fanatically bent upon the expansion of value, the capitalist relentlessly drives human beings to production for production's sake."[101] Analyzing the capitalist economic structure in terms of internal relations, Marx treats it as a socially-lived contradiction. He criticizes the bourgeois economists for their inability to understand the historically unique significance of capital as a form of socioeconomic life and their inability to realize that labor is not only a commodity, sold freely and bought in exchange as the equivalent of its price, but that it is also the source of surplus value that generates capitalist profit. In his early works, Marx agrees with Ricardo that there is always a strict "inverse relation between profit and wages." In *Grundrisse*, however, he argues against Ricardo's theory of profit, indicating that "surplus value—in so far as it is the foundation of profit but still distinct from profit commonly so-called—has never been properly explained."[102] Distinguishing here between profit and surplus value, he maintains that the rate of profit as explained by the bourgeois economists actually falsifies the rate of capitalist exploitation. "The rate of profit never expresses the real rate at which capital exploits labour but always a much smaller relation, and the larger the capital, the more false is the relation it expresses. The rate of profit could express", he adds, "the real rate of surplus value only if the entire capital were transformed solely into wages or exchanged for living labour."[103]

Marx's theory of surplus value is an extension of the labor theory of value advocated by classical economists. In both cases commodities exchanged in the market are seen as the products of labor. Unlike the economists, however, Marx concentrates his economic research on the "domination of accumulated, materialised labour over direct, living labour which turns accumulated labour into capital."[104] What is new in his theory of value is not the theory itself but rather his insistence that capitalist economists have formulated human relations in terms of a "cash nexus" that is strikingly indicative of alienation. Even "Ricardo who alone among all the economists understood the conception of surplus value often goes astray in conceiving the multiplication of values on any basis other than the investment of additional objectified labour time in the same product. Hence the absolute antithesis in his thinking between value and wealth."[105] Contrary to the bourgeois economists, Marx contends that the labor power of alienated workers used in the production of commodities generates value beyond its cost. What is tragic, Engels contends, is that the "values produced by the workers do not belong to the workers but to the owners of the raw materials, machines, tools and the reserve funds which allow these owners to buy the labour power of the working class."[106]

In his analysis of value, Marx follows Aristotle and Adam Smith and differentiates between use value and exchange value. Every commodity, he says, has a "twofold aspect—use value and exchange value."[107] Use value is a relation that exists only between the potential use and a commodity. As an aspect of the commodity "it coincides with the physical palpable existence of the commodity." In *Contribution to the Critique of Political Economy*, Marx says that "a commodity can only become a use value if it is realised as an exchange value" and that "it can only be realised as an exchange value if it is alienated and functions as a use value."[108] Exchange value is a social relation. "The exchange value of commodities," according to Marx, "is nothing but a mutual relation between the various kinds of labour of individuals regarded as equal and universal labour, i.e., nothing but a material expression of a specific social from of labour."[109] The commodity must have use value if it is to realize its exchange value. Thus "use value as an active carrier of exchange value becomes a means of exchange. The commodity is a use value for its owner only in so far as it is an exchange value."[110]

Marx sees use value and exchange value as related yet incompatible categories. "The commodity is the direct unity of use value and exchange value, and at the same time it is a commodity only in relation to other commodities."[111] To become use values, commodities must be alienated. This takes place in the exchange process. Exchange, in Marx's view, "is concerned only with their aspect as exchange values." In *Grundrisse*, Marx notes that capital and wage labor are forms of developed exchange value and of money that is the incarnation of exchange value. "It is the elementary precondition of bourgeois society that labour should directly produce exchange value, i.e. money."[112] Money can buy labor directly and thus also the "labourer but only in so far as he alienates his activity in the exchange." As use value for capital, labor is a mere exchange value for the worker.

The capitalist uses labor for more than its exchange value, and it is the misuse of this value that creates surplus value that, in Marx's view, is the direct opposite of equivalence. Indicating that the use value that the worker offers in the exchange with capital only exists as an ability of his bodily existence, he defines surplus value as "value in excess of the equivalent."[113] Surplus value "can never sprout out of the equivalent" because in the exchange process of strict equivalence only equal values are exchanged. Analyzing the creation of surplus value and its alienating effects in capitalist society, Marx argues that surplus value is the opposite of equivalence. The capitalist gets this value because the value of the worker's wage is smaller than the amount of working time for which the worker is paid. "The only thing which can make man capitalist is not exchange but rather a process through which he obtains objectified labour time, i.e. value, without exchange. And the multiplication of values can take place only if a value in excess of the equivalent has been obtained and created."[114] Contrary to Smith who believes in the "natural rates of wages and profits," Marx contends that as long as men remain within the relation of capital and wage labor, the interests of capital and labor will remain diametrically opposed. In capitalist alienated production, the "rates of wages and profits" are always in "inverse proportion." "If capital is growing rapidly, wages may rise but the profit of capital rises incomparably more rapidly."[115]

Capitalist alienation of the worker, according to Marx, is based on the "theft of alien labour time," which always generates economic inequality. A rapid increase in capital is equivalent to a rapid increase in profit, and this leads to economic alienation.[116] Surplus value that the worker produces in excess of the equivalent is profit. "The capitalist is quite unaware," Marx says in *Capital*, "that the normal price of labour includes a definite quantity of unpaid labour and that it is precisely this unpaid labour which is the normal source of his gain."[117] He adds that even the "extra pay for overtime includes unpaid labour" and thus entails alienating profit. Unlike Smith who defends the capitalist's profit as "his revenue" or the "proper fund of his existence," Marx argues that profit, involving all the surplus value extracted by the capitalist in the exchange process with the worker, is the source of alienation. There is no law that determines minimum profits. Fixation of the profit rate in capitalist productioin is settled only by the "continuous struggle between capital and labour, the capitalist constantly tending to reduce wages to their physical minimum and to extend the working day to its physical maximum, while the working man constantly presses in the opposite direction."[118]

Marx is almost obsessed with the idea of profit and contends that it is not the employing capitalist but the alienated worker who adds an arbitrary value for his profit to the value of the commodity sold in the market.[119] Whereas in the pre-capitalist economic structure "even that part of the worker's labour which is paid appears to be unpaid," in capitalist alienating production the reverse occurs so that "even the unpaid labour seems to be paid labour."[120] In "Wage, Price and Profit," Marx reiterates the view expounded in *Grundrisse* that in production based on slavery, the slave is not considered as being engaged in exchange whereas in production based on capital the whole economic system is mediated by exchange and labor is always treated merely as a means for promoting the self-expansion of alienating capital.[121] He criticizes the bourgeois economists for failing to realize that in alienated capitalist production the paid and unpaid portions of labor are so inseparably mixed together that it is easy to confuse reality with appearance and exploitation with equivalence. Smith's view that "equal quantities of labour, at all times and places, must have the same value for the labourer" is rejected. So is his "dogma" that wages determine the prices of commodities.[122] According to Marx, the alienated laborer in capitalism is always cheated by the employer. "The money price of labour, nominal wages, do not coincide with real wages, that is, with the sum of commodities which is actually given in exchange for the wages."[123]

The value of labor power used by the capitalist always contains unpaid labor or surplus value that is "pocketed by him" as profit. The capitalist employer is not interested in any equivalence. He buys labor to produce goods or products that can be sold for a higher price than the real cost of their production. When the price of a commodity falls below its production cost, the capitalist employer will withdraw his capital from its production.[124] The purpose of alienating capitalist production is always the production of goods for sale to make a profit. Thus the capitalist process of production, Marx points out in *Capital*, "reproduces, of its own accord, the divorce of labour power from the means of labour. It reproduces and eternalises, therewith, the conditions for the exploitation of the worker. It perpetually forces the worker to sell his labour power that he may live, while perpetually enabling the capitalist to purchase labour power that he may enrich himself."[125] The alienated worker only produces for the capitalist. The wealth he produces as capital or money is expressed tragically as power that is alien to the worker, controls him, and exploits him.[126]

The central point in Marx's economic theory of alienation is that when a capitalist converts a portion of his capital into labor power, he augments his total capital by extracting surplus value from the alienated laborer. Thus economic alienation is the result of commodity production and capitalist exchange. These processes are complete when the means of production are transformed into commodities whose value exceeds their total production cost or, as Marx states, whose value "contains the capital primarily expended plus surplus value."[127] The capitalist's passionate hunt for value and his "inextinguishable passion for gain" create a division between labor and capital and lead to exploitation and alienation of the worker. Exploitation always involves expropriation of the surplus product of labor power and only occurs when the worker is separated from the conditions of production. Exploitation is the distinguishing feature of the production process in which a "relation between people is expressed as a relation between things." As capitalism develops, the worker is more dehumanized, reified, and alienated. The only way to achieve a meaningful existence, according to Marx, is by substituting non-alienated labor for alienated labor.

Capitalism, in Marx's opinion, is a destructive and alienating force. As such, it has, he says in *Capital*, not only created "two sorts of people: some of them, the chosen few, industrious, intelligent and, above all, thrifty; the others, lazy rascals, wasting their substance in riotous living." It has also created the "mass of poverty, oppression, enslavement, degeneration and exploitation."[128] The difference in alienation of the capitalist and the worker is expressed most vividly in their behavior in the exchange market. "The one who comes to the market as the owner of money leaves it striding forward as a capitalist; the one who comes to the market as the owner of labour power brings up the rear as a worker. One of them, self-important, self-satisfied, with a keen eye to business, the other, timid, reluctant, like a man who is bringing his own skin to the market and has nothing to except but a tanning."[129]

In *Grundrisse* and *Capital*, Marx focuses his criticism on the alienating power of money. Money, like capital, reflects social relationships, yet they are distinct economic categories based on "different laws." Representing the "divine existence of all commodities," money, Marx says in the *Grundrisse*, is the "treasure which neither rust nor moths eat up. All commodities are only transitory money; money is the permanent commodity."[130] Like Smith, he realizes that money has become the universal instrument of commerce in all civilized nations. Unlike Smith, however, he focuses on the alienating effect of money "as something posited by society and the expression of a social relation."[131] In *Capital* Marx indicates that money is the first phenomenal form of capital. The primary distinction between money as money and money as capital is merely a difference between their respective forms of circulation.[132] Analyzing its corrupting power, he notes that money is alienating because it reverses the natural properties of things, breeds dishonesty, and prostitutes almost everything it can buy. The money that the worker earns as wages is a symbol of his alienation.

In money wealth loses its social and objective value and assumes an independent existence. The ownership of values in exchange is private ownership of money. For Marx, wealth as "something outside man and independent of him" represents an alien power and must be condemned. Private wealth, as opposed to social wealth, divides men into rich and poor, into owners and non-owners. Seeing in money the "alienated ability of mankind," Marx states in all his major works that contradictions are immanent in money relations. In the essay *On the Jewish Question*, he uses the concept of alienation in his description of money as the way the capitalist employer alienates and dehumanizes the worker. "Money," he writes here, "is the universal self-established value of all things. It has therefore robbed the whole world—both the world of men and nature—of its specific value."[133] To emphasize the alienating effects of monetary greed and avarice, Marx adds that "money is the estranged essence of man's work and man's existence" and that "as an alien essence it dominates man and he worships it."[134]

Analyzing the appearance of money as an autonomous entity, Marx argues that money is not a natural object but rather a historic product of exchange. The transformation of a commodity into money and the retransformation of the money into a commodity he calls "metamorphosis." Both "phases of this metamorphosis are transactions effected by the owner of the commodity. He sells, exchanges his commodity for money and he buys, exchanges his money for a commodity."[135] It is the sale in order to buy that unifies these two transactions. The capitalist is always the owner of money and thus the principal actor in both transactions, whereas the worker merely owns the labor power. Yet paradoxically, the worker's surplus labor creates the capital that is easily transformed by the capitalist into alienating money. The tragedy involved in these transactions is that the fruit of the worker's labor power actually goes to the capitalist employer. The products of labor that belong strictly to the worker are taken away from him and ultimately turned against him. By robbing the worker, the capitalist creates his private capital and becomes "enriched in proportion to the extent to which he can put the screw on others' labour power."[136]

Marx calls the capitalist a shrewd thief who mercilessly exploits and robs the poor and low-paid workers. "In the capitalist's breast there develops a Faustian conflict between the passion for accumulation and the desire for enjoyment."[137] In this conflict the desire for accumulation prevails. Facing the choice between "being and having," his choice is always fixed on mere "having," on accumulation and fetishization. Because the capitalist is merely "capital personified" interested in producing surplus value and transforming it into "additional capital," Marx likens him to the fetish worshipper. Analyzing the "mystery of the fetishistic character of commodities" in *Capital*, he argues that capitalism is a version of fetishism. In capitalism as in fetishism, the whole emphasis is on man's dependence on the magic efficacy of objects. These objects are seen as separate natural entities existing outside man and independent of his existence. The value of objects appears to reside in them rather than in the social relation of the producers of commodities. Using the analogy of religion, Marx stresses that the "fetishistic character of the world of commodities is the outcome of the peculiar social quality of the labour which produces commodities."[138] The capitalist form of fetishism is alienating because it transforms living human relations into the relations of inanimate things and because it attributes to the products of labor the qualities that only humans can possess.

In *Capital*, Marx criticizes the classical economists for treating capital as a natural and immutable product rather than the product of the social relations of the labor process. Socioeconomic relations provide the irreducible context of meaning for understanding all historical productions. The categories of bourgeois economics, like other economic categories, bear the stamp of history. They are the "socially valid thought forms which serve to express the relations of production peculiar to one specific method of social production, namely commodity production."[139] Marx assumes that by taking away the relations of exchange and commodity production, the capitalist unit of exchange will cease to be money. "Nature does not produce money any more than it produces a rate of exchange or a banker."[140] In capitalist production, he believes, everything is upside down and an object, which in reality is a historically created product, is falsely acknowledged as existing in a fetish. The product or commodity produced by alienated labor power is called a veiled phenomenon characterized by metaphysical charms. Marx adds that "all the mystery of the world of commodities, all the sorcery, all the fetishistic charm, which enwraps as with a fog the labour products of a system of commodity production, is instantly dispelled when we turn to consider other methods of production."[141]

In communism in which the means of production would be socialized, there will be, according to Marx, a great accumulation of productive resources but no room for the accumulation of private capital produced by alienated labor power. It is interesting to note, however, that he only predicts the new economic structure without describing it clearly and without mystification to ensure that it is easily recognizable from the "non-collectively controlled" economies.[142] Marx, of course, could not observe the application of his economic theory in practice. He has merely predicted that when the capitalist monopoly becomes a fetter on production, centralization of the means of production and socialization of labor will reach "incompatibility with their capitalist husk" and the "expropriators will be expropriated."[143] His persistent dislike of the capitalist division of labor, private ownership, exchange, and money has led him to maintain that in a socialist controlled economy, labor would never be treated as a commodity and that economic alienation would end.

Marx rightly emphasizes that in capitalist production labor is not receiving its fair share, and his attack on industrial capitalism is in many ways convincing. Capitalism is condemned because it overvalues external wealth and undervalues "inner wealth." It is alienating because it deliberately creates the conditions for exploiting workers, transforming their whole life into working time. As a result of capitalist accumulation, the condition of the worker, whether his wages are high or low, necessarily grows worse. Using an ancient Greek metaphor, Marx stresses that under capitalism the alienated worker is "chained to capital even more effectually than Prometheus was fastened to the rock by the fetters forged by Hephaestus."[144] Alienation of the worker frequently leads to unemployment and intolerable poverty. The unemployed worker, he says, is driven into the "industrial reserve army," enabling the capitalist employer to lower wages further.[145] Although Marx exaggerates the capitalist's treatment of the workers when he speaks of them as "mere objects of exploitation," his attack on unrestrained capitalism based on unpaid labor is morally justified. However, he fails to see that exploitation, oppression, and alienation cannot be confined to capitalist society alone.

Many modern writers observe that although ownership in communism is "social or collective" in form, actual control of ownership in practice is in the hands of "party bureaucrats."[146] The fact that the decisive control of communist ownership is located in the hands of these bureaucrats can only mean that the collective control of production will remain a dream. Although workers here are less exploited and their products are less alien to them than those produced under an alien power generated by competition and monetary greed, exploitation is not the social evil that could easily be limited to capitalist exchange or the commodity mode of production. In his analysis of alienation, Marx fails to appreciate the seriousness of inherent human badness. All men, the exploiting and the exploited, are of the same nature, of the same proclivity to self-interestness, and of the same passions for "monetary greed." Even Marx mentions the workers' mania for riches and possessions that seems to suggest that the innocence of the exploited proletariat is only a lack of opportunity, reflecting the manipulated appearance rather than the "inner substratum" of communist goals.[147] Basically, however, he attributes innocence and humanism to the owner of labor power, just as Rousseau attributes it to "natural man." The main difference between them in this respect is that Rousseau blames civilization for alienation whereas Marx blames "blood sucking capital and avarice."[148]

Analyzing the role of machinery and automation in capitalist production, Marx argues that here the machines are only a means for producing surplus value and thus profit for the capitalist. "Machines are not wage earners," he writes in the *Grundrisse*, and "capital employs machinery only to the extent that it enables the worker to work longer for the capitalist."[149] Openly displaying his animosity against the alienating power of capital, he adds that the most developed machinery merely forces the worker to work harder and longer than the "savage does or he himself did with simplest, crudest tools."[150] For Marx, machinery is a productive force, but in capitalist production only the bourgeois economists imagine that machines aid the alienated worker. Here, on the contrary, machinery depreciates the worker's labor power, lengthens the working day, increases the rate of exploitation, intensifies economic alienation, and produces poverty.[151] By reducing the need for any considerable expenditure of labor power, "machinery produces a surplus working population which is compelled to submit to the dictation of capital."[152]

Marx sees the object of capitalist automation as simply "economic power," always reflected in the political domination over the laboring classes. Machines are introduced by capitalist employers to destroy the bargaining advantages of skilled wage earners and thus to maximize the chances for creating surplus value. Machinery can only increase the rate of surplus value by diminishing the number of workers employed by a given amount of capital and consequently by reducing the price of labor power below its value.[153]

Like any other constituent of constant capital, machinery, according to Marx, does not create value but merely transfers its own value to the product "it serves to beget."[154] Thus surplus value is the result of the exploitation of human labor power and the machine cannot be a source of surplus value. Marx could not deny that machines also could indirectly be a source of surplus value, but his reasoning here ends in a contradiction that neither he nor his followers can explain. Not surprisingly, therefore, his idea of surplus value is regarded by modern Marxists as an object of respect or a relic of the founder of communist ideology rather than an intelligible and convincing part of the theory of value. For this reason, Lenin hardly mentions it in his elaboration of the exploitation of man by man.[155]

The fact is that Marx's economic theory as a whole is based on moral and metaphysical as well as economic assumptions. In spite of his pretensions, his theory of economic alienation is far from being "purely scientific." The idea that capitalist profit rests on a surplus value of labor can be neither proved nor disproved simply because Marx's theory of value, as Croce indicates, is metaphysical and essentialist. By definition, surplus value is "extra value" and as such lies outside the sphere of pure economics.[156] Constructing his abstract theory of surplus value on an ethical basis, Marx is guilty of treating value in the manner of Plato as an objective reality and prices as a form of appearance, thus entirely separating the essence of value from experience and empirical facts. Because a surplus value as an extra value is a metaphysical category, the Marxian idea of surplus value is meaningless in the analysis of purely economic categories. The belief that the value of products depends on the human labor spent can be traced beyond Smith and Locke to Aquinas. Marx concentrates on the capitalist's "theft of alien labour time" and concludes that "surplus value is exactly equal to surplus labour and that the increase of the one is exactly measured by the diminution of necessary labour."[157]

Marx could not foresee that automation and mechanization of productive forces would alter the relation between dead and living labor in such a way that the very measurement of individual output would become practically impossible. Many modern economists maintain that automation is the end of measuring the output of any individual laborer.[158] It is even less possible to measure the rate of surplus value or labor power embodied in it. Being untestable, Marx's theory of surplus value is divorced entirely from experience and, like any other theory of value, is bound to be metaphysical, abstract, and confusing. As a metaphysical category, it can hardly be of any scientific relevance in the measurement of the rate of exploitation. Haunted by the ghost of capitalist surplus value and chimera of a natural, immutable, and unhistorical economy, he fails to realize that surplus labor and surplus value cannot be confined to capitalist production. It is well known today that considerable profits can be paid to men who are not engaged in productive work not only in capitalism but also in socialist-controlled economies. If profit originates from the exploitation of labor power, as Marx argues, then profit exists in collectively controlled production because labor power is also exploited here, although to a lesser extent. There is no human society, communist or capitalist, in which the worker is not really separated from the conditions of production and thus somehow is confronted by an alien power. It is only unfortunate that the worker does not produce for himself but always for the bosses who are frequently unsympathetic to his suffering and manipulate his products for their private ends.[159]

Production of surplus value is not an "absolutely necessary law" of any specific method of production; it is inherent in man's economic life. Marx is right in criticizing capitalism for "proclaiming the making of surplus value as the sole end and aim of mankind," and in denouncing the capitalist monetary greed and theft of the surplus value for purely egoistic ends. Yet Marx is not an egalitarian. Arguing against Proudhon's economic egalitarianism, he believes that this egalitarianism could not change the fundamental aspects of alienation but that it would rather reduce all men to worker status and transform the whole society into an "abstract capitalist."[160] Marx's economic theory is frequently ambiguous and inconsistent. Sometimes he speaks of both the labor and the capitalist "being under the sway of inhuman power" and sometimes he speaks only of the alienated worker as being "a mere fragment of a human being" but never says anything about the alienation and fragmentation of the peasant or the intellectual. It is really the alienation of the worker that is always in his mind because the non-worker or capitalist is regarded to be merely in a "state of alienation."[161]

Considering the analysis of Marx's economic alienation as a whole, one can see that the use of the concept of alienation in his later writings is practically synonymous with that of exploitation, dehumanization, and impoverishment. In these writings, especially in *Capital*, the worker is treated as a member of a class that will utlimately rise to the consciousness of its own degradation and destroy the underlying causes of economic inequality. In *Grundrisse* and *Capital*, alienation of the worker is not explained by the unchanging qualities of human nature but rather by the "concrete category" of social relations. Relying more on dialectical forces than on technology, Marx does not maintain that technological progress is a necessary or effective means for the transformation of a technologically backward society into communism. This transformation depends primarily on the mode of production that conditions the social, political, and intellectual process of human life. Although his description of the capitalist world cannot be disregarded easily, Marx's economism fails to account for the existence of economic alienation because this alienation is a complex phenomenon, partly involving social and historical relations and partly entailing psychological and superstructural aspects of human life. Although avarice and greed may be minimized or maximized by a definite socioeconomic development, they cannot be entirely, as Marx claims, the product of this development. They are "natural" and exist naturally in some form or another in all human beings—capitalist and proletarian alike. Yet, although Marx's criticism of capitalist avarice and greed is sometimes exaggerated, it is impossible to ignore his great courage in denouncing the dictatorship and alien power of capital and his burning desire to improve the living conditions of alienated and dehumanized workers.

4
Self-Alienation and Self-Realization

Philosophers, theologians, psychologists, and sociologists differ considerably not only in their definitions of the concept of self-alienation but also in their assumptions involved in these definitions. On the one hand, self-alienation is presented as a spiritual, mental, and psychological phenomenon reflected in the loss of personal identity, a confused mind, a divided self, or in deviation from normality. On the other hand, self-alienation is conceived to be primarily an economic, ethical, and socio-political concept, a fact of man's phenomenal rather than of superstructural or spiritual life. The unifying factor in all theories of self-alienation or self-estrangement is the belief that human individuals have become divided within and have lost touch with themselves. Most theoreticians maintain that self-estrangement is an ontological fact, rooted in human nature. The core of the Judeo-Christian tradition is that man is a fallen being, that he was good originally but now is a sinner. Mankind not only suffers the effect of original sin but also shares in the sin itself. All men, according to this tradition, are guilty and estranged because the whole human race is mysteriously involved in a history that has failed to observe the laws of free will. Man's estrangement from God has resulted in the imperfection of his essential powers and in the evils of history. Above all, it has resulted in a dislocation of his inner life and in a divided self.

Postulating man's self-estrangement as an inherent phenomenon, Judaism and Christianity give specific prominence to the negative aspect of this estrangement, to the removal of obstacles, and urge men to renounce their pretensions to self-mastery, self-centeredness, and impious godlessness. The process of overcoming the deep gulf between self-estranged man and his creator is possible only through reconciliation. Alienated man is expected to repent his sins, but God alone can provide the means of reconciliation. Natural man can exist without grace, but it is emphasized that he cannot fulfill his true life purposes and realize his essential being without divine assistance. Mediation plays a significant role in the Judeo-Christian tradition in relation to man's reconciliation to God. In this tradition the concept of self-estrangement is always related to the dichotomy of sacred and profane, holy and sinful, divine and alienated rival kingdoms. The relation between man and his creator is believed to be moral. Only men who have learned to will what God wills, love what God loves, and hate what God hates are able to enter into the fullness of divine life. God is exalted above finitude and limitation as well as above sin and evil. The idea of ethical end in man's life is connected with a religious ideal that expresses the ultimate goal of personal aspirations.

From the point of view of Christian theology, self-estrangement is inherent in human nature and linked with a loss of moral freedom. The originally non-self-alienated individuals have misused their moral freedom and thus become alienated. Having become divided within himself, man feels powerless to realize his essential being. Although he is aware of the conflict between different aspects of his conscious being, his self is so split that one part claims to have more right to represent the whole self than the other part. By becoming alien to each other, the two hostile parts of the same self necessarily become alien to the entire self. St. Paul is well aware of this conflict when he speaks of "doing the things he should not be doing and of not doing the things he should be doing."[1] Whenever moral principles are deficient, whenever the will of God is violated, then selfishness, profligacy, vanity, and evil practices are abundant. The regulation of passions and instricts is the secret of self-control. Without a permanent organic center of unity, the organization of meaningful moral life is impossible. This entails a mind or self through which man becomes aware of his divine origin and of his divinely ordained ends. What matters in human creative activity, according to Christian teaching, is the realization of valuable ends. Regardless of the actual facts involved in the process of moral progress, the idea of a rational end is the only principle that can make evolution fully intelligible.[2]

Christians believe that creative power on which man's development depends is inseparable from the deliberating activity of the mind. Creativeness implies that man's moral activity must spring from his conscience. Moral progress is neither mechanical nor fortuitous. Only through conscious harmony of the self can man attain his higher spiritual goals. The free, contemplative, and unitary self provides human life with its goals and justification. Generally speaking, the good outweighs the manifestations of evil. Taken as a whole, self-alienation does not constitute a realm of its own but plays a subordinate role in divine providential rule of the universe. Irrational impulses overpowering rational judgment are some of the immediate antecedents of bad acts that may lead to human misery. The important function of reason is to control these impulses and reveal to men the situation in which they ought to act. Men will best overcome alienation and minimize suffering when they act reasonably and according to moral laws that are themselves manifestations of divine perfection. In his analysis of self-alienation, Marx rejects entirely the religious conception of self-estrangement, because he thinks this conception is based on illusory reality. According to him human nature is neither good nor bad but amoral, and estrangement of human life cannot be regarded as a divine process.[3]

In Marx's view, all forms of idealism fail to realize that self-alienation is a historical phenomenon that must be traced to the processes of work and to the effects of forced labor on the development of human nature in society. Yet, in spite of essential differences between St. Paul and Marx's ideas of self-alienation, they both believe that alienation is a negative phenomenon leading to significant changes in human life, and that, as a result of alienation, everything in the world of men is somehow different from itself. St. Paul sees alienation affecting both men and nature, stating that all men are under the power of sin.[4] Marx describes the same situation as being "under the sway of inhuman power."[5] The most visible manifestation of self-alienation is seen in human suffering. Although Marx rejects the view that self-alienation is an inherent phenomenon, he still maintains paradoxically that man's productive activity is stimulated by his congenital suffering. This suffering, he thinks, is a natural and inherent characteristic of all natural, corporeal, and sensuous beings, including men.[6] This apparent contradiction in Marx's theory of alienation between congenital suffering and uncongenital self-alienation has led some commentators to assume that humans have always been self-alienated.

The fact is that Marx's theory of self-alienation is far from being clear and consistent. He seems to suggest that self-alienatiion is a temporary phenomenon with its origin in the institution of private property and division of labor. In his more general view, the phenomenon of self-alienation must be associated with man's socioeconomic relations and occurs when he fails to realize his historically created essential powers and potentialities. Because man's socioeconomic relations are alienated, "he is estranging himself from himself."[7] In alienated labor, every man is separated from his fellow-men, split and alienated from himself. All genuine human needs, including creativity, are suppressed and their desire for self-fulfilment and expression of essential powers and capacities is sadly denied. "The greater and the more developed the social power appears to be within the private property relationship, the more egoistic, asocial and estranged from his own nature does man become."[8] Capitalism is the incarnation of inhumanity and prevents "free manifestation" and realizatioin of man's essential capacities. In capitalist alienated society, "human morality itself has become an object of commerce." Here, "a good man is considered to be a man who is able to pay."[9] All human values are transformed into monetary categories and all human activity is submerged in avarice.

Marx's ideas of self-alienation as expressed in his early works represent a synthesis of Hegel's and Feuerbach's reasoning about the essence and nature of man. Rejecting their abstract and mystical concepts of human nature, he argues that self-alienation is the expression of real, sensuous man. Man not only alienates himself in the form of consciousness and spirituality but also more importantly in the products of his physical labor. Hegel wrongly concentrates on the estrangement of self-consciousness; thus, in Marx's view, he ignores entirely the alienation of the products of man's socioeconomic activity in art, philosophy, and material commodities. Hegel believes that the process of self-alienation can only be understood in the light of human development. Self-alienation is a process of self-development in which the obstacles and limitations of one's self-realization are transcended gradually and overcome. The alienated self reflects a disharmony between its conflicting parts and also the obstacles facing it in its striving for true selfhood. To realize himself, man must endeavour to subjugate his particularity to the supreme authority of the universal. Only in the totality of selves is self-realization possible. The contradiction between self-assertion and self-realization is transcended only in the mind of society. Here the principle of subjectivity is no longer evil and alienating because it is universalized. "The systematised whole," he says, "is independent of the opposition between a merely subjective aim and its realisation and is the same in both despite their difference in form."[10]

As long as individuals fail to realize that they are part of the totality of selves, Hegel believes they cannot fulfil their moral and rational goals, and they inevitably become alienated. The transcendence of alienation depends on pure intellectual insight and knowledge of the Absolute or God. The realm of alienation is the realm of particularity, a realm of self-betrayal of man's self-fulfillment. Rejecting the validity of individualism, Hegel maintains that the moment of individuality is intelligible only when regarded as the social moment. The Greeks, he remarks, "knew neither God nor man in their true universality." "Only in Christendom is man respected as man in his infinitude and universality."[11] Indicating that self-alienation in the sense of *Entäusserung* is the process through which the finite self appropriates its own qualities forfeited in the separation from its true nature, Hegel believes that the alienated self can return to the unity with the totality of other finite selves only in the realm of society and developed culture. "The fancies, which the individual in his isolation indulges, cannot be the model for universal reality."[12] The nature of human individuals, Hegel says, is "essentially universal" and social.[13] Men depend on one another and relate reciprocally in their work and in the satisfaction of their needs. Social individuals are determined by the developing actuality of society in which they live, and only in society can they attain moral and rational ends and fulfill their social functions in the interests of all members.

Hegel sees the processes of self-alienation and its transcendence as necessary moments in the externalization and re-internalization of Absolute Spirit. The final goal of infinite spirit in history is self-knowledge. The goal, which is "spirit knowing itself as spirit," finds its pathway in the "recollection of spiritual forms as they are in themselves." Reason becomes spirit when it achieves the full consciousness of itself as being all reality. "Self-consciousness lives outside of itself in another self-consciousness in which it at once loses and also finds itself."[14] The real world is inseparable from the world of spirit because, Hegel maintains, the spirit of the world constitutes the essence of the history of the natural world. The natural world, he says, "obtains its existence through self-consciousness's own externalisation and separation of itself from its essence."[15] Nature is the idea or spirit in the form of externality or mere objectivity. "The distinction between nature and mind is not improperly conceived when the former is traced back to reality and the latter to ideality as a fundamental category."[16] Because nature is a partial expression of the Absolute Idea, it also goes through alienation. External nature is not merely an alienated mode of existence in which consciousness and self-consciousness have to realize their spiritual goals—it is also relevant to the existence of consciousness itself. Nature is the "work and the negative of self-consciousness" and thus contains the principle of unity concealed.[17] Like consciousness, nature also is a posited existence that has its true meaning only when it is regarded as a part of the process in which conscious mind expresses itself, "reflects on it and converts it into something it has itself posited."[18] The phenomenon of consciousness, in Hegel's view, is both natural and contingent. In the final analysis, alienated nature, which has no history without alienated consciousness, has its own teleology and this teleology is primarily moral.

Hegel believes the primary purpose of man's endeavors must be to understand the natural world and to appropriate and dominate it. In this respect, it is important to remember that man cannot advance to his true self-fulfillment except by the way of the divine ideal. "The self knows itself as actual only as a transcended self," and it is through culture that the "individual can acquire standing and actuality" and overcome alienation.[19] The difference between the divine and human mind is rooted in the self-differentiation of the Absolute or Spirit. Finite mind is limited and imperfect because the conditions of its existence lie beyond itself and are imposed on it from without. "Absolute mind knows that it posits being itself, that it is itself the creator of its other, of nature and finite mind."[20] Man is distinguished from animals and nature by knowing himself as "I." Man is a thinker and universal, but he is a thinker only because he feels his own universality. "The animal too is by implication universal but the universal is not consciously felt by it to be universal; it feels only the indivdual."[21] Man alone knows that he is "I." Hegel distinguishes between consciousness and self-consciousness. Consciousness is awareness of objects that are regarded in sense perception as different from the self; self-consciousness is the negation of "otherness" that leads to the internal unity of the divided self. In the dialectical process of development, self-consciousness is faced by another consciousness and thus it must supersede the otherness of itself and eliminate the alien selfhood. After this elimination, the self can return freely to itself. As simple being-for-self, self-consciousness must be willing to sacrifice everything concrete for its own infinite self-respect and the respect of all others.[22] Both divine and human life imply self-alienation and self-reconciliation. These processes are essentially those of self-consciousness and express the dialectical moments in the development of the "self-alienated Spirit" and its return to itself.[23]

The main theme of Marx's criticism of idealist monism as expounded in

Hegel's philosophy is that it posits ultimate reality in the Absolute Spirit, resulting in an incorrect conception of man and the surrounding world. Marx accepts Hegel's notion of the human individual as a social being and his idea of history as a dialectical process but rejects his idealism and concept of self-alienation. Although Hegel grasps the alienation of man's essence, Marx believes he fails to realize that the estrangement of self-consciousness is not the expression of the real alienatioin of the natural human being.[24] In Hegel's philosophical system, real man and real nature are reduced to mere symbols of spiritual reality and the material, objective, and concrete bases of alienated forms of human self-consciousness are ignored and left in the realm of mental reality. Marx argues that Hegel's conception of the alienation of self-consciousness and Feuerbach's conception of the alienation of the abstract and non-historical man are equally unsatisfactory because they either under-estimate or ignore the significance of "actually existing men." While Hegel regards the sensuous world as merely a manifestation or externalization of the eternal Idea or Spirit, Feuerbach never manages to conceive the sensuous world as the total living sensuous activity of the real human individuals who compose it.[25]

Marx rejects emphatically the passive content of Feuerbach's pseudo-materialism, although he has previously praised his great service in emphasizing the claims of the real man against the idealist thought-estranged world. He says that although Feuerbach is dissatisfied with abstract thought and wants empirical observation, he fails to conceive the sensible and real world as practical, human sensuous activity. Feuerbach's assertion that the "anti-thesis of divine and human is altogether illusory" and that it represents nothing but the "antithesis between the human nature in general and the human in-dividual" has Marx's approval. In drawing his picture of self-alienated man, he constantly has before him the Feuerbachian model of religious self-estrangement.[26] Attracted initially by Feuerbach's inversion of Hegelian transcendentalism, Marx later rejects his pseudo-materialism and his religious model of self-alienation. Feuerbach, in Marx's view, merely registers the fact of religious self-alienation and confines himself to mere contemplation of its existence. The whole history of self-alienation in Feuerbach's system, he believes, is seen as the history of the production of abstract, unreal, and contemplative man. Abstracting from the historical process and presupposing the imaginary individual, Feuerbach is compelled to take refuge in the "higher perception" and in the ideal "compensation in the species" and thus relapse into idealism similar to that of Hegel.[27]

In spite of Marx's opposition to Hegelian idealism, he remains loyal to Hegel's dialectical reasoning and uses his metaphysical categories in the direction of his dialectical materialism. Unlike Feuerbach, who thinks of man in terms of "contemplation," Hegel regards man as an active being.[28] As described in *Phenomenology*, self-alienation is essentially the expression of human activity, although this activity, Marx rightly indicates, is primarily spiritual and divine. In opposition to idealism and "all previous materialism in which everything is conceived in the form of the object or of contemplation," Marx argues for "real, objective, material activity" that proceeds from man as a real, corporeal being. Feuerbach indicates correctly the essential connection between man's material and social realms, but because "he does not conceive human activity as objective activity," he fails to explain the origin and real nature of self-alienation.[29] Marx sees man as essentially an objective, sensuous being who can realize himself only in a historical nature. In the state of self-alienation, he is alienated, dehumanized, and enslaved because he is dominated by the alien powers of alienated society. In Marx's opinion, matter is the subject and essence of all changes in the world. It is impossible "to separate thought from matter which thinks." Rejecting all forms of previous materialism, he believes that only dialectical materialism is capable of comprehending the movement of world history and the "real estrangement of human beings."[30]

At the center of all forms of alienation, Marx argues, lies man's alienation of his essential powers that has its origin in productive activity. In capitalist market economy, man has never been fully himself in his creative activity. This activity, he says, has always been involuntary and coerced rather than self-activity, which alone can realize his human potentialities. Man would not be facing the product of his activity as a stranger unless he were estranging himself from his essential being in the act of production.[31] In capitalist society, Marx notes, the alienated worker experiences not only alienation of the thing that is expressed in the loss of the product of his labor but also the alienation of self. Alienation of the object of labor merely expresses the "alienation of activity, active alienation or the activity of alienation."[32] Capitalist production, Marx believes, is the first movement in human practical activity to develop the alienating conditions of the labor process on a large scale. It develops these conditions in the form of powers that control and cripple individual laborers and that are essentially alien and hostile to their essential being. All products in capitalist production confront the workers as hostile and alien entities. As objects, they are independent of their producers. "The relation of labour to the act of production within the labour process," Marx writes, "is the relation of the worker to his own activity as an alien activity not belonging to him; it is activity as suffering and activity which is turned against him, neither depends on nor belongs to him. Here we have self-estrangement as we had previously the estrangement of the thing."[33]

In capitalist economy, the worker's productive activity appears only in the "form of wage-earning activity." Bourgeois economists, according to Marx, do not consider the worker "when he is not working as a human being."[34] They know the worker only as a working animal and the seller of labor in the process that alienates his essential powers. By reducing the worker's needs to the most miserable level of physical existence, capitalism alienates his spiritual and economic activity and subordinates it to the avaricious instinct of "having." In Marx's view, capitalist greed and rapacity are the real ground and source of self-alienation. Infatuated by the acquisitive mania for wealth and luxury, the capitalist enslaves the worker; prevents him from being a natural, human, and social individual; degrades him to the level of animal needs; confines him to merely "having"; and forces him to lose and alienate himself from his essential being.

The development of production, Marx maintains, is always involved with the forms of ownership and productive relations. It is in the light of these relations that he analyzes the phenomenon of man's self-alienation. Rejecting Hegel's idealist view of self-alienation, he believes that man is alienated from himself whenever he is denied the possibility by the economic system to realize his work capacities. Self-alienation cannot be intelligible unless it is connected with man's work and his relations with other men. Marx argues that the division of labor and private ownership are alienating powers that make man an "extremely abstract being" and lead inevitably to an arrested development of his intellectual and physical faculties. "Presupposing private property", he writes, "my work is an alienation of life" and "my individuality is alienated to such a degree that my life activity is hateful to me, a torment and the semblance of an activity. It is a forced activity imposed on me through an external fortuitous need rather than through an inner, essential need."[35] It is impossible to be truly human in capitalist market economy. Here man is alienated from his own essential nature and from productive activity. His work becomes an activity without meaning and fulfillment. The worker, in Marx's view, produces no personal value for himself but only exchange value for his selfish employer. The external and meaningless character of labor for the alienated laborer in bourgeois society is demonstrated easily by the fact that it is not labor for self-fulfillment or self-realization but for "someone else."[36] The owners of capital know the workers only as "instruments of production which have to yield as much as possible with as little cost as possible." They only let them live and work while they need them, and they make them redundant "without the slightest scruple."[37]

When labor is treated merely as a means to satisfy needs external to it, human beings cannot realize their true nature and essential powers. Under capitalism, Marx maintains, man can never be truly human in his productive activity. Because working people are treated by their greedy employers as mere means rather than what Kant calls "ends in themselves," and their lives depend almost entirely on the "whim of the rich," this leads inevitably to their degradation, loss of dignity, and "active alienation." Although the rich and the poor, the property owners and the propertyless workers represent the same human self-alienation, the poor are devastated by it and see in it their powerlessness and misery expressed in their suffering and inhuman existence.

The distinguishing mark of Marx's social theory is the belief that self-alienation is always expressed in man's powerlessness, in his inability to control his productive activity, and in the loss of self. Instead of being the realiza-

tion of man's essential powers, productive labor in capitalist acquistive society
has been transformed into "slave labour" for the benefit of "capricious and
pleasure-loving capitalist masters."[38] Here man's life is nothing but the
reification and alienation of his life. His essential reality assumes an inhuman
existence and becomes an alien and dehumanizing reality. Those controlling
capitalist production are always motivated by the striving for material possessions and think only of the "realisation of their own excesses."[39] They disregard the interests of the poor and underprivileged and ignore the totality of
human needs that can only be satisfied by activities related to the essential
and social nature of real man. The complete domination of alienated objects
over man in capitalist society reduces him to "commodity man, man in the
role of commodity." This commodity or instrumental man is alienated from
his own products and from his essential being. The tragedy of the "activity of
alienation" or of the "alienation of activity," Marx believes, is reflected in
man's inability to free himself from his economic slavery and to realize his
genuinely essential powers. By alienating these powers, man inevitably becomes a stranger to himself and to others. When he alienates his own free
activity from himself, he also consciously or unconsciously "confers to the
stranger activity which is not his own."[40]

Marx maintains that self-alienated man is degraded and impoverished because he loses his own independence and is dominated by an inhuman power
and a being outside himself. Just as he begets his own products as the "loss of
his reality," he involuntarily "begets the domination of the one who does not
produce" anything but private profits for personal enjoyment.[41] Alienated
activity of self-alienated man is that of a tormented, sacrificed, and empty
being. It appears only as the "expression of man's loss of self and of his
powerlessness" to realize his truly human potentialities. Saying that man is
alienated from himself, Marx maintains, simply means that his own activity
has become an "alien, coerced activity," that "his production appears to him
as the production of his nullity, his power over an object as the power of the
object over him, and that he himself, the lord of his creation, has in reality
become the servant of this creation."[42] In self-alienation, man always becomes an object manipulated by alien and inhuman powers. As a result, his
productive activity "belongs to another man, someone who is alien, hostile, powerful and independent of him."[43]

When alienated from himself, man is powerless to exercise his free activity
in any but his animal manners. "The animal is immediately identical with its
life activity. It does not distinguish itself from it. It is its life activity." Man,
Marx points out, is different from animals because he "makes his life activity
itself the object of his will and of his consciousness. He has conscious life
activity which directly distinguishes him from animal life activity."[44] After
learning from Feuerbach that "consciousness in the strictest sense is present
only in a being to whom his species, his essential nature is an object of
thought" and from Hegel that only man is a "being that perceives and wills,"

Marx maintains that only a "being that thinks and wills" can be alienated from his essential being.[45] Animals act from immediate impulse and cannot be credited with any direct consciousness of an end of their activity. Although the activities of animals may be adjusted to an end, they cannot be regarded as purposeful activities. Even the higher animals, insofar as they are guided by mere physiological tendencies to certain action, cannot be supposed to have any idea of an end. They move instinctively toward certain ends, but they do not will them.

According to Marx's anthropology, which partly reflects Feuerbach's conception of man, man's activity is capable of spontaneous and free movements that are not given to other species. The action of animals is only a physiological reaction to external stimuli; their movements are never self-determined or self-willed. They have a certain spontaneity, but they are not moved by self-willed ends. Man's life is an object for his consciousness. His intellectual, spiritual, and physical life is normally self-conducted. Unlike animals that cannot think and unify their instinctive activity, man is self-conscious and a center of action that has a certain relative permanence. Recalling Hegel's definition of "man as a thinker and universal," Marx says that man, unlike animals, "treats himself as universal and therefore a free being."[46] The universality of man is manifested in practice "in the universality which makes all nature his inorganic body."[47] Without self-consciousness, Marx admits, man could not be aware of his self-alienation.

The distinguishing characteristic of man's life is that activity of will in which, as Feuerbach states, the powers of thought and will are contained, constituting the elements of his essential nature.[48] The tradegy of man's conscious life activity, Marx believes, is expressed in the enslavement of this activity by "alien and inhuman powers," reaching its peak in the capitalist mode of production. Capitalism is a barrier to man's independence and self-fulfillment. It creates and maintains the conditions for self-alienation by subordinating human beings to the alien power of capital. "A being only considers himself independent when he stands on his own feet; and he only stands on his feet when he owes his existence to himself. A man who lives by the grace of another regards himself as a dependent being."[49] In capitalist alienated society, no worker is guaranteed employment. He can be laid off and made redundant without any rational explanation and for any reason. The capitalist system implies a hierarchical social relationship in which the minority possessing economic power dominates the poor and underprivileged. Here the needs of the majority depend on the initiative of private egoistic individuals and financial conglormerates. The concentration of wealth and power in fewer and fewer hands entails the alienation of the producers of general wealth. The mechanism by which private capital is accumulated makes it possible for egoistic individuals to transform everything that is indispensable to communal life into private property and to pursue selfish goals. Because capitalist society is ruled by the blind law of competition, it is necessarily devoid of any conscious governance of its ends. Capitalism is the first economic system in history that totally lacks a concept of the relation of truly human ends to society as a whole. Marx argues that capitalism is an alienating force, recognizing no laws but its own and subjecting all social relationships to itself. Under the guise of morality, the capitalist practices immorality.

Marx maintains that everything is upside down under capitalism and its ethics, like political economy, are a "specific estrangement of man."[50] According to these ethics, all human values become commercial values and are always subject to bidding and selling. Being commercialized, the values of human culture are merely a saleable commodity and only express in different forms the alienating relations of capitalist society. The only conscious productive relation between human individuals is the "private exchange of all products of labour, all activities and wealth."[51] In capitalist society, there can be no human activity unless labor power is first sold in the exchange between the buyer and seller. Here the quest for private profit becomes the supreme motive behind every enterprise. Marx states that capitalist production develops the conditions of the labor process, which inevitably create and maintain man's self-alienation. Forced labor cannot belong to man's "inner nature." In capitalism, money is the estranged essence of man's existence, and this alien essence dominates and alienates all human activity. Both human beings and money are subject to the laws of the market and are manipulated by those who control the means of production. Everything in capitalist society has its price and everything, including humans, can be bought and sold. Everything, Marx points out, must be "saleable and useful," otherwise capitalist production could not survive.[52] Capitalism and profit-making are always joined.

Because of the existence of the uncontrollable alien forces of productive activity in capitalist society, the self-alienated man is forced to take refuge in his private autonomous world. In this realm of privacy and pseudo-independence, the "rich, living, sensuous, concrete activity of self-objectification is reduced to its mere abstraction, absolute negativity—an abstraction which is again fixed as such and thought of as an independent activity."[53] In *Manuscripts*, Marx argues that the "real human person" does not exist in capitalist society except in alienated and dehumanized form. In self-alienation that peaks under capitalism, "man becomes an abstract activity and a stomach, being ever more dependent on every fluctuation in market price, on the application of capitals and on the mood of the rich."[54] In the abstraction that separates man's genuinely human functions from the sphere of all other human activity, man feels he is his own enemy, a stranger to himself.[55] He feels alienated from himself because his activity is forced on him by an external alien entity instead of being motivated by genuine human needs in response to an "inner necessity." Self-alienation, as Marx understands it, is the expression of the "abstract existence of man" and of his "externalisation in the thing" that "confronts him as something hostile and alien" and belongs to somebody else.[56] The abstract existence of alienated man in capitalist society reflects his suffering and the possibility of his "daily fall from his filled void into the absolute void—into his social non-existence."[57]

In *Manuscripts*, Marx maintains that self-alienation is man's loss of his essential human capacities. As a result of his self-alienation, man cannot realize his essential powers and natural being. In self-alienation, the appropriation of "man's total essence in a total manner" is impossible. Arguing against Hegel's conception of "man's self-estrangement," Marx firmly believes that man is a "sensuous, human natural being" and that his self-alienation cannot be merely a "thought-form or logical category." Man's world is composed of objects and rhythms that are produced in nature. Although these objects and rhythms exist outside man and are independent of him, they are still essential to the satisfaction and manifestation of his essential powers.[59] As man lives on nature, Marx maintains that nature is gradually "humanised," becoming a rational life force that is expressed in his physical and spiritual activity. Although remaining natural, man also transcends nature and in his specifically human manner becomes an active, self-conscious "human natural being."[60] He merges with nature which, Marx claims, becomes "his inorganic body." Yet, in the conscious elaboration of the world of things he realizes his essential powers and affirms himself as a unique being.

Marx believes man could realize his essential powers and appropriate "essential objects" in a universal and objectively human manner if man's essence were not alienated. The fact that man's essence has been alienated simply means the loss of his spontaneous activity.[61] Alienated man does not fully understand his own essence and is hardly aware of the "loss of his self." Once the creative activity of natural and sensuous man has been alienated, he is unable to distinguish between the sense of being and the sense of having, between the subject and the object, between self-fulfillment and self-alienation. In self-alienation, appropriation and estrangement express the same relationship.[62] In capitalist alienated society, appropriation has lost its positive denotation. Instead of leading to the enrichment of man's inner wealth and stimulating his creative activity, it sadly has become the avenue by which self-alienated man gratifies his bodily needs. Abolition of the conditions of self-alienation will make possible the "real appropriation" by man of objects and of his essential being. As the essence of man is indissolubly social, human, and natural, he can and must appropriate the totality of the world in a social, human, and natural way.

Analysis of the production of man by himself indicates that human development corresponds to moments of his production. Marx believes that all production is an "appropriation of nature by an individual within and with the help of a definite social organisation."[63] In capitalism human life is not produced consciously, appropriation is always motivated by greed, and alienated man does not comprehend his true historical goals. The objects produced by human labor are passed continually from some private individuals to others who are equally keen on private ownership. Man's essence, in Marx's view, is alienated because social and economic organizations make it very difficult, if not impossible, for a human individual to appropriate human objects and nature in an objective and creative way. "It is clear", he writes, "that wherever ownership of the instrument of production is the relation to the conditions of production as property, there, in the real labour process, the instrument appears only as a means of individual labour."[64] In capitalist appropriation, human life appears only as a means and man is reduced to thinghood. Production and appropriation are always connected with the interests of "private individuals who work independently of each other." When the relations of human individuals are enveloped in inhuman relations and supplanted by abstract and selfish relations expressed in economic fetishism, man is unavoidably alienated from his self.

Labor must not be reduced to its purely instrumental, utilitarian values. In its higher forms, total human labor is a creative force. Marx indicates that in work man "realises his own purpose, the purpose which gives the law to his activities, the purpose to which he has to subordinate his own will. The less attractive he finds the work in itself, the less he enjoys it as something which gives scope to his bodily and mental powers."[65] There can be no "purposive activity" if human life is reduced to the consciousness of suffering, poverty, and slavery. These categories express self-alienation and "general exploitation of communal human nature."[66] Man can develop his essential powers only when allowed to act as a free member of the community. Although Marx's conception of freedom is obscure and inconsistent, and, as in Hegel, associated with necessity and determinism, he still maintains that creativity and purposive activity are possible only in the realm of qualified freedom. Here his metaphysics faces a contradiction between personal freedom and necessity that neither his materialist dialectic nor his logic can solve. In *Manuscripts*, he definitely speaks of free activity of man that distinguishes him from animals. Unlike animals, man is a conscious species being who creates an objective world by his practical activity and, to satisfy his needs, he produces things in freedom. "An animal's product belongs immediately to its physical body while man freely confronts his product."[67] Besides being "conscious and free," man's activity is the "object of his will," although this will, as Marx says in *Capital*, must always be "subordinated to a higher purpose."[68]

The source of man's activity that leads to his creativity, Marx sometimes indicates correctly, lies within man himself. Yet, Marx does not believe in individual freedom. As a materialist, he regards man as a part of nature and always subject to its laws. Human nature is only a part of the natural world, and the inner and outer forces of human life are ultimately one. Marx sometimes states that the necessity, so evident in Hegel and Engels, that entwines man's life is an inner rather than an outer necessity. In the ultimate analysis, however, inner and outer necessity are seen as the same. In Marx's view, freedom lies beyond the sphere of actual material production. The realm of freedom can only be meaningful when associated with the realm of necessity as its basis.[69]

The obscurity and inconsistency that characterize Marx's conception of freedom demonstrate his inability to bridge the gulf between man's autonomy and his dependence on external objects. Because the problem of freedom is ultimately a metaphysical one, he simply fails to find a way out of metaphysical confusions and consistently treat human freedom in a purely deterministic and necessitarian way. Similar to Hegel, he identifies freedom of will with the knowledge of natural necessity. "Those who fancy they honour Divine Providence by excluding necessity from it," Hegel writes, "are really degrading it by this exclusiveness to a blind and irrational caprice."[70] While Hegel resolves freedom into a higher necessity, a transcendental version of determinism, Marx resolves it into a lower necessity, a historical version of determinism. Hegel depersonalizes man into God or the Absolute; Marx depersonalizes him into nature. Because Marxism, like Hegelianism, has no place for the personality of man, it is hardly possible to speak of human freedom in communism as being anything but compulsion. Marx fails to harmonize his belief that man, alienated or not, is endowed with freedom of choice with the belief that he is determined by the external world of nature and the mode of production. In *Holy Family*, he refers to man's freedom as the "positive power by which he asserts his true individuality." What this "true individuality" is, he does not explain. If man is "determined by the objective world" outside himself, as Marx indicates in the same work, then, surely, human freedom must be an illusion.[71] Anxious to avoid this conclusion, some of Marx's followers prefer using the phrase "being conditioned" to "being determined," although this linguistic sophistry does not explain anything. The ambiguous relation between freedom and necessity still remains. In the absence of metaphysical proof of freedom, Marxism has no option but to adhere to determinism. In this case, dialectical materialism cannot offer any satisfactory explanation of the estrangement of man. If man is merely a part of nature and is "determined by the objective world," then self-alienation is necessarily a purely natural phenomenon and no man, capitalist or proletarian, can ever be responsible for it.

Some exponents of Marxism, including Bukharin, aware of Marx's inconsistent interpretation of human freedom, explicity deny the freedom of the will. On the whole, they treat freedom in the light of economic determinism as compulsion and the conscious surrender of the individual activity to the total activity of the whole community. Marx indicates that it is only in the "real community that the individuals obtain their freedom."[72] Like Hegel, he believes that the individual is real only as a member of society. The individual alone can never become a complete, harmonious system: only in society, in the totality of individual and common interests, can unity between freedom and necessity be possible. The individual realizes his freedom by identifying his will with the collective will. The main difference between them is that Hegel associates personal freedom with the evolution of divine reason and Marx usually connects it with the uniformity of nature and the mode of production. In both cases, necessity is the inseparable condition, or, as Marx states, the basis of freedom. Without the co-element necessity, human freedom is totally incomprehensible and illusory.

Apparently aware of the contradiction between freedom and necessity in his philosophical system, Marx assumes that only naturalism as expressed in practice can resolve this contradiction. He does not elaborate on how this goal is exactly attained; he merely indicates that the total man is "all nature" and that only the "total man," not the individual man, can transform nature into " will and freedom." All human activity, in his view, constitutes a conscious and irresistible analysis of nature, seeking to attain the living reality expressed in the total praxis. This activity moves from the abstract to the concrete and, as in Hegel's system, reverts dialectically back again. The anlaysis can never be complete. The totality of human activity, in Marx's view, lies in the future; and in the future, when the multiplicity of physical and social determinisms will hopefully decrease, man will return to himself and overcome his self-alienation.

Marx's analysis of man and his self-alienation in *Manuscripts of 1844* is predominantly metaphysical in spite of his linguistic emphasis on humanism and "the true anthropological nature of man."[73] Yet, much of this work is devoted to the critique of Hegel's metaphysical conception of self-alienation. Hegel's ideas of self-alienation, he argues, are defective because they are related only to man's consciousness, and this consciousness is nothing more than thought, metaphysically dissociated from nature that is disguised as a purely external existence. In Hegel, thought or mind constitutes the whole of life. The alienated life of man is regarded as the torment of unrealized being and this being, according to Marx, exists "only in the shape of mind." "Having posited man as equivalent to self-consciousness, Hegel regards the estranged reality of man as nothing but consciousness or the thought of estrangement."[74] Marx maintains that Hegel does not understand man's self-alienation simply because he "turns man into the creature of consciousness instead of turning consciousness into the consciousness of real men." Both Hegel and Feuerbach, in his view, fail to explain self-alienation historically because they both ignore the "humanness of man's senses" and "sensuous human activity."[75] For Feuerbach, human activity is only theoretical and abstract. Marx overlooks that his own conception of man as a "species being" is equally abstract and theoretical. Like Feuerbach, he is also involved in the metaphysical generalization about the "essential being of man" and also postulates the existence of a non-observable human "species essence."

Rejecting Hegel's conception of man, Marx proclaims the universality of man who in himself somehow includes society and nature. Men, he believes, are the visible and yet, paradoxically, invisible subjects and objects of historical becoming. They can live and develop only within the life of their own species, that is, within human life. For Marx, "species being" is a being that is characterized by a number of distinguishing powers and needs. As a being for himself, man is a species being who "confirms and manifests himself" in his specifically human life activity and self-consciousness.[76] Unlike animals, man knows that he is different from other species and that his specificity consists in his unique universality as opposed to the particularity of other beings in nature.[77] The actions of men proceed from their specifically human talents that are expressed in the process of knowing. "An animal forms things in accordance with the standard and the need of the species to which it belongs, while man knows how to produce in accordance with the standard of every species and knows how to apply everywhere the inherent standard to the object. Man therefore also forms things in accordance with the laws of beauty."[78] As a species being, man is unique and universal, the wonder and glory of the universe. Yet, in alienated society the "consciousness which he has of his species is transformed by estrangement in such a way that the species life becomes for him a means." When man's spontaneous and free activity is alienated, his species life is degraded and becomes a "mere means to his physical existence."[79]

In *Manuscripts of 1844*, Marx maintains that the fully developed and free individual lives a life that is harmonious with the life of the species. "Man's individual and species life," he writes, "are not different, however much— and this is inevitable—the mode of existence of the individual is a more particular or more general mode of the life of the species, or the life of the species is a more particular or more general individual life."[80] What is interesting in this statement is Marx's inability to decide whether the priority should belong to the human individual or to his species. Feuerbach believes that the species is the real being and that individual man is only a particular instance of the species. "The measure of the species", he says, "is the absolute measure, law and criterion of man."[81] Hegel rejects the notion of man's species being as a hopeless abstraction. For him, an individual is a specific existence, not man in general.[82] Man in general has no real existence. Only a particular human being exists, and his existence must be seen in the context of his activity in society. It is not the Absolute Spirit that creates history but it is rather the concrete action of men that is the creative agency in history. "Being in themselves powerless, the Idea and abstract characteristics generally are realised and actualised only by the activity of man."[83] Marx insists on the unity of man with man, which can be expressed and confirmed in man's consciousness of his species being. Human species being stands for the actuality of man's existence in society and for the conscious and purposive activity in the process of production. Without this activity, man sinks to the level of an animal and his activity becomes "active alienation."

Aware of his species, man goes beyond his narrow and short-sighted individual life and, unlike animals, can realize his essential powers and needs with species powers and needs. "The real, active orientation of man to himself as a species being or his manifestation as a real species being (i.e., as a human being)," Marx indicates, "is only possible by his really bringing out of himself all the powers that are his as the species being—something which in turn is

only possible through the totality of man's actions."[84] As a species being, man
has his essential nature inherent in the capacities that distinguish him from
other living beings. With the coming of man, the whole evolutionary process
has entered a new historical phase. For the first time in the history of life,
humans have developed powers to control nature and the course of historical
development. "In his consciousness of species man confirms his real social life
and simply repeats his real existence in thought, just as conversely the being
of the species confirms itself in species consciousness and is for itself in its
generality as a thinking being."[85] Consciousness is only present in a being
whose essential and species characteristics can be the objects of thought and
of knowing. Man, in Marx's view, is the universal being of nature because he
is a species being. "He first proves himself to be a species being in the working
up of the objective world." His productive activity is "his active species life"
and the "object of labour is, therefore, the objectification of man's species
life."[86]

In estranging man from his essential being, estranged labor, Marx argues,
also alienates him from his species being. Whenever man's capacities to produce freely for himself and his species are inhibited in society, then his species
life is fragmented and dehumanized. "In tearing away from man the object of
his production," he writes, "estranged labour tears from him his species life,
his real species objectivity and transforms his advantage over animals into the
disadvantage that his inorganic body, nature, is taken from him,"[87] depriving
him of his unique potentialities for self-fulfillment. When man's productive
acitivity is restricted by an alien power and his control over his own products
is eliminated, the human species is inevitably deprived of its reality and alienated. The division of labor and private ownership, Marx believes, give rise to
a social system which creates and maintains the conditions of alienated labor.
As soon as work is divided, man's spontaneous activity is directed toward an
inhuman end, and his energies are only concentrated on securing physical
survival. Labor can be creative only when man freely makes his life activity an
object of his will and consciousness. In capitalist society, self-alienation is a
mutilation of man and his species being. As an inhuman force, capitalism is
inimical to man's development as a free being.

Alienation from the species, according to Marx, is an aspect of historical
reality in which the individual is alienated from himself and the products of
his labor.[88] In the economic system of avaricious exchange, the whole emphasis is on the "sense of having." The separation of labor and capital and the
inhuman domination of one person over another demonstrate clearly man's
degradation in capitalism. When human actions are motivated by deception
and plundering, man loses control over the "product of his labour" and "produces only in order to possess for himself." The object he produces is only the
objectification of his selfish need. By producing alienated objects, man is unable to appropriate his "total essence in a total manner." Because his products
belong to the capitalist, he "feels outside himself" and utterly dependent on

alien powers that cripple and impoverish him.[89] Human activity, Marx believes, is alienated when it becomes opposition between "being and having" and between individual and social life. Under capitalism, where this opposition reaches its highest dimensions, "being" is always subordinated to "having" and social life is always sacrificed to private egoistic life.[90]

Living in the world of private ownership and motivated by greed, humans are so estranged that they lose most of their awareness of self-knowledge and self-doing. Their activity is so fragmented and crippled that they find no creative purpose or self-fulfillment in it, because these are only possible in freedom. "Estranged labour," Marx says, "turns man's species being, both nature and his spiritual species property, into a being alien to him, into a means to his individual existence. It estranges man's own body from him, as it does external nature and his spiritual essence, his human being."[91]

In the inhuman realm of private capital, man is the prisoner of alienating socioeconomic forces that form his objective content. He will realize his essential being only by overcoming these forces. "The rich human being," Marx indicates, "is the being in need of a totality of human life activities." It is the "man in whom his own realisation exists as an inner necessity, as need."[92] The mania for material possessions and wealth, on the one hand, and human misery, slavery, and oppression, on the other, are the alienating forces that tear human reality into conflicting parts. Under a system of private property, man is not conscious of the need to produce for the species. Here all production is motivated by self-interest. In a society dominated by alienated wealth, men behave as egoistic individuals and do not recognize the needs of others. By individualizing what is essentially social, capitalism creates the conditions for "greedy self-indulgence, selfishness, sectional interest and evil intent."[93]

Under the reign of private property, Marx maintains that man is deprived of humanity and gradually becomes entirely indifferent to the needs of others. The indifference and hostility characterizing capitalist particularity are typical expressions of man's self-alienation that is connected closely with social alienation. "In fact," he says, "the proposition that man's species nature is estranged from him means that one man is estranged from the other, as each of them is from man's essential nature."[94] In the alienation of human species being and in self-alienation, each human is separated from other society members. Man is transformed into an empty being and becomes the essence of private property and wealth. Because capitalism is based on mutual competition and class antagonism, Marx believes it reduces man to a narrow and selfish particularity, distorts and brutalizes his productive activity, and turns him to a means and an object. In capitalist society the sensuous appropriation of the "objective man" is conceived only as "having" and "private possession." When man is alienated from himself and his products, he cannot treat himself as the "actual, living species" and unavoidably lives as an abstract being. Self-alienation and species alienation produce a "bestial barbarisation,

a complete, unrefined, abstract simplicity of needs" and, by divorcing individual life from social life, they transform them into abstraction.[95]

In money-orientated society, man's worth is always seen in the light of
private possessions. Here the right to self-interestedness and self-seeking gratification is identified with morality. This right sadly ignores the rights of all
men to self-fulfillment. "Only when the real, individual man reabsorbs in
himself the abstract man and as an individual human being has become a
species being in his everyday life, in his particular work and in his particular
situation, only when man has recognised and organised his own powers as
social forces," only then, Marx says, will he be able to realize his human
potentialities in a positive way.[96] Just as "every self-estrangement of man
depends on his relation to other men," so every self-realization must depend
on man's readiness to treat others as ends in themselves. Man's personal life is
essentially a life of relations among people. Only the person who stands in the
right relation to others will positively fulfill his own obligations toward himself. Self-realization cannot be attained in a society of "egoistic individuals."
To realize his true self, man must help others to realize their own potentialities. Thus Marx contends that self-fulfillment is impossible outside the socio-
historical framework, because man is a social being and can only develop in
society.

Individual expression of life, Marx believes, must be related to the expression of other people's lives.[97] Man's fulfillment cannot be conceived in abstraction from nature and society. As a part of nature, man cannot be reduced to
something abstractly spiritual. Hegel's idea that man is a non-objective,
spiritual being is rejected, because he believes erronously that the spiritual
self is the equivalent of the real, sensuous man. Because this "self is only
the abstractly conceived man," Marx believes Hegel's conception of self-
realization is also abstract and unsatisfactory.[98] Yet, he shares Hegel's view
that without a certain amount of deliberate reflection, human individuals
could not be regarded as fully human and thus would be incapable of their
own spiritual and physical improvement. During the learning process, the
self-conscious individual becomes familiar with external nature and with society that is itself the product of human activity. Self-realization is not merely
the satisfaction of private needs; it also must include the satisfaction of spiritual and physical needs of other members of society. Selfish individualism
expressed in alienation is the enemy of self-realization.

Both Hegel and Marx maintain that society can only exist when it satisfies
the conscious needs and desires of all its constituent members. The self being
realized can only recognize itself and its activities in a whole. This whole or
totality to which individuals belong is a unity of "homogeneity and specification," and it is in this unity that a "perfect self-realisation" can be attained.
Totality is not only an assembly of individuals connected externally by some
alien force as in capitalism. True human society, Marx states, is constituted of
"conscious individuals," each seeking the fulfillment of the totality of men.

Disregarding entirely "egoistic naturalism," as expressed, for example, in Hobbes's doctrine of exclusive egoism, with its emphasis on the impossibility of a disinterested regard for the good of others, Marx's optimism leads him to believe that the social relation of the human individual to others can only be realized in communist society. In capitalist alienated society, in which the elementary principles of morality are either absent or distorted, humans are treated as means and commodities, never as ends in themselves. Every human action, thought, and vital manifestation of man's life has been "alienated and individualised." Selfishness, the only objective principle of capitalist ethics that is in harmony with itself, separates man from man, transforming him into a hostile object.[99] Means become ultimate ends and, conversely, human ends are transformed into inhuman means.

The real world of capitalism, as Marx sometimes indicates, is neither the Christian nor Feuerbach's world of love or benevolence but the world in which egoism is the ruling passion. Here men in power never desire the good of others, and the "appropriation of the human world" is transformed into the appropriation of private possessions.[100] The capitalist is always a "dried-up twister without honour, a person estranged from the community who breeds competition and the dissolution of all social bonds."[101] Dead capital is indifferent to both human self-alienation and his self-realization.[102] Capitalism proclaims the making of surplus value or profit to be the "sole end and aim of mankind."[103] It ignores that man is social and consequently can only "confirm and realise his true nature" by giving up his egoistic desires and identifying his will with the will of the community. Under the domination of egoistic need, individuals alienate themselves and turn their essential being into something alien that separates them from social and "communal nature."[104] Marx believes avarice thwarts man's realization of his essential powers. As long as there is a separation between the particular and the common interests, human individuals will remain self-alienated. "Active alienation" will be overcome when "human *praxis*" provides an opportunity for individual self-assertion and when man's work is a "free manifestation of life."

Admittedly, men are self-assertive in all societies, although only in some can they assert themselves in a truly self-creative way. Both Hegel and Marx believe that man's self-assertion and self-fulfillment are essentially phenomena of social intercourse. Where Marx differs considerably from Hegel in this respect is in the meaning of the self and reality. For Hegel, the spiritual alone is the real, and the self is a spiritual entity that is simultaneously particular and universal. Mere particularity is a realm of negativity, a denial of the individual's infinite nature. The distinguishing mark of self-consciousness is that it expresses "a being-for-itself" and that its object is an immediate unity of "being-in-itself and being-for-itself."[105] The real being of man's mind is its activity, and the controlling principle of this activity is always teleological. Self-realization in Hegel's system, however, is determined rigidly by the whole. Reality of the human person is found only in the totality of "beings-in-themselves." The only real individual is the universal Spirit that realizes and sustains the whole realm of meanings in the movement of its own self-alienation and dealienation.[106] "The single individual," he says, "is incomplete Spirit, a concrete shape in whose whole existence one determinateness predominates, the others being present only in blurred outline."[107] Marx rejects Hegel's "spiritual or religious" anthropology and its implication that the processes of self-alienation and self-fulfillment are only the expression of a "divine process."[108] This anthropology, he says, moves "within the sphere of abstraction."

In opposition to Hegel, Marx argues that man is an "objective, sensuous being" who "owes his existence to himself." The objective world is not the realm of the all-pervasive Spirit but the realm of material things and living beings in which "sensuous man" fulfills himself and realizes his capacities. Because man is a real sensuous being, Marx believes, he can confirm and express his being in real sensuous objects. Man's relation to the world of objects is always reflected in *praxis*. As in Hegel's spiritual development, in Marx's materialist evolutionary movement progress consists in the transition from man's capacities toward practical results that in turn are expressed in his self-satisfaction and self-realization. In Marx's naturalistic monism, however, self-fulfillment is not seen as an ideal to be realized in a logical or transcendental structure. He maintains somewhat inconsistently and contradictorily that there are no *a priori* goals and no abstract ideals.[109] Men belong only to this material, visible world and can only realize themselves in the same world.

According to Marx, self-fulfillment cannot be explained fully by any *a priori* logical pattern. He believes that it can be explained only materialistically and dialectically in the light of purely physical and social development. Self-fulfillment does not depend "on consciousness but on being, not on thought but on life."[110] "It depends," Marx says, "on the individual's empirical development and manifestation of life which in turn depends on the conditions in the objective world. If the circumstances in which the individual lives allow him only the one-sided development of one quality at the expence of all the rest, if they give him the material and time to develop only that one quality, then this individual achieves only a one-sided, crippled development."[111] The difficulty with Marx's conception of self-realization is that he never explains its real meaning in his materialistically orientated philosophy. He indicates vaguely that the basis of this philosophy is the concrete human situation in which the conditions of production determine all human development. This development is not related to personal aims but rather to universal and "coming-to-be" objectives. Man's self-fulfillment always depends on external forces, and there is no reference to the internal factors, human nature itself, playing any significant role in the process of self-realization. It is true that in his early writings, Marx accepts the reality of human nature and thus the possibility of its change and gradual improvement.

In *Manuscripts of 1844*, he writes about the human essence conjoined with man's total essence and says that, when expressed in a "total manner," human life is an "enjoyment of self."[112] What this self is, Marx never explains. It is because of his obscure and ambivalent references to human self and human nature that his usage of such terms as self-alienation, self-fulfillment and self-realization is far from being coherent and intelligible.

In Marx's anthropology, the human self is never represented as the indivisible subject of feeling, knowing, willing, and acting. It is never the universe in which man habitually lives and rationally chooses his ends. Never defined, his self only seems to be a "real sentient" entity that feels its needs and strives for their satisfaction, as in animals. Marx believes will is connected intimately with consciousness, but consciousness is always the expression of the "material conditions in which man lives."[113] All mental states are either emotion or sensuous desire.[114] Man's free activity proceeds from his "sensuous being" rather than from the thinking mind. The whole emphasis is on sensibility and satisfaction, although Marx categorically rejects hedonism. Purposeless cupidity and momentary gratification as final aims in human life are condemned, but "man's feelings and passions" are still the main factors in the process of self-fulfillment. There is an assumption, as in Hume, that "reason is the slave of the passions and can never pretend to any other office than to serve and obey them."[115] In Marx's analysis of self-alienation and self-realization, reason cannot form any new motive, but in the form of consciousness, it can show how existing motives can be pursued to the best advantage of human beings. "Man's passions and feelings are not merely anthropological phenomena in the narrower sense but truly ontological affirmations of his essential being."[116]

Arguing against Stirner's superficial interpretation of Stoicism and Epicureanism, Marx indicates that the maxim of Epicurean life, like that of the Stoic, is the tranquillity of the soul or "ataraxia," something "higher" than mere pleasure.[117] It is implied that the pleasures of the mind are superior to those of the body. Epicurus recognizes the indispensableness of reason in the conduct of human life to be realized. The end of this life is a kind of pleasure, but the pleasures accompanied by pains must be avoided. Self-realization, in Epicurus's view, cannot be attained without the guidance of reason. Unlike Epicurus, Marx rarely appeals directly to reason for its guidance in the process of true self-fulfillment. His appeal in this respect is usually to "real, objective, natural and sensuous man" or to a "conscious species being," living in nature and society. Only as a "sensuous man," he says, "can he confirm and realize his essential powers.[118] He obviously shares Hegel's belief that consciousness is synonymous with reason, but he denounces categorically Hegel's psychology with its emphasis on man as a purely rational, non-objective, and spiritual being.[119] While Hegel starts from the postulate that the real is rational and that self-realization is the conscious realization of rational will, Marx begins from the diametrically opposite premise, insisting that real man is "man in the flesh." This man has been dehumanized and needs redemption.

Basically, Marx's conception of self-fulfillment is so obscure that it is almost impossible to find its equivalent in the three main theories of the moral standard. In his anthropology, human goals and ends are analyzed in terms of socio-historical development, and such ideals as perfection, happiness, and duty are not his primary concern. Self-fulfillment is never conceived as a "direct, one-sided gratification."[120] Momentary gratification, he believes, is not identical with self-realization, and crude hedonism is incompatible with the dignity of man. This suggests that Marx, like Aristotle, advocates eudaemonism in which the rights of reason and the rights of sensibility are fully recognized and harmonized. Human happiness or self-fulfillment must be regarded as the synthesis of reason-guided pleasures, not as the enjoyment of individual pleasure or "the satisfaction of a single passion."[121] Marx admits that although man is a creature of impulse and a subject of direct wants and instincts, he is also a rational animal. As a rational and conscious being, man is called upon to bring impulse under the rational control. Both Hegel and Marx believe in the essential rationality of the life of sensibility, but Marx's reductioin of man's essence to the ensemble of social relations and to "forces" that are "impulses" clearly implicate him in naturalism that is not always easily distinguished from some forms of hedonism.[122] Marx has never explained how the self, which is merely the ensemble of social relations, can be alienated from itself, act freely, and be realized in any but a sensuous way.

The truth is that Marx definitely fails to give a satisfactory account of the self and, by ignoring psychology, he cannot explain clearly and consistently the processes of self-alienation and self-fulfillment. Hume rejects the idea of a "substantive ego" on the ground that such an entity is unobservable, but he at least admits, although reluctantly, that personal identity cannot be explained easily away. Marx rejects the existence of "transcendental ego" in any form but never says anything about personal identity. Following Hegel, he merely asserts, "I am not alone, I am another reality than the object outside me."[123] Again, Marx does not elaborate on the properties of his "I," except its awareness of itself. There is hardly any room in his anthropology for permanent self and, as a result, no place for moral values, without which self-realization is meaningless. Both Marx and Engels argue that all moral values are relative and instrumental, and belief in eternal moral principles is condemned. "We reject every attempt," Engels writes, "to impose on us any moral dogma whatsoever as an eternal, ultimate and for ever immutable ethical law on the pretext that the moral world has its permanent principles which stand above history. All moral theories have hitherto been the product, in the last analysis, of the economic conditions of society. And as society has hitherto moved in class antagonisms, morality has always been class morality."[124] Marx similarly stresses that the "communists neither preach morality nor impose on people any moral demand."[125] He does not deny directly the significance of morality in human life, although he also treats moral values as the product of the economic conditions of society. In his view, morality, like law and religion, has no independence and is conditioned by a definite development of productive forces. As a form of social consciousness, morality reflects the human effects of socioeconomic conditions and expresses them in a relative way as ideals, norms, and values. Men are both "subject" and "object" of moral consciousness, but Marx maintains that this consciousness is neither transcendental in its origin nor inseparable from man's practical life.

While Kant's moral man cannot fit the moral imperative and the need for happiness into a coherent moral activity in which complete self-realization is possible, Hegel's conception of moral consciousness revolves around the unity of perfection and happiness as a practical end of morality. "The final cause or Good" in Kant's theory of morality, Hegel indicates, "is a vague abstraction."[126] Marx also rejects Kant's moral formalism and his belief in a noumenal realm beyond time and space. "By transferring the realisation of good will to the world beyond," Marx believes, Kant has overlooked entirely the concrete forms of human suffering expressed in exploitation and alienation.[127] He agrees with Kant that men should not be treated as things or means but insists that real self-realization cannot exist independently of the totality of men living in society. In opposition to Kantian and Hegelian humanism, which is based on transcendental values, Marx's humanism is identified completely with this world in which "man has become for man the being of nature, and nature for man as the being of man."[128] In this world men must realize themselves materially, naturally, and socially. Marx is not concerned with normative morality, although it is implicit sometimes in his discussion of humanism or naturalism. The normative character of Marxist ethics, according to some modern Marx's followers, originates from the totality of the Marxist view of society and from the categorical imperative that men must eliminate "bourgeois egoistic morality" and replace it with communist morality.[129] Morality becomes normative only when it is subordinated to the interests of "proletarian humanism." The common interests in the class society are always expressed in illusory ideals that lead to self-alienation and imaginary self-satisfaction.

Abstract, ideological, and theological morality, based on purely abstract values, is rejected by Marx. In Marxism, the main emphasis is on instrumental values that must be associated closely with practical results. Because of the dichotomy of "is" and "ought," the idealist and bourgeois morality is regarded as "impotence in action." "Every time it fights a vice, it is defeated."[130] Moral obligation is meaningless unless it leads to positive action. Marx regards Christian morality as no less hypocritical than bourgeois morality because it preaches universal love but practices hucksterism, supports bourgeois exploitation, and opposes political economy only in appearance.[131] He overlooks that the contradiction between the ideal and the practical is not the distinguishing feature of any specific morality. Surely,

Christianity condemns moral preaching dissociated from moral practice. The human way to the moral goal, it is emphasized consistently, is through complete faithfulness to the practical. The ideal, if it is going to have any real meaning in self-realization, must be found in the actual and expressed in practice. Because of the complexity of moral life, however, conformity of moral ideas to moral action is frequently absent. Marxist morality is not different in this respect. Like any human society, communist society is far from being perfect and is frequently involved in moral pathology.

In his hatred of bourgeois and theological morality, Marx tends to exaggerate vices and evils of non-proletarian ethics. Much of what he says about capitalist egoism is true, and most reasonable people agree with his depiction of a greedy capitalist as a "sly, deceitful, heartless and soulless individual without honour and moral principles."[132] It is true, in capitalist society "human individuality and human morality itself have become merely objects of commerce."[133] This does not mean that all morality is egoistical and relative. Like others, Marx and Engels observe that moral principles and attitudes differ considerably from society to society, but they fail to realize that the world's moral systems and standards also show striking similarities. Good will, friendship, honesty, courage, respect for human life, and self-control are respected and approved almost universally; selfishness, lying, cowardice, and murder are almost universally condemned. The great moral and religious systems in human history have been united in the view that mental satisfaction is more noble than momentary bodily pleasures. In these systems, human dignity is always united powerfully with the ideals of moral freedom, perfection, progress, and self-realization. Its emotional expression is sympathy, its moral quality is respect for persons, and its practical expression is care and concern about individuals and social fulfillment of all members of society.[134]

Naturalism analyzes moral concepts only in terms of the descriptive sciences. Moral ideas are regarded as the product of feelings, instincts, and desires that originally have had no moral predicates. Hobbes, for example, derives the principles of morality from the natural instincts of self-preservation and self-assertion. Hume derives them from a variety of feelings, including sympathy and pleasure, and explains their moral significance by custom and tradition. In all systems of morality, he believes, men start with certain factual statements. Initially, these statements are not judgments of value, but gradually and "imperceptibly" the "is and is not" change into "an ought and ought not."[135] Marx and Engels analyze moral concepts mainly in terms of social and economic relations and thus are led to the conception of morality that is always class-orientated. "When we see that the three classes of modern society, the feudal aristocracy, the bourgeoisie and the proletariat, each have a morality of their own," Engels writes, "we can only draw the conclusion that men, consciously or unconsciously, derive their ethical ideas in the last resort from the practical relations on which their class position is based— from the economic relations in which they carry on production and exchange."[136] Engels fails to prove that "morality has always been class-relate." Assuming, like Marx, that primitive societies were without classes, he concludes without any empirical evidence that they were also without morality. Many social anthropologists reject categorically this very tendentious and misleading view. The origin and development of morality, they believe, are closely connected with the general development of social life, and the ideas of right and wrong, like the ideas of the sacred and numinous, have never been absent from the consciousness of men.[137]

Unaware of contradiction, Engels also speaks of "progress in morality" and predicts the coming of "a really human morality which stands above class antagonisms."[138] In what respect the human morality of the communist future differs from class morality, he does not explain, Lenin is equally obscure and inconsistent in this respect. "Communist morality," he says, "is subordinated to the interests of the proletariat's class struggle" and is "based on the struggle for the consolidation and completion of communism."[139] Rejecting "eternal morality," he still asserts that "morality serves the purpose of helping human society rise to a higher level." The phrase "higher level" is left unexplained, but it is clear that he consciously or unconsciously has in mind some absolute and objective moral ends toward which even communist men and women should aim. In spite of Marxist denials of the existence of moral ideals, Marxist communism always has been inspired by such ideals as progress, freedom, social harmony, classless society, collectivism, and humanism. If communism could be ideal free, there would be no need to appeal to "communist goals" or to such virtuous moral activities as "social duty, honesty, truthfulness, loyalty and voluntary consciousness of justice."[140] Only on the assumption that Marxist ethics contains normative elements can Engels speak of "a really human morality" that will guide men toward realizing their "higher" ends and can Lenin visualize "a higher level" of moral standards in a new communist society. Without this assumption, the whole indoctrination of Russian youth "with communist ethics" would be meaningless.

Marx and Engels lived in an age of utilitarian ethics that takes the principle of utility as the ultimate ethical standard. Originally these ethics attracted many naturalists, but as soon as Bentham's inconsistencies were revealed, the "greatest happiness principle of the greatest number" lost much of its original appeal. After all, as Marx remarks, the "principle of utility was not discovered by Bentham." "He merely reproduced in a dull and spiritless fashion what Helvetius and other French writers of the eighteenth century had said before him so brilliantly."[141] In Marx's view, Benthamism is the negation of "human morality" and the real expression of bourgeois class morality based on exploitation and alienation. In his analysis of utility, Bentham assumes that the "modern petty, bourgeois and, above all, the modern English petty bourgeois is the normal man."[142] Helvetius believes that the sole motive of human acts is egoism and self-interest and that the exalted virtues can be explained in terms of self-love and pleasure. For Bentham, egoism and free competition, as Engels remarks, are the essence of morality.[143] Marx criticizes Bentham for "indulging in lengthy moral reflections" only to justify bourgeois egoistic morality. "Remaining within the confines of bourgeois conditions," Benthamism "could criticise only those relations which had been handed down from a past epoch and were an obstacle to the development of the bourgeoisie."[144]

In advocating alienated ideals for human life, capitalist morality, according to Marx and Engels, is opposed to the full development of human capacities. This morality keeps all persons living under capitalism in the alienated role of slave, preventing them from satisfying their elementary needs and desires. The ethics of political economy, Marx indicates, "is based on pure self-interest and has no regard for those who are regressing to the cave dwelling in an estranged form" and no sympathy for the weak and poor.[145] It is the ethics in which money takes the place of virtue and plays the role of the "highest good." Bourgeois morality is reflected in the deepest degradation of man and in total dependence on free competition. Capitalism "expresses moral laws in its own way," and therefore it is utterly immoral.[146] Here all man's passions and moral ideals are "submerged in avarice."[147] In capitalist society, morality is always ego-centred and closely bound up with hypocrisy, cynicism, indifference, excess, and intemperance.[148]

It is impossible to read *Manuscripts* and *Capital* without being aware of Marx's enmity toward capitalist morality. This morality is always motivated by the alienating powers of having rather than by any truly human considerations. Moral conscience of the capitalist is one of the forces of alienation that prevents the human being from realizing his individual and communal nature. Because the capitalist is frequently pleasure-orientated and becomes the "prey of his cupidity," both Marx and Engels maintain that capitalist morality is the "misuse of morality for immoral purposes" and the expression of the hedonistic principle of self-pleasing.[149] Their ideas of happiness are associated with the struggle for the liberation of alienated man. Naturalistic utilitarianism, expressed in capitalist morality, and idealist perfectionism, expressed in Christianity and Hegelianism, entirely ignore this struggle. Even if there is any meaning in pursuing happiness as a merely moral end, Engels says, the "urge towards happiness of the oppressed class must not be ruthlessly sacrificed to that of the bourgeoisie."[150] Inspired by Hegelian anti-hedonism, Marx asserts that the "philosophy which preaches enjoyment has never been anything but the clever language of certain social circles who have had the privilege of enjoyment."[151] Marx categorically rejects both the hedonistic principle of self-gratification or self-pleasing and the purely rationalistic principle of self-sacrifice or self-denial. The historical appearance of dialectical materialism "has shattered the basis of all morality, whether the morality of ascetism or of enjoyment."[152]

In spite of Marx's criticism of various moral theories and his occasional rejection of all morality, he occasionally assumes that there is an "independent morality which is based on the consciousness of human dignity."[153] On this assumption he condemns the "increasing value of the world of things and the devaluation of the world of men."[154] Without the assumption that alienation, exploitation, and human degradation are intrinsically morally bad, he would have no ground for condemning the capitalist system as evil. If moral propositions were purely empirical and historically conditioned, as he seems to maintain, then there would be no rational justification for condemning capitalist immorality as being anything but an error or defect in human behavior. Yet, Marx's and Engel's condemnation of capitalist morality is essentially a moral one. Confusing descriptive and normative propositions, they are unable to realize that if moral statements are simply empirical propositions that describe the reactions of men to their socioeconomic conditions, they can only indicate why men act in a certain way. They cannot command that men ought to pursue any particular moral aim. Self-alienation can be condemned only on the assumption that morality is somehow absolute and universal. The fact is that many of Marx's and Engels's references to morality do contain a mixture of normative and descriptive sentences. Modern Marxists either accept them as such or simply ignore them. They all reject the "emotive and attitude theories" on the grounds that they reflect in a bourgeois or capitalist way the alienating and purely individualistic class morality.[155]

In his analysis of self-alienation and self-fulfilment, Marx often uses such moral expressions as "brutal exploitation," "alienation," "oppression," "dehumanisation," "slavery," "degradation of personal dignity," "moral conscience," and "morality" without ever defining them. He has promised to write an "independent pamphlet" on ethics but this has never materialized.[156] He must have realized that ethics, like religion, is closely connected with metaphysics and this probably explains why he has avoided an explicit moral theory. As a result, his references to moral problems are obscure, ambivalent, and frequently contradictory. As Plamenatz rightly indicates, Marx and Engels say little about the origin, nature, and difference of moral standards and make no attempt even to distinguish between the moral standards of primitive and civilized societies.[157] They ignore completely any constructive analysis of the development and significance of moral judgment, treat moral phenomena as the mere expression of social relations, confuse the realm of appreciation with the realm of description, identify moral values with economic values, and simply do not refer to moral obligation and moral pathology. They start from the premise that ethical properties such as "goodness and rightness" are essentially similar to natural properties such as "useful and powerful." Moral ideas, in their view, have no independent status. They are made by individuals living in society and like all other ideas, they are "conditioned by productive forces."[158]

Marx believes that "metaphysics has in practice lost all credit" and cannot accept any moral standard that is related to metaphysical or pseudo-materialist values. While Hegel relates morality to universal objectives and transcendental purposes,indicating that moral ideals are internal and rational creations, Marx always relates it socioeconomic objectives and revolutionary purposes. He hates morality of the capitalist oppressors but fails to realize that the ethics of domination and submission are also inherent in his historicist ethical theory. If capitalist morality is based on the principle that the end justifies the means, Marx's revolutionary ethics are also based on the same principle. It is only "revolutionary terror," he says, "that can shorten the murderous death agonies of the old society and the bloody birth throes of the new society."[159] Hegel regards "morality as a specific form of feedom," but Marx regards it as a mask that merely opposes the full unfolding of man's essential powers.[160] In both cases, however, might is right and force is the cardinal virtue. What differentiates Marx's moral theory from Hegel's is the belief that moral alternatives must always be resolved into alternatives of external conditions, including wealth and poverty. Whether an action is right or wrong can only be decided by proletarian class consciousness.[161] Marxism identifies the good with the proletarian class interest and thus with the interests of the revolution. All forms of "abstractly conceived morality" must be discarded because they have no room for revolutionary practice. It is only "revolutionary ethics" that, Marx claims, are capable of eliminating self-alienation or the alienation of activity and can guide individuals to the realization of their essential powers.

5
Religious Alienation

The whole movement of thought in Western Europe during the nineteenth century was hostile to the narrow rationalism that was the atmosphere in which deism flourished. The modernist view of God was dominated by the concept of evolution that made common a way of regarding the world and life unfavorable to the deistic conception of God. As men of letters became familiar with the notion of a development, they sought for evidence of deity within the world process rather tahn without it. For some modernists God became an impersonal cosmic force, but for most the traditional concept of a personal God was retained, although His relationship to man and the world was modified. The unity of God, man, and nature was emphasized and any dualism of natural and supernatural spheres was attacked. Monism, which asserts that the universe is in some sense a whole and that the apparent plurality of things is ultimately illusory, was a view held widely during the nineteenth century. In Germany Fichte, Schelling, Hegel, and the Young Hegelians were monistic philosophers, advancing a variety of arguments in support of essentially similar, although in some respects different, metaphysical positions. By the close of the century, the fact of evolution was accepted by most scientists and theologians.

Writers of the nineteenth century tended to deify the evolutionary process, making it the source of progress. Darwin denied that he had ever been atheistic in thought, although occasionally he had been agnostic. Evolution, according to him, is not incompatible with theism. Engels, however, saw incompatibility between evolution and deism. "In our evolutionary conception of the universe," he writes, "there is absolutely no room for either a Creator or a Ruler; and to talk of a Supreme Being shut out from the whole existing world, implies a contradiction in terms, and, as it seems to me, a gratuitous insult to the feelings of religious people."[1] The term *deism* came into use about the beginning of the eighteenth century, and the phrase "God but not the Gospel" was used by deistic opponents to characterize the nature of deistic beliefs. Deism stood for a purely rationalist religion, and its adherents were anxious to set forth an idea of God that would appeal to abstract understanding. According to deism, God is not immanent in things; he exists outside them and does not continuously sustain them. Eighteenth-century deistic writers emphasized the theory of a transcendent God who set the world process going and then left it to its own devices. As rationalists, the deists rejected revelation and argued that God endowed man with natural reason that is the light of natural religion. Along with their idea of a natural religion as the embodiment of the natural human reason, they stressed that free thought had in every way made for progress. Deists stood for a rationalizing rather than a spiritual impulse. Yet, they believed God was not a shadowy Absolute but a determinate Being in determinate relations to the world and man.

The defects of deism were conspicuous, and thus its demise was unsurprisingly sudden. The last phase of the deistic controversy centered around the attack on miracles. Criticism of the deists was marked by the defect in historical insight that was common to the whole eighteenth century. It was an unhistorical assumption that Christianity was the corruption of an original "natural religion" and that this natural religion was the original religion of man. The waning of deism as a living force must be attributed primarily to its own weaknesses. Deism was too abstract and rationalistic to capture the hearts and minds of contemporary believers. The deists attacked the institutional church, and traditional Christianity was frequently represented as the enemy of the religion of reason. Just as later in the writings of Marx, Engels, and the Young Hegelians, miracles were rejected as primitive superstitions, and cases of cruelty and immorality in the biblical record were cited sarcastically. In France, attacks on Christianity were often vehement and bitter, in England they were restrained and moderate. Most people did not care to join in a disreputable attack on Christianity. In Germany many thinkers, like Goethe, gave voice to the disrepute into which the conception of an extra-mundane God had fallen. In England, Carlyle spoke scornfully of an "absentee God, sitting idle, ever since the first Sabbath, at the outside of his universe," and in France the deist Voltaire was more interested in combating "atheism and fanaticism as the two monsters" than in propagating "natural religion."[2] Of all the philosophers of the Age of Reason, only Rousseau, the founder of the romantic movement, remained loyal to natural religion. Rejecting a purely rational interpretation of religion and referring to Voltaire as "the trumpet of impiety," Rousseau emphasized the religion of the heart that appealed to most Protestant theologians.

The change in temper and ideals that marked the transition to the nineteenth century had important effects on religious conceptions. The sympathetic study of Spinoza, introduced by Lessing, stimulated poets and thinkers to see the immanence of God in nature and in man. The new modern attitude was favorable to the better understanding of religion because it meant a deeper insight into the motives and forces that were at work in the evolution of religion and a somewhat broader way of looking at religious phenomena as a whole. The view of man differed considerably from the classical doctrine. Human nature was regarded as essentially divine, but emphasis was laid on man's moral and spiritual progress and unity with God rather than on his sinfulness and opposition to God. Religion was seen as being rooted in human experience, and theological interpretations were treated with suspicion. Geothe, the best-known literary exponent of the ideals of the Enlightenment in Germany, gradually realized the shortcomings of rationalist teaching; in the end, he declared that "Christianity is far above all philosophy." Both Hegel and Schleiermacher represent a view of life and the world inherited from Goethe. Although in point of speculation they are contrasted as antipathetic types, it would be easy to prove a close relation between their conceptions of the essence of religion. Romantic pantheism haunted both of them. The main difference, however, between them is that Schleiermacher expressed his romanticism in terms of feeling whereas Hegel construed it in the severer categories of pure thought.

Schleiermacher, the father of liberal theology, appealed to religious experience and held that the basis of religion is distinctive religious awareness and not revealed doctrine as in traditionalism, nor ethical will as in Kant's moralism, nor cognitive reason as in natural theology. Like the Romanticists, he held that God is known by immediate apprehension rather than by indirect inference. Theologies are local and transitory. Religious experience is before its intellectual interpretation. Recognizing early the importance of feelings in religion, he continued to treat the feeling experience as fundamental and religious dogmas as the outcome of reflection on this experience. Schleiermacher's interest in historic religion was centered in Christianity. He helped to make theology Christocentric, but his own theology was not Christocentric enough. Although he sought to free theology from its servitude to philosophy, he was bound to a preconceived philosophy of religion. In tracing the psychological origin of religion to the feeling of dependence, he tried unsuccessfully to reach a universal principle that is constitutive of the religious consciousness. Schleiermacher's treatment of religion as a "feeling of absolute dependence" provoked Hegel's well-known retort that Schleiermacher's dog was more pious than his master. Hegel grew up when the Age of Reason was in decline and when the age of feeling and imagination was invading Germany.

Although Hegel questioned many of Kant's doctrines, he remained a Kantain throughout his life. Kant's ideal was a rational and ethical religion, purged of alien elements and freed from everything that savors of superstition and intolerance. According to him, the content of religion is the performance of moral duties conceived as commands of God. However, Kant's theory of religion suffers as much as his moral theory from his neglect of psychology. Taking up in a higher sense the tradition of eighteenth-century rationalism, according to which Christianity is doctrine, Hegel welcomed the Christological dogma as embodying the true philosophy as imaginative intuition. While still a Romanticist, like Schelling, he appealed to a realm beyond reflective thought that for him was religion. Hegel recognizes that religion is a universal attitude of the human spirit and that Christianity is the best representation of God's effort to reveal Himself. Although Hegel cannot hide his antiecclesiastical, if not anti-Christian, sentiments in his early essay *The Positivity of the Christian Religion*, later in *The Spirit of Christianity* and other works he indicates deep sympathy for the doctrine of the Gospel. In the concept of Spirit he finds the inseparable connection between mind and spirit and between the divine and the human. There is no loftier truth than that God and man, so far from being essentially different, are a rational and intrinsic unity. Religion, inferior to philosophy as an exponent of this unity, is still expressing this unity in the ecclesiastical dogma of the God-man. The moments in Jesus' life are grand pictures of ontological ideas, because they speak to us that man, viewed in his alienating finitude, is the prey of dissolution and negation. To save man from his state of alienation and division, God must objectively enter this empirical world as man's equal. Thus the Divine and the human natures are not different but alike and in unity.

Hegel's Christology affirms that "God comes to be Spirit," and this can take place only in man, in finite spirit. Christianity receives absolute praise but at the cost of its tie with history. It is only the world process as a whole rather than a single point or person in it that can be the true manifestation of the Absolute. Everything in his philosophy of religion as expressed in the *Phenomenology of Spirit* (publ. 1807) appears as Christian as his exposition of it in *The Spirit of Christianity* (1798), although in *Phenomenology* the emphasis is on "religion as consciousness of Absolute Being" rather than on Christology and Christian soteriology and the development of religion is associated with the dialectical "movement of the universal moments." Whereas Hegel's essay *The Positivity of the Christian Religion* (1795) is permeated with hostility to Christian institutions, and the essay *The Spirit of Christianity* is full of praises for Christ and the Gospel, the *Phenomenology of Spirit* is concerned with "the religion of the ethical Spirit." Here, Hegel argues, the truth of religion must be based on the speculative Idea of God. Hegel's theory of religious development as a dialectic process led to much arbitrariness in the construction of historical materials. The shortcomings of his religious philosophy are well known. He certainly overlooks the importance of psychology and exaggerates the function of thought in religion. Yet, a philosophical achievement of such magnitude as Hegelianism necessarily leaves a permanent mark on theology. Certain minds became so intoxicated by the new system that they hardly believed that the world could ever get beyond it. Soon after Hegel's death in 1831, however, differences of opinion began to appear within the Hegelian school. Even Hegel's followers began asking whether he was not really a pantheist.[3] The interpretation of religion has varied considerably, depending on whether stress was laid on the unity of the whole or on the rality of the differentiations within it. Differences in the Hegelian school became more pronounced in 1835 and after publication of *The Life of Jesus* by David Strauss. As a Hegelian, Strauss maintains that Christianity is the first great religion to claim that it has overcome metaphysical dualism. This claim, according to him, is the substance of the doctrine of the unity of divine and human consciousness in the person of Christ.

Strauss was anxious to combat the alienating effects of religious dualism.

The only method to conquer this dualism, he believes, is to substitute human-ity, the species, and the race as the exemplification of the God-man. The apotheosis of the God-man is then transformed into the apotheosis of human-ity or race. Unlike Hegel who is more interested in "God as activity and the Essence of Essences" than in the historicity of the Gospels, Strauss believes that the Gospel narratives are the essence of Christianity.[4] Many items in the Gospels—the supernatural birth of Jesus, his resurrection and ascension and even miracles—apparently remain eternally valid truths, as symbols of a metaphysical idea. Conceived as in an individual, a God-man, the attributes and functions ascribed to Christ are mutually contradictory, but according to Strauss, they harmonize in the idea of the race. Strauss's book came under attack from the orthodox Lutherans as well as from Hegel's followers who were anxious to defend the Hegelian reconciliation of religion and philoso-phy. They argued that Strauss no longer saw the very idea of religion as con-sisting in personal union with God. Yet, a Christian might somehow accept Strauss's theology expounded in *Life of Jesus*. He cannot, however, bridge the gulf that inevitably separates him from the anti-dogmatic naturalistic theology of Bruno Bauer. In *Critiques of St. John's* (1840) and *The Synoptic Gospels* (1841–1842), Bauer maintains that neither the fourth gospel nor the three synoptic gospels possess historical validity. He believes that St. Mark's gospel, which he regards as the earliest and the source of the others, is full of lies and inventions. He denies the historicity of Christ as well as His divinity. Indeed, he soon came to believe that Christianity preaches nothing but hypocrisy and falsehoods. The open implication of Bauer's exegesis is de-finitely atheism.[5]

The only principle to which Bauer remained loyal during his lifetime is the principle of criticism. For him, criticism is activity that transforms all human aims and acts into self-consciousness, and the whole development of self-consciousness depends on this activity. Like the other Young Hegelians, Bauer believed criticism was a powerful weapon for destroying all those obstacles that impede the progress of history. As a trained theologian, he accepts Christianity as a necessary stage in human development; like Hegel, he gives prominence to the world-process as a whole. According to Bauer, Christianity has subjected humanity to dogmas and an arbitrary God and thus has opened the door to religious alienation. Religious alienation in Chris-tian faith is total, and this total alienation impedes the progress of self-consciousness. Religious consciousness is a negative aspect of human life be-cause it deprives individuals of their own attributes and places them in an illusory realm. This view of man dominates Feuerbach's *Essence of Christian-ity*, published in 1841. The principal aim of this controversial book, according to Feuerbach, is "to show that the true sense of theology is anthropology and that there is no distinction between the predicates of the divine and human nature, and, consequently, no distinction between the divine and human subject."[6]

Feuerbach's book was received by Marx and Engels with unconcealed joy.

According to Engels, this enthusiasm was general. "We all became at once Feuerbachians."[7] For Feuerbach, God is only a projection of human nature onto a mythical being who exists only in the imaginary world. "The Divine Being is the human being glorified by the death of abstraction; it is the departed spirit of man."[8] Religion, on the other hand, is "human nature reflected, mirrored in itself."[9] The time has come to reject hypocrisy and falsehood of the past and reclaim the alienated attributes of man. Feuerbach refuses to be called an atheist, however, denying emphatically that in his view religion is an "absurdity, a nullity, a pure illusion." It is probably true to say that his opposition to religion is more anti-Hegelian than anti-Christian. Hegelian theology, essentially the traditional Christian theology seen in the light of dialectic development, is a religious affirmation of pride, whereas in Feuerbach's theology there are elements of a critique of pride. Moving from the standpoint of pride to that of love, he points out that "Christianity is not only a religion of faith but also of love."[10]

Hegel's rationalist philosophy may be seen as the final rational support of theology. His religious philosophy may be interpreted as the final engulfing of the divine by the human, thus expressing manifestly the pride of man. It could also be seen as the final engulfing of the human by the divine, thus involving the denial of human personality. Hegel tends to see the world process as the becoming of God. It is in man as a finite spirit that God finally becomes conscious. According to Hegel, God arrives at self-consciousness in man. Feuerbach, on the other hand, believes the self-consciousness of man is enough. The self-consciousness of Absolute Spirit or God in man is merely the self-consciousness of man himself and of his nature. In Feuerbach's theology, the absolutely divine is replaced by the absolutely human. "The grand characteristic of religion, and of the Christian religion especially", he writes, "is that it is thoroughly anthropotheistic, the exclusive love of man for himself, the exclusive self-affirmation of the human nature, that is, of subjective human nature."[11] For Schleiermacher, religion is the feeling of absolute dependence of human beings on the cosmic ineffable whole; for Feuerbach, it is the projection of experienced human needs. Like Schleiermacher, however, Feuerbach also finds the origin of religion in human feeling. He argues against Strauss that religion is a product of real human need rather than of fancy mysticism and against Bauer that religion is not a need of the human reason but of the heart. Religious judgments as expressed in wishes reflect man's desire to control his natural surroundings in harmony with his emotions and, above all, his helplessness in the world of nature. Starting in his study of Christianity from the notion of religious alienation, Feuerbach is anxious to show that the essence of religion is the essence of man himself reified and projected outside himself. The powers and qualities attributed to God are man's own powers.

Feuerbach's *Essence of Christianity* had a more lasting effect on Engels than on Marx, although initially Engels's religious view had been more influenced by Schleiermacher and Strauss. Marx's idea of the naturalization of man and the humanization of nature—the idea of "true anthropological nature"—is based on Feuerbach's assertion that the "divine being is nothing but the human nature purified."[12] In *Holy Family*, Marx praises Feuerbach for being the first to complete the criticism of religion and for overcoming the "old antithesis between spiritualism and materialism."[13] Later, when Feuerbach was pushed into the background, both Marx and Engels were struck suddenly by his astonishing poverty when compared with Hegel. Feuerbach's assertion that the "periods of humanity are distinguished only by religious changes" is, in Engels's opinion, "decidedly false." Feuerbach has no wish to abolish religion but to perfect it.[14] Marx's criticism of Feuerbach's doctrines implies that they are contemplative and give no guidance to action. Contemplation has to be supplemented by deeds. According to Marx, Feuerbach does not understand human activity itself as objective activity, and he always takes refuge in external nature that has not yet been subdued by men.[15] Starting from religious alienation, he merely duplicates the world into religious and secular worlds. Marx's main objection is that Feuerbach's reduction of theology to anthropology is not radical enough. The mere assertion that the attributes of God, such as goodness, love, providence, justice, holiness, and prescience, are in fact reifications of human attributes does not put an end to religion and religious alienation. Feuerbach has believed that his main service to alienated humanity has been in emphasizing that man is alienated from himself only when worshipping the imagined alien higher being. Man objectifies himself in the form of a divinity because it is in his nature to seek self-objectification. "God is born in the misery of man." God, Feuerach says, is "man's highest feeling of self, freed from all contraries or disagreeables." As God is the highest being, to feel God is the highest feeling of self as well.[16]

Feuerbach's influence on the Young Hegelians has been attributed almost exclusively to his critism of religion and religious alienation. Although there were other critics of religious alienation, Marx was regarded in late 1844 as being a disciple of Feuerbach. Max Stirner more than anybody else successfully convinced Marx to go beyond the static humanism of Feuerbach. Stirner is very critical of Feuerbachian theology, and in his book *The Ego and His Own* he points out that the "humanist religion of Feuerbach is only the last metamorphosis of the Christian religion."[17] Unlike the other Young Hegelians who have either proclaimed a religion of humanity or atheism as their main concern, Stirner rejects both the divine and the human. "The divine is God's concern and the human, man's. My concern," he writes in the preface to his book, "is neither the divine nor the human . . . but solely what is mine, and it is not a general one, but is—unique as I am unique." In *German ideology*, Marx criticizes Stirner for reproaching Feuerbach on the ground that he turns the predicates of God into subjects, although he himself "is far less capable of arriving at anything" and accepts these predicates, merely attaching to them the predicate "holy," i.e., "doing exactly the same as that for which he reproaches Feuerbach."[18] Of all the Young Hegelians, only Arnold Ruge remained loyal to Feuerbach, advocating a new idealism that would transform alien religion into a truly new religion of humanity.

Following Marx's quarrel with Ruge and the end of their friendship in mid-1844, the entire Young Hegelian movement ceased to be a unified and coherent force by the end of the year. The origins of this movement were theological, and Strauss's theology and ideas about religious alienation filled them with Hegelian attitudes and simultaneously made them "more and more disillusioned with Protestant theology." Summarizing the disagreements, ideals, and differences of outlook among the Young Hegelian members, Marx assails all of them, except Engels, for merely staying at the level of criticism or of critical criticism. "The Old Hegelians," he says, "had understood everything as soon as it was reduced to a Hegelian logical category. The Young Hegelians criticised everything by ascribing religious conceptions to it or by declaring that it is a theological matter. The Young Hegelians are in agreement with the Old Hegelians in their belief in the rule of religion, of concepts, or of a universal principle in the existing world. Except that the one party attacks this rule as usurpation, while the other extols it as legitimate."[19] The total damnation of religion was presupposed and religious concepts dominated all ideas and realities. "The entire body of German philosophical criticism," Marx continues, "from Strauss to Stirner is confined to criticism of religious conceptions. The critics started from real religion and theology proper."[20] They wanted to free men from their religious bonds and religious alienation, yet Marx claims their negation of religious alienation remained merely abstract, ideologically critical, and theological in an anti-theological form.

On close insepection, Marx writes in *Manuscripts of 1844*, "theological criticism—genuinely progressive though it was at the inception of the movement—is seen in the final analysis to be nothing but the culmination and conseqence of the old philosophical, and especially the Hegelian, transcendentalism, twisted into a theological caricature."[21] Engels's criticism of the Young Hegelians' cult of abstract man and of their inability to combat effectively religious alienation is similar to that of Marx. "The step which Feuerbach did not take," he says, "had nevertheless to be taken. The cult of abstract man, which formed the kernel of Feuerbach's new religion, had to be replaced by the science of real men and of their historical development. This further development of Feuerbach's standpoint beyond Feuerbach was inaugurated by Marx in 1845 in *The Holy Family*."[22] Both Marx and Engels point out in various ways that all religious experience is illusory and alienating and therefore must be eliminated. They accuse Bauer, Ruge, and Feuerbach as well as Stirner for being religious, merely substituting the old Hegelian transcendentalism by the religion of humanity and theological atheism without ever considering seriously the social effects of religious alienation itself. While Bauer concentrates his criticism on biblical Christianity and biblical theology, Strauss analyzes dogmatic Christianity and dogmatic theology, Feuerbach

proclaims the religion of humanity, and Stirner declares that the self is God—
not the self in general and not humanity within the self as in Feuerbach, but
the separate unique ego.

Early criticism of religion in Germany as exemplified in the writings of
Hegel, Schleiermacher, and Strauss could not, according to Marx and Engels,
transcend the realm of the "pure spirit" and thus made "religious illusion"
the driving force of history. This criticism merely showed some deficiences of
past religious ideas, indicating that these ideas were in contradiction with
development toward the social harmony and human happiness. Bruno Bauer
moved further toward a radical form of criticism, but even this criticism was
"through and through theological." Herr Bauer, Marx writes, "has really made
the 'creative' power of the Lord Jesus and of his principle so evident that his
'infinite self-consciousness' and the 'Spirit' are nothing but creations of
Christianity."[23] Rejecting Hegel's "apparent criticism," Bauer's theological
criticism, and even Feuerbach's "humanistic criticism," Marx and Engels
advocate the relevance of radical social criticism. In *Introduction to the Cri-
tigue of Hegel's Philosophy of Right* (1843–1844), Marx stresses that criticism
of religion is the beginning of all criticism. The basic postulate of his criticism
of religion is that man makes religion, man here meaning the world of man,
the state, and society. "The basis of irreligious criticism," he says, "is that
man makes religion, religion does not make man."[24] The criticism of religion
therefore is in embryo the criticism of the vale of tears, the halo of which is
religion. For Marx, religion is the first and primordial form of ideological
alienation. In the state of religious alienation, all forms of ideology are most
active as destructive, antisocial forces. In religious alienation, individuals
creates an illusory world, representing objects and ideals that constitute
their earthly lives as part of divine wisdom.

Because religion is the expression of alienation and impotence, Marx believes it alienates man from his essential powers as well as from his social life.
Religion, expressed in man's frustrations, his ignorance, and his weakness, is
explained as a reflection of the economic structure and as consolation. "Religion is the general theory of that world, its encyclopaedic compendium, its
logic in a popular form, its spiritualistic *point d'honneur*, its enthusiasm, its
moral sanction, its solemn complement, its universal source of consolation
and justification. It is the fantastic realisation of the human essence because
the human essence has no true reality."[25] Marx overlooks the fact that religion is a basic constituent of human culture and thus is amazingly complex. It
touches human life on every side and embraces belief and conduct, reason
and emotion. It is enshrined in creed and custom, morality and science, and
yet lives independently of them in the minds and hearts of men. As a human
phenomenon it is both individual and social, and its manifestations range
from the orgies of savages to Spinoza's "intellectual love of God." The fundamental fact is that behind the rise of religion man is an incomplete being,
and his incompleteness is revealed in the constant upspringing of lofty desires

that call for satisfaction. Many wise men throughout history have emphasized
that man's consciousness of his insufficiency creates that longing for fel-
lowship with a Reality beyond him, through which religion is realized. Even
animals distinguish between their own movement and the movement of an
object and are instinctively aware that they can affects surrounding objects.
Without this awareness they could not survive in the struggle for existence.
However, only man can give meaning to his world.[26]

Man realizes his nature as man when the subconscious is related to the
conscious as means to end, and the end dominates the means. Apart from a
conscious mental activity, instinctive feelings can never be elevated into religious motives. Using thought, man emancipates himself from bondage to the
immediate present. Looking before and after this present, man adopts means
to ends and thus attains the status of a voluntary agent and a socially responsible being. In Marx's naturalism, however, man stands alone in a predominantly hostile nature. Unlike Hegel who believes that "nature and the finite
spirit are a product of God," Marx rejects abstract theodicies and argues that
the very idea of religious man corresponds to a reified conception of man. As
a biophysical being, man can only be understood when described in terms of
economics. Here is the material root of his real life, and here "criticism by
weapons" must be rooted. Marx deviates from Romanticism in that he
accepts the Promethean imperative that man should become God. Man is
everything insofar as he forms, controls, and dominates his natural and social
environment. His attitude is obviously one of pride, defiance, and self-
sufficiency. This certainly is implied in his criticism of religious alienation.
"The criticism of religion," he writes, "ends with the teaching that man is the
highest being for man, hence with the categorical imperative to overthrow all
relations in which man is a debased, enslaved, forsaken, despicable being."[27]

Man's consciousness of himself as the highest being is the essence of Marx's
"ought-to-be-everything" imperative. This imperative is a function of his
Promethean complex, and the purpose of the theory embodied in this complex is to enable Marx to continue his dreams of human divinity. His essentially romantic conception of religious belief is seen in his love for the myth of
Prometheus who in his dissertation is represented by Epicurus as the real hero
in the rebellion against the mythical gods. Marx is captivated by Aeschylus's
tragedy *Prometheus Bound*, although his story, like Shelley's in *Prometheus
Unbound*,[28] has been transformed in allegory to fit his faith in the regenera-
tion of humanity. It is assumed that real victim is not Prometheus but the gods
whose dominance has been shaken by man's disbelief. By exposing the God-
illusion, Marx hopes to free man to revolve around himself as his real sun.
"Religion," according to Marx, "is only the illusory sun which revolves round
man as long as he does not revolve round himself."[29] In Hegel's and Feuerbach's theological theories, religion belongs to man's essence. Marx believes
that religious sentiment is always a social and economic product. While Hegel
indicates that God makes history and Feuerbach is satisfied with "contempla-

tive materialism," Marx insists that the central issue in the criticism of religion is to eliminate religion altogether. "The struggle against religion is therefore indirectly a fight against the world of which religion is the spiritual aroma."[30] According to Hegel and Feuerbach, the divine object is one that satisfies a personal and spiritual need and primarily represnets a value. Pure facts alone have no religious value. Thus the supramundane object of religion is conceived as a supreme and ultimate value that finally satisfies human needs. Marx's Promethean humanism questions all absolutes, all temporally conditioned conceptions, and all values. It eliminates any transcendence imposed from below and above in the sense of an absolute value. It also rejects the view that a deliberate, purposive, and meaningful life of man is made possible by his perception of values that presuppose a pre-existing teleological adaptation or harmony between the reality seen as a good when it enters consciousness and the psychical nature of man. In place of these arbitrary transcendental values, Marx affirms man's self-transcendence, identifying transcendence with attributes that are specifically human in man. Man cannot be fully human unless he strives to go beyond himself and form his own identity in the struggle with negative forces of nature and with alienating forces of the world of which religion is the spiritual aroma.

In drawing his picture of man alienated from himself in servitude and worship to a superhuman Being, Marx constantly recalls the Feuerbachian analysis of religion. Feuerbach has argued that religion is man's search for a "supernatural being in the fantastic reality of heaven" in which he actually finds no reality but "a reflection of himself."[31] Religious man invests all the attributes of human nature in the image of himself as God, thus impoverishing his empirical self as a result of imagination. In his early writings, Marx retains Feuerbach's ideas of projection and alienation, reiterating that the superhuman being is only the externalized mental activity of self-worshipping alienated man. "Man, who looked for a superhuman being in the fantastic reality of heaven and found nothing there but the reflection of himself, will no longer be disposed to find but the semblance of himself, only an inhuman being, where he seeks and must seek his true reality."[32]

In Hegel's theodicy, the facts of religion are markedly different from the facts in the sphere of physics or biology. Religious facts are the expression of conscious minds; the latter are not. "It is only a thinking being that can have a religion." Development of thought is the key to the development of the objective world. Man reflects alienation of the alienated Spirit. For Marx, religious alienation is intrinsic to the socioeconomic process. The essential difference between him and Hegel is that Marx rejects the inherent religiosity of man and human nature itself. Hegel indicates that apart from living minds, historical data could not become spiritual values and assume a religious significance. The inner witness of the spirit is essential, and without it historical proofs for the existence of spiritual values count for very little. Hegel's conception of religious alienation leads Marx to point out that "the religious man can find in Hegel his final confirmation."[33] Marx rejects any validity of theistic proofs and the validity of any speculative reasoning about man and his real world. Analyzing Stirner's ideas about the realm of essences and the supreme being, he states emphatically that to try "to prove the existence of God is merely a waste of time," because the superhuman being is in fact the estranged form of man himself. In religious alienation, men always make their empirical world into an imagined entity, confronting it as something foreign.[34]

Strictly speaking, the idea of God is incapable of proof and equally of disproof. Nothing that is ultimate can be proved or disproved. Religious philosophers emphasize rightly that it is impossible to meet all the objections that can be raised against any hypothesis about the existence of God just as it is impossible to meet those that can be raised against fundamental hypotheses of modern science. These hypotheses are accepted, however, not because they can necessarily be undeniably demonstrated but rather because they have the capacity of explaining certain known facts and possess sufficient evidence to give them preference over alternative explanations. In this way, theists and atheists alike must regard the question of the divine existence. Marx is not a theologian and has no interest in the "fantastic reality of heaven." For him, religious sentiment is a social product and the denial of God is a condition of the very possibility of the affirmation of man. By orienting man toward the fictitious happiness of the heavenly world, religion distracts him from his earthly functions and creates in him the psychology of an enslaved, despicable, and alienated being. "To abolish religion as the illusory happiness of the people is to demand their real happiness. The demand to give up illusions about the existing state of affairs is the demand to give up a state of affairs which needs illusions."[35]

There are not many religious philosophers today who maintain that it is possible to prove the divine existence from an abstract conception of God or from an abstract conception of the world. Even Hegel indicates that the "proofs presuppose the world and its contingency."[36] Assuming that duty and happiness must coincide in the end of human endeavor, Kant insists that it is morally necessary to believe in God because without God there is no guarantee that the inexorable sense of duty is not an illusion. Duty cannot be illusory because it speaks with an authority that nothing else possesses. Kant believes in the existence of God as a postulate of practical reason, although he dismisses the idea that reason could afford a ground for this belief. According to Hegel, God is expressly what can only be "thought as existing and His notion involves being." Man's happiness conceived as an abstract and unrealized unity of particular satisfactions involves a contradiction and cannot express the true nature of the spirit. Moreover, happiness regarded as the satisfaction of all desires is only imaginary. This Hegelian idea of religious happiness permeates Marx's school essay, the "Union of Believers with Christ," in which bodily pleasures are denounced and Epicurean hedonism is rejected. In

Berlin Marx undergoes a radical conversion and Epicurus becomes his hero. In *German Ideology*, he praises Epicurus as "the hero who was the first to overthrow the gods and trample religion underfoot." For this reason, he adds, "Epicurus has always had the reputation of being the philosopher *par excellence*."[37] Yet, strictly speaking, Marx, unlike Epicurus, is as anti-hedonistic as Hegel. In this view, crude pleasures are degrading and alienating phenomena in human life. Although passion is the "essential force of man," Marx regards man as a suffering being.[38] What Marx and Epicurus share in this respect is strong pity for the sufferings of mankind and an unshakeable conviction that these sufferings and human alienation as a whole would be reduced greatly if men would adopt materialistic philosophy. Unlike Marx, Epicurus believes in the existence of gods because he cannot otherwise account for the widespread existence of the idea of gods.

Marx's atheism is grounded in the affirmation of man's autonomy rather than in scientific negations of religion. Both he and Engels reject the primitive and negative character of pure atheism that is based on mere speculation, emphasizing that dialectical atheism as opposed to theoretical atheism should be grounded in practice. Because Marx's dialectical epistemology is rooted in man's relations to nature and society, it follows that atheism must be a corollary to human practice. Marx rejects Feuerbach's atheism because of its theoretical character and because it is linked to his speculative theory of man. This atheism, according to Marx, is inadequate to eliminate religious alienation.[39] Feuerbach's dissolution of God into man is only another form of religious alienation. While retaining Feuerbach's ideas of projection and alienation, Marx argues that Feuerbach's theory of religious alienation only touches the theoretical side of this alienation and ignores entirely the practical solution. In the struggle against religious alienation, it is not enough to become aware of it and speculate about it. This struggle necessitates the transformation of the world that generates it. Marx and Engels see all things in the world of man and nature in the process of change, and in this process of change men must eliminate the social roots of religion and thus conquer both the alienation within and around them. There is always an assumption that atheism cannot be regarded as an end in itself once religious alienation is seen as a reflection of social alienation. Theoretical atheism negates neither religious insights nor religious alienation. "As soon as the idealistic folly is put into practice," Marx says, "its malevolent nature is apparent: its clerical lust for power, its religious fanaticism, its charlatanry, its pietistic hypocrisy, its unctuous deceit."[40]

Man, according to Marx, takes his refuge in a fantasy world of religion because he is frustrated, dehumanized, and alienated in this real, pragmatic world. "Religious distress is at the same time the expression of real distress and also the protest against real distress."[41] The task of history must be to establish the truth of this visible world. It is only when the real existence of man and nature has become practical that the question about an alien being, one above nature and man, will become impossible in practice.[42] Marx's theory of religious alienation is dominated by the idea that man is essentially a creator. This alienation is seen as an alien power dividing man himself and attributing to God the human act of creation. The creative act of man attributed to the alien being above nature and man must be restored and treated as a distinguishing feature of man alone. Marx never doubts that man will overcome his religious alienation by himself. Even in some of his early poems he points out that "man's supreme prayer" is always for his own greatness. Mortal man, seeing his most cherished ideals in ruins, must take revenge and build a throne for himself.

The tragedy of religious alienation is exemplified by the false separation between the absolutely divine and the absolutely human attributes. Marx's purpose is to liberate man from religious alienation and thus reunite him with the world of nature and other men. As man owes his existence to himself, the dignity of man requires recognition of his true humanity and rejection of the false separation of his essential powers into human and divine elements. Like Feuerbach, Marx indicates that the qualities ascribed to God are really the attributes of man. Man's being can be found in his real life process that is shaped primarily in the production of the means of existence. Marx insists that man is a natural, not an abstract, being who objectifies himself in work. He is not lost in his object only when the object becomes for him a truly human object.[43] He rejects Hegel's personification of the world spirit that externalizes itself as the world of nature and man. While Hegel is the exponent of a rational theology, Marx is an exponent of a naturalistic philosophy, according to which man can realize his true nature only in the setting of society. Hegel sees human activity as always spiritual or mental; for Marx, it is essentially natural, practical, and material. The main difference between Marx and Hegel is that Hegel speaks of alienation of the spirit whereas Marx speaks of alienation of the "world of man" in which religion is the "spiritual aroma." Marx believes the distinguishing feature of religious alienation is the "duplication of the world into a religious world and a secular world."[44] This duplication is unnecessary and should be rejected. There is only one world and that world is secular, pragmatic, and historical.

The basic assertion of dialectical materialism is that whatever exists is of the same sort as matter. No new kinds of entity can ever be formed because every new phenomenon is the equivalent of a rearrangement of existing entities. Eighteenth-century abstract materialism is seen only as an antithesis to abstract spiritualism, positing Nature instead of the Christian God as the Absolute facing man.[45] This abstract materialism, according to Marx and Engels, is inadequate to solve the problems of evolution in nature and history. Being essentially fatalism, it leaves no room for the conscious historical activity of thinking human beings. Abstract materialism does not eliminate religious alienation. Because it is based on dualism, Marx claims, it is unable to explain man's intellectual and social development in terms of material needs. The main error of abstract materialism is similar to that of Hegelian idealism and consists in positing the relationships between men and objects in thought rather than in socioeconomic reality. Marx is anxious to emphasize that dialectical materialism is immersed in the historical process and that in practice it becomes coextensive with the reality of the world of men that is in continuous becoming. Thus all ideologies, including both abstract materialism and abstract idealism, are subjected to the relentless critique of practice. History is the unfolding of creative human activity that entails the work of the ensemble of social relations in their historical becoming. It is with the positing of a definite form of activity and a definite mode of life that true history begins. Man within the context of history must extend his creativity beyond the control of his narrow private world, but in doing so he must endeavor to avoid alienating himself in the products of his physical and mental efforts.

Marx's interest is confined to this planet and within this planet to man. The ideologists, he indicates, turn everything upside-down.[46] Instead of discovering the origin, nature, and goal of an institution such as religion by studying the history of the institution, they postulate religious man as the primitive man and make religious illusion the driving force of history. When the religious production of fancies is put above the real production of the means of life itself, then men are inevitably plunged into an inverted world, into the world of illusions and religious alienation. Religion in this world, according to Marx, is only "the sigh of the oppressed creature, the heart of a heartless world, just as it is the spirit of spiritless conditions. It is the opium of the people."[47] Whether Marx intended this statement to be a definition of religion, it is impossible to say. A good definition of religion must contain some reference to all the psychical factors that operate in religious experience. Hegel defines religion as "the knowledge possessed by the finite mind of its nature as absolute mind."[48] Hegel's definition is in terms of intellect; Marx's pseudo-definition is in terms of pure feeling. In this respect, Marx follows Feuerbach who bases religious experience on the feeling of love—"feeling intoxicated with joy, blissful in its own plenitude."[49] Marx's definition, however, is logically obscure, a striking example of *obscurum per obscurius*. Its defect arises from the use of eccentric and metaphorical expressions that are irrelevant to an adequate definition of religion. As far as the term "opium" is concerned, it has been established that Bauer originated it and Marx only popularized it. Marx uses the word for the first time in his letter to Feuerbach in October 1843.[50] Referring to religion as opium, he obviously suggests that religion is a mark of alienation, weakness, abasement, and helplessness. At the root of all religion lies man's sense of helplessness and the sense of living in a hostile world. In religious alienation, man's main concern is to banish the cause of his fears. Fears drive men to religious illusions; smitten with terror, they instinctively turn to God or gods for help.

According to Marx and Engels, man can be truly satisfied only in the secular world. Religion diverts him from seeking real satisfaction here on earth by offering an illusory satisfaction. The desire for goods and objects belongs to man's nature as an active being, and the existence of desire is linked inseparably with the sense of need and the "genesis of human society." Instead of projecting the ideas of himself into the fantastic reality of heaven, man must try to realize these ideas in the real history of human society by transforming society and himself with it. As a natural and productive social being, man is never simply the result of past and present conditions but rather the totalization of these conditions. Producing the conditions needed for his existence in an inherently social way, man's task is to transform the world around him and overcome alienation. Criticism and speculation are not sufficient to overcome religious alienation when humans are totally immersed in alienation. This alienation, according to Marx, can only be overcome by "material force." All solutions must be seen in practical terms. The main task is establishing a society in which genuinely human functions are not alienated from man. Marx and Engels, of course, assume that only in a communist society, in which men work together toward a common goal, can all forms of alienation be robbed of their significance, power, and dehumanizing effects.

Analyzing the "nebulous world of religion," Marx notes that "religious reflections of the real world will not disappear until the relations between human beings in their practical everyday life have assumed the aspect of perfectly intelligible and reasonable relations between man and man, and between man and nature."[51] Both he and Engels maintain that the idea of God is developed in the medium of socioeconomic conditions and that the religious world is "reflex of the real world." In *Capital*, Marx clearly makes a difference between primitive or tribal religion and sophisticated or modern religion, adding that Christianity with its cult of the abstract human being is the most suitable religion for bourgeois societies.[52] There is an assumption that the whole life of primitive man is ruled by convention and that the religions bond becomes more important in giving unity to the tribal system as a whole. In this primitive system of production, man does not initially think of himself as an independent individual but rather as a part of his community. The organic and inorganic, mind and matter are normally fused together and treated as if there were no essential differences between them. Marx assumes wrongly that fetishism is the lowest form of religion. Fetishism is the outcome and expression of a fully articulated spiritism. The background of fetishism is always a well-developed spiritism, and fetish-worship is an attempt of primitive man to control the spirits for his own purposes. Speaking of the general movement of alienation, Marx sometimes gives the impression that primitive man is less alienated than bourgeois man. Logically, religious alienation in primitive society should be less dehumanizing and less degrading than religious alienation in capitalist society, but he makes no qualification in this respect. One must conclude, therefore, that Marx is either unable to make any significant differentiation in religious alienation at different stages of human development or simply assumes that "the religious reflex" and thus religious alienation are biological as well as socioeconomic phenomena.

Marx and Engels always reject the abstract approach to the problem of alienation, indicating that this approach itself is alienated. In religious aliena-tiion, they emphasize, speculation and abstraction merely confirm the religious reflex, and instead of abolishing religion they even "perfect" it. In *Anti-Dühring*, Engels speaks of religion in almost the same way as Marx does in the *Introduction to the Critique of Hegel's Philosophy of Right.* "All religion," according to Engels, "is nothing but the fantastic reflection in men's minds of those external forces which control their daily life, a reflection in which the terrestrial forces assume the form of supernatural forces."[53] In the same work, unaware of the contradiction, he says that monotheism is a "reflection of the abstract man." Engels's ideas about the origin and nature of religion and about religious alienation are not original. He takes for granted Feuerbach's doctrine that God is only a "fantastic reflection of abstract man" and that religion is merely the outcome of human feeling. Religion will continue to exist as "the sentimental form of men's relation to the alien, natural and social forces which dominate them so long as men remain under the control of those forces."[54] Like Marx and Feuerbach, Engels fails to trace the origin of the religious reflex to any particular stage of evolution. He only says that at a certain stage primitive man assimilates the alien, mysterious, and superior forces of nature by means of personification. It was man's urge to personify and project his own ideas about the formidable forces of nature "that created gods everywhere."[55] What exactly is this urge, Engels does not explain.

The fact is that the origin of religion is beyond the comprehension of man; men can only speculate as to how it may have arisen. Anthropologists now believe that religion in the sense of a belief in spirits or higher powers is a universal phenomenon. Ethnography is unable to show any race devoid of religion but only differences in the degree to which religious ideas are represented. In every form of religion, man seeks to establish a self-satisfying relationship between himself and higher powers. The impulse or urge to form this relationship proceeds from a felt need that, as theologians and most anthropologists confirm, is inherent in human nature. The universality of this urge, which even Engels cannot explain away, is the secret of the universality of religion.

Analyzing religious alienation in primitive society, Engels insists more than Marx on man's feeling as being controlled by natural forces. This has been a favorite idea of those who, like Petronius and Lucretius, have tended to identify religion with superstition. Feeling in the form of fear, however, only partially explains the religious reflex.[56] Reflection shows that the motive of fear of natural forces in abstraction from other motives is inadequate to explain the origin of religion; therefore, it must be linked with elements derived from the cognitive and conative side of human consciousness. Engels is right in suggesting that the impulsive and emotional factors are more active in the earlier stages of evolution and that thought and the cognitive factor are only servants of the immediate purpose. He is very wrong, however, in assuming that religion and religious alienation are exclusively the products of socioeconomic relations, and that in a communist society the alien forces or religion will altogether disappear and "there will be nothing left to reflect."[57] Engels's naive optimism about the disappearance of religious beliefs merely expresses his wishful thinking. When discussing religion, he and Marx always give free rein to their speculative tendencies, inventing "projections, urges, functions and analogies" that lack foundations in individual psychology. They overlook that religion at all stages of its development bears the impress of the human mind. The broad similarities evident in the religions of the world originate in the common mental structure of man. Religious development reveals religion as an increasingly inward and spiritual phenomenon. The growth of human religious consciousness is a process of momentous significance. Many thinkers believe this growth means man's progress in the knowledge of himself, of God, and of the world. The force of religious conviction does not depend, as Marx and Engels maintain, on man's socioeconomic conditions. As Hegel indicates, man is by nature a religious being. There is nothing arbitrary and evanescent in religion that is a dominant aspect of man's experience. Referring to religion as an illustion, Marx never explains what he means by it.[58]

Both Marx and Engels are frequently sarcastic about dogmatic pronouncements of their ideological opponents. Engels, for example, accuses Dühring of claiming to be "no less infallible than the Pope" and of believing that his own doctrine is "the only way to salvation."[59] He also criticizes Feuerbach's conception of man who "always remains the same abstract man occupying the field in the philosophy of religion."[60] Surely, similar objections could be made against Engels and Marx. They have always insisted on the infallibility of their own doctrines, believing firmly that their ideas of the new communist future represent the whole truth. Their new future is immanent in the historical process, and in that sense it is a human future; but it is still envisaged to be an absolute future, mysteriously projecting itself beyond the present into a humanist pseudo-transcendence. Neither Marx nor Engels can explain how religious alienation could vanish in this pseudo-transcendence and why "there would be nothing left to reflect in it." It is clear that all attempts to reify the horizon of the future, whether through a static and projectionist concept of supernatural Being or through the establishment of an "absolute communist future" or a final humanist utopia, are equally illusory, unhistorical, and abstract. In opposition to theological projectionism and idealist transcendentalism, Marx and Engels are pleading constantly for a purely naturalistic interpretation of all aspects of human thought and behavior. They maintain that the horizon of the future is open to all men and that the creative overcoming of historical contradictions and religious alienations by generating a new classless future is the basis of human freedom. Like Spinoza, they believe that men can attain satisfaction and dignity only by identifying themselves with the whole order of nature and by submerging their private interests in the world of all human beings. The enlightened and free man, therefore, is urged to do everything possible to work for his complete return to himself as a social being and in that way contribute to the emancipation of his fellowmen from the blind hatred generated by superstitious beliefs and religious alienation. Yet, there is no comfort for individual man in this dialectico-materialistic teleology. The horizon of the future envisaged by Marx and Engels has great limitations and in many ways restricts the full play of man's creativity, responsibility, and freedom.

Marx's proclamation of man as the highest being for man offers no security against the domination of man by an alien power similar to that existing in capitalism. The substratum underlying Marx's anthropology is far from being favorable for any form of dealienation. In this anthroplogy, man is dragged away from the spiritual world and is subjected to the alien power of the dictatorship of the proletariat. Marx observes correctly that man is an alienated being, but he believes wrongly that man's alienation is caused and maintained by religious ideas. The religious urge may be indicative of alienation, but it cannot be its cause. Religion is not the first form of ideological alienation, although it probably is its earliest indicator. Like Feuerbach, Marx starts with the deification of humans, but his humanism soon evaporates and passes into anti-humanism. After denying the divine, he ultimately denies the human as well. In his anthropology, humans appear in the form of the impersonal social collective. Here the realm of God takes the form of the classless and stateless condition of the human community in which the world of man is seen only as "the ensemble of the social relations." In criticizing Feuerbach, Marx fails to realize that he himself is abstracting from the historical process when presupposing an abstract society of the absolute future. This presupposition, dressed in his materialistic theory of history and society, conceals an eschatology. The traditional faith in the redeeming power of a supernatural being is replaced by a belief in the inevitability of social progress that will eliminate religious alienation and bring about man's redemption from self-estrangement. The meaning of history consists in the elimination of religious alienation that, Marx believes, debases man, cuts him off from the perceptible external world, and throws him back into his abstract inner nature for the sake of illusory perfection.[61] According to Marx and Engels, in religion men transform their empirical world into a mere thought-world, an illusory world of ideas that confronts them as an alien reality. In their eschatological scheme, however, the world of the absolute future is neither a mere thought-world nor an illusory world of ideas, concepts, and abstractions.

Analyzing the world of men and religious alienation in his early writings, Marx refers to the phenomenon of death as a "harsh victory of the species over the definite individual."[62] He adds that the determinate individual is only a determinate species being and as such mortal. Like Hegel and Feuerbach, Marx approaches death from a social perspective. Hegel argues that being must pass into nothing to become existence and reality. Being and nonbeing, life and death are inseparably bound together. Hegel's dialectical process passes through contradictions as through its death, but it does not end in them.[63] The dialectical process transforms them into being. Engels quotes Hegel as saying that "no physiology is held to be scientific if it does not consider death as an essential element of life."[64] The dialectical conception of life is nothing but the assertion that the negation of life is contained in life itself. In evolution, death is as vital as birth. In Christianity, the negation of life is an indispensable means to the historic life.[65] Individual life would be absurd if it went on endlessly; that would not be eternal life. Christianity, however, links the phenomenon of death with the immortality of the soul that Marx and Engels reject. For Christians, the meaning of human life lies beyond the confines of history, and the paradox of the relation between humans and the divine, between time and eternity, is fundamental. Everything moves through the antithesis of the human and the divine. For Marx and Engels, the meaning of life and history is the work of men in the totality of their history, and the immanent presence of the totality of being in each finite being is the source of its development, death, and transcendence. This transcendence, however, does not entail individual immortality.

Throughout centuries, philosophical thinkers have believed that there is something absolute and eternal in the very nature of the self. The idea that there is an intrinsic spiritual value in the soul that guarantees its immortal life is as old as humanity itself. In Christianity, death is the condition of a spiritual transformation of the natural. Only through death can man become capable of a glorified and supramundane life. On the whole, it is evident that a belief in immortality has played an immortal role in the history of religion, especially in the higher religions. The movement of the religious mind, reflecting, as Hegel puts it, the "Spirit of God Himself," is naturally linked with the belief that the personal spirit has a destiny beyond the temporal order of things.[66] As a materialist, Marx maintains that personal consciousness is bound up with the bodily organism and that the hope of survival after death is the expression of religious alienation. In religion, he indicates, all reality emerges as a distortion and senseless abstraction of concrete facts.[67] Belief in immortality reflects the alienated reality of man who is under "the domination of an alien being" and "revolves round the illusory sun."[68] If the transcendent world could be rationalized fully and connected with the visible world, it would cease to be transcendent. Marx claims that representations of the supramundane in terms of this world are illusory, alienating, and unrealistic.

For Marx, as for Feuerbach, it is the species being that is immortal. In his materialistic teleology, the interest of the species or of humanity is always supreme. The goal of history lies in the full development of the supra-individual entity. Every philosopher and sociologist has found some relationship between man and nature, on the one hand, and between human individual and society, on the other. In Marx's anthropology, the emphasis is on man's externalization in nature and society so that his inner nature can become accessible to others and take its place in the realm of the social world.

The purpose of the individual creative process is to create objects "corresponding to the need of another man's essential nature."[69] Like Feuerbach, Marx indicates that "man is not only something for himself but also for others, for the general life, the species."[70] The communist individual, freed from religious alienation and from the domination of alien beings, will somehow realize his true nature in "communal nature." However, his idea that the communist individual will eliminate "the strife between man and nature, the individual and the species," and appear to have neither superego nor *id* is a mystical absurdity. In some respects, Marx's individual is reminiscent of Stirner's unique ego.

Speaking about religious alienation, Marx argues that religion always remains "the ideal, non-secular consciousness, reducing man to an alien being different from the real man."[71] Beliefs are socially caused. Men think and act in relation to their conditions of existence by means of ideologies. In all ideologies, including religion, men and their relations appear upside-down as in a *camera obscura*. This inversion, according to Marx, "arises just as much from their historical life process as the inversion of objects on the retina does from their physical life process."[72] He never departs from the view that ideologies are internal to the social relations of which they are the ideological manifestations. There is no awareness that religion and ideology derive their spontaneity and naturalness from the fact that they are not merely a discourse of social description but also a discourse of self-realization, self-affirmation, and self-identification within the human social system. Marx's analysis of religion in terms of ideology is fragmentary and inferential resisting any coherent analytical reconstruction. Man's beliefs are colored by his social and political environment, but religion is not generated by this environment. The religious reflex has its origin and focal point in the spiritual structure of man. The presence of the religious reflex expresses man's psychical incompleteness and does not depend on economics. Regardless of the magnitude of conscious human efforts to eliminate all contradictions between individuals and the given form of society, the religious reflex is unlikely to disappear from human consciousness. The universality and permanence of this reflex are now admitted by many Marxists.[73] What is entirely lacking in Marx's and Engels's criticism of religion is the fact that religion sometimes expresses a happy acceptance of the world and delight in being alive.

Progress in civilization creates new desires calling for satisfaction, and modern man may feel miserable by the absence of some comfort or convenience that his ancestors were content to do without. The suffering caused by oppression and violence, familiar in the past, has not been eliminated from modern society. Phenomena like these should warn us against an exuberant optimism. Man's attitude to life will depend on whether he takes it as something ultimate and complete, earthly and mortal, or as something pointing beyond itself. The conception of progress requires some notion of the goal to which history is moving for its justification. The real significance of any process of development cannot be discerned apart from its goal or completion, because development is far more than change. Marx, unlike Plato, advocates the inevitability of change, indicating that material development results from the capacity of matter to change, not from any supernatural creative principle. Material movement, which can neither be explained in terms of anything else nor denied, is the only principle from which all change is derived. Marx and Engels deny emphatically that spirit precedes nature or that it is the cause of change in matter and, indeed, in society. To attribute separate existence to anything in the nature of thought, mind, and life necessarily opens the door to a superstitious belief in supernatural beings or transcendental forces. Nature, they believe, is remarkable for presenting us with the paradox of continuity and change, unity and difference. The emergence of novelty even in the world of man is the mode of existence of matter.

Marx and Engels maintain that every dialectical movement is an impersonal progress that will ultimately eliminate both the religious reflex and religious alienation. They speak of progress as a necessary law of human history and as an immanent principle that carries human society inevitably toward some high destiny. Their conception of an immanent necessity controlling the movement of history reflects the evolutionary ideology of the Enlightenment. Like the philosophers of the Age of Reason, they overlook that human development does not always mean amelioration or improvement. Progress in one respect may be accompanied by regress in other respects. There may be technological progress and moral regress and, paradoxically, scientific progress resulting in the use of poisonous gas and thus in the destruction of human life. Progress is not a law; it is a task. It is also the fruit of human wills freely and responsibly dedicating themselves to making things better. Believing in the inevitability of progress, Marx and Engels fail to realize that progress presupposes spiritual freedom rather than an impersonal force molding human wills to predestined utopian ends. Their attempt to treat religion in its constructive form as being hostile to all progress is extremely tendentious exaggeration based on no proven facts. They ignore religion as a characteristic activity of the human mind and religious development as a special case of spiritual development. Although man does not create religion, he develops it as an element in his complex spiritual life. Marx and Engels overlook that the human spirit, which is at the center of religion, is active in science, art, history, and social life. These manifold activities interact and influence one another, and no positive religion finds it necessary to inhibit their rational expression.

For Marx and Engels, the driving force in history is man's relation to matter of which the mode of production is the most important. They think that religion, like philosophy and art, of any epoch in human history is the product of the methods of production and is inevitably linked to class structure and class ideology. There is no hint of the mechanism by which the class structure promotes the emergence and growth of religious consciousness. Analyzing religious phenomena in terms of socioeconomic structure, Marx assumes that religious alienation is a consequence of socioeconomic causes. Alienated and class-divided society, he states, "produces religion and inverted world consciousness."[74] Because of their preoccupation with ideas, some people in this society believe that ideas dominate the world; others, because of their miserable socioeconomic conditions, are led to invest the idea of a transcendental being. Both classes, Marx thinks, live in a world turned upside-down.[75] He fails, however, to explain the existence of religion not only in class-divided but also in primitive societies. Religious origins cannot be confined to class consciousness. Yet, he maintains that religious alienation is worst in societies divided into antagonistic classes and that it is in these societies that religion can become class ideology.

Marx and Engels, like Hegel and Feuerbach, know Christianity in its Lutheran form, which is inspired by St. Augustine and schoolmen like William of Ockham. In *Capital*, Marx speaks of the cult of the abstract man, indicating that deism and Protestantism are the most suitable religions for the borugeoisie.[76] Forming his religious convictions when a state religion was imposed upon the German people and the Lutheran clergy frequently sided with the ruling classes, it is not surprising that Marx is hostile to Christianity in both its idealistic philosophy and practice. Both of these, he says, serve a definite class interest in dulling the social feelings of the workers and binding the oppressed classes to submission to their oppressors. Both Christian principles and practice have alienating effects, leading to a complete severance between the earthly and heavenly life, between this world and another world beyond the grave. When the idea and the actual fact of human nature have been separated as completely antithetical and when the perception of the essence of humanity as free and dealienated faces a humanity completely enslaved and alienated, men must realize that they are engaged in a struggle with the illusion and inertia of religion. The fact that religion not merely expresses but also sustains and perpetuates that dualistic habit of mind that wishes to maintain the purity of the heavenly world from contamination by the secular world is enough to justify a complete break with religious illusions. Practice, according to Marx, is the only tool that will eliminate religious alienation. In the context of praxis, religion and the religious reflex will necessarily disappear.

Engels believes that early Christianity was most attractive to the oppressed and exploited classes, especially slaves, and only later became the religion of the bourgeoisie. He does not say explicitly that Christianity ceased to be the ideology of the oppressed. The idea of religion, especially Christianity, as class ideology has received more attention from Marx and Engels than the idea that it is a fantasy of alienated man. There have been phases in human history when the oppressed and exploited classes fought their class struggle for emancipation under the banner of religion. Basically, however, they think religion has hardly tried to end class divisions and economic exploitation. Marx refers to religion as "the heart of a heartless world" and to Christianity as a spent force in the sense that it serves the interests of the bourgeoisie. Overlooking the strong social sympathies of Christianity and its condemnation of the unrighteous arrogance of the wealthy, Marx attacks the social principles of Christianity because "they are capable, in case of need, of defending the oppression of the proletariat even if with somewhat doleful grimaces."[77] "The social principles of Christianity," he adds, "declare all the vile acts of the oppressors against the oppressed to be either a just punishment for original sin and other sins or trials which the Lord, in his infinite wisdom, ordains for the redeemed." Above all, he attacks the social principles of Christianity because they advocate "cowardice, self-contempt, abasement, submissiveness and humility, the qualities of the rabble."[78] This line of thought is similar to that of Nietzsche whose main objection to Christianity is that it accepts slave morality and that the God of the Christians is the God of the poor in spirit and of the humble rather than of the strong. Both Marx and Nietzsche condemn Christianity for glorifying modesty, chastity, and the morality of weaklings; for denying the value of pride; and for changing impotence into goodness, ignoble cowardice into humility, and the fighting instinct into submission and servility. They glorify the will to power and emphasize that the essence of reality is brute force. Unlike Nietzsche, who wants to use this force for creating an aristocratic and heroic race of supermen, Marx maintains that it should be used by the proletariat "which needs its courage, its self-confidence, its pride and its sense of independence even more than its bread."[79] Engels refers to this force as the "instrument with the aid of which social movement forces its way through and shatters the dead, fossilized forms" of man's social life, thus eliminating religious alienation.[80]

Marx never discusses religion in general. With the exception of a few references to deism and some rhetorical and unrestrained utterances about Judaism, all his comments and effusions concern Christianity. Most of these comments are superficial, inferential, and frequently contradictory. The idea that there is an affinity between capitalism and Christianity in the form of "English Puritanism or Dutch Protestantism" is based on purely arbitrary analogies.[81] Any philosophical person can invent such analogies between a set of mental attitudes and some socioeconomic structure. Marx merely states that the Christian religion, like Judaism, is useful for the ruling class, suggesting but not explaining a causal link between Puritanism or Protestantism and various aspects of capitalism. He believes this link plays an important role in religious alienation. Because capitalism is an alienating force, any religion associated with capitalism also must be alienating. Marx takes for granted that Christianity, like Judaism, is the "special religion of capital." In *Theories of Surplus-Value*, he indicates that in capitalism all depends on whether or not man has credit; in Christianity, it depends on faith. While the hoarding of gold and silver is associated especially with Protestantism, the monetary system is associated with Catholicism. One should note that Marx often writes about religion without considering seriously its origin, nature, or purpose;

therefore, it is not surprising that these analogies are totally arbitrary, fictitious, tendentious, and mutually inconsistent.[82] He never explains why the ruling classes also entertain religous beliefs. After all, religion is much older than any form of social organization.

Admittedly, Christians have sometimes been bourgeois in attitude, and Christian practice has sometimes, as in other human institutions, including Marxist praxis, contradicted the theory. Marxists argue that the contemporary character of organized Christianity links it with alienated bourgeois society, thus making it incompatible with humanism. Christians can answer this by saying that, in that case, contemporary Christianity is incompatible with true Christianity. In Marx's view, Christianity and humanism are incompatible. Believing that Christianity is essentially individualistic and egoistic, in opposition to all statements in the Gospels to the contrary, he argues that all forms of Christianity, like Judaism, are hostile to the working classes, and that, for that reason, the French proletariat has become irreligious.[83] This contradicts Engels's statement that the "French communists, being a part of a nation celebrated for its infidelity, are themselves Christians. One of their favourite axioms," he says, "is that Christianity is communism."[84] Like Marx, however, Engels is inconsistent, and in the "Condition of the Working Class in England in 1844" he also indicates that the "modern proletariat cannot believe in God because money is the god of this world and the bourgeois, having taken it from the worker, has made him an atheist."[85]

Speaking of religious alienation, Marx and Engels reject entirely the view that religion is rooted in the eternal aspect of human life. They claim there is no supernatural, supersensible, and heavenly world standing over and dominating the secular realm. The external world exists antecedently to and independently of a "divine" mind or any other abstract entity. Therefore, it is meaningless to talk about a divine Creator of man and nature. The majority of theologians are now satisfied that there is no necessary contradiction between the Christian doctrine of creation and the idea of evolution. Most modern scientists admit that the origin of the cosmos and the causal principles of its history will remain, unexplained and inaccessible to science. The contribution of fossils to the problem of the origin of life, they say, is a limited one. Fossils are unlikely to help, and the transformation of non-living material to living is not known to be occurring today. They emphasize that any hypothesis concerning the origin of life must depend chiefly on our knowledge of existing physico-chemical reactions, genetic and physiological processes, and the recorded development of life. Existing hypotheses are no more than intelligent guesses. Modern scientists, unless they are hostile to religion, like Marx and Engels, cling to the belief that the world is the work of some creative power, and that matter has a beginning and will have an end. They also believe in cosmic purpose. Human history is not a meaningless movement resulting from the dialectical confrontation of man's creativity with the restriction of his socioeconomic context.

Marx's materialistic theory of evolution is an unwarranted dogma. He overlooks the important link between the evolution of religious beliefs and the psychological structure of man. The phenomenon of religion is not a fortuitous or accidental aspect of man's being. Religion evolves as an aspect of the larger culture, and in its development it influences and is influenced by other aspects of culture. The present century has seen a significant change in the work of social anthropologists. Early anthropologists like E. Tylor and J. Frazer were mainly theoreticians who ignored the practical aspect of religious belief.[86] Modern anthropologists base their theories on objective investigation of religious beliefs and practices rather than on perfunctory observatioins of a tribe. Many of them reject almost entirely the ideas of Tylor and Frazer, stressing the significance of religious feeling among primitive men in contact with a supersensible power believed to control nature and human life.

Religion, of course, is related to other systems in society, but in itself it is a system of symbols and categories by which human individuals make sense of experience in terms of basic goals and spiritual needs. In the absence of these goals and needs, the destruction of religious beliefs would be justified, and "the religious reflex" could not exist.[87] Marx's analysis of religious alienation ignores the existence of religious experience that dialectical materialism will never dispel. The sense of helplessness and a feeling of dependence on a spiritual power are important biological characteristics of human beings in any social life. Marx takes for granted that religious feelings are merely the product of society. He overlooks the fact that, although religious emotions are stimulated by the social setting, they are not created by society. The religious life implies the existence of irresistible inherent forces that cannot possibly be illusory. An illusioin is short-lived and cannot last throughout human history. The Marxist view over-stresses the reflex character of religion and ignores entirely the contribution of man's own mental and spiritual activity. If man merely passively reflected the world in his mental life, he would have no internal impulse to compensate for his powerlessness before natural and social forces and no urge to create religion. The superhuman power, whether it be God or the world spirit, is not an expression of human self-alienation: it is the expression of his spiritual and mental needs. Marx and Feuerbach have failed to prove that "man makes religion." Religion is a part of human nature, and man cannot create religion any more than he can create hunger.

In their attempt to demolish the Hegelian abstractions, Marx and Engels, like Feuerbach, Bauer, and Stirner, have created new abstractions of their own—the species, "man," social individual, communal human nature, human essence, etc. One can argue that the existence of God cannot be taken for granted. It is possible to deny the existence of God. The question whether God exists or not is not amenable to any scientific method and obviously cannot be decided by observation or experiment. Natural tests, as Polanyi indicates, can only establish the natural aspects of an event and can never represent it as supernatural; thus, it is illogical to attempt to prove the supernatural using natural tests.[88] Marx and Engels totally ignore that religion, like science, is an organized body of insight, a way of thinking and knowing, a point of view and a way of life. It also has fought superstition and ignorance. Science and religion represent different aspects of man's quest for reality. In the true sense, there can be no more conflicts between these two aspects of social life. In his philosophical comments on religion and science, Bertrand Russell stresses that of these two aspects of social life, religion has been important since we have known anything about man's mental history.[89] Darwin himself is cautious in his criticism of religion. He moves from a vague belief in a supreme power when *The Origin of Species* was published in 1859 to an indifference to religious questions that marks his last years.

For Marx and Engels, science is primarily the *uncilla ideologiae*, and proletarian science always must be based on the materialist conception of history. Only "proletarian science" can eliminate the religious reflex from the minds of alienated men and thus terminate religious alienation that exists in "the realm of consciousness." Most scientists in the western world during the last two centuries have been religious men. Many of them have written about the philosophical or religious meaning that they have experienced in their research. Like theologians, they believe that the harmony and order of the Newtonian universe could be a valuable model for a society torn by social chaos and revolution. In later years, Einstein indicates that "all those individuals to whom we owe the greatest achievements of science were imbued with the truly religious convicion."[90] Niels Bohr points out that religion and science represent different sides of the human psyche, the emotive and the cognitive, and that they are deeply complementary. Arthur Eddington, Max Planck, M. Faraday, J. Thomson, and W. Heisenberg were all religious men. To them, the spiritual element in human experience is the only creative element. Like Newton and Bacon, they had no difficulty in reconciling their deeply religious beliefs with the principles of science. A small minority of scientists have been atheistically orientated. A materialistic form of naturalism, known as evolutionary monism and similar to that of Marx and Engels, has been defended by Erns Haeckel. His theory that the atom may have a simple soul and rudimentary psychic qualities has considerably influenced Engels's scientific outlook.[91]

Both Marx and Engels manipulate scientific ideas for ideological ends. One of these ends is the destruction of religious beliefs, assuming that it would be followed by the return of man from his illusory and alienated world to the world of "reality." They believe the denial of God is a prerequisite to "proletarian scientific" research. Like religion, science is treated in terms of class consciousness. Instead of simply being neutral with respect to all values, science, in Marxist ideology, must serve the interests of the proletarian class. Only in that way will science be successful in the struggle against religious alienation. Science must be class conscious as long as there are classes in the social structure. Mindful of religious alienation, Lenin urges that "the proletariat must enlist proletarian science in the battle against the fog of religion.''[92] In the struggle against the world in which religion is "the spiritual aroma," Marx does not rule out religious persecution. Although his ideas about the exact method of eliminating "the opium of the people" are far from being clear and consistent, the praxis in communist countries is full of religious persecution. Modern Marxists justify this persecution on the ground that religion is anti-scientific, parasitic, and intolerant. They refer frequently to the persecution of scientists at the time of Inquisition, especially that of Copernicus, a faithful Christian, and Giordano Bruno, who unfortunately was burned alive in 1600. They overlook, however, that there is a Marxist "Inquisition." Marxism, as many modern scientists indicate, is hostile to science and persecutes scientists. Although Antoine Lavoisier, the founder of modern chemistry, could not have been guillotined by the Marxists, his executioners were atheists inspired by persecuting tendencies similar to those of modern communists.[93] One can add, however, that just as the Church did not persecute scientists for their vocational calling but only for acting against a specific doctrine, so does the Marxist state act in regard to its own beliefs.

The distinguishing mark of Marx's theory of religious alienation is the assumption that this alienation is the outgrowth of specific historical conditions molded by man's unwitting activity. The view of theologians, philosophers, existentialists and many sociologists and anthropologists that alienation is essentially a psychological phenomenon is treated as a superficial approach. Marx shares Feuerbach's view that the gods are human wish-projection and that religious ideas have their sole origin in the social intercourse of man with man. He thinks that insofar as religion had any reality, it is the product of this world. It is always assumed that the fantasy, dream, and postulate of religion are the aspects of the sovereignty of man but of man as an alien being. Marx has no doubt that after eliminating "the fantastic reality of heaven" men will be capable of producing a compensatory consolation that will consist of "real happiness."[94] There is hardly anything convincing in this vague and metaphysical prediction of self-realization. Rejecting all absolute values and cosmic teleology, Marx fails to offer any consolation to the communist man except that he will survive death in the form of the species being.[95]

Marx's criticism of religion follows the critiques of religious thought by Feuerbach and the Young Hegelians. The most striking feature of this criticism is the assumption that religious beliefs are merely the projection of the essence of man onto an imaginary heavenly being possessing supernatural qualities. Religion, Marx argues, has nothing to do with human nature. Religious phenomena can only be understood in the light of the real conditions of man's empirical life. The theories that postulate religious man as "the starting point of history" and "put the religious production of fancies in the place of the real productioin of the means of subsistence and of life itself" must, in his view, be rejected.[96] Marx takes for granted that Hegelian idealism is absolutely wrong and that his own theory about religion is absolutely correct. He blames the German thinkers for failing to solve the problem of religious "illusions" without realizing that he also has failed to penetrate the mystery of the origin of religion.[97] It is important to remember that Marx's criticism of religion revolves round the function, practice, and effects of the belief in supernatural powers. He says nothing about the origin of religion. In his brief references to religion as "the heart of a heartless world, the spirit of spiritless conditions and the opium of the people," the origin of religion is never explained. He rejects the view that religion is a basic fact of human culture and speaks inconsistently of religious beliefs in terms of socioeconomic relations, social practices, real life, illusions, illusory happiness, fantastic projections, and class domination. Max Weber, admitting some connection between Protestantism aned capitalism, rejects the view that religion is ever a simple function of social position. Capitalism and proletarianism, he says, are "not expressible in a religious form" and the origin of religion cannot be related to either of them.[98] The fact remains that the origin of religion cannot be a matter of precise historical knowledge but merely of conjecture.[99] Yet, there is no reason to think that anthropological and philosophical conjectures, affirming the universality of religion, are less trustworthy than similar hypotheses regarding the origin of species.

Comte indicates that the "scientific spirit" would not have arisen without the protection and stimulation of the "religious spirit." Like Comte, Durkheim is convinced that the "demonstrative value" of religious experience is not inferior to that of "scientific experiments." Durkheim's main error, however, lies in the belief that religion originates in "collective states of mind, not in individual feelings."[100] Arguing that religious problems are primarily psychological problems, Jung rejects the view that all religions are "concocted out of the head."[101] The human head, he says, is inadequate when it comes "to thinking up" religious ideas and symbols. Marx's theory of religious alienation makes no attempt to explain the psychological origin of religious needs. Thus his tendency to lapse into functional explanation makes his theory of religious alienation myopic, illusory, and worthless. The distinguishing mark of this theory is the belief that religion originates merely as a compensation for the economic suffering of the oppressed classes. It is in this sense, he thinks, that religion is the "opium of the people." The view of those who maintain that this and similar descriptions of religion are not Marx's call for religious destruction and persecution cannot be supported. He frequently associates some religions with capitalist greed and egoism and "demands" their destruction. He advocates "the struggle against religion" and insists that man must "shake off the chains of religious enslavement."[102] Everyone knows that many religious practices are repugnant and alienating, but this does not mean that religion as such is an invention either of the rulers or of the ruled. In human history, religion sometimes may have been class-orientated, but positive religion always rises above class. Identifying the nature of religion with religious practices, Marx concludes falsely that socioeconomic change can eradicate religion itself.

6
Philosophical Alienation

The generation of philosophers that succeeded to Kant's heritage sought to complete his philosophical work on its positive side. Kant had originally been an adherent of the school of Wolff, who had attempted to systematize the philosophy of Leibniz. Leibniz's philosophy was popular and influential in Germany, but outside Germany it had little influence. His contemporary, Locke, dominated British philosophy; in France, Descartes continued to influence French philosophy until he was overthrown by Voltaire and the Encyclopaedists, who popularized English empiricism. As in England, the rationalists in France directed their criticism against the religious beliefs that seemed to them to be superstitious and irrational.[1] The strife against irratioinalism and the forces of obscurantism took a sharper and more virulent tone in France than in England, where Locke appealed to the religious men and women to leave theology and return to the simplicity and reasonableness of the New Testament. Reasonableness was the dominant note of Locke's life and work. His writings were not intended as a systematic study of rules and laws to which thinking should conform but rather as a description of the ways in which human beings proceed when they are thinking about the social, political, religious, scientific, and moral problems of life. Nor were they intended to be a logical or ideological analysis of the elements involved in human understanding, although they contain a partial analysis. The victory of Locke's empiricist philosophy in England and France resulted largely from the prestige of scientific researches of Newton whose cosmogony somewhat minimized philosophical respect for Cartesian philosophy.

Hume's skepticism was too far from common sense to appeal to the French philosophers of the Enlightenment. In reaction against both Berkeleyan idealism and Hume's skepticism, the French Enlightenment tended to a thorough materialism that, as Marx and Engels indicate, merely substituted the nature goddess for the Christian God. In *Holy Family*, Marx rightly points out that the French Enlightenment of the eighteenth century and particularly French materialism were not only a struggle against the existing political institutions and the existing religion and theology but also an open struggle against all metaphysics, in particular that of Descartes, Malebranche, Spinoza, and Leibniz. Philosophy, he states, "was counterposed to metaphysics just as Feuerbach, in his first resolute attack on Hegel, counterposed sober philosophy to wild speculation."[2] In *L'Homme Machine* (*Man a machine*), La Mettrie reduced man, as Descartes had reduced the animal, to a mere automaton or a body governed by purely physical laws.[3] Helvetius carried Condillac's principle of sensationalism into the moral and practical realm, stressing that egoism or self-interest is the sole motive of all our action. A similar view is expressed by Holbach in *System of Nature*.[4] "Nature," he says, "invites man to love himself incessantly to augment the sum of his happiness; religion orders him to love only a formidable God who is worthy of hatred, to detest and despise himself."

Marx vaguely refers to materialism as the "natural-born son of Great Britain," indicating that the Franciscan schoolman Duns Scotus attributed the power of thought to matter.[5] Nothing is said about materialism of Democritus. Duns Scotus was not a materialist but a moderate realist who denied the validity of natural theology, believed in the divine origin of truth, and even defended the doctrine of the Immaculate Conception.[6] Marx rightly states that Francis Bacon is the first scientifically minded philosopher who has emphasized the importance of induction as opposed to deduction. He is wrong, however, in referring to Bacon as "the real progenitor of English materialism." Bacon believed that reason could prove the existence of God but that other truths in theology could be known only by revelation. Philosophical truths, however, depend only on reason. In his essay "Of Atheism," Bacon points out that "those who deny a God destroy man's nobility and are ignoble creatures." Unaware of his inconsistency, Marx is simultaneously affirming and denying Baconian materialism. This materialism, he says, contains "theistic prejudices" and "inconsistencies imported from theology."[7] It was Hobbes, "Bacon's continuator," who had shattered these prejudices." Although Hobbes was a materialist in some respects, he felt passionately about religion and God. The nature of God is incomprehensible. "We know nothing of what he is but only that he is." In *Leviathan* he maintains that God is the cause of the world.[8] Under Galileo's influence, Hobbes arrived at the view that motion is the fundamental conception for explaining not only the physical world but also the reactions of man and society.

Leibniz's optimistic philosophy continued to influence German thinkers during the entire German Enlightenment. The philosophic systems of Leibniz and Wolff crystallized into a modern scholasticism that opposed the orthodox theology. Unlike the philosophical systems of the French materialists of the Age of Reason, Leibniz's philosophy is based on metaphysics that is well expressed in his spiritual pluralism and in his definition of substance as activity, energy, and force. In opposition to Spinoza, Leibniz makes of the individuals the unique centers of life and energy. Kant, aware of the "fashion of the French philosophers to despise metaphysics," firmly believed that it is only the "science" of metaphysics that can solve the problems of God, immortality, and freedom. His philosophy is widely known as formal, logical, or critical idealism and most commonly as the critical philosophy. This philosophy postulates a unitary and substantial soul behind the changing content of experience and thus attempts to render conceivable, through the idea of God, the totality of existence, self, and world. The metaphysical development of post-Kantian German idealism, as represented by Fichte, Schelling, and Hegel, ended in monism, pantheism, and evolutionism. The new German speculative philosophy not only eliminated the "thing in itself," but it also substituted immanence for transcendence and necessity for freedom.

At the beginning of the nineteenth century, philosophers were much concerned with epistemological problems involving the relationship between knowledge and ultimate reality. Fichte's philosophy starts from the attempt to take seriously Kant's conception of the unity of experience. "A philosophical system", he writers, "is not a piece of dead household furniture which one can use or lay aside at pleasure, but is animated by the soul of the man who has it." The fundamental fact in the universe is free spirit. The world is a creation of spirit rather than, as the materialist holds, its source. Fichte reads the riddle of human life by viewing it as a moral conflict between the forces of the ideal self and the non-self, a world of unspiritual material things. While Kant's categories and principles play a significant role in the unification of human experience and originate in the mind rather than in objects, Fichte finds their source in the pure activity of the Ego. The Absolute Ego is very different from the individual self. The individual transcends his finitude and knows what he really is only when he has recognized his identity with the infinite Ego. The Ego is not merely consciousness because it also includes will, and the two sides are inseparable. Whereas Fichte subordinates the object to the conscious subject, Schelling seeks a higher unity in the Absolute. For Schelling, the "universal organum of philosophy is the philosophy of art."[9] The "ideal work of art and the real world of objects", he says, "are the products of one and the same activity." The meeting of the conscious and the unconscious gives without consciousness the real and with consciousness the aesthetic world. Schelling is ultimately led to postulate a common source for nature and intelligence. In this source the differences between the two disappear in an abstract identity, suggesting Spinoza's position. Unlike Fichte and later Marx, Schelling argues that speculative knowledge cannot be subordinated to practical knowledge because this knowledge is an end in itself. Like Hegel, he points out that the knowledge of the Absolute is the highest end of thought and action. In the consciousness of the self as a part of the Absolute, all contradictions and difficulties of life must disappear.

Marx's letter to Feuerbach in 1843 suggests that Schelling was a popular philosopher not only in Germany but also in France. "To the French romantics and mystics," Marx writes, Schelling presents his idealism as "the union of philosophy and theology," to the French matrialists as "the union of philosophy and theology," to the French materialists as "the union of flesh and idea," and to the French skeptics as "the destroyer of dogmaticism."[10] He was regarded by some French writers as the "man who replaced transcendental idealism by rational realism, abstract thought by thought with flesh and blood, specialised philosophy by world philosophy." Marx indicates that Schelling's philosophy is "Prussian policy *sub specie philosophiae.*" In his later writings Schelling definitely became more mystical and held, like neo-Platonists, that the highest end is the immediate vision of God or the Absolute and that such vision is higher than reflective knowledge.

The movement of philosophical thinking from Kant to Hegel revolved around the idea of man's self-realization as a godlike being. Hegel views experience as the self-evolution of Absolute mind in which the logician, historian, clergyman, scientist, and transcendental philosopher go through the same stages of development. The main difference in their self-realization is that some proceed to the goal of perfection empirically, in space-time fumbling, whereas others approach that goal in metaphysically self-conscious reflection. In *Phenomenology of Spirit*, Hegel indicates that philosophy does not move in the inert and abstract realm of mathematics but rather in the actual and organic progression of distinct phases, some of which negate what went before and are themselves later negated in the final unity of opposites. Negation is essential to both conception and being, but it operates within a unity. The sequence of phases involves a blend of the contingently historical and the logically necessary. The method of philosophy must be set forth by logic and, for Hegel, logic is the same as metaphysics.[11] Marx rejects Hegel's logic as "alienated thinking" that merely abstracts from nature and from real man.[12] In his *Logic*, Hegel defines logic as the "science of the pure Idea."[13] Logic deals with universal concepts, and thought itself is primarily universal. Logic begins with pure Being, the most universal and abstract conception, and ends with the Absolute Idea that entails all conceptions in a complex totality. For Kant, the inner reality is so different from its phenomenon that it cannot be known; for Hegel, the phenomenon manifests its essence and the essence is the truth of its appearance. Hegel sees the world of experience as a progressive embodiment of reason. Nature receives its true meaning when it is recognized as a part of the process in which Mind expresses itself and asserts its own freedom. Mind or Spirit entails the union of nature and consciousness.[14]

Like Marx, Engels praises and criticizes the Hegelian system of philosophy. "In this system—and herein is its great merit," he writes, "for the first time the whole world, natural, historical, intellectual, is represented as a process, i.e., as in constant motion, change, transformation, development, and the attempt is made to trace out the internal connection that makes a continuous whole of all this movement and development."[15] Hegel is regarded as the "most encyclopaedic mind of his time" who "had freed history from metaphysics and made it dialectic." Yet, "Hegel was an idealist. To him the thoughts within his brain," Engels adds, "were not merely abstract pictures of actual things and processes but even worse things and their evolution are only the realised pictures of the Idea, existing somewhere from eternity before the world was. This way of thinking turned everything upside-down and completely reversed the actual connection of things in the world."[16] While Marx speaks of Hegel's philosophy as the expression of "the alienation of human thought," Engels prefers a milder criticism and refers to it as a system of inversion. There is no explanation of what is meant by saying that Hegel has "freed history from metaphysics." Surely, Hegel's philosophical system is metaphysical *par excellence*.

Analyzing atomism in *Logic*, Hegel argues that it is impossible to escape metaphysics and cease to trace nature back to terms of thought by throwing ourselves into the arms of atomism. "The atom," he points out, "is itself a thought; and hence the theory which holds matter to consist of atoms is a metaphysical theory. Newton gave physics an express warning to beware of metaphysics, it is true. But, to his honour be it said, he did not by any means obey his own warning. The only mere physicists are the animals; they alone do not think, while man is a thinking being and a born metaphysician."[17] Because philosophy, in Hegel's view, is the unity of "art and religion" and as such "not merely keeps them together to make a totality but also raises them to self-conscious thought," the objects of philosophy, on the whole, are "the same as those of religion. In both the object is Truth, in that supreme sense in which God and God only is the Truth. Both in like manner go on to treat of the finite worlds of Nature and the human mind, with their relation to each other and to their truth in God."[18] Philosophy, according to Hegel, does not move in the "inert, abstract realm of mathematics" but rather in the "actual world." "As the thought of the world, it appears only when the actuality is already there."[19] If philosophy merely projected abstract ideals or images beyond real social relations rather than thought, it would no longer be philosophy but a medium of religion or art. Hegel criticizes Kant's philosophy of consciousness, not because it grants too much importance to sense perception but because it grants it too little importance. The object of consciousness, he says, is a "combination of sense qualities with attributes or wider range by which thought defines concrete relations and connections."[20]

In his criticism of Hegel's philosophy, Marx argues that this philosophy "transforms everything into thought, into the holy, into apparition, into spirit, into spirits, into spectres."[21] The distinction between consciousness and its object is practically eliminated. Nature and materiality become the inverted appearance of self-consciousness. Hegel, he says, makes man the man of self-consciousness instead of making self-consciousness the self-consciousness of man, of real man living in a real, objective world and determined by that world.[22] Hegel's *Encyclopaedia*, Marx adds, is in "its entirety nothing but the display, the self-objectification, of the essence of the philosophic mind, and the philosophic mind is nothing but the estranged mind of the world thinking within its self-estrangement, i.e., comprehending itself abstractly."[23] Instead of setting out from the estrangement of the real man with his feet on the solid ground, Hegel starts from the estrangement of substance and self-consciousness.

For Hegel, substance is spirit, the self-conscious unity of the self and essence. Each has for the other the significance of alienation. In its simple being, spiritual essence, he says, is pure consciousness, and this pure consciousness is self-consciousness.[24] The process by which the substance becomes actual entails the alienation of man. In the process of dividing itself, self-consciousness establishes the object as the reverse of itself; thus inversion results from estrangement of self-consciousness. According to Marx, Hegel identifies alienation with objectification insofar as consciousness recognizes itself as alien to itself. The reappropriation of self-consciousness is for Hegel the transcendence of the objective world, a process of incorporation into self-consciousness. "The man who takes hold of his essential being is merely the self-consciousness which takes hold of objective essences. Return of the object into the self is therefore the reappropriation of the object."[25] Objects in the Hegelian world are strictly thought-entities and as such can only express the estrangement of pure, abstract, and philosophical thinking. "It is precisely from abstract thought that these objects are estranged and which they confront with their arrogation of reality." Objectivity itself is alienated self-consciousness. This means that for Hegel overcoming alienation is the transcending of objectivity, a process that takes place in consciousness. Identifying being and thought, Hegel is led necessarily to analyze the history of the abstract Idea as if it were the real, corporeal, and material entity. In his philosophical system, empirical reality assumes the character of being the real truth of the Idea or God, and real human practice is transformed into a mere manifestation of this Idea. Hegel's idealistic philosophy, according to Marx, is, like his religion, an inverted consciousness of the world produced by an inverted world. In Hegelianism, the philosopher, who is himself an abstract form of estranged man, becomes the measuring rod of the estranged world. The whole history of the process of alienation and the whole process of the transcendence of alienation, therefore, are only the history of the production of abstract, logical, and speculative thought.[26]

Analyzing the inversion of being and consciousness in Hegelian philosophy, Marx argues that Hegel's conception of alienation and the inversion it entails indicate clearly that he "stands the world on its head" and that the real subjects are turned into the predicates.[27] Appropriation of man's estranged and objectified essential power, he says, only occurs in consciousness, in pure thought, or abstraction. In Hegel's mind, both alienation and inversion are inherent conditions of self-consciousness; inversion is given in the breaking-up of self-consciousness. Spirit, Hegel says in *Phenomenology*, "constructs for itself not merely a world but a world that is double, divided and self-opposed." Equilibrium of the whole is not the unity that remains within itself, nor the contentment that comes from having returned into itself, but rests on the alienation of opposites. The whole, therefore, like each single moment, is a self-alienated actuality. It always splits into self-consciousness and pure consciousness that is not a present actuality but exists only for faith.[28] For Marx, it is not the alienation of self-consciousness that generates an inverted objective reality, but the other way around—it is an inverted reality reflected in thought-entities that generate an inverted consciousness. In Hegel's conception of alienation, the sensuously concrete particulars are taken up as abstractions of themselves, and their real material generation together with their material existence leave the picture altogether. Contrary to Hegel's "abstract universal," Marx advocates "concrete universal" that is a determinate mode of being of things only when it has a material, corporeal, and sensuous basis. In Hegel's philosophy of concepts, ideas, and thought-entities, everything is upside-down, and for this reason Marx scorns the abstract philosopher who pretends to be the measuring rod of the estranged world.[29]

Examining Hegel's conception of alienation, Marx points out that self-consciousness divorced from the world of objects confirms alienation. Human consciousness is the consciousness of sensuous and natural human beings, not the consciousness of abstract, unreal men created by estranged philosophers. "Sensuous consciousness," he adds, "is not an abstractly sensuous consciousness but a humanly sensuous consciousness."[30] Because men's activities are necessarily expressed in a social framework, real sensuous consciousness must be their consciousness of being involved in a socioeconomic structure. Any abstraction or inversion from these fundamental realities of life can only result in an alienated self-consciousness. Marx criticizes Hegel for inverting the real relationship between the concrete and the abstract, giving the existential status to the products of the mind and making the actual world of particulars the mere hypostasis of the abstract essence. He insists that the relations of these particulars are not logical but material. Hegel has mistakingly identified all externalization of man's essential powers with alienation. These two processes are meaningless when associated with the Absolute. From Marx's point of views, the objectification of man's essential powers and capacities is perverted into alienation only under certain historical conditions.

Marx praises Hegel for realizing that man is the result of his labor conditions. The positive feature of *Phenomenology*, he indicates, is that Hegel "conceives the self-genesis of man as a process, conceives objectification as loss of the object, as alienation and thus grasps the essence of labour."[31] However, Marx criticizes Hegel for seeing only one side of this process—the alienation of self-consciousness—and neglecting the alienation of the actual man who produces the commodities of life and has sensuous objects outside himself rather than in his mind. Whereas Hegel thinks of labor in terms of mental, conceptual activity, Marx sees it in terms of material production and class society. Examining the secrets of capitalist production, Marx develops the forms and features of labor into a constellation of diversified alienation, reflecting various facets of the relations of production in their historical development. The process by which man becomes alienated in the product of his labor passes through distinct stages of socioeconomic development. For Marx, alienation is above all a social expression of man's inability to build an integrated, harmonious, inwardly stable, and constantly developing system of socioeconomic relations. It is only when all inequalities in social and economic conditions of human life are eliminated that the gap between actual and potential self-realization will be transcended and men will be able to realize their creative potentialities.

Beginning with the fact that man is a specific part of nature, Marx argues against Hegel that "abstractly mental labour" cannot generate "essential objects, indispensable to the manifestation and confirmation of man's essential powers."[32] On the materialist basis of reality, he thinks, it is not difficult to account for the genesis of "abstractly mental labour." Although Hegel conceives man's act of self-genesis in labor, for him the movement of self-genesis in the form of self-alienation is "regarded as a divine process, a process traversed by man's abstract, pure, absolute essence that is distinct from him."[33] According to Marx, alienated labor or the alienated form of man's productive activity is the key to all alienation. Slavery is the first organized system of alienated labor and wage labor will be the last. Because philosophic alienation, like that of religion, occurs only in consciousness and economic alienation is that of real life, the influence of spiritual and psychical factors in the genesis of alienation is insignificant compared with its economic causes. The real basis of alienation within non-communist society is found in the contradictory relations of its mode of production and in the class antagonisms arising from these antagonisms. Criticizing Stirner's conception of the "alienation of the ego," Marx definitely links the "inverted world" of ideologists and philosophers with the division of labor and class structure. "The philosophers," he says, "have only to dissolve their language into the ordinary language from which it is abstracted, in order to recognise it as the distorted language of the actual world and to realise that neither thoughts nor language in themselves form a realm of their own, that they are only manifestations of actual life."[34]

"The immediate task of philosophy," according to Marx, "once the holy form of human alienation has been unmasked, is to unmask estrangement in its unholy" ideological forms.[35] He adds that "philosophy cannot be made a reality without the abolition of the proletariat and that the proletariat cannot be abolished without philosophy being made a reality."[36] The general idea expressed here is that philosophy, like religion, science, and law, is class-orienated and that a new materialist philosophy must be based, as Althusser puts it, on a proletarian class position.[37] In Marxist terminology, the proletarian-orienated theory of philosophical thinking must be joined with a new practice of philosophy. While Hegel and his followers define philosophy as the "exploration of the rational" and deify it as a cosmic force that makes and unmakes an unfolding series of historic developments, Marx defines it in terms of the "real existence of man and nature," stressing its dependence on the existing social relations and productive forces.[38] By inverting and misrepresenting the real relationship between the production of ideas and material production, bourgeois philosophers, in Marx's view, have blinded themselves in believing that their philosophical ideas and principles could be divorced from the social relations they express. These ideas and principles, Marx says, are "historical and transitory products."[39]

Marx rejects all philosophy that is opposed to "concrete, historical thinking." Philosophy as idealism is alienating and incompatible with the historical world. The alienated world must be changed, but it cannot be changed by theoretically criticizing its existing structure. It must, he admits, be understood and then transformed by effective revolutionary action. Marx insists on the unity of theory and practice. Proletarian philosophy needs both practical and theoretical knowledge. Although all philosophies, including Hegel's, claim to be ultimately practical, Marx believes that his philosophical theory is the first to become aware of the importance of practice. Thinking and being, he indicates in *Manuscripts*, are indeed distinct, but they are still in unity with each other. Idealism has developed the active side of the subject but only abstractly. It is self-evident, he thinks, that idealism explains practice from the idea rather than the idea from practice. The belief of philosophers that ideas rule the world originates in the division of society into classes. The formation of ideas, Marx claims, can only be "explained from material practice."[40] Any attempt to draw a picture of reality from ideas and concepts alone can only produce "false consciousness" and alienation.

Although Marx's philosophic thought has been shaped by Hegel's metaphysics with its emphasis on the alienation of self-consciousness, he criticizes Hegelian philosophy for systematizing and confirming philosophic alienation in all its forms. Metaphysical thought expressed in the conception of the alienation of self-consciousness, Marx believes, confuses the abstract and the real: it takes the abstract for the real and translates the real abstractly. The solution of theoretical riddles must be the task of practice, and true practice is the condition of a real and positive philosophical theory. The comprehension of "material practice" can easily replace any abstractly conceived logic. Abstract spiritualism and abstract materialism, being merely theoretical, cannot penetrate into the secrets of philosophic alienation. Specializing in the production of general ideas, philosophers and abstract thinkers, Marx argues, are the heroes of the alienation process. They imagine they are the true makers of history and the "measuring rod of the estranged world." In opposition to old mechanical materialism and abstract idealism, he defends practical and dialectical materialism, and in the name of this materialism he condemns all speculative philosophy. He sees both philosophy and religion as manifestations of the same estrangement. They are in an alienated form because of their interconnection with alienated forms of productive activity. The philosophy of pure thought merely reflects real, sensuous, and material practice; therefore, it must be transcended. The transition from Hegelian philosophy to "practical materialism," Marx believes, is equivalent to the transition from speculation to "practical science." What this science is, he has never explained. He merely associates the false consciousness of philosophy with non-scientific forms of consciousness and the alienation of self-consciousness with the alienation of other forms of the superstructure.

In his analysis of philosophic alienation, Marx's thought vacillates continually between "practical materialism" and "scientific realism," always assuming that they are synonymous. Engels has failed to clarify the similarity between "modern dialectical philosophy" and "proletarian science" as expressed in Marx's writings. He indicates that Marxism is "no longer a philosophy at all but simply a world outlook which has to establish its validity and be applied not in a science of sciences standing apart, but in the positive sciences. Philosophy is therefore sublated here, that is, both overcome and preserved; overcome as regards its form and preserved as regards its content."[41] The fact is that Marxism is not science in any real science. Despite the claim of "scientific Marxists" that Marxism is science, it is not, and many commentators rightly emphasize that Marx's philosophical ideas are predominantly class-orientated.[42] Marx admits that his philosophy tands or falls on Hegel's philosophy, and he never claims to be more than a critic of mystifying ideas, alienated concepts, and abstractions. In his criticism of speculative and alienated philosophy, Marx frequently accuses Hegel and his followers of inversions and prides himself on his own reversions. By making the material the foundation for the spiritual as opposed to the abstract the foundation for the physical, he believes he has successfully eliminated Hegel's metaphysics. Yet, he assumes incorrectly that the transition from idealism to practical materialism is necessarily the transcendence of philosophy and that his own ideas are free from alienating effects.

Before the final split of the Young Hegelians near the end of 1844, Marx and Engels, the most radical of the left-wing movement, insisted that the function of philosophy must be critical. Criticism of religion is not enough. Although criticism of religion is the starting point of the Young Hegelian movement, this criticism, in Marx's view, "does nothing but construct formulae out of the categories of what exists, namely out of the existing Hegelian philosophy and the existing social aspirations. Formulae, nothing but formulae. And despite all its invectives against dogmatism, it condemns itself to dogmatism. It is and remains an old woman—faded, widowed Hegelian philosophy which paints and adorns its body, shrivelled into the most repulsive abstraction."[43] He remarks sarcastically that in "critical criticism" of the Young Hegelians, "everything that is real and living is un-critical" and that only the ideal, fantastic creatures of critical criticism are "everything." Rejecting the view of Edgar Bauer about human nature, Marx accuses him of transforming all the "attributes and manifestations of human nature into their negation and into alienations of human nature."[44] Marx apparently agrees with Bruno Bauer that the criticism of religion is the premise of all criticism and that the criticism of religious alienation leads to the criticism of other forms of alienation. Yet, Marx viciously attacks Bauer's philosophy of self-consciousness and his conception of "metaphysical alienation." The theological antithesis of faith and reason in Bauer's philosophy, according to Marx, has been resolved into the critical-theological antithesis of common sense and pure critical thought. "What he combats in substance is not the metaphysical illusion but its mundane kernel-nature, nature as it exists outside man and as man's nature."[45] Because Bauer's criticism ends up in Hegelian idealism, Marx points out that he, like Hegel, gives priority to self-consciousness rather than to conscious being, the being of men in their actual life process. Thus Bauer's "metaphysical-theological caricature of man in his severance from nature" necessarily leads him to speak only of the alienation of self-consciousness.[46]

It is ironic that *The Holy Family* has been written under the influence of Feuerbach's materialistic or rather pseudomaterialistic views expressed partly in *Essence of Christianity*, *Theses*, and *Principles*. Although impressed by Feuerbach's endeavor to formulate the philosophy of man without any link with the philosophy of the Absolute and "to demonstrate that the essence of speculative philosophy is the same as that of theology," Marx could not resist also criticizing Feuerbach's philosophy. This criticism appears mainly in *German Ideology* and "Theses on Feuerbach." According to Marx, Feuerbach "realises that man too is an object of the senses." However, Feuerbach "still remains in the realm of theory and never arrives at the actually existing active men."[47] In *Manuscripts*, Marx praises Feuerbach as the conqueror of the old philosophy. Positive, humanistic, and naturalistic criticism begins with Feuerbach alone. One of Feuerbach's great achievements, he adds, is the "proof that philosophy is nothing else but religion rendered into thoughts and that it has therefore to be condemned as another form of existence of the estrangement of the essence of man."[48] A similar commendation appears in *The Holy Family*. Feuerbach, Marx writes, "did away with the very categories with which Criticism now operates—the real wealth of human relations, the immense content of history, the struggle of history, the fight of the mass against the Spirit, etc."[49] Marx also points out that Feuerbach is the first to describe philosophy as speculative and mystical empiricism and the first to insist that philosophy must come down from the heaven of speculation to the depth of human misery.[50]

In "Theses on Feuerbach," Marx argues against defects of all previous forms of materialism, including that of Feuerbach himself which is the particular target. In contradiction to practical materialism, Feuerbach, according to Marx, does not conceive human activity itself as objective activity. Instead, his materialistic views are inconsistent and essentially metaphysical. He conceives of practice only "in its dirty Jewish form of appearance."[51] In many ways, Feuerbach is still an idealist. He fails to draw his attention to the role of human practice in the critical comprehension of the objective world and its forms of alienation. Having only an abstract conception of man in isolation from historical reality, Feuerbach does little more than indicate religious self-estrangement in an estranged world. He never asks why the process of estrangement occurs or tries to explain it. From Marx's point of view, Feuerbach is merely rejecting the Hegelian conception of the estrangement of self-consciousness. Marx agrees with Feuerbach that the beginning of philosophy is not the Absolute, not being as the predicate of the Absolute but rather the finite, the definite, and the real. However, he entirely rejects Feuerbach's conception of alienation. The phenomenon of alienation, he indicates, must be seen as the result of the real living conditions of men. Neither Feuerbach nor traditional, mechanical materialism can provide an adequate basis for a struggle against the estranged forms of consciousness. Both fail to see that the essence of man is the ensemble of social, economic, and class relations.

In *Poverty of Philosophy*, Marx remarks that Feuerbach's talent is poor compared with Hegel's. Yet, he adds, Feuerbach "was epoch-making after Hegel because he laid stress on certain points which were disagreeable to the Christian consciousness but important for the progress of criticism, points which Hegel had left in mystic semi-obscurity."[52] The distinguishing mark of Marx's judgment of Feuerbach is ambivalence. This ambivalence persists in most of his major philosophical works. Even in *Manuscripts*, in which Marx's assessment of Feuerbach's achievements is definitely the most favorable, he does not spare Feuerbach from his negative criticism.[53] Because Feuerbach's philosophy affirms theology and transcendentalism, his position remains fundamentally dualistic, offering no solution to the problems of alienation. He, according to Marx, deals with these problems only in a theoretical, abstract way. Preoccupied with religious alienation, Feuerbach cannot concentrate on the perceptibly alienated expression of human activity. His main error, Marx remarks in *Theses*, is that he conceives reality and sensuousness "only in the form of the object or of contemplation," thus entirely ignoring practice.[54] Marx maintains that the truly materialistic conception of practice should be analyzed in terms of observable changes in the objective world and that the materialist conception of alienation should never be divorced from the material basis and "revolutionary practice."

Engels holds a similar ambivalent view about the relevance of Feuerbach's role in materialist philosophy. Indicating that Feuerbach's philosophy is in many respects an intermediate link between Hegel's philosophy and Marx's and his own, Engels, unaware of inconsistency, simultaneously refers to him as a materialist and an idealist. Feuerbach's *Essence of Christianity*, he writes, "placed materialism on the throne again," and even Marx "was influenced by it" in writing *The Holy Family*.[55] As a materialist, Engels says, Feuerbach realizes that "the Hegelian premundane existence of the absolute idea, the pre-existence of the logical categories before the world existed, is nothing more than the fantastic survival of the belief in the existence of an extramundane Creator; that the material, sensously perceptible world is the only reality and that our consciousness and thinking are the product of a material, bodily organ, the brain."[56] While still a materialist, Feuerbach has rejected both

Hegel's speculative philosophy and his idea that nature is a mere alienation of the Absolute. However, Engels argues that Feuerbach is not a consistent thinker. Believing that philosophy must be absorbed in religion, he can only think in terms of religious alienation. He cannot, in Engel's view, overcome the customary philosophical prejudice against materialism.[57] Feuerbach lumps together the materialism that is a general world outlook, resting upon a definite conception of the relation between matter and mind and the special form in which this world outlook was expressed in the eighteenth century. Like Marx in *Theses*, Engels indicates that Feuerbach appeals to sensuous objects but fails to conceive human activity itself as activity that belongs to the objective world. Engels concludes that Feuerbach, in fact, is an idealist. His idealism, Engels argues, is reflected in his refusal to accept "mutual relations based on reciprocal inclination between human beings" without associating them with a particular religion. "The chief thing for him is not that these purely human relations exist but that they shall be conceived of as the new, true religion."[58] Like Marx, Engels refers to Feuerbach's "astonishing poverty" when compared with Hegel.

Many commentators, including theologians and philosophers, indicate that Feuerbach is not a materialist but a humanist. In his Introduction to Feuerbach's *Essence of Christianity*, Karl Barth states that Feuerbachian philosophy is not an entirely negative phenomenon. He wrongly assumes, however, that Feuerbach's "frankly sensuous philosophy" is in some respects superior to Kant's and Hegel's philosophies. Feuerbach merely criticizes these philosophies for "separating essence from material sensuous existence, from the world, from man," but this does not make his philosophy less mystifying and alienating and in profundity infinitely inferior to Hegel's and Kant's idealism.[59] Feuerbach's hatred of transcendentalism and speculative philosophy often led him to seek the complex explanation in purely physical terminology. His teaching, as Marx and Engels remark, aims to be "a frankly sensuous philosophy" as opposed to the shadowy phantoms of supernaturalism and idealism. Marx thinks Feuerbach is right to protest against the power exercised over man by all forms of objectification and alienation that claim to be transcendental, metaphysical reality. He is also right in stressing that the main task of truly materialist philosophy is to unmask human alienation in its secular form. Marx argues, however, that Feuerbach is far from being a positive and consistent philosopher. In fact, his philosophy contradicts the essentially historical character of practical and dialectical materialism, ignores entirely the relevance of practice, and fails to trace the origin of alienation to alienated labor and alienated social relations.

Marx analyzes the genesis of philosophic alienation in terms of practice, not in terms of consciousness or contemplation. Alienation of man's consciousness is not at the root of the process of alienation. The alien power that confronts man originates in estranged human relations and in the objective material world. Transcendental alienations are the illusory expression of a material alienation. Marx has inherited from Hegel the conception of history as a dialectical development through the process of alienation to restitution and as "the beginning and end of all actuality." Having inverted the Hegelian philosophy from the realm of Spirit to material reality, his principal aim is to avoid "theological" mystifications, abstractions, and *a priori* constructions. Yet, paradoxically enough, he falls prey to these mystifications, *a priori* constructions, and intellectual dogmatism without being aware of it. Marx's criticism of Hegel's idealism is philosophical and frequently *a priori* rather than empirical and *a posteriori*. He is, after all, neither a scientist nor a consistent philosopher and has never conducted scientific experiment. His opposition to "contemplative philosophies," like Hegel's and Feuerbach's, overlooks that these philosophies are not removed entirely from real life. They may go too far from the real, secular basis, but they still represent a way of life. The scientific outlook, which Marx and Engels claim as the only possible historical objectivism, is itself a philosophy, and it is important to remember that it has been brought into being mostly by philosophers. Marx fails to see that science cannot replace philosophy because natural science raises philosophical problems. No scientific laboratory can demonstrate whether or not the universe is a unity, if and in what sense men are free, and whether and when the process of alienation will be overcome. The mechanistic view of the universe characteristic of science during the last few centuries is derived chiefly from Descartes. Although mechanical French materialism adopted, as Marx puts it, Descartes's physics in opposition to his metaphysics and his followers were anti-metaphysicians,[60] "mechanical French materialists" still claimed to be philosophers who aimed at giving a systematic and consistent picture of human experience and the world. The value of philosophy, as Bertrand Russell indicates, is to be sought largely in its very uncertainty and in its critical approach.[61] Scientists cannot start their scientific research without tacitly assuming answers to some philosophical questions.

In his theory of philosophic alienation, Marx sometimes maintains that critical materialism entails the end of all traditional philosophy. In his contemplation of a classless society, he goes as far as to say that in that society there will be no need for philosophy. He indicates that philosophical problems cannot be "dissolved" in thought but only in "social practice" because they are expressions of material reality. In ideologies, this reality is always alienated, mystified, and inverted. For him, criticism of traditional philosophy with all its phantoms of alienation is equivalent to a truly scientific approach to reality only when criticism has become revolutionary and radical. He takes for granted that his philosophical criticism is based on the identity of the theoretical comprehension of social contradictions and class practice. It is interesting to note, however, that Marx's own criticism is frequently vicious, tendentious, one-sided, and inherently dogmatic. It is possible to argue that just as "absolute criticism proceeds from the dogma of the absolute competence of the spirit,"[62] to use Marx's own words, so his own criticism proceeds similarly from the dogma of the absolute competence of "thinking matter." Marx has criticized all philosophical points of view as being theological, ideological, dogmatic, speculative, and illusory, but he has refused consistently to subject his own philosophical and other theories to the same criticism. His own ideas about the relevance of philosophy are so obscure and inconsistent that it is practically impossible to ascertain whether he speaks of the end of all philosophy or merely of "abstract philosophy." In the introduction to his *Critique of Hegel's Philosophy of Right*, he definitely speaks of the need "to negate not only hitherto existing philosophy" but also "philosophy as such." A similar idea is suggested in the eleventh thesis on Feuerbach. Marx does not explain what is meant by "an end of all hitherto existing philosophy." His ambiguity in this respect is reflected in the contradictory views of his followers. Some commentators, like Karl Korsch, maintain that Marxism has no room for "philosophy as such" because all philosophy is alienating. Others, like John Hoffman, argue that Marx had no intention of abolishing "philosophy as such" at all.[63]

Engels similarly fails to clarify the role of philosophy in communist society. Analyzing the significance of dialectical philosophy as a whole, he stresses that this philosophy "reveals the transitory character of everything and in everything; nothing can endure before it except the uninterrupted process of becoming and of passing away, of endless ascendancy from the lower to the higher." Dialectical philosophy itself, he adds, "is nothing more than the mere reflection of this process in the thinking brain."[64] Unaware of any inconsistency, he still sticks to "revolutionary absolutes." He never defines the meaning of these "absolutes" nor the meaning "from the lower to the higher." Because Engels is not speaking here of the negative and positive pole in electricity or of the relationship between oxygen and hydrogen in water, but rather about the existence of contradictions in the realm of metaphysical absolutes, he cannot appreciate the specificity of this complex realm. Like Marx, Engels believes that his view of reality is essentially materialistic, an inversion of the Hegelian idealism. "The Hegelian system," he says, "represents merely a materialism idealistically turned upside down in method and content."[65] According to Hegel, nature, as a mere alienation of the Idea, is condemned to an eternal repetition of the process of development. The same unhistorical conception of development is seen in history. Hegel's dialectics, Engels points out, entails the self-development of the absolute concept that is believed to be the actual living soul of the whole existing world. The absolute concept alienates itself by changing into nature and finally coming to self-consciousness in man. This conception of alienation and development, Engels states, is an ideological perversion that must be rejected. The concepts in our heads must be comprehended materialistically as images of real things instead of regarding the real things as images of this or that stage of the absolute concept. Thus, in dialectical materialism the dialectic of concepts becomes merely the conscious reflex of the dialectical motion of the real world, and

Hegel's dialectic "is turned off its head on which it is standing and is placed upon its feet."[66] Whether Engels's inversion of Hegelian dialectics makes any sense depends on whether one believes or not in the significance of any dialectic at all, be it idealistic or materialistic.

The conception of "*L'homme machine*," prominent in traditional materialism of the eighteenth century, has already been discredited in the Kantian system of critical philosophy. In this sytem the Cartesian principle, which gives consciousness its fundamental place in the interpretation of the existing world, is reaffirmed in a new form.[67] The world is seen as the product of the laws of our own understanding, reacting in accordance with fixed principles that are not peculiar to our separate individuality. The field of values is more rational than the field of science. Within its phenomenal limits, science is absolute. Truth, God, beauty, the self, the values which make life, however, lie beyond these limits. Kant is interested in reason with its logical immanence, rigid necessity, and perfect universality; yet Kant's philosophy is supremely metaphysical. Hegel condemns all earlier metaphysical systems on the ground that they give an incomplete and subjective picture of reality. One of the main errors of these systems, he believes, is that the reality they describe is static and dualistic in nature. Their descriptions of reality are a symptom of abstraction. The structure that Hegel believes he discovered is dynamic and monistic. If there is to be a metaphysical structure of reality at all, it has to be one in which change, growth, movement, and development are explained rather than explained away. Hegel takes over from Plato the conception that ideas alone possess reality; unlike Plato, however, he indicates that ideas themselves are not fixed and static but rather in a continuous state of change and development. Basing his conception of reality on Aristotelian rather than Platonic lines, Hegel argues that "the real" is equivalent to "the concrete" or to "what a thing is capable of becoming." The idealism that merely asserts an immediate certainty confronted by other immediate certainties without going through the relevant dialectical preparation can neither explain nor understand itself.[68]

The crucial point in both Hegelian and Marxist philosophy is in the discovery of the dialectic in which, Engels says, "the things apparently stable no less than their mental images go through an uninterrupted change of coming into being and passing away."[69] Although Hegel's philosophy represents the alienation process idealistically, Engels still stresses that "there has never been, ever since man began to think, a system of philosophy as comprehensive as that of Hegel."[70] In spite of the materialistic conception shared by Marx and Engels with Feuerbach, the philosophical relationship of Marx and Engels is incomparably rooted more deeply in the basically monistic philosophy of Hegel than in the dualistic philosophy of Feuerbach. The principal difference between the Hegelian and Marxist philosophies is defined by Marx in the preface to the second German edition of *Capital* in which he indicates that in Hegel's works dialectic stands on its head. "You must turn it right way up again if you want to discover the rational kernel that is hidden away within the wrappings of mystification." It is significant here that Marx does not reject the importance of the dialectic as a method for understanding the world reality—he merely criticizes the "mystifying aspect of the Hegelian dialectic." He does not hide that his own materialist dialectic has been inspired by Hegel's dialectical idealism. Lenin confirms the view that "Hegelian dialectics was considered by Marx and Engels as the greatest achievement of classical German philosophy and as the most comprehensive and profound doctrine of development."[71] The philosophy of Marxism, he says, is materialism, but this philosophical and dialectical materialism has been "enriched with the achievements of German classical philosophy, especially of Hegel's system."

Rejecting Hegel's conception of reality as the Absolute, Marx exaggerates the difference between Hegel's and his own ideas of man and nature. He complains that Hegel reduces the realities of man and nature to "thought entities" and treats the estrangement of man merely as a reflection of real, existing man. Marx tends to overlook that Hegel's philosophy is not only the "study of the universe of mind" but also the "study of the universe of nature."[72] It is absurd, Hegel indicates, "to fancy that a philosophy can transcend its contemporary world." Hegel's thought, no less than Marx's, is directed against the dichotomy of theory and practice, because it is this dichotomy that prevents the realization of philosophy as a "single science."[73] When dissociating himself from Hegel's "actuality," Marx relies on abstract dichotomies between theory and practice. He fails to notice the extent to which Hegel, when speaking of dialectical processes in which nature is involved with man, is also speaking about man and society in ways not necessarily incongruous with Marx's monistic philosophy. The conception of the whole or unity is very prominent in both Hegel and Marx's monistic philosophy. Marx accepts Hegel's view that all development, whether of things or thought, is brought about through a conflict of opposing forces. For Hegel, the development of things and the discovery of truth are aspects of the same reality. The difference between him and Marx in this respect is that Hegel gives logical priority to the discovery of truth. Marx, holding that thought is a reflection or manifestation of things, emphasizes the priority of the development of things. The principal agencies of the movement in Marx's dialectic are not ideas, concepts, and thought entities, as they are in Hegel, but material forces. Marx locates the alienation process itself in these material forces rather than in concepts.

Marx agrees with Hegel that reality is a dialectical process but differs from Hegel in holding that this process is of a material, not of a logical, character. When speaking of reality as material, Marx does not mean that it is physical as distinct from mental. He believes that all mental processes are associated with corresponding physical processes and that the physical and mental interact according to laws that can be discovered "empirically." Marx is not an empiricist, however. As Lenin indicates, "Marx decidedly rejected, not only idealism, but also the views of Hume, Kant, agnosticism, criticism and positivism in their various forms."[74] He adds that Marx and Engels are partisans in philosophy from start to finish, able to detect the deviations from materialism and concessions to idealism and fideism in all of the recent trends.[75] This surely suggests that Marx's and Engels's form of materialism is as speculative and metaphysical as that of the old "abstract materialism." Being unscientific, the postulates of their materialism can never be tested. In spite of his emphasis on human sensible activity or practice, Marx's dialectical philosophy, like Hegel's, cannot be considered as anything but a purely metaphysical invention. The assertion that the development of things and the discovery of truth are brought about by a conflict of contradictory forces and that all human, social, economic, political, and cosmic processes develop dialectically can never be proved in any empirical or scientific way. Marx and Engels, like Hegel, take for granted that as enlightenment increases, human ills, including philosophic alienation, will get progressively better, although, in the absence of empirical facts, they naturally have different ideas about what "getting better" really means. Rejecting Hegel's philosophy on the ground that in it "object in the last analysis is alienated subject" or externalized world spirit, Marx assumes that monistic materialism can offer a coherent and valid differentiation between object and subject and thus a concrete and historical solution to the problem of alienation. As long as man does not recognize himself as "real man" and the human self is conceived only abstractly, Marx thinks social relations and the whole superstructure, including philosophy, will appear in the form of estrangement because its subject, man, living in an estranged world, is inevitably estranged from himself.[77]

In their analysis of the dialectic forces in man and nature and of necessity, which they disclose in historical development, Marx and Engels clearly rely on Hegel. It is important to remember that Marx and Engels have not changed the metaphysical foundation of Hegel's dialectic. In fact, they retain the main outline of his dialectical thinking. When they speak of "turning Hegel's dialectic right way up," they do not mean they have altered the dialectic as a system for understanding the conflict of opposing tendencies but rather a metaphysical interpretation of it. What Marx and Engels have "turned right way up" is the order of priority. In Hegel, the driving force of the dialectic process is engendered by the developing ideas themselves. For Marx, the ideas are merely part of the material world "reflected by the human mind."[77] In his analysis of alienation, he gives prominence to the forces of production that in his philosophical system remain a material equivalent to Hegel's infinite Spirit. Thus the final causes of all religious, social, political, and philosophical changes, according to Marx, should be sought in the economics of each particular epoch of human history, not in speculative philosophy.

Marx's belief that change in the socioeconomic conditions of men is always effected by the conflict of contradictions originates from Hegel's conception of the dialectical process representing everything as being in the state of becoming something else. Hegel maintains that the idea is composed of a unity of contradictory elements. The idea develops through negation. "When the result is conceived as a determinate negation, a new form has thereby immediately arisen, and in the negation the transition is made through which the progress through the complete series of forms comes about of itself."[78] The contradictory character of the idea produces motion that entails progress. As the idea always necessarily contains its opposite, it will always be capable of further development through the dialectical process. This evolutionary and, indeed, revolutionary aspect of the dialectic of Hegel's idealism is also a distinguishing mark of Marx's dialectical materialism. Marx merely eliminates "the wrappings of mystification" but leaves the evolutionary aspects of Hegel's dialectic intact. Whereas for Hegel the idea is composed of contradictory elements, for Marx it is matter that is composed of contradictory elements and also matter that is self-sufficient. Its contradictory nature provides it with a motive force of development. Yet, unlike Hegel who states explicity that spirit is self-active and self-energizing and that matter has "its essence out of itself and is self-destructive,"[79] Marx merely assumes that matter possesses the qualities similar to those that Hegel attributes to spirit and that matter develops as ideas do. There is no basis, however, for maintaining that material things develop in the same way as Hegel's ideas and that everything that happens in the material world must be explicable by the laws deducible from the dialectic process. The dialectic, whether manipulated by Hegel or Marx, is incapable of providing good reasons for understanding the development of the universe. In their materialist deliberations, Marx and Engels lay more emphasis on the dialectic than on materialism. Lenin confirms this in his analysis of the materialist conception of history.[80] Engels's argument that contradictions are present objectively in all spheres of real life is based on purely metaphysical assumptions. Mindful of both Hegel's and Marx's dialectic, Eugene Dühring rightly argues that "contradiction is a category which can only appertain to a combination of thoughts but not to reality. There are no contradictions in things, or, to put it another way, contradiction accepted as reality is itself the apex of absurdity."[81]

When Marx's and Engels's dialectical philosophy is analyzed either logically or scientifically, one is immediately struck by its extreme vagueness and the extreme generality they attribute to words difficult to define. The words "contradiction," "self-genesis," and "materialism" have many meanings, and both Marx and Engels use these words so vaguely that many commentators are left in doubt as to their true meaning. They tend to describe as contradictory almost any sequence of phenomena that are contrary to one another in some vague sense, implying that these contradictions are always reconcilable. Although Marx is not really very concerned with an objective dialectic of nature but rather with social contradictions, he, like Hegel and Engels, argues that everything is inherently contradictory and that things and events can move only if they have a contradiction within them. Whatever is meant by materialist dialectics, in both Marx and Hegel, contradiction is a metaphysical principle present in all existence. Marx fails to realize that some contradictions, because of their nature, cannot be reconciled at all. To be meaningful, the statement that "all men are biped" must exclude the contrary statement that "some men are quadruped." These cannot be reconciled. Like Hegel, who regards the dialectic not only as a method of thinking but also as a law of being, Marx and Engels also assume the universal presence of a movement of opposites in all things and living beings. Their dialectical method involves the consideration of things and human society in terms of their change, growth, and development.

Having turned Hegel's dialectics "right way up," Marx could not avoid doing something similar with Hegel's theory of knowledge. Hegel argues that experience is a system of reason with its own laws and that thought and reality are identical. There is no fictitious entity in itself beyond experience and no transcendent truth distinct from the reason that lies in things and events themselves. The problem with the relationship between the knowing mind and known objects is strictly insoluble, although Hegel approaches this problem through the axiom of internal relations and the concept of the whole. He believes knowing mind and known objects constitute an example of a whole or unity. With the system of significant experience reality is absolutely coextensive. Whatever does not enter into experience is meaningless. Knowledge, according to Hegel, begins with sense perception, and through skeptical criticism of the senses it reaches the stage of self-knowledge, in which the distinction between subject and object is finally transcended.[82] However, the distinction is not something that is outside the act of knowledge. It is a distinction within a whole between parts of the whole. Only the whole of knowledge is real. Treating all acts of knowledge as wholes, Hegel emphasizes self-consciousness as the highest form of knowledge.[83] Only the whole is reality, and partial facts are abstractions that need to be brought into connection with the whole to gain validity. Marx's theory of knowledge, despite his boasting of inversion, is in many respects similar to that of Hegel. Both systems regard knowledge as an aspect of the dialectical process. Because reality is dialectical, valid thinking must be dialectical, and thus the rules of thought necessarily reflect the laws of contradiction in all things. Engels indicates that the whole process of knowing things and facts in nature is made easier "if one approaches the dialectical character of these things and facts equipped with an understanding of the laws of dialectical thought."[84] We cannot escape contradictions, he adds, even in the sphere of thought. For Marx, as for Engels and Hegel, the dialectic controls all things and all men. Only in the light of the dialectic process can human knowledge of reality and alienation be perceived.

Knowledge in the sense of passive contemplation is abstract and unreal. "The chief defect of all previous materialism, including that of Feuerbach," according to Marx, "is that things, reality and sensuousness are conceived only in the form of contemplation, not as human sensuous activity or practice."[85] Marx obviously believes that we cannot apprehend an external object merely as object. He seems to suggest that we apprehend it only when we react to it in some ways. The key to his criticism of "all previous materialism" is the idea of practice. In Marx's view, all perception is an inter-action between subject and object. The object apart from the activitiy of the percipient is only a raw material. Strictly speaking, knowledge does not occur independently of its relation to practice, and the object of action is to change what is known. Practice or action involved in the process of knowing changes both the percipient and the object perceived. There is no such thing, he points out, as knowledge that is a mere contemplation of the external world. All knowledge is a form of action and for the sake of practice. Practice changes at the same time the knower and the known. Marx rejects the views that ignore the role of practice in bringing about perception and knowledge of the external world. "The question whether objective truth can be attributed to human thinking is not a question of theory but a practical question. The truth, i.e., the reality and power of thought must be demonstrated in practice. The dispute over the reality or non-reality of thinking which is isolated from practice is a purely scholastic question."[86] Because the purpose of knowledge is to change matter, there is an assumption that knowledge is true only when it promotes that change. The percipient and the object known are in a continuous process of mutual adaptation which, being dialectical, is never completed fully.

Marx rejects both idealism and mechanical materialism, insisting that men are not ideal or machine-like entities who automatically detect their difference from the external objects around them. They are objective, sensuous beings in an objective, sensuous world where there is reciprocal stimulus and response. Human beings, Marx believes, have bodies that are active, passionate, self-moving, and responsive to sensuous nature. "Man is affirmed in the objective world both in the act of thinking and in the act of perception."[87] Basing his theory of knowledge on sense perception and practice, he is wrongly led to the conclusion that the knowing subject and the known object are practically indistinguishable in any cognitive process. His activist theory of knowledge is based on the assumption that knowledge is indissolubly bound up with practice and thus possible only to those who participate in the movement of objects. Mental life is primarily practical in that our ways of thinking have grown to be what they are because of their utility in shaping our reactions to the external world. In the human mind, which develops slowly in response to practical needs of the body as a whole, the measure of value of an intellectual process will consist in its specific efficiency to satisfy the human need from which it originates. Marx sometimes goes as far as to obliterate the difference between man and his objects. Man himself is part of the same objective world. "The manner in which objects become his depends on the nature of the objects and on the nature of the essential power corresponding to it; for it is precisely the determinateness of this relationship which shapes the particular, real mode of affirmation."[88] Marx does not realize that if the knowing subject and the objects to be known are the same dialectical process, then the demand that the knowing subject must change the world is meaningless.

Dialectical idealism may be described as a method of justifying beliefs by making them conform to logical forms and axioms already established. Empiricism can analogously be described as a method of testing beliefs and hypotheses by their agreement with immediate present experience, either internal or external. Dialectical materialism, however, tests beliefs and hypotheses by the consequences that will flow from them in the future. If the future consequences of holding a theory are satisfactory, that would indicate its truth. Unsatisfactory or harmful consequences indicate its falsehood. If the theory makes no difference in the life of those who hold it, it can be treated as meaningless. In Marx's view, no theory can be properly regarded as true unless it yields practical concrete consequences that will be valuable to those who use it. The futuristic attitude expressed in Marx's practicalism originates in the philosophy of August Cieszkowski who, as a member of the Young Hegelians, was anxious to replace speculative philosophy with a practical philosophy.[89] The future role of philosophy, according to Cieszkowski, must be that of practical activity, of praxis, in which there is a synthesis of thought and action. Marx's view of the relation of theory and practice or of thought and action is essentially the same as that of Bauer, who seems to follow Cieszkowski in this respect. Strictly speaking, Marx and Bauer are merely exponents of Cieszkowski's belief that philosophy must descend "from the heights of theory into the fields of practice." What transcends practice and concrete sensuous experience is alienated; thus, Marx states, it must have alienating effects. The rational comprehension of practice can transcend all rationalist logic and in that way help us to understand the estranged world as a whole. Speculative philosophy, according to Marx, has separated consciousness and reality. This led to a general acceptance of the alienated world as it is. When he speaks of reality, he always means material, concrete, "objective" reality. It is this reality that must be regarded as the basis of "material practice."

Marx's dialectical materialism is not concerned so much with cosmic matter as with matter that is relevant to human needs. In his view, the needs peculiar to men as self-conscious and social beings can be more fully satisfied when they are better understood. Contemplative materialism, like mechanical materialism, is rejected because it is still "bound by the traditional idealist fetters" and the ideals of its philosophy still retain a mystical color.[90] Marx urges men to understand the sensuous world, presently alienated, as human sensuous activity. This means that they must become conscious of themselves as social beings, developing simultaneously as subjects and objects in the dialectical process of history. Marx is at pains to distinguish the speculative methods of philosophy from his own which implies that the "concrete totality is a totality of thoughts, concrete in thought, in fact a product of thinking and comprehending; but not in any way a product of the concept which thinks and generates itself outside or above observation and conception."[91] The method of abstraction, however, is never absent from his "practical materialism." Even in his "Theses on Feuerbach," Marx tends to counterpose theory to practice in an abstractly theoretical way. In the first thesis, he claims to be transcending the abstract oppositions between idealism and materialism, theory and *praxis*, but he is actually reinforcing them. By taking activity from idealism and sensuousness from materialism, he presents his own position as the combination of theory and practice expressed in "actual sensuous activity." Because actuality is dissolved in activity, he claims that his materialism consists solely in the sensuousness of activity. The nature of practice itself is never explained, and the reference to sensuousness is abstract because the idea of activity of a "human, natural being" already includes it.[92] Marx's notion of practice is based on the abstract opposition between being and consciousness. As a result, the antithesis between theory and practice is mere appearance of human reality. Maintaining that the essence of reality and being lies in material production, he then refers to something that lies "beyond the realm of material production." In his ontology, he has, in fact, produced an ambiguous dichotomy of human activity and nature, of being and consciousness, and of theory and practice that relies entirely on a historical beginning and a utopian end.

Marx is not an empiricist, although he sometimes claims that his epistemology is "based on empirically verifiable facts." The empiricists insist that all our knowledge is derived from experience. Locke minimizes the extent of human knowledge, indicating that our ignorance is greater than our knowledge. Only "intuitive and demonstrative knowledge are properly so called." Sensitive knowledge of particular existences "only passes under the name of knowledge."[93] Bishop Berkeley goes deeply into the problems of perception and indicates the difficulties involved in the concept of objects as opposed to their qualities. Although matter is mind-dependent, he does not deny that the physical world exists independently of the human mind. The mind in question "need not necessarily be mine; it may be God's." The ideas known, according to Berkeley, exist independently of our knowledge as they continue to exist as ideas in the mind of God.[94] The true essence of the physical world is to manifest the activity of spirit. Hume's theory of perception eliminates the concept of God on the ground that we have no sense experience of any transcendental being. Like Locke and Berkeley, Hume takes for granted that what we perceive directly in the process of knowing is our own mental states. He concludes broadly that there is no reason to believe in the existence of anything but in what is perceived immediately. Hume's analysis of experience leaves us no ground for a belief in the existence of a permanent identical self. In the history of philosophy, he is commonly represented as a sceptic. On the whole,

Marx tends to belittle the importance of British empiricism. "As soon as the active process of human life is described,' he writes, 'history ceases to be a collection of dead facts, as it is with the empiricists (themselves still abstract) or an imagined activity of imagined subjects as with the idealists."[95] Marx frequently associates the British empirical philosophy, especially that of Locke and Hume, with political economy, alienation, and abstract thinking.

The main issue of the theory of knowledge today, as it was in previous centuries, is the issue between the philosophy of pure reason or mind and the philosophy of experience. The British empiricists maintain that although we can attain adequate knowledge of the particular facts of nature and of the relations of sequence and co-existence between them, it is impossible to know the reality underlying the phenomena of sense perception. Marx and Engels do not share this view. They insist that neither idealism nor empiricism can give us true knowledge of the external world and that only dialectical materialism "constitutes the unifying truth of both."[96] They criticize not only idealism but also empiricism and all previous forms of materialism for their failure to grasp the external objects in the world as materializations of man's activity. Feuerbach is reproached for looking at these objects only through the spectacles of the philosopher or estranged thinker. Marx insists it is impossible to apprehend these objects "only in the form of sense perception." It is equally impossible, he thinks, to understand man as a mere "object of the senses." Both man and the external objects in the world can be understood only in the light of "man's sensuous activity." The way men think about themselves and the outside world is influenced profoundly by the form of production and class structure. "Communist workers do not believe that they will be able to argue away their industrious masters and their practical debasement by pure thinking."[97] They know, Marx says, that "property, capital, money, wage labour and the like are no ideal figments of the brain but very practical, very objective products of their alienation."[98] Here human knowledge is degraded to what Bertrand Russell calls mere acquaintance as opposed to knowledge of truths. There is a false assumption that the self-knowledge of the proletariat is somehow representative of the cognitive stage of all society and that "practical materialism" is the truth because it is the ideology of the proletariat. Unlike Francis Bacon, who treats human knowledge both as a means and an end, Marx regards knowledge only as a means and as a weapon of partisan ideology.

Marx's theory of knowledge is far from being clear and consistent. Indeed, it is possible to argue that it does not even exist. Some philosophers, including the logical positivist A. J. Ayer, deny the existence of Marx's philosophy in any meaningful sense. Marx himself says nothing explicitly either about the perceiving mind or about the objects revealed to us in perception. Commentators base their analysis of Marxist epistemology mainly on Marx's random phrases, which are subject to various interpretations. Frequently, they read into Marx what he does not say and *ex nihilo* create epistemological theories that do not represent his view. Lenin is probably the first important analyst of Marxist epistemology. However, Marxists themselves cannot agree to what extent his analysis represents Marx's ideas. Some of them maintain that the theory of reflection, for example, as defended by Lenin is illusory and indefensible. Arguing against Ernst Mach, whose theory of knowledge stems from Hume and Berkeley, Lenin notes that to be a materialist one must acknowledge the existence of a material world beyond the mind. The epistemology of dialectical materialism, he insists, must start from the axiom that the knowing mind in sensory experience always makes contact with something other than itself and that "something other" is directly revealed to the mind.

Lenin's interpretation of Marx's and Engels's epistemology leads him to advocate naive realism or objectivism. Physical objects, he believes, do not depend on our perception of them for their existence. "They exist independently of our sensation, of our consciousness, of our self and of man in general" and are revealed to us by our senses exactly as they are.[99] Asking whether in perception one "should start from things to sensation and thought or the other way around," he asserts categorically that the "first line is the materialist line, adopted by Engels, and the second line is the idealist line, adopted by Mach and idealists."[100] It is interesting to note that he does not refer here to Marx, although he obviously assumes that reflection theory is essential to Marxist materialism. How do we know that the objective world exists independently of what we think it is and how are we to explain the fact of differing perceptions of the same objects, neither Marx nor Engels nor Lenin can explain. They merely assume that physical objects in the external world are primary and that "sensation is a result of the action of matter on our sense organs."

Believing that the external world is objectively real, Marx seems to suggest that in perception we notice objects as part of the process of acting on them. He also seems to suggest that sense perception gives us faithful images of the external world. A sensation has a cause in the outside world, and it is a sensation of that which causes it. Because sensations must have an external reference to objects that cause them, human knowledge is never of mental states alone. Knowledge is always about objects.[101] In opposition to Feuerbach, Marx argues that the "object can only be apprehended as human sensible activity or practice."[102] There is no such thing as a knowing that is a mere contemplation of the external world. Human knowledge neither occurs independently of its relation to action nor, in Marx's view, can it be intelligible in the "form of contemplation." In his early writings, especially in *Manuscripts*, he is still under Hegel's influence and speaks of man in terms of "spiritual essence," "free activity," and "contemplation." In objectifying himself, he says, "man duplicates himself not only, as in consciousness, intellectually, but also actively in reality, and therefore he contemplates himself in a world which he has created."[103] Man is active as a spiritual being, as a being conscious of himself as an individual. In this quotation man bears traces of the

Hegelian Spirit that "obtains its existence through self-consciousness's own externalisation and separation of itself from its essence."[104] By being active, Marx's alienated man, like Hegel's spirit, "duplicates himself" in consciousness and in reality or nature. There is an assumption that man's ideas and the outside world in which they objectify themselves reflect one another and are interconnected.

The reflection theory, advocated by Engels and later by Lenin, is only implicit in Marx's epistemology. Whenever he makes a distinction between the real and the apparent, as he does in *Manuscripts*, *German Ideology*, and *Holy Family*, he is assuming the theory of reflection. There would be hardly any knowledge, he seems to suggest, unless appearances reflect or mirror reality and unless sensations copy physical objects. In Marx's epistemology, concerned primarily with finding ways to eliminate philosophic alienation, knowledge is seen as both reflection and projection in a "unity of practice." The errors in previous forms of materialism consist in neglecting the active side of knowledge. On the other hand, he says, the idealist interpretation of activity is only abstract, and speculative knowledge based on this activity therefore must be alienated. Marx's own ideas of human activity, whether conceived as social activity or as sensuous activity, remain abstract and metaphysical. The basic premise in Kant's epistemology is the thesis that the self creates the laws of nature by applying pure forms of the mind to its sensory material. Nothing can ever be perceived as a natural object unless it has been through the mill of rational faculties.[105] The mind, he maintains, imposes its own forms of synthesis on the objects perceived, and it is mental activity that plays the decisive role in cognition. Hegel also ascribes knowledge to the activity of the mind. "The examination of knowledge", he says, "can only be carried out by the act of knowledge."[106] This is possible because thought is active. Marx does not dispute the activity of reason. He merely argues that "mental activity and physical activity" must be unified in practice.[107] His argument in favor of this unification, however, is ambiguous, inconsistent, and superficial. As a result, his epistemology vacillates from idealism and rationalism in early writings to pseudo-materialism in mature writings.

A close examination of Marx's epistemology in his early writings, including the *Critique of Hegel's Philosophy of Right*, reveals that, in spite of his forceful attack on Hegel's epistemology, he elaborates an alternative that is still within the confines of idealism. In *German Ideology* and later works, however, the emphasis is on materialist epistemology and material activity. Yet, in all Marx's reflections on the basis of knowledge and philosophic alienation, there is a continuing rejection of the empiricist account of knowledge that claims that sense experience alone is an adequate ground for all human knowledge. In his view, knowing is not merely perceiving. Perception depends on both experience and thinking. In *Contribution to the Critique of Political Economy*, Marx rejects the positivist-empiricist account of knowledge with the same force as in the early writings. "The concrete concept," he writes, "is concrete because it is a synthesis of many definitions, thus representing the unity of diverse aspects. It appears therefore in reasoning, as a summing-up, a result, and not as the starting point, although it is the real point of origin, and thus also the point of origin of perception and imagination."[108] Knowledge of reality, Marx at least sometimes believes, is obtained by reason rather than by the mere passive reception of sense data. The cognitive process is always "from abstract definitions by way of reasoning to the reproduction of the concrete situation as a concrete mental category."[109] The concepts that give a knowledge of reality cannot be the result of the passive reception of sense data. "The concrete totality regarded as a conceptual totality, as a mental act, is indeed a product of thinking and of the thinking intellect which assimilates and transforms perceptions and images into concepts."[110] It is because of the existence of rationalist elements in his philosophy, that Marx is sometimes regarded as a pseudo-materialist as well as a pseudo-empiricist.[111]

In his opposition to idealism, Marx argues that the world of objects cannot be reduced to the status of total dependence on the finite conscious self and that the truth of a practical, non-alienated philosophy depends on its realization in action. He is equally opposed to a dualistic orientation that separates man from nature. For him, both man and nature are objects. As in Hegel, object and subject, being and consciousness, matter and mind are not, strictly speaking, considered to be separate entities. In Marx's analysis of philosophic alienation, man is conceived as a being of practice, capable of changing the world. The world is a historical phenomenon, the product of man acting on his natural environment. Changing the conditions in which "man is debased, dehumanised and alienated" requires conscious action. Abstract idealism and abstract materialism are rejected as being theoretical only. Marx claims they both maintain the illusions of metaphysical speculation and fail to grasp the significance of "revolutionary activity."[112] The task of philosophy must be "to unmask alienation in all its forms." This requires the destruction of the whole edifice of speculative philosophy and "abstract empiricism." According to Marx, speculative philosophy, abstract materialism, and abstract empiricism, like theology, depend on alienation. The very process of thinking in these inverted spheres of human activity has given expression to the world of alienation. Once this alienation is abolished, men will be able to realize themselves as social beings and "to prove the truth in practice."

Emphasizing that the question of "objective truth" must be analyzed in terms of practice, Marx does not deny the reality of epistemological distinctions between truth and falsehood. He accepts the concept of truth, although he never defines it. On the whole, his ideas of truth are similar to those of Hegel. In spite of his criticism of Hegel's idealism, he never explicitly rejects Hegel's definition of truth. In Hegel's monistic system, the correspondence of judgment with fact cannot be the meaning of truth. "In common life," he writes, "truth means the agreement of an object with our own conception of it. In the philosophical sense, however, truth is the agreement of a thought-content with itself."[113] The truth of isolated facts can only be established when those facts are analyzed as part of the totality or whole.[114] In the absence of Marx's explanation of his meaning of truth, it is difficult to say whether by truth he means "coherence" or "correspondence." The fact that he, like Hegel, maintains that everything that exists must be seen in relation to a system or a whole or a totality of things and that he also is a monist suggests that the meaning of truth is coherence. Considering Marx's criticism of "abstract empiricism," it is wrong to treat his theory of truth in terms of Lockean or Humean "correspondence." Some commentators fail to realize that the correspondence theory is held by empiricist philosophers and thus is foreign to the monists.[115]

The criterion of theoretical truth, in Marx's view, belongs to practice. Because no man in practice can ever attain a completely coherent system or, as Hegel puts it, the "thorough harmony of notion and reality," no judgment about a fact or part of reality is absolutely true. Yet, paradoxically enough, both Marx and Engels sometimes claim that their own judgments are "absolutely true." Any suggestion that there are divine, sacred, or merely abstract truths is rejected as a figment of imagination. These imaginary truths, they believe, are the product of alienation. Philosophic alienation, like religious alienation, is the illusory expression of a real alienation. The phantoms formed in the human mind cannot be dissociated from the "sheer estrangement of all physical and mental senses, the sense of having."[116] Theory that originates from alienated practice is inevitably alienating and deceitful and, vice versa, practice that originates from alienated theory is equally alienating. In Marx's theory of philosophic alienation, the separation of theory from practice, of consciousness from being, also entails alienation. True thought reflects a theory that is in coherence with a nonalienated practice.

Whether Marx has succeeded in establishing the unity of theory and practice is a matter of argument. Many commentators rightly maintain that he has failed to transcend the dichotomy of theory and practice and that his inversion of Hegel's idealism has not eliminated dualism. Abstract dichotomies between theory and practice, mind and matter, consciousness and existence have never been transcended.[117] As a result, his "human natural being" is as much a "theoretical idealist" as a "practical materialist," as much an individual who thinks, contemplates, and "duplicates himself in consciousness, intellectually" as he is a "sensuous" or "social being." The conscious and sensuous, rational and material, ideal and real, theoretical and practical remain only in an abstract and illusory unity. The union of the particular with the concrete universal is conceived only theoretically in the form of an utopian end.

Marx's philosophy, like Hegel's, is dogmatic, speculative, and obscure. The premises of his philosophical theory could never be "verified in a purely empirical way." He rightly says that developments in human history, science, morality and philosophy do not spring from contemplation alone. Instead they spring from man's creative relations with nature and the world around him. He is wrong, however, in assuming that philosophy can be transcended by the "science of man," which is nothing but "partisan ideology." Infatuated with Marx's theory of praxis, both scientific and critical Marxists uncritically assert that praxis is the only real basis for all forms of "active and militant humanism" and, of course, the only real basis for eliminating alienated philosophy. Marxist critics, on the other hand, emphasize that Marx's philosophy is class-orientated and that it tends to undermine the rationalist belief in reason. They also indicate the alienating effects of Marxist determinism on human freedom. Marx has definitely failed, they believe, to formulate a theory in which decision-making is not dominated by "absolute necessity." Analyzing his reflection theory of knowledge, one can say that its weakness lies in its failure to account for the relativity or subjectivity of the contents of illusions, dreams, and hallucinations that may be real as appearances to the perceiving mind without corresponding to any external reality at all.

Some modern Marxists deny that the reflection theory is either explicit or implicit in Marx's epistemology. They are critical of Engels's and Lenin's reflection theory on the ground that it cannot be reconciled with praxis. The reflection theory, in their view, relegates ideas and concepts to the role of passivity so that consciousness is negated its "active side" in the transformation of the world. However, they go too far in the attempt to represent Marx's activist epistemology as being totally opposed to the reflection theory of knowledge. This theory is implicit in Marx's writings; otherwise, it is very unlikely that Lenin would be defending it in his own theory of knowledge. Whatever one may think about Marx's ambiguous and inconsistent epistemology, he has been acclaimed as the "great proletarian philosopher" who has appealed directly to the heart of the alienated worker. It is sad to note that his interest in Brisith empiricism is insignificant and that his knowledge of it is superficial. All indications are that he has distrusted empiricism and positivism because of their relativism, skepticism, and subjectivism. The Humean stand that all ideologies are equally bad and that the absolute nature of the reality that expresses itself in human experience is demonstrably unknowable is definitely alien to Marx's "practical and dialectical" orientation. By creating a metaphysical barrier between "reflection and experience," theory and practice, Marx believes, empiricist philosophy easily degenerates into a self-defeating relativism which, in its turn, inevitably leads to intellectual paralysis. He could never accept the skeptic claim that the riddle of the world is insoluble. His philosophical orientation has been molded by German rationalism and Hegelian dialectical thinking in which the universe is pictured as an interlocking system and all the elements are related by absolute necessity. As a dogmatic thinker, Marx is far removed from Baconian empiricism and Comtean positivism. His idea of progress is bound up with the idea of alienation which, in its different forms, has haunted him throughout his life.

7
Scientific Alienation

Science in the eighteenth and nineteenth centuries was largely concerned with digesting and later utilizing the approach that emerged in the seventeenth century in the works of Galileo, Newton, and their contemporary scientific investigators. The seventeenth century was remarkable not only in astronomy and dynamics but also in a series of revolutionary discoveries in other scientific fields. There was already a profound change in the conception of man's place and his purpose in the universe around him, and almost all traces of animism were removed from the laws of physics. Scientists were looking for better ways of communicating with one another, and they formed scientific societies in England, France, and Italy. With mathematics now finding wide application in physics, Galileo's mathematics was supremely importtnat in the use of the pendulum to give greater precision to his proofs. Good mathematical and experimental tools were created, leading to increased sea trade and exploration. Instrument makers, geographers, map-makers, and astrologers turned to mathematics for assistance in their scientific researches. While Newton was doing his important work in optics that was destined to provide a firm basis for better compound microscopes and new astronomical telescopes, Leeuwenhoek began using his simple microscope, which helped him to discover unicellular organisms.

It is important to realize that during the seventeenth century, science was still of secondary importance, and most men and women still saw the meaningful life in personal rather than in impersonal terms. The unviersities were expected to conform to ecclesiastical or Aristotelian dogma. There was a continuous antagonism between the Renaissance spirit and religious beliefs. Although men of science were anxious to maintain only those doctrines they believed could be demonstrated by scientific facts, the conflicts between religion and science were comparatively insignificant. The Protestant astronomer Kepler, persecuted by the protestant University at Tübingen for defending the heliocentric theory of Copernicus, took refuge with the Jesuits in 1596. Both the Roman Catholic Galileo and the Protestant Kepler ventured into theology only to indicate that the Copernican system is consistent with an objective interpretation of the words of Scripture. Galileo was convinced that his work glorified the majesty of God, and Kepler was an intensely earnest Christian. Like Newton, Leibniz, and most scientists of this period, Descartes was a religious man. Robert Boyle, the father of modern chemistry, wrote considerably more about the Christian faith than about science. Part of Newton's preoccupation was theological, and his acceptance of atomism and rejection of atheism was essentially the guiding principle in the mechanistic philosophy of the eighteenth century. Newton believed that God designed and created the world machine and that His system of the universe illustrates the grandeur of God's works.

Today the work of Galileo and Newton is of supreme importance in the physical sciences, but for most of the eighteenth century it had little effect outside astronomy. Natural philosophy, however, which in Newton included heavenly and terrestrial bodies in a single picture, affected all subsequent thinkers. It led directly to the empirical philosophy of Locke and Berkeley and also to attempts to deal similarly with economic and social questions. Galileo and Newton had also developed the old technique of representing physical problems by models of mathematical equations. Newton and Leibniz demonstrated how to model changing situations in this way when they developed calculus. The fusion of mathematics with theoretical physics appeared more strikingly in the early nineteenth century at the hands of men like Laplace and Fourier. Given models, scientists were able to think about heat and combustion, to devise experiments, and to conceive theoretical and practical uses for heat and combustion. In theoretical physics there were no models such as atoms or molecules. Heat, magnetism, and static electricity were discussed in terms of imponderable fluids. Ideas in physics, chemistry, biology, and geology, as well as in theology and philosophy, were ripened and digested during the eighteenth century. The old medieval encyclopedic tradition began to split up into different forms. France led the scientific world in pure science throughout this century. The great advances in applied science were made in England. With the coming of the industrial revolution, the manufacture of fundamental reagents in chemistry increased sharply. The experiments of Joseph Priestley and Lavoisier with combustion and the identification of oxygen marked the beginning of modern chemistry. Underlying the oxygen theory is the scientific principle that the total quantity of matter in an isolated system remains constant during chemical changes.

Chemical scientists in France were reluctant to abandon phlogiston, and they finally rejected it near the end of the eighteenth century. Priestley, Cavendish, and many other scientists in the century never abandoned it. The supersession of phlogiston by oxygen attracted scientists to the importance of researches in the fields of chemistry and physics. In the middle of the nineteenth century, the concept of a heart fluid was abandoned and the energy principle was extended to incorporate the heat phenomena previously explained with the help of the principle of conservation of heat fluid. This extension clarified and unified several energy concepts and finally led to the formulation of the first general principle of conservation of energy. In a short essay in 1842, the young German physicist Julius Mayer definitely suggested a general equivalence and conservation of all forms of energy of which the equivalence of heat and work is only a special case. In the nineteenth century, physics expanded considerably with theories about light, electricity, and thermodynamics. When the interchange of heat and mechanical energy is involved, the principle of conservation of energy is referred to as the first law of thermodynamics. The wave theory of light, revived by Young and his contemporaries at the beginning of the century, led to a series of mechanical models for ether. These proved unsatisfactory, although Young's experiments on the interference between beams of light and those of Fresnel, who developed a theory that satisfactorily described many diffraction effects, gave a strong impetus to the wave theory. This was later brought to an apparent state of perfection by Maxwell's electromagnetic theory. Newton preferred a corpuscular theory of the transmission of light. Nobody knows what light really is. All that is known is that sometimes its behavior can be explained by wave theory and sometimes it can be explained by particle theory.

From the time of the earliest philosophic speculations, thinking people have been intrigued by conflicting hypotheses about the structure of matter. Democritus maintained that matter is divisible into atoms and that the "atoms and empty space are the only existing things." Plato, Aristotle, and many of their followers rejected atomism. Newton occasionally used the atomistic picture and, like Francis Bacon, Descartes, and Gassendi, seemed to believe that atomism explains various phenomena, despite its speculative character. From ancient times to the beinning of the nineteenth century the words "atom," "particle," "corpuscle," and others were used more or less interchangeably to designate invisible and indivisible constituent parts of material objects. No conceptual scheme of the structure of matter emerged, however, that could be called reasonably unambiguous and precise. While Boyle saw atomism as the best method of explaining physical and chemical changes, John Dalton gave it its definite specification by saying that the atoms run in classes and that each class constitutes a chemical element. Chemistry grew from its foundation in Dalton's atomic theory early in the nineteenth century to Mendeleev's formulation of the periodic table and to the rise of organic chemistry by the end of the century. Toward the end of the nineteenth century, the synthesis of numerous compounds became the distinguishing feature of organic chemistry, especially in Germany, where the vitalist Liebig believed that putrefaction is a form of chemical breakdown that follows the withdrawal of the vital force from living bodies. In 1836 Theodor Schwann, an outstanding German experimenter, showed that putrefaction is caused by some living microorganisms. This later was elaborated by Pasteur. In 1839, Schwann announced the general theory of the cell as the basis of all life. A number of biologists before Schwann and Schleiden wrote about the cellular organization of animals and plants, but the research of these two men crystallied the basic concept and inaugurated a new fruitful period of cellular studies.

In the mid-nineteenth century, a new and most important province had been conquered for the cell theory. Rudolf Virchow had made a detailed examination of the histology of diseased tissues and thus became the founder of cellular pathology.[1] Von Baer applied the new microscopy to embryology and found that the further back he traced the development of the embryo, the more resemblance could be seen between embryos of different species. There was no basis for a descriptive model of electricity until the electron was identified in 1896, but the development of current electricity coincided with the rise of mathematical physics. Electrical and electromagnetic phenomena could apparently be completely understood in terms of the hard work of such physicists as Faraday and Ampère. These phenomena were finally unified in the monumental electromagnetic theory of Maxwell. The crowning achievement of this theory is the emergence of a complete account of all optical phenomena, resulting from its description of light as an electromagnetic wave. In the nineteenth century, industrial invention and scientific theories were in every respect more remarkable than in the preceding period. The science of electricity initiated the corresponding industry, and the steam industry gave prominence to thermodynamics. The history of technology is international, but an account of developments in the eighteenth and nineteenth centuries has a marked British flavor because many developments were British. No country in the world was as statistically minded and mechanized as England. The new industries that appeared as the nineteenth century advanced owed everything to science. Chemicals and electrical engineering attracted many scientists. William Thomson (Lord Kelvin), known for his major contributions to physics, also contributed to the design of Field's Atlantic cable and the associated equipment between 1853 and 1866. Science and technology were independent activities. In Germany in 1820, Peter Beuth established the Association for the Promotion of Indsutrial Knowledge in Prussia and launched the Industrial Institute in Berlin. Between 1810 and 1826, four research institutes were set up in Germany; between 1822 and 1835, ten technical high schools were also founded. It was in the light of these scientific advances that Marx and Engels were attracted by natural sciences.

Both Marx and Engels claim to be scientifically orientated, but whether they can be considered as scientists depends on the meaning of *science*. The term *science* is used in many senses, but is generally agreed that science is knowledge of natural phenomena and the rational study of the relations among the concepts in which these phenomena are expressed. Like philosophy, science is primarily knowledge of learnable facts, which means the wisdom of the ancients. The main aim of science is to trace in the chaos of phenomena a consistent structure with order and meaning. The object of all sciences, according to Einstein, is to coordinate our experiences and bring them into a logical system. Philosophy, theology, and art can claim the same goal. Some philosophers define speculative philosophy as the endeavor to frame a coherent and logical system of general ideas in terms of which human experiece and human life can be analyzed and interpreted. In science, as in philosophy, theology, and art, human intellectual efforts are directed toward the discovery of order, system, structure, and pattern. Thus, science is only an aspect of the great intellectual adventure and a form of human activity, through pursuit of which humanity acquires an increasingly richer and more accurate knowledge and understanding of nature. The origin of the term *science*[2] indicates the extent of its appeal and the depths of its roots. Among the great early men of science, Leonardo da Vinci and the Polish churchman Nicolaus Copernicus indicate the absence of sharply distinct boundaries between science and non-science.

There are certain differences separating the natural sciences from the non-sciences which cannot be denied. Traditionally, scientists have been regarded as possessing practical reason, as being driven by emotional motives, and using their intellect to realize practical aims. Attention has been concentrated on logic and mathematics as their important intellectual devices in learning. In the past, experiment and theory have always been linked by philosophy. In modern times, however, there has been a tendency to distinguish science from both logic and philosophy. Science, it is stressed, uses operationally defined concepts and works toward theories that are useful and falsifiable.[3] While philosophers are mostly concerned with logical deductions from self-evident principles, natural scientists concentrate principally on such concepts as mass, force, motion, gravitation, valence, and energy. Some modern scientists indicate that philosophy has been significant for developments in science only in that science has been affected by the general pool of ideas in society, and philosophers contributed to that pool. In practice, they argue, it is difficult to demonstrate a causal connection between modern physics and modern philosophy. Although it is easy to trace the roots of positivism in the philosophies of Locke, Berkeley, and Hume, it is difficult to trace its connection with the works of Priestley, Cavendish, Dalton, or Einstein.

The distinction between science and philosophy is comparatively recent. Newton was called a natural philosopher. In the seventeenth and eighteenth centuries, the physical world was allotted to science and the spiritual to theology. Science and religion represented different aspects of man's quest for reality. All definite knowledge belongs to science and all transcendental and speculative knowledge to theology. Philosophy basically occupies an intermediate position between science and theology, but philosophical knowledge does not differ essentially from other forms of knowledge. There is no special source of wisdom that is open to philosophy but not open to science. The scientists, like ordinary people, take for granted that every normal human individual possesses a certain amount of valid knowledge. The essential characteristic of philosophy that distinguishes it form science is criticism. Philosophy critically examines the principles used in science and daily life. It is, in fact, the critical method of philosophy that dominates Marx's epistemology and his scientific outlook. In his letter to Ruge in 1843, he emphasizes critical philosophy, insisting on the importance of criticism in theology, philosophy, and science.[4] In another letter to J.B. Schweitzer in 1865, Marx criticizes Proudhon and "the utopians" for their interest "in a so-called science by means of which they want to devise *a priori* a formula for the solution of the social question instead of deriving their science from a critical knowledge of the historical movement which itself produces the material conditions of emancipation."[5]

The scientist restricts himself to some simple aspect of reality and deals strictly only with a part of it. He adopts the method of induction and verification to explain the part of reality. The philosophical method, however, is applied to the whole of reality. Scientific method is primarily experimental. In philosophy, however, experiment is impracticable in view of the very general and comprehensive problems that are always involved. The philosopher deals mostly with concepts, ideas, or categories rather than with facts or concrete events. A man is a scientist when he tries to formulate the actual laws that explain facts and sequences in the world. He enters the field of philosophy as soon as he undertakes to lay down the general propositions about the ultimate nature of the universe. Men have believed many things about the relationship between ultimate reality and human knowledge of the external world. Most scientists believe that the experiences that come through the human senses correspond exactly to a real world that exists independently of our interpretations. This scientific "realism" is opposed not only to idealism, which maintains that "ideas and impressions" are the only realities, and to positivism, which rejects speculation about ultimate causes or origins and regards nothing as ascertainable or meaningful beyond sense data and concepts that refer to sense data, but also to dialectical materialism that is primarily concerned with social and economic relations not open to any direct observation. Unlike Marxism, modern science repudiates the "truth" view of the universe and resists referring to things as "being real or being true." In science as in philosophy and theology, an objective universe is always assumed, but its nature and purpose are rarely discussed.

The view that science is primarily a search for truth has had most of the attention in the past history of scientific research and probably still has except among a minority of well-informed critics. This approach takes as its starting point an external world of objects governed by natural laws. Once the obstacles to discovering these laws are removed, some physicists take for granted that truth will be visible to all who are genuinely interested in it. Modern critics repudiate this approach to natural science as negative and unscientific. Natural science, unlike logic and mathematics, is not concerned primarily with the logical deductions of consequences from the general premises of reasoning, and yet science can be regarded as a route to truth. Most thinkers, scientists and non-scientists alike, realize that while mathematical propositions are certain or absolutely true, scientific propositions can only be probable. In his conception of "a single science," Marx confuses these propositions, indicating that his science is of absolute validity. His utterances on truth in "Theses on Feuerbach" have a distinct philosophico-speculative meaning. This understanding of truth, inspired by Hegel's ideas, reappears in Engels's analysis of "ultimate truths." In *Anti-Dühring*, Engels defends the view that "in the exact sciences certain results are eternal, final and ultimate truths."[6] Lenin, basing his conception of truth on Engels's utterances, reproaches "the dogmatic, metaphysical materialist Dühring for being unable to apply dialectics to the relation between absolute and relative truth. To be a materialist," he says, "is to acknowledge objective truth which is revealed to us by our sense organs."[7] No positivist could ever believe that "our sense organs" can "reveal to us objective or absolute truths."

Today the claim that matter, space, time, evolution, motion, and inheritance are "eternal, final and ultimate truths' is rejected by many philosophers and scientists. J. Bronowski rightly indicates that today there is almost no scientific theory that was held when the Industrial Revolution began about 1760. Present theories usually flatly contradict those of 1760, and many contradict those of 1900.[8] Hardly anybody now engaged in the research in cosmology, quantum mechanics, genetics or even sociology holds the beliefs that appeared unshakeable 70 to 80 years ago. Arguing against idealism and positivism, Lenin, like Marx and Engels, disregards all positive criteria for natural science and simply insists that "the Marxist doctrine is omnipotent because it is true."[9] Science is the search for order within facts that are commonly regarded as simple units of knowledge issuing from pure perception. The truth of science in a wider sense, however, is not truth of facts but truth of laws that are contained within the facts. Many facts can be patterned into laws, but generally scientists try to pattern or classify all facts into still more complex wholes called scientific theories. Scientific facts are not essentially dependent for their use in the scientific world on the work of any individual. Although scientific facts are discovered and formulated by individual scientists, they have to be presented so that other scientists may examine the alleged facts. On many occassions, there have been conflicts and disagreements between scientists and non-scientists about the relevance to human knowledge of these alleged facts.[10] There have been and still are disagreements in this respect among scientists themselves. These diagreements, however, can be minimized more successfully in the scientific world than in the non-scientific field when different observes of facts judge coincidences and experimental values of scientific theories. There is no claim that a technically verified theory represents "final and absolute truth" or God-like knowleddge. Because there is always an endless number of theories that can account for all known facts, scientists judge between what matters and what does not matter and thus refer to some theories as more coherent or truthful than others.

There are no self-evident principles in natural sciences. Marx and Engels fail to realize that even Newton's theory of gravitation is liable to revision, although the law of gravitation remains "absolutely true." Earlier in this century, the German physicist Heisenberg has shown that every description of nature, not just of an electron, contains some persisting uncertainty. Science, like theology and philosophy, begins with the belief that humans can orderly arrange the natural world. The purpose of science is to describe the natural world in an orderly pattern that will assist scientists as they forecast the future behavior of observed phenomena. Unfortunately, this is a very limited activity as entailed in the uncertainly principle in modern physics. The inadequacy of experiments, microscopes, and observation in scientific research has been indicated and stressed by many scientists and philosophers, including Marx. Speaking of difficulties facing the research worker in economics, Marx indicates rightly that in "the analysis of economic forms we have neither microscope nor chemical reagents to help us out. The power of abstraction has to take the place of both these expedients."[11]

It is widely believed that facts are the foundation of science and that these facts are observable. Yet, as Poincaré points out, an "accumulation of facts is no more science than a heap of stones is a house." The assumption of persistent features in the natural world is not an adequate premise for the establishment of natural science. Both Newton's dynamics and Einstein's theory of relativity essentially go beyond all observations.[12] Modern theories of physics are highly speculative and abstract, far removed from observable facts. Modern physicists advise us not to picture atomic particles. The search for a visual electron, they say, easily leads to confusion. The impossibility of visualizing ultimate matter is an essential feature of atomic explanation. The philosophical assumption of Marx's theory of knowledge is that the universe is a process of which empirical knowledge is the only possible knowledge. Yet, he is neither a consistent materialist nor a consistent empiricist. Sometimes he realizes that the inference in induction is not a merely empirical matter and that some *a priori* principle about the world is needed if induction is to be justified. Engels rightly points out that "induction can never prove that there will never be a mammal without lacteal glands."[13] Like Hegel, who maintains that the inductive conclusion is essentially problematic, he argues that induction is not an infallible method. "A striking example of how little induction can claim to be the sole or even the predominant form of scientific discovery occurs in thermodynamics."[14]

Marx's and Engels' interest, like Hegel's, is principally in the dialectical method, because this alone in their view can prove necessity. In his *Encyclopaedia*, Hegel maintains that "mere experience affords us only perceptions of changes succeeding each other but gives us no knowledge of necessary connection."[15] Like Hegel, Engels reaffirms that "the empiricism of observation alone can never adequately prove necessity."[16] Marx seems to realize that necessity can characterize only analytic statements, and that from these nothing can be known about the material world. The part played by deduction in scientific reasoning is greater than Bacon had supposed. Both Marx and Engels realize that thought as the source of the *a priori* and sense experience are different capacities and have separate, although essential, functions in scientific knowledge. Rationalist thinkers of the seventeenth and eighteenth centuries reduced sense experience to confused thinking, but modern philosophers and scientists do not share this view. Hume maintains that only analytic propositions are *a priori* and that all necessity is merely conditional. Kant and Hegel argue that although synthetic or *a posteriori* propositions alone may be devoid of logical necessity, they are characterized by transcendental necessity derived from the mind itself. Hume's skepticism rests entirely on his rejection of the principle of induction. If this principle is false, then all attempts to arrive at any general scientific laws from particular observations must be fallacious, and skepticism is inescapable for empiricists.

Unlike rationalist philosophers, Hume argues that all factual propositions are ultimately reducible to statements about simple impressions and that these are devoid of any necessary connection. Scientists, however, are not interested in Humean scepticism. Einstein, attracted initially by the skeptical and analytical philosophies of Ernst Mach and David Hume, has found these philosophies inadequate for recognizing the place of hypotheses in science. Thus he has moved away gradually from positivism to ontological assertions of the existence of a physical reality entirely independent of man. Physical reality and causality, which Hume and Mach regard as purely speculative and unfounded concepts, become very significant components of Einstein's philosophy of science. In Marx's view, science alone can extend man's understanding of the real world. Other sources of knowledge, including philosophy and theology, are of no importance except in providing relevant data for scientific generalizations about practice and thus influencing action. It is for this reason that he foresees the elimination of philosophy and its replacement by science. "Where speculation ends," he writes, "where real life starts, there consequently begins real, positive science, the expounding of the practical activity, of the practical process of development of man. Empty phrases about consciousness end, and real knowledge has to take their place. When the reality is described, a self-sufficient philosophy loses its medium of existence."[17]

Feuerbach rejects *a priori* propositions as products of speculative philosophy. Defining science as the "cognisance of species," he does not realize that his own "science" is only a reflection of pseudo-scientific orienation characterizing German *Naturphilosophie* and that his claim to be a "natural philosopher in the domain of mind" is essentially idealistic.[18] Like Feuerbach, Marx states emphatically that the premises from which he starts in his "science" are neither Hegelian abstractions nor abstract formulae of the Young Hegelians. This claim is exaggerated, and Marx's "science of man," in many respects, reflects the alienated *Naturphilosophie*. The "science of man," unlike Einstein's science, is entirely man-orientated and ideologically motivated. Like most scientists in democratic countries, Einstein has stated explicitly that the content of natural science cannot have any relevant bearing on the social sciences. "Science can only ascertain," he says, "what *is* but not what should be the case." Genuine scientists, he says, are reluctant to participate in philosophical and sociological controversies and "the practical scientist may appear to trained philosophers and sociologists as a type of unscrupulous opportunist."[19] Marx's approach to his science is entirely different. Starting from the premise that man is the immediate object of natural science, he subordinates the investigation of nature to the investigation of the "human essence of nature or the natural essence of man."[20]

Marx is not really a scientist at all. After all, his knowledge of natural science is rudimentary and, not surprisingly, he says very little about it. Without defining his own "science," he uses the term in many different ways. Sometimes he speaks of a "single science," "the science of history," and sometimes, like Plato and Feuerbach, of the "science of man." He takes for granted that dialectical materialism agrees fully with natural science. Preoccupied with "scientific truths," Marx admits that "scientific truth is always a paradox, if judged by everyday experience, which catches only the delusive appearance of things."[21] Only materialist dialectics can lead us to truth. In Marx's and Engels's view, an understanding of the world must include a knowledge of its historical development, not just its functional behavior. The material world is an interconnected whole, and man's knowledge is derived from existing matter. The motion in matter and the changes that occur in it are entirely self-generated and in accordance with overall regulatities or laws which are dialectical. Matter is infinite in its principles, and man's knowledge of matter can only be intelligible in the light of dialectical laws. Just as biological phenomena cannot be reduced to physical ones, so social phenomena cannot be reduced to biological or psychological phenomena. Marx treats psychology as an alienated bourgeois science, and for this reason psychology "cannot become a genuine, comprehensive and real science."[22]

In all his brief references to natural science, Marx speaks of a "genuine and real science," but he never describes this science except in unscientific terms. In fact, his analysis of "science" is always colored by political and ideological overtones. He criticizes "true socialism" for eulogizing "German science". In his view, "true socialism which claims to be based on science" is only alienated and "esoteric science." "Its theoretical literature is intended only for those who are initiated into the mysteries of the thinking mind."[23] Believing that his own ideas of reality are derived from "scientific facts," Marx criticizes Proudhon for sharing the illusions of speculative philosophy and for his inability to penetrate the secret of "scientific dialectics." Proudhon and the utopians, he says, are hunting for a so-called science and, by ignoring "scientific dialectics," they only find "alienated science." Proudhon's "science reduces itself to the slender proportions of a scientific formula; he is the man in search of formulas."[24] Marx believes Proudhon is not the only *parvenu* of science. The ideas of Bauer and other Young Hegelians are equally "unscientific," reflecting the "twaddle about science" and alienated science.

Engel and Marx share a similar view of science. Both are interested in "scientific dialectics," and both are history-orientated. Criticizing Dühring's "scientific" method as nothing but the method of German *Naturphilosophie*, Engels indicates that Dühring's science is "one of the most characteristic types of pseudo-science which in Germany nowadays is forcing its way to the front everywhere and is drowning everything with its resounding-sublime nonsense."[25] This sublime nonsense, he says, is "the most characteristic mass product of Germany's intellectual industry." Attracted by Hegelian dialectics, Engels rejects all science that is not connected with dialectical laws. For Engels and Hegel, dialectical laws are ubiquitous. They regulate the whole universe and are relevant equally in history, sociology, economics, physics, and chemistry. Marx certainly bases his philosophical and scientific ideas on Hegel's dialectics, but it is difficult to know whether he has accepted all that Engels advocates in his dialectics of nature. Many commentators, including George Lichtheim, argue that Engels has ventured into the field of pure speculation where Marx has feared to tread, and that the outcome is "dialectical materialism" that will continue "to weigh heavily on his followers." Engels is blamed for his attempted synthesis of positive science and speculative philosophy. Marx's views, they say, cannot be identified with Engels's theories as described in *Anti-Dühring* and *Dialectics of Nature*. The fact is that both Marx and Engels claim to be materialistically orientated, and that their "science of history" cannot be understood in non-dialectical terms. The most fundamental aspects of the materialist conception of history, a theory with which Marx and Engels are closely associated, cannot be grasped except on the basis of "scientific dialectics."[26]

Marx and Engels both indicate that scientific thought is distinguished from other modes of thought by being proved valid in practice. They reject the view, however, that there can be "real science" unless its content is applied to practical life. Unlike natural scientists, they believe that real science cannot be neutral with respect to human values, whatever these may be. This science, Marx says, must "transform human life practically through the medium of industry."[27] Its immediate object must be man in his relationship with nature and other men. It is in the sources of "the science of man" that those interested in the knowledge of reality will find the source of truth and the moral inspiration for a "scientific" socialist humanism. There is a hint of French Enlightenment in Marx's conception of positive science. Positive science and enlgihtenment, he believes, are the same thing. It is to "real science" that we owe the liberation of mankind from alienated forms of thought. There is, however, a considerable difference between Condorcet's positive science and Marx's science of man. Underlying Condorcet's analysis is the assumption of a link between the "true" and the "just."[28] He starts from the premise that ethical facts are as general and constant as those of the physical order. Marx rejects these facts, and instead of trying to use the probability theory to rationalize legal, political, and economic decision-making, he uses the Hegelian dialectical method to revolutionize political, ideological, and socioeconomic decision-making. Marx and Engels have always seen positive science as merely a weapon in the struggle against capitalist alienation, believing that this science could aid the workers in their class war toward liberation from capitalist enslavement.

In the practical sense, science is the necessary basis for abstract and theoretical scientific orientation. The successes of modern science probably would not have been achieved if scientists had not taken from great philosophers certain assumptions on which they based their theories. Science involves the abstractions of some variables from complex reality and the attempt to establish laws about the probability of regular relationship between such variables. Scientists have learned that science thrives when it stays clear of social, political, and ideological criticism.[29] Mixing issues of science with those of ideologies leads invariably to controversies as is clearly illustrated in the Galilean and Darwinian episodes. The claim by sociology to be a science does not go unchallenged. This claim implies that it is possible to construct models and formulate theories that allow us to predict the behavior of men and social systems as a whole. Many scientists reject this claim. Some modern scientists, especially physicists, restrict the denotation of science to such branches of knowledge as physics and chemistry.[30] Much that has passed for science is now felt by some scientists to be dubious philosophy, sociology, or even theology. Indeed, in the *Oxford Dictionary*, theology is still defined as "the science of religion." Engels defines dialectics as "the science of universal interconnection."[31] Much that is held to be "real science" is often felt to provide only confused fragments of the realities that affect the life of man. There are philosophers, economists, and sociologists who speak in the name of real science, although their "science" is nothing but, to use Marx's phraseology, "the twaddle about science and sham display of it."[32] Marx's "science of man," unfortunately, is open to the same charge.

French thinkers have created sociology, and their contributions are unrivalled for their scope and originality. Auguste Comte, who coined the term *sociology*, is well aware of the difference between natural sciences and sociology. In the inorganic sciences, he indicates, the elements are much better known than the whole. In these sciences, research must progress from the simple to the complex, whereas in the study of man and society the reverse method is necessary. In Marx's and Engels's theories, the positivist conception of science is defective and alienating like any "bourgeois science." They believe that "proletarian science" must be based on a "critical knowledge of the historical movement" and that the interpretation of social phenomena in relation to social change is of primary importance. They contend that the role of theoretical thought in the description of social phenomena and human involvement in the process of "scientific" understanding are much greater than it is assumed in positivism. In *Manuscripts of 1844*, Marx denounces the illusion that the philosophy of nature is of primary importance in the development of natural sciences and insists that "industry is the actual historical relation of nature and therefore of natural science to man."[33] Indicating that "philosophy has remained alien to the natural sciences as they remain alien to philosophy," he envisages the elimination of philosophy and a reciprocal intertwining of physical sciences with "the science of man." As a result, he says, natural science will lose its abstractly material or its idealistic, speculative tendency.[34] As long as natural science is manipulated by bourgeois scientists, it will remain alienated. In confused language, Marx concludes that the "social reality of nature and human natural science of the natural science about man are identical terms."[35]

In his theory of alienation, Marx argues that the subjection of natural science to alien capitalist interests necessarily reflects alienated productive activity. In the framework of the capitalist mode of production, the natural sciences and philosophy manifest the same process of alienation. Bourgeois science, in Marx's view, is always in the service of alienated, inhuman, and fragmented ends. Moreover, alienated science is unavoidably "unnatural" and class conscious. In opposition to "bourgeois alienated, abstracat and idealistic natural science," he advocates the creation of a "human science or the science of man."[36] Here, Marx obviously means a "science" that is linked closely with socio-political developments. "The science of man" must be in close correspondence with the stages of man's social development. There is no such thing as science *in vacuo*. There is only the science of a particular society at a particular time and place. The history of science, according to Marx and Engels, can only be understood as a function of the total life of society. To understand the historical development of science, it is necessary to know the evolution of society and its political structure. Private property and division of labor have an important influence on the development of science. The emergence of a class society, they indicate, is responsible for scientific alienation.

The roots of alienated science, Marx and Engels state, are found in the existence of classes and in the alienation of consciousness resulting from alienated class society. Scientific alienation in this society reflects the interests of the dominant class, which are opposed to the interests of the workers. Only science produced by the "historical movement and consciously connected with it" is, they say, "positive science." Marx writes, "We know only a single science, the science of history. One can look at history from two sides and divide it into the history of nature and the history of men. The two sides are, however, inseparable. The history of nature and the history of men are dependent on each other so long as men exist."[37] Because he is not well versed in the history of nature or natural science, he naturally decides to examine the history of men, stressing that "the whole ideology amounts either to a distorted conception of this history or to a complete abstraction from it."[38]

Marx's examination of the history of men is ideological and not always based on the empirical study of socioeconomic processes in modern society. He has little direct knowledge of workers and their alienated conditions. However, he claims to have direct insight into the alienation of the proletariat and, as a reuslt, describes his own representation of socioeconomic reality as "real positive science." This reality is in many respects distorted, ideological, subjective, and inferential. Marx and Engels do not, of course, consider their own theories as being part of any ideology. For them, ideology is social consciousness alienated by class orientation. Human relations in this orientation, they argue, are always presented in a fragmented, mystifying, and distorted manner. However, even some modern Marxists admit that Marxism itself is also an ideology. Consciousness that uses sociological laws to predict the future is, they say, necessarily ideological. Marxism is an ideology because its theories subordinate science to politics, putting political objectives before scientific, moral, and ontological objectives. Unlike Einstein, who has insisted that scientists should leave politics to the politicians, Marx and Engels insist on the opposite. Not surprisingly, their science is a "malady of contemporary scientific philosophising." It is moved by emotions, class-hatred, and subjectivity and it is based on patchy evidence and metaphysical assumptions. There are certainly differences between Marxist and non-Marxist ideologies. From the point of view of objective science, both of these ideologies are beyond the boundary of constructive science. If non-Marxist ideology is alienating, mystifying, and unscientific, Marxist ideology is the same.

Many accounts of the social significance of science are infused with social philosophies that are based on the idea of a continuous creation of absolute values.[39] Needless to say, these philosophies are frequently speculative, abstract, and irrelevant to man's practical life. While natural sciences are normally based on verifiable facts and assert nothing that is not observable, social philosophies are based on social phenomena that cannot always be verified. It is the abstraction of meaning related to these phenomena and the speculative aspect of analysis, that separate sociology from the natural sciences. The tendency of some sociologists to reduce sociology to the realm of natural science has been resisted successfully by natural scientists. Many scientists, deeply concerned about social problems, regard science as a tool rather than an integral part of society. The character of products of natural science depends, as Einstein points out, on the nature of the goals alive in the minds of men. "Once these goals exist, the scientific method furnishes means to realise them." This method, he adds, cannot furnish the goals. Unlike a scientist, a sociologist cannot take an entirely impersonal and neutral approach to his sociological object. The discovery of uniformities of human behavior is an essential task of sociology. It may be possible to express these uniformities in terms of causal laws, but there are considerable differences between uniformities of nature and uniformities of social behavior. Human beings differ significantly from atoms, molecules, and celestial bodies. Although the relevance of atomic physics is considerable for understanding life and social processes, the essential characteristics of living beings, as the physicist Niels Bohr points out, have "no counterpart in inorganic matter."[40]

In his theory of scientific alienation, Marx rejects any sharp distinction between natural sciences and sociology. He insists that "positive science" must always yield practical results and also be able to predict the future. Under the influence of French materialism and determinism, he overlooks that society is never static and that most human actions are unpredictable. Even in natural sciences, predictions have only a limited value.[41] The limitation of predictability is much more obvious in social systems. In describing the future behavior of these systems, mistakes are made frequently in assuming that future behavior will resemble the present and that by logical reasoning one can make inferences from the general to the particular. In fact, it is hardly possible to predict any particular social behavior from a generalization alone. Marx and Engels assume that prediction based on generalizations is sufficient for a favorable assessment of social development. They associate this process with deterministic or, as Marx calls it, "scientific dialectics." The laws of dialectics, according to Engels, are the "most general laws abstracted from the history of nature and human society."[42] Believing that Hegel has "freed history from metaphysics by making it dialectic," he points out in a very metaphysical manner that "Hegel is capable of giving the most striking individual illustrations of the dialectical laws from nature and history in hundreds of passages."[43] The law that impresses most strongly the minds of Marx and Engels is that of the transformation of quantity into quality and vice versa. Marx admits that this law is drawn from Hegel's philosophy and believes, like Engels, that it holds good in economics and sociology as well as in the world of nature. In sociology and economics, in the science of man, "just as in the natural sciences," he writes, "we find confirmation of the law discovered by Hegel in his *Logic*, that, at a certain point, what have been purely quantitative changes become qualitative."[44] The importance of this law and the purpose for which it is used in Marx's positive science are obvious. His interest in this law is primarily ideological. In his struggle against capitalist alienation, he maintains that the "scientific dialectics" will inevitably produce radical social changes and lead to the elimination of all forms of alienation.

Under Hegel's strong influence, Marx and Engels never doubt the objective validity of "inexorable laws" in nature and society. Many modern critics, including some liberal Marxists, reject the existence of any inexorable laws in society, indicating that the natural laws cannot reveal the economic law of motion of modern society.[45] The fact is that Marx and Engels, in their criticism of alienated science, rely more in their researches on Hegel and Feuerbach than on such distinguished scientists as Newton, Priestley, Lavoisier, and Dalton. Marx criticizes Proudhon for rejecting Hegel's dialectics,[46] and Engels states explicitly that Hegel is a greater authority on natural sciences than Newton. "As far as Hegel is specifically concerned," Engels writes, "he is in many respects head and shoulders above his empiricist contemporaries who thought that they had explained all unexplained phenomena when they had endowed them with some force or power—the force of gravity, the power of buoyancy, the power of electrical contact, etc." He adds that "in contrast to the deification of Newton, Hegel brought out the fact that Kepler was the real founder of the modern mechanics of the celestial bodies and that the Newtonian law of gravitation was already contained in all three of Kepler's laws."[47] Goethe has attacked the Newtonian theory of colors as an intrusive dissection of perfectly natural phenomena into component parts in a way that he had considered alien to nature. Engels ranks Newton lower than Hegel only because Hegel has formulated the laws of dialectics which, in his view, can satisfactorily explain the history of nature and human society. Without Hegel, Marx's and Engels's "positive science" simply could not exist. Hegel's error consists in picturing reality in idealistic, estranged forms, not in describing it as inherently developmental and dialectical.

Marx and Engels, like Hegel, believe that the dialectical laws constitute the life and soul of scientific progress.[48] Every motion in man and nature is a dialectical process. "We have to agree with Hegel," Plekhanov writes, "that dialectics is the soul of any scientific cognition. This applies not only to cognition of nature."[49] Plekhanov overlooks the very important fact that Marx's dialectic gives prominence to inherently materialistic development for which Hegel's idealist dialectic gives him no justification. Marx is interested primarily in the dialectic that, he thinks, can resolve the historical contradiction underlying alienated class societies. He believes that the development of history is dialectical, always stimulated by the conflict of opposing economic interests. He sees the alienation of the production of life as the principal source of scientific alienation. The abolition of economic alienation in general and of capitalist alienation in particular would eliminate all traces of scientific alienatioin. The positive abolition of scientific alienation cannot be the result of the superficial modification of ideas. It is only "positive science" in its practical form that offers the elimination of both real alienation and alienation in consciousness. Marx's primary concern is the formulation of a social and political theory embracing a revolutionary program that must lead to radical social and cultural change. His science of man is in fact nothing but an integral part of a wider revolutionary ideology. This science is simultaneously a critique of capitalism and a philosophy of communist practice. There is always an assumption that "proletarian *praxis*" is always right and that it can never be an alien force.

Marx's tendency to represent history as an exact science and his belief that the main task of science is to predict the future lead him to the false belief that the natural world and society are equally governed by "inexorable laws." This implies that positive science is capable of attaining some form of absolute truth. To scientists, absolute truth, like absolute relativity, is a metaphysical, not a scientific conception. Natural scientists neither deny the existence of absolute truth nor affirm it; they merely ignore it. A scientific law, unlike economic or sociological laws, is not an order that must be obeyed—it is only a statement of fact. There is no way of obeying or disobeying it; and because disobedience is impossible, there is no penalty involved. Failing to distinguish between laws of nature that are simply general statements about certain regularities in nature and laws of society that are valid only on the assumption that certain conditions are present and remain unchanged, Marx and Engels overlook that the "laws of society" are always hypothetical in nature. They cannot be characterized as permanent, immutable, and all-pervading. Even "the inexorable laws of nature," according to some physicists, are neither eternally true nor unchangeable.[50] Thus predictions in sociology are hardly possible. Laplace's claim that all future events could be predicted from knowledge of the present has definitely been abandoned in the quantum theory.[51] As Heisenberg indicates, we cannot predict both exact position and exact velocity of the electron, and can calculate only probabilities for the future. Although he speaks primarily of the difficulty involved in predicting the exact position and velocity of an electron, he does not deny the validity of his observations in the physical realm for non-physical reality.

Prediction is not a regular aspect even of scientific laws. Kepler's first law specifies the shape of the orbit in which the planet moves, but it says nothing about the speed with which it moves in that orbit. His laws and Darwinian theory predict nothing. Many modern physicists are convinced that uncertainty is a fundamental limitation of human knowledge; and because of this limitation, we are unable to know whether events and phenomena in the atomic domain are determinate or not. The paradigm of a conception of science pursuing the ideal of extreme determinism has been formulated by Laplace. He believes that the future is fully and definitely determined. If and when we know the present completely, we can completely determine the future.[52] The nineteenth century has been dominated by Laplace's materialistic and deterministic theory that everything can be described in terms of causality. He has advanced the hypothesis that the solar system has condensed out of a vast rotating gaseous nebula and that what is now the system of the planets and the sun was originally a single diffuse nebula. Both Marx and Engels are fascinated by Laplace's ideas, especially by his determinism, materialism, and atheism. These concepts dominate their positive science. They are pleased that in Laplace's *Treatise on Celestial Mechanics* "the Creator is not even mentioned."[53] They do not realize that the acceptance of a scientific outlook based on the Laplacean fallacy not only imperils scientific freedom, it also destroys the conditions for any rational explanation of social behavior. No strictly deterministic analysis can give us a model for social analysis. In the non-Marxian picture, human individuals perceive the world around them, select features to the perceived, discriminate among them, judge them, change them, and are held responsible for their actions. In the Marxian scientific picture, however, they are members of a species shaped by evolutionary contingencies of survival, displaying social processes that bring them under the control of the environment in which they live. Here voluntarism is replaced by determinism, and the direction of the controlling relation is reversed in such a way that human individuals do not, strictly speaking, act on the world but the material world acts on them.

Marx's deterministic and materialistic view of science, like the Laplacean mechanistic conception of man with which it is associated, subordinates all scientific and cultural activities to the controlling agency of the state. Here scientific values are discredited and their appreciation is suppressed and alienated. Communist praxis is, in fact, a vivid example of human activity in which there is no room for free science. Marx insists that opposing realities can never be reconciled in practice. This means that bourgeois alienated sceience must be eliminated and replaced by the science of man. In the Preface to the second German edition of *Capital*, he associates the critical and revolutionary character of his science of man with his form of dialectic. Being deterministic, materialistc, and revolutionary, his dialectic is strongly opposed to the division of positive science into the natural sciences and the science of human history. This division, he believes, is unnecessary, irrelevant, and alienating. "One basis for life and another basis for science is *a priori* a lie."[54] The division of human knowledge into competing disciplines can be maintained only by alienation. The capitalist division of labor not only alienates the worker from his essential being, it also distorts reality in the interests of capitalist domination and thus causes and maintains scientific alienation.

As part of economic alienation, scientific alienation, according to Marx, reflects the real estrangement and fragmentation of human activity. Whenever "the science of man" is removed from the totality of cognition, it necessarily loses its objectivity and its determination to liberate man from alienation. Marx is convinced that soon "natural science and the science of man will become one science."[55] Scientific alienation will be transcended when the whole movement of scientific orientation is conceived as a social movement serving social ends. Attempts to isolate any aspect of the science of man from the socio-political movement are condemned. The claims of non-Marxist science to universal validity are revealed as erroneous, deceptive, mystifying, and class-orientated. The unmasking of alienated bourgeois science is regarded as an example of dialectical objectivity. The science of man must always be in the service of revolutionary politics. The victory of this science is identified ultimately with the victory of socialism.[56] Capitalism is wrong, decaying, and alienating. It is only "socialism" that is "always right," always progressive, and always "scientifically-orientated." Within a society based on dialectical materialism, the forces of coercion, anchored to the central political power of the proletariat, become in reality the agents of Marx's critical and revolutionary science.

In Marx's science of man, the class struggle motivates scientific progress. This progress is not spontaneous but must be organized on the basis of the scientific theory of historical materialism. Advances in scientific research in bourgeois societies have been made possible by the increasing mechanization of industrial production. Large industrial corporations have promoted the kind of scientific knowledge that could be transformed profitably into technological innovation. Scientific products could only be appropriated by industrial enterprises and, to some extent, individual inventors. The introduction of professional careers in the natural sciences and the establishment of allocation funds for scientific research have always depended on political and economic priorities. After the emancipation of scientific orientation from the tradition of Aristotelianism, scientific research gradually became susceptible to integration into the capitalist mode of production. Profit-motivated industrial capitalism, according to Marx and Engels, has been the first socioeconomic formation in history that has applied very successfully scientific knowledge for production purposes. In their view, however, bourgois science serves the interests of the ruling class only. Representatives of bourgeois science have become the "undisguised ideologists of the bourgeoisie," distorting and misinterpreting scientific facts to suit their own goals and to maintain alienation. The subsumption of natural sciences under profit and their separation from dialectical materialism inevitably lead to alienation.[57] Marxist science must be class conscious and defend the interests of the workers. "The more ruthlessly and disinterestedly this science proceeds," Engels says, "the more it finds itself in harmony with the interests and aspirations of the workers."[58]

The dialectical principle that Marx applies in his science of man to history and economics is applied by Engels to the sphere of nature. Assuming wrongly that modern science has furnished the convincing proof that nature works dialectically, he concludes that "nature itself is the proof of dialectics."[59] Engels does not realize that all scientific discoveries were made without any reference to the dialectical laws of nature. Galileo's laws of motion, Kepler's laws of planetary motion, Newton's law of gravitation, Boyle's law of gaseous pressure, Dalton's law of multiple proportions, the kinetic theory of matter and heat, the quantum theory, and Einstein's theory of relativity have nothing to do with dialectic. No scientist, working in countries in which science is a free activity, has ever invoked the principles of dialectic to support his scientific theories. Virchow, referred to in Engels's old preface to *Anti-Dühring*, has made a detailed examination of the histology of diseased tissues without appealing to dialectical principles. In addition, he has defended freedom and independence of science in the modern state, indicating that scientific research must be independent of state control and revolutionary politics.[60]

In Marx's view, scientists must be active in the struggle against alienating bourgeois science. The sceience of man should not simply be a method of research and political action but also the theoretical expression of solutions in any given socioeconomic structure. Theoretical practice must be taken seriously. It requires real, class-conscious, and revolutionary investigators, and must include both ideological and scientific theoretical orientation. Hegel's "science of logic" is concerned only with theoretical, philosophical, and ontological issues and with specific alienated needs rather than with practical issues. This science is alienating, Marx argues, because it is irrelevant to practical human problems. Like any other "bourgeois science," it maintains the alienating division of social activities and professionalism as the condition

for "scientific theoretical practice." Marx claims that in his system of historical materialism, the science of man and the natural sciences will be integrated
and harmonied with the totality of social practice. Non-Marxist scientists,
however, do not share this view. They point out that in the absence of an
objective scientific method, the claim that the Marxian dialectic will resolve
the historical contradiction of alienated society and shatter the contradictions
involved in the alienation process is purely inferential and scientifically un-
sound. Natural science is distinguished from pseudo-science and Marxist
ideology by its empirical method, which is essentially inductive.[61]

Marx never explains how the development of material forces can proceed
in the same way as the development of spiritual forces through the conflict of
opposites. Assuming, like Hegel, that the dialectic gives the clue to the whole
process of development, he takes for granted that material things are capable
of self-development like ideas and spiritual entities, whatever these may be.
He also assumes that the historical method is synonymous with the scientific
method and thus adequate for the analysis of socioeconomic totalities. The
fact is that no scientific method can ever be adequate for the predictive analysis of Marx's socioeconomic totality, which is as metaphysical and mystical as
any Hegelian totality. Defending dialectical materialism in Marx's science of
man, some modern Marxists justify their standpoint even by quoting such
non-scientifically orientated dialecticians as Plato, Aristotle, Schelling, and
the German theosophical mystic, Jacob Boehme.[62] One could well add to
these dialecticians the scholastic philosopher and theologian Pierre Abélard,
who was also interested in dialectic as the road to truth. Marx fails to see that
his "scientific dialectic" is in substance similar to other forms of philosophical-
ly and theologically orientated dialectics. In Marx's dialectic, as in Plato's and
Hegel's, "the real and true," "science and truth" are always the distinguishing categories of the knowing process.

Although Marx is not opposed in principle to the study of the history of
nature, his main interest is in the history of man or in "the science of history."
Real history, he says, begins when men "start to produce their means of
subsistence."[63] It must include the history of how nature becomes man, the
genesis of its empirical existence, as well as "the comprehended and known
process of its becoming."[64] In the process of historical becoming, all branches
of knowledge, theory, and practice, must become "science." The science of
history, in Marx's view, will become "one science" embracing simultaneously
the science of nature and the science of man.[65] Marx does not explain the
difference between "the science of man" indicated in *Manuscripts of 1844*
and "the science of history" advocated in *German Ideology*. Both of course,
are based on dialectical and materialistic philosophy and are linked closely
with the economic, social, and political position of the working classes. They
could really be defined as the science of communism, which is destined to
replace alienated bourgeois science. Marx's science, "which directly serves to
enlighten and organise the advanced class in modern society," Lenin writes,

"indicates the tasks facing this class and demonstrates the inevitable replacement (by virtue of economic development) of the present system by a new order."[66] Because this science reveals the mechanisms of alienated bourgeois science in theory and practice, it is misunderstood and resisted by all bourgeois scientists. "Throughout the civilised world," he says, "the teachings of Marx evoke the utmost hostility and hatred of all bourgeois science which regards Marxism as a kind of pernicious sect. There can be no impartial social science in a society based on class struggle. In one way or another, all official and liberal science defends wage slavery, whereas Marxism has declared relentless war on that slavery."[67]

Following this line of thinking, some modern "scientific Marxists" reduce Marx's science almost entirely to the science of communism. Marx has established, according to Althusser, "a new science: the science of the history of social formations."[68] This science "cannot be a science for everyone." Because it brings "the social classes face to face with their truth," he says, "it is unbearable for the bourgeoisie." Althusser admits frankly that Marx's science is "only acceptable to the proletariat whom it represents."[69] The struggle for Marxist science is regarded as a form of political and ideological class struggle. The unique character of dialectical science consists in the fact that it is linked with the real becoming of productive activity, that it reveals alienation, and that it can be used by the revolutionaries in their struggle against the alienating forces of capitalism. The real revolutionary power, Marx believes, is found in the products of science and technology. Technology forms the rhythm of historical development and provides the "earthly basis for history." "Steam, electricity, powered machinery were revolutionists of a rather more dangerous character than even citizens Barbès, Raspail and Blanqui."[70]

Technology is always more important in Marx's mind than natural science. "Technology," he says, "reveals man's dealings with nature, discloses the direct productive activity of his life, thus throwing light upon social relations and the resultant mental conceptions."[71] The revolutionary force of technology creates a new class-conscious world in which industrialization must spread and the number of alienated workers must inevitably increase. Alienation of the forces of production necessitates the disappearance of the structures of capitalism. Marx's interest in technology must be connected with his belief that technological progress can be an effective method in the transformation of alienated science. Man produces himself as man and nature becomes history through technological processes. "Industry," he says, "is the actual, historical relation of nature, and therefore of natural science to man. If, therefore, industry is conceived as the exoteric revelation of man's essential powers, we also gain an understanding of the human essence of nature or the natural essence of man.[72] Only when science and technology are freed from the bonds of alienating private property and class division and are united in the science of history will there be any real significance in the elimination of scientific alienation. Technology constructs the bridges between different stages of historical development and reveals the contradictions in alienated activities.

Marx is well aware of contradictory effects of technology within a condition of alienation. Although automation creates new opportunities that lead to overcoming alienation, it also produces many undesirable side effects and far-reaching changes in the pattern of employment. Workers accept technological change when they are consulted in advance and are allowed to participate in decision-making. In the bourgeois system, however, this happens rarely. The distinguishing mark of bourgeois technology, Marx claims, is that it alienates and poisons everything. In spite of its achievements reflected in the "subjection of nature's forces to man, machinery and application of chemistry to industry," capitalist technology has intensified and extended the human drama of alienation. "Machinery, gifted with the wonderful power of shortening and fructifying human labour but in the property system of profit-markers, leaves man alienated and enslaved to other men or to his own infamy. Even the pure light of science seems unable to shine but on the dark background of ignorance."[73] Comforted by his oracular gifts, Marx is confident that the capitalist mechanization of labor that "destroys every connection of the product with the direct need of the producer" and reduces the worker to a "conscious appendage of a machine" for the sake of profit necessarily leads to its own negation. As part of the unified science of man, it is envisaged that the techniques of the communist future, will be the antidote that will eliminate alienated science and alienated techniques. Scientific and technical knowledge that in the capitalist system is "alien and external to the worker" will not only "cease to be doctrinaire" and alienating but will also become the property of all revolutionary men and women.[74] The antagonism between alienated science and alienated industry "stultifies human life into a material force."[75] In classless society, this antagonism is bound to disappear.

In *Manuscripts of 1844*, Marx is optimistic about the positive potential of technological development in providing the means for satisfying human needs and in preparing the ground for human emancipation.[76] In his mature works, however, there is a mixture of optimistic and pessimistic statements about the side effects of automation. In *Grundrisse*, his view of the qualitative tranformation of labor in the communist-controlled technological process is relatively optimistic.[77] In *Capital*, he indicates that even under communism there might be a residue of intrinsically disagreeable labor. There are no explicit statements about alienation and unemployment in the communist future. He observes correctly that the contradiction involved in automation in its capitalist form "works itself out disastrously in the incessant sacrifice of workers and in the reckless squandering of labour power "for the benefit of profit-makers.[78] Marx does not foresee the possibility of alienation in the communist system. In communist praxis, however, workers are alienated and frequently experience unemployment as well. Of course, their position is considerably more alienating under capitalism where they are mercilessly left to "sink gradually into the proletariat and be involved in a constant battle with the bourgeoisie."[79] Marx overlooks that progress of automation necessarily entails unemployment in all societies. In communist countries, technological unemployment is somehow "spread out in space," and unemployed workers are directed by the central authority to move, when necessary, to distant locations. Such a procedure seems to be just as inhuman as the capitalist indifference to the suffering and alienation of redundant workers.

Technology is not an offspring of science; it is a separate activity that may be stimulated by scientific research. Traditionally, science is aristocratic, intellectual, and speculative, whereas technology is seen as lower-class, empirical, and action-orientated.[80] Primitive technology may be treated as a mere extension of bodily skills used to satisfy bodily appetites. It is life-centered rather than power-centered. Modern inventors and controllers of computer intelligence, supersonic transportation, instantaneous planetary communication, nuclear energy, and military techniques, however, are haunted by delusions of omniscience and omnipotence. The concepts of absolute power, culminating in the invention of nuclear weapons, are reminiscent of the conception of divine omnipotence and omniscience. Modern man's state of mind is dominated completely by technical values. The monstrous power of technological inventions originates in capitalism. Communism has simply taken over these inventions and, as Berdyaev states, "worships them as a totem." The tragedy is that Marx's science of man is, in fact, nothing but a form of revolutionary technique aimed at reshaping capitalist science and technology. In opposition to capitalist alienating science and technology, he develops his single science with all the necessary rigor and enthusiasm, linking it closely to the requirements of revolutionary class struggle. In *Poverty of Philosophy*, he indicates that automation is capable of transcending the alienating division of labor and specialization. "What characterises the division of labour in the automatic workshop is that labour has there completely lost its specialised character. But the moment every special development stopps, the need for universality, the tendency towards an integral development of the individual begins to be felt. The automatic workshop wipes out specialists and craft-idiocy."[81] Proudhon is criticized for failing to understand "even this revolutionary side of the automatic workshop." Marx does not see that scientists have always defended specialization.[82]

Reducing science to technology, Marx takes for granted that the technological progress in communist society will lead to the conquest of the world by and for man. He does not always realize that advanced technology creates social problems and may also have alienating side effects in communist-controlled systems of production. Central planning may increase effiiciency, but scientific planning and state control are inadequate measures when dealing with human individuals. The complete fusion of science and technology creates the dependence of scientific development on technological invention. Marx does not see that science and technology have different aims. Whereas science aims to enlarge our knowledge through devising better theories, technology aims to create new artifacts through devising means of increasing effectiveness.[83] The factual restriction of science to political reasoning makes the search for truth meaningless. In politically controlled science, truth becomes a medium of organizational integration rather than an objective aim and an inspiration of the scientist in his search for scientific knowledge. Speaking of "proletarian science" in terms of "truth," Marxists argue that "bourgeois science" is a distortion of truth and "true ideas" always serve the interests of the alienated class. For Lenin, "communist theory—the science of communism formulated by Marx—is an *a priori* truth.[84] Rejecting Einstein's theory of relativity, he insists that the "natural scientist must be a modern materialist, a conscious adherent of the materialism represented by Marx, i.e., he must be a dialectical materialist."[85]

Marx believes scientific truth is always paradoxical when judged by the mere "appearances" of things. Bourgeois scientific truths, based on appearances rather than on reality, are a distortion of the whole truth that can only be found in the "science of communism." Marx's science of history and Engels's science of dialectics are commonly associated with the Darwinian theory of evolution. "Logically," according to Plekhanov, "the investigation of Marx begins where the investigation of Darwin ends." The spirit of their research is the same. "That is why one can say that Marxism is Darwinism in its application to social science."[86] Initially, Marx and Engels have been enthusiastic about Darwinism, but this enthusiasm has not lasted long. Having read Darwin's *Origin of Species* in 1860, Marx has written to Engels indicating the importance of Darwin's discovery for dialectical materialism. "This is the book," he says, "which contains the natural-history foundation for our viewpoint."[87] In *Capital*, Marx also stresses the importance of Darwin's theory in the history of natural and human technology.[88] At first, Engels is equally impressed by Darwin's *Origin of Species*. Darwin's theory of evolution, the Kant-Laplace nebular theories, Lyell's *Principles of Geology*, and Lamarckism lead him to the conclusion that the "old teleology has gone to the devil." Like other materialists of his time, Engels takes for granted that dialectical materialism has become the only rational explanation of the origin of life. "It is now firmly established," he says, "that matter in its eternal cycle moves according to laws which at a definite stage necessarily give rise to the thinking mind in organic begins."[89]

Marx's and Engels's enthusiasm for Darwin has evaporated somewhat abruptly. Rejecting Marx's revolutionary ideas of science and his dysteleology, Darwin has declined Marx's intention to dedicate his *Capital* to him. As a result, Marx has reacted quickly, denouncing Darwin's discoveries and his biological science as being overlaid with Hobbesian and Malthusian bourgeois ideology. Even the work of such insignificant scientists as P. Trémaux is now superior to that of Darwin.[90] Engels's criticism of ideological Darwinism is expressed even more strongly. "The main reproach levelled against Darwin," he writes, "is that he transferred the Malthusian population theory from political economy to natural science and that in his theory of the struggle for existence he pursued unscientific semi-poetry, and that the whole of Darwinism, after deducting what had been borrowed from Lamarck, is a piece of brutality directed against humanity."[91] In the eyes of Marx and Engels, Darwin's biological science has suddenly become as unscientific, fragmentary, unhistorical, bourgeois, and alienating as the "esoteric science" of "True Socialists" and the "unedifying science" of Proudhon.

Darwin's evolutionary theory, according to Marx and Engels, is inadequate for explaining social and economic life because it lacks dialectical elements. In the absence of an exhaustive physical and chemical explanation based on dialectical laws, Darwinism in their view, fails to explain satisfactorily the origin of life. Marx and Engels say very little on the origin of life, and what they say is unclear and unconvincing.[92] Like other materialists, they assume that the material of inanimate things and animate beings is qualitatively the same and that the differences between them are merely differences of arrangement. The difference between mind and body, in their opinion, is only a difference of complexity. Mental processes are always associated with corresponding physical processes. There is no consciousness without its material background, and nothing happens in the world without the expenditure of physical energy. The mechanistic conception of life is the only conception that can lead to an understanding of ontogenesis. The evolution of consciousness is explained in purely materialistic terms. Contrary to the Judeo-Christian tradition stressing the genesis of life from the living God, Marx and Engels advocate the materialistic version of spontaneous generation that in principle is similar to Aristotle's dualistic theory of spontaneous generation. Their conception of creation is based almost entirely on the "science of geology" which, according to Marx, "presents the formation of the earth as a process of self-generation." "*Generatio aequivoca*," he says, "is the only practical refutation of the theory of creation."[93] Refusing to involve himself in the controversy about the First Cause on the ground that it is "non-existent," Marx leaves the problem of the origin of life unanswered. As a result, modern Marxists differ widely in this respect. Without abandoning his idea of spontaneous generation, some support it with Darwinian theory of evolution, others with Lamarckian theory, and yet others with "dialectical jumps."

In spite of Redi's and Spallanzani's experimental demonstration that microbes originate from pre-existing life like plants and animals, the idea of spontaneous generation persisted among scientists. Justus von Liebig, Marx's and Engels's favorite scientist, has refused to believe that fungi and yeast are living organisms. Spallanzani, a Roman Catholic abbot and biologist, has demonstrated that heating a meat broth, then sealing the flask to exclude airborne organisms, effectively prevents microscopic life. In 1861, Pasteur has carried general conviction against spontaneous generation, which has continued to appeal to Liebig, Buffon, Marx, and Engels. They have refused to accept Pasteur's findings on the ground that, as Engels states, the only alternative to spontaneous generation would have to be the belief in a divine creator and a separate act of creation.[94] Engels admits there are "enlightening aspects" of Pasteur's experiments, but because they are associated with a religious ideologist, promoting alienated bourgeois science, he thinks they are "useless."[95] Like Marx, he firmly adheres to Liebig's hypothesis that "organic life could be thought of as present from the very beginning in life-less matter just as much as carbon and its compounds." "With regard to the origin of life, natural science is only able to say with certainty that it must have been the result of chemical action."[96]

As many non-Marxist scientists indicate, it is impossible to have any clear conception of living beings so long as one insists on defining life in terms of physics and chemistry. The rise of new forms of life is undefinable in terms of physical and chemical processes. There are no processes and events occurring according to the known laws of physics and chemistry that can be conscious. One could, like alchemists, attribute conscious desires to the mating of acids and bases, but this would not solve the problem of the origin of life. A physical-chemical explanation of life is incomplete as a causal explanation. A complete explanation of biological systems requires a reference to laws at a considerably higher level of organization. The spontaneous rise of sentient, creative, and conscious beings can only be attributed to the operations of an orderly innovating principle. Naturally, Marx and Engels reject this view. "The lowest living beings known to us," Engels writes, "are in fact nothing but simple particles of albumen and they already exhibit all the essential phenomena of life. Undoubtedly," he adds, "the presence of other chemical combinations is also necessary in a living body in order to induce particular differentiations of these phenomena of life."[97] Following Engels's view that thought and consciousness "are products of the human brain and that man is a product of nature," some dialectic materialists express their doubts about the validity of explaining the genesis of life in terms of physics and chemistry alone.[98] They argue that biological laws are essentially different from physical and chemical laws and that biological and social phenomena, including life itself, are unique and specific. According to modern biologists, living beings, are unique because they are self-maintaining systems or "homeostats," able to correct any outstanding internal imbalance to survive.[99]

The key tenet of Marx's and Engels's dialectical materialism, at the base of their "dealienating science," is the recognition of a development in which the qualitative changes of living organisms occur abruptly rather than gradually. The Darwinian theory, they argue, fails to explain the origin of life.[100] Darwin, Marx says, attributes everything to chance and nothing to necessity, and he "cannot explain degeneration."[101] "It is dialectics," Engels points out, "that constitutes the most important form of thinking for present-day natural science, for it alone offers the method of explaining the evolutionary processes in nature, inter-connections in general and transitions from one field of investigation to another."[102] This view is opposed to Darwinian gradualism and is based on Hegel's belief that qualitative increase and development often are the result of a sudden leap rather than the result of gradual evolution as in Darwinism. In a very few references to Hegel's saltatory hypothesis, Marx and Engels merely express their admiration and approval of it.[103] Darwin's evolutionary theory is not rejected entirely, but it is the "Hegelian law of the qualitative leap in the quantitative series" that they believe offers more convicing proof for a sudden leap from alienated bourgeois science to proletarian science, from capitalism to communism. "In spite of all gradualness," Engels writes, "the transition from one form of motion to another always remains a leap, a decisive change. The transition from the physics of molecules to the physics of atoms—chemistry—in turn involves a decisive leap."[104]

In recent years, there have been attempts among some English biologists to discredit Darwinian gradualism altogether and to promote the saltatory view of development. They deny any connection with dialectical materialism, however, indicating that "there are several, quite different, philosophical and sociological schools of thought" in this respect, and that Marxist application of political criteria in the assessment of scientific theories is detrimental to neutral science and must be resisted.[105] They argue that Marx's and Engels's dialectical revolutionary science is alien to natural sciences because it violates the principle of objectivity and inhibits scientific freedom. Marx's science of history is based on the principle that the true interests of science always coincide with the interests of the proletarian class. Historical materialism, in Marx's view, is a science of history that is guided by socialist aspirations and political aims. He underrates the importance of biology and practically ignores psychology because of its failure "to feel its own incompleteness."[106] Marx's belief that biological determinants of human behavior totally neglect socioeconomic determinants has later led to the controversy between classical geneticists and Lamarckism, culminating in the dispute between "bourgeois eugenics" and "proletarian eugenics." The concept of a communist eugenics, whether derived from Lamarck, Darwin, or Mendel, was finally condemned by Soviet political leaders in the early 1930s. It has been felt that one-sided biologism, especially the theory of the inheritance of acquired characteristics, might have negative effects on the social structure and even increase alienation. Being afraid that all socially or physically deprived and alienated classes might inherit the alienating and debilitating effects, communist rulers in the Soviet Union have rejected both "bourgeois genetics" and alienating "bourgeois eugenics." Lysenko and Stalinist genetics, notorious throughout the world, represent the last attempt in biological science to deviate from the statistical evidence for Mendelism.[107] The issue of Lamarckian inheritance has been settled by August Weismann, who has found that the nature of the reproductive cell is not affected by environment and that bodily modifications are not inheritable.[108] In the noncommunist world, Mendel's theory of inheritance has been generally accepted as correct. In communist countries, however, Mendelian genetics are regarded as a bourgeois product, inadequate for explaining such phenomena as alienation, dehumanization, and unemployment.

In his science of history, Marx realizes that scientific and technological research may have negative side effects not only on employment but also on human health and environment. However, his writings tend to confine these effects to alienating capitalist mechanization and automation. Although critical of alienating science and technology in capitalist society, he is totally indifferent to the potential ill effects inherent in the technological process per se. He has failed to anticipate the creation of a new technological ethics with its own values that may be as alienating as those of fetishism. There is no awareness that the technological world is the world of material things and that technological society is not a genuinely humanist society. Technological society, Marx overlooks, puts material objects rather than man, in first place. In a purely technologically orientated society, whether it is alienating capitalist society or classless society, man's conquest of nature easily becomes, as C.S. Lewis remarks, "nature's conquest of man."[109] Once technology has become indifferent to spiritual values, it necessarily generates alienation and leads to dehumanization.

Marx takes for granted that technology integrated into the communist system of production will become humane and dealienated and that the contradiction between the base and the superstructure will disappear. He has failed to anticipate that new technology will augment the bureaucratic character of the modern state and that the use of destructive technology, especially in the military and biomedical fields, is bound to lead to alienation, ill-health, environmental pollution, and accidents. During Marx's time, scientists have believed that the universe is eternal, indestructible, and without beginning. This is Marx's and Engels's view as well. Most modern scientists, however, maintain that such a view is no longer tenable. In the light of modern physics, the belief in the eternity and indestructibility of the universe is incompatible with the second law of thermodynamics and the principle of entropy. The principle of entropy implies that the universe must have begun in a condition of a minimum entropy or maximum available energy and must end in a condition of maximum entropy or minimum available energy. Eventually, all things and living organisms will be exposed to the same temperature, and all life activity will end.

Without invoking the principle of entropy, Engels presents a very pessimistic and apocalyptic picture of that end. "Millions of years may elapse, hundreds of thousands of generations be born and die," he writes, "but inexorably the time will come when the declining warmth of the sun will no longer suffice to melt the ice thrusting itself forward from the poles; when the human race will no longer find even at the equator enough heat for life and gradually even the last trace of organic life will vanish."[110] This view of dialectical regression is difficult, if not impossible, to reconcile with Marx's optimistic prediction of the communist future, in which the dealienation of man and the dealienation of nature will occur at the same time. He speaks of the end of prehistory but not of the end of the "history of the world which is nothing but the coming-to-be of nature for man"—an unending process.[111]

Modern scientists, unlike Marx, resist the implication of science in socioeconomic problems. Many of them, including Einstein, Bohr, and Eddington, indicate their interests in spiritual values rather than in politics and existing ideologies. Those interested in socioeconomic problems, however, believe that many social ills, including scientific alienation, can be solved by peaceful and legisltive means without invoking "dialectical weapons" and destroying the independence of science. By contrast, scientific Marxists always regard science as a weapon, not an end in itself. Emphasizing the practical value of modern physics as a means of defense, they follow the traditional expansionist aspiration inherent in Marx's science of history. This science entails the belief that all of nature—factual and normative, physical and social, material and spiritual—can be brought under the sway of a single scientific approach.[112] Scientists in democratic countries reject Marxist attitudes to science. They oppose the view that scientific research must be directed centrally as part of economic planning. The ideals of objectivity and universality in science, they argue, can only be realized in a society that respects the independence of science and freedom of thought.

8

Social Alienation

The nineteenth century began in the aftermath of the Industrial and French revolutions that were destined to transform the basic economic and social structure, first of Western Europe and then of the rest of the world. The Industrial Revolution is the name given to the great change in industrial methods and the vast growth of industrial production that occurred in Britain between about 1760 and 1840, and which in some ways continued long after 1840. The intellectual life of the nineteenth century was definitely more complex and more advanced than that of any previous age. Science made new and triumphant conquests in many fields, especially in organic chemistry, physics, and biology. Philosophy was treated as a kind of scientific psychology. In France the dominant trend was in favor of analyzing everything into ultimate, irreducible atomic constituents, whether psychological or physical. La Mettrie believed that the true philosopher is an engineer or anatomist who can explain rational processes in terms of physiology. There was a profound revolt against traditional systems in politics and economics. In Britain and France, new technology and machine production profoundly altered the socioeconomic structure and made men aware of a new conception of their powers in relation to their physical and social environment. Thought in England was considerably affected by the French Revolution; unpopular views were identified with those of French extremists and frequently suppressed. The period was marked by continuous debate about religious toleration. As Marx and Engels remark, all sects united in condemning and persecuting the minority of agnostics and free thinkers who doubted whether any theological view could be uniquely right. The majority of the population were brought up with no doubts about the literal truth of the book of Genesis. The prevailing attitude of scientists and others who supported evolution was anti-orthodoxy rather than anti-religious.

Politics in the nineteenth century, as in the past, became a matter of intrigues and personalities, and the political system was openly corrupt. The "English revolution" of 1640–1688 and the French Revolution of 1789 had left a capitalist society in which, as Marx indicates, freedom to profit from enterprise was almost a sacred notion. Social disturbances were either local and temporary or inevitable and incurable. In Britain, there was almost an acceptance of the Marxist view that the state could wither away leaving "inexorable" and even divinely ordained laws of economics to control all human affairs. The possibility that society might continue to change and would need certain mechanisms for regulating change was hardly discussed, let alone accepted. Herbert Spencer supported the unrestrained action of economic individualism, and he could not accept the realism of Adam Smith or that some public acts might be objectively positive and socially beneficent.

Considering that the early nineteenth century was technologically orientated, it was easy to believe that the laws of economics were as certain and inexorable as the law of universal gravitation. Already in Spencer's writings, *laissez faire* was taken as a law of nature. Rejecting the premise of the political economists that economic laws are universal, Marx himself focused his attention on the specific laws of capitalism and assumed that these were a special case of a more general set of laws that are easily obervable in class-divided societies.[1] A movement of thought, originating from Darwin's theory of evolution and inspired by writers like Spencer and Malthus, gradually became a significant intellectual force destined to play a considerable role in the second half of the nineteenth century. Social Darwinism was essentially an attempt to justify in Darwinian terms the existing individualistic *laissez faire* and competitive system of society. Social Darwinism, it must be emphasized, was entirely opposed to French collectivism and to Comte's and Durkheim's belief that society is superior to the individual. Unlike Comte and Durkheim, Spencer argues that "a society is but a collective name for a number of individuals." "Thus," he says in *The Principles of Sociology*, "the units of a society alone exist, while the existence of the society is but verbal."[2]

Although Spencer claimed to be a positivist, his positivism is opposed diametrically to Comte's positivism. As an evolutionist, he believed that evolution works well, even if with cruelty to those who compete incompetently, when it is left alone. The fittest societies are those with the fittest individuals: only the fittest survive. The belief that "all social suffering is removable and that it is the duty of somebody or other to remove it is false." The command "if any would not work neither should he eat," he says, "is simply a Christian enunciation of that universal law of nature under which life has reached its present height—the law that a creature not energetic enough to maintain itself must die."[3] Spencer's sociology is grounded on egoistic principles. Inequalities among human beings, he contends, are natural. He takes for granted that only those possessing and controlling property are entitled to hold political power and exercise social domination. That is their "natural" prerogative and their "natural" civil right. In his agnostic mood, Spencer mocks "ardent philanthropy" and Christian "timid sentimentality." In *The Man versus the State* he shows no sympathy for the unemployed. They, he says, "either refuse work or quickly turn themselves out of it. They are simply good-for-nothings, vagrants and sots and those on the way to crime."[4] As Marx and later Max Weber remark, this attitude fits very well with some aspects of puritanism, although it is very repugnant to a larger

Christian charity and conscience. Luckily, human society has not gone as Spencer wished. The trend to socialism has continued in many parts of the world, and about half of the human race lives under régimes dedicated to democratic socialism or to a form of collectivism. In Germany, as in Britain and France, sociological thinking continues to move in the direction of democratic socialism. On the whole, revolutionary socialism is rejected. As Weber remarks, "there is no clearly discernible tendency towards proletarisation today."[5]

Marx's social theory is a synthesis of ideas that originate from political economy, materialist philosophy, and Hegelianism. St. Simon's industrial prophetism and social democracy as well as Hegel's ideas of dialectical development were always dear to his heart. Marx's conception of social reality, like his conception of reality in general, is essentially Hegelian. He does not deviate from Hegel's dialectical thinking in philosophy but simply gives a revolutionary turn to his line of reasoning. As in Hegelianism, his dialectic represents the fundamental law of historical and social progress. Marx's principal complaint is that Hegel denies that social reality is generated in the empirical world through the realization of man's essential powers. Hegel, he insists, wrongly maintains that the appropriation of these powers "is only an appropriation occurring in pure thought."[6] In opposition of Hegel's belief that the dialectic operates in the realm of Spirit, he argues that the dialectical process of history is only intelligible when seen as operating in man's social relations. Men, he says, make their own history. In producing their material life, they enter into relationship with the means of production and in that way generate productive relations. These relations are conditioned by human needs and the mode of production. "Life involves before everything else eating and drinking, housing, clothing and various other things."[7] In capitalism, Marx states, human needs are always one-sided, directed toward accumulation rather than toward "inner wealth." While accepting Hegel's idea of collective sociability, Marx rejects its idealist basis. Social reality, he thinks, cannot be derived from the Absolute but must be derived from man's empirical existence.

The error in Hegel's account of human development in society, according to Marx, is that he treats man as a predicate of universal determination rather than its subject. In Marx's social theory, dialectical movement is always linked with "the existing empirical world" as well as with "tendencies which work out with an iron necessity towards an inevitable goal."[8] Like Hegel, he regards dialectic as a powerful method for understanding the opposing tendencies in human history. Dialectical analysis alone can reveal the necessity inherent in all historical and social development. Marx's social theory, like Hegel's, incorporates the concept of a conflict between opposing tendencies. The correct interpretation of history is reached through rational analysis of both the opposing elements involved in development and their results. Although empiricism is rejected as the embodiment of abstractions, Marx still argues that "the connection of the social structure with production" and material reality "must be brought out empirically."[9] It is the reality of "existing men" engaged in the productive process, not the reality of ideas, that dominates his sociology. The distinguishing mark of Marx's historical materialism is the belief that workers as producers of social wealth and as the most alienated class in capitalism must become the protagonists of a new dealienated society in spite of their alienation. The oppressed elements of alienated society must be seen as the conscious heroes of the total liberation of all alienated men. "The weapons with which the bourgeoisie felled feudalism to the ground" will have to be used by the creators of the new communist society "against the alienating forces of the bourgeoisie itself."[10]

The social world of industrial capitalism, Marx argues, is a perverted and alienating world of the "fetishism of commodities" in which the products of labor become alien to the producers and rule the producers instead of being ruled by them. Under capitalism, social relations become entirely inverted. In *Capital* he indicates that in capitalist society "every element, even the simplest, the commodity, for example, is an inversion of social relations." Here the social relations of persons are transformed into saleable objects. The alienated "worker is constantly producing objective wealth in the form of capital and, as a result, in the form of power which controls and alienates him."[11] Individual man in an acquisitive society dominated by exchange values and greed cannot avoid feeling controlled by impersonal, external, and alien forces rather than by personal creative and human processes. The primary aim of the capitalist, Marx stresses, is the ongoing process of profit-making. This orientation entails the creation of capital and wealth by inhuman means and merciless exploitation of labor power. The extraction of surplus value by the capitalist necessarily leads to the development of a social world in which human life is progressively alienated, devalued, and fragmented. The resultant alienated worker is "transformed into a conscious appendage" of an automatic structure, "a bond servant of capital which piles up dangerously over against him."[12]

Capitalism is a negative, inhuman, and alienating force. Given the choice between accumulation and pleasure, the capitalist, Marx says, prefers accumulation and wealth. All of his social activities are always profit-oriented. The real social foundation of the unequal exchange between capital and labor is hidden and mystified. Yet, the fact is that "the mediating process between men engaged in exchange is not a social or human process, not human relationship; it is the abstract relationship of private property to private property."[13] Exchange in capitalist society, Marx believes, is one of the main causes of social alienation. The phenomenon of individualism that permeates the social theories of Smith, James Mill, Ricardo, and Bentham is treated as the product of exchange. Unlike Smith, who maintains that exchange cannot be the basis for distinguishing the modes of production, Marx argues that exchange corresponds to a definite mode of production. By exchange he means capitalist market exchange, and in this exchange "men do not relate to each other as men and things lose the significance of human, personal property."[14]

Criticizing political economists, Marx rejects the view that the bonds of private interest are simultaneously social bonds. He argues strongly against the social theories of Smith, Ricardo and James Mill, which, in his view, are egoistic, inhuman, and anti-social. Marx rejects Smith's conception of "every man becoming in some measure a merchant" and his ideas of "society becoming a commercial society."[15] Smith maintains that a socioeconomic system in which individuals are all pursuing their own selfish interests will still produce, by some beneficent law of nature, a happy and harmonious community. In his *Theory of Moral Sentiments*, Smith regards sympathy as the ultimate element into which "social and moral sentiments" can be analyzed. "Our approval or disapproval of the conduct of others," he says, "depends on the extent to which we are able to sympathise with them."[16] All liberally minded economists have believed that private and public interests always coincide in practical life, and that it is impossible in practice to distinguish between one's own interests and those of society. Marx criticizes these economists for claiming that "self-interest or self-love" is the basis of society. Self-interest, he claims, is the direct opposite of humanism and socialism and the cause of social alienation and human misery.

Any attempt to establish "society through unsocial, particular interests" must be rejected. Sympathy, as expounded by Smith and Hume, cannot be the real bond between human beings in their social relations. The claim of political economists that individual relations in capitalist society are real social relations, Marx argues, is a figment of the imagination. The social theories of these economists are based on egoism and greed, not on humanism and social feelings. The surrender of social interests to the interests of private individuals, he thinks, is practical proof that political economy regards "egoism as the only motive of those engaged in exchange" and in socioeconomic relations in capitalist society.[17] The basis of these relations is "mutual plundering." "The intention of plundering, of deception," Marx points out, "is necessarily present in the background because capitalist exchange is selfish, inhuman, and alienating."[18]

Devaluation of the human world under capitalism is in direct correlation with the increase in value of the world of man-produced objects. In capitalist society, "the value of the worker as capital rises according to demand and supply, and even physically," Marx says, "his existence, his life, was and is looked upon as a supply of a commodity like any other."[19] The worker's human qualities exist only insofar as they exist for capital, which alienates him. It is an irony of history that the "monstrous objective power which social labour itself erected opposite itself as one of its moments belongs not to the worker but to the personified conditions of production or capital."[20] Every form of society, Marx believes, is always related to a specific mode of production. Production by isolated individuals outside of society is absurd. When men speak of production, they always have in mind production at a certain stage of social development or production by social individuals. In a primitive society, he maintains, the relations of production have been those of co-operation. By contrast, in capitalist society the relations of production have been transformed into relations of "having." Under the sway of private ownership, the propertyless worker becomes an alien object, and his role in the industrial process is transformed into that of a commodity.[21]

Under capitalism, the right of property, Marx maintains, undergoes a dialectical inversion "so that on the side of capital it becomes the right to an alien product or the right of property over alien labour and, on the side of labour capacity, it becomes the duty to relate to one's own labour or to one's own product as to alien property."[22] Abolition of the relations of private property, he claims, is the abolition of the conditions that produce alienated individuals and aliented society. The new communist society can be created only after the transcendence of private ownership. Regarding private property as the material expression of alienated human life, Marx sometimes stresses that communism is the "transcendence of private property only." "Self-acquired, self-earned property" will not be abolished and "the right of personnally acquired property" will be respected in communist society.[23] Like private property and exchange, division of labor in capitalist production also creates social antagonisms and class conflicts. As soon as the division of labor emerges, each man pursues his own selfish interests. The division of labor, Marx states in *German Ideology*, "implies the contradiction between the interest of the separate individual and the common interests of all individuals."[24] The concept of division of labor is central to his social theory of alienation. Intensification of the division of labor, he believes, not only increases the productive power of labor but it also increases the division between the rich and the poor. By increasing the quantity of wealth for the owners of the means of production, the division of labour is bound to intensify social alienation.

The division of labor as conceived by Marx is a major driving force in the production of private capital and wealth. Although his ideas of the division of labor "as the expression of the social character of labour within the estrangement" are frequently obscure and inconsistent, this division as a category of social life remains an important feature in his social analysis in most of his writings. In *German Ideology*, Marx indicates that the division of labor is "the first indicator of a cleavage between the individual and the public interests."[25] In communist society, he stresses, there will be no division of labor and no conflict between these two spheres of interests. Here human needs and capacities will never become one-sided, and "nobody will have one exclusive sphere of activity." Society, he writes in a typically romantic and utopian way, "will make it possible for me to hunt in the morning, fish in the afternoon, rear cattle in the evening, criticise after dinner without ever becoming hunter, fisherman, shepherd or critic."[26] What is striking in this passage is the appeal to romantic ideals. All romantics have admired rural scenery, fishing, rich pastures, and individual freedom. In their revolt against social bonds, they show no sympathy with professionalism, industrialism, and capitalism. Like the romantics, Marx believes that the idea of an occupation reflects a reified conception of man.

Marx's description of communist man in *German Ideology* is definitely reminiscent of the romantic conept of "pantisocracy," a community in which all have similar talents. Some English romantics have evolved the concept of society in which every individual would somehow be free to cook, gather wood, fish, or write poetry according to an agreed plan for a given day. Unfortunately, the scheme failed because the members of this romantic community could not even agree among themselves which food to cook and who should be eligible for membership. Like the romantics, Marx is interested principally in the "non-professional" man. His model for "communist man" is neither Raphael, one of the three great artists of the High Renaissance, nor John Milton, the author of *Paradise Lost*, but Leonardo da Vinci, the well-known painter, architect, philosopher, composer, poet, and sculptor. Criticizing Stirner's conception of the "organisation of labour," Marx underrates the creative genus of Mozart and Raphael simply because they, unlike Leonardo da Vinci, are incapable of excelling in many arts and dexterities. "Sancho," he says, "could surely have known that it was not Mozart himself but someone else who composed the greater part of Mozart's *Requiem* and finished it, and that Raphael himself completed only an insignificant part of his own frescoes."[27]

Considering Marx's criticism of the division of labor and professionalism as a whole, it is clear that he has failed to formulate any convicing alternative to professionalism. It is only by ignoring the realities of life and using utopian thinking with its millenarian fantasies that Marx is able to postulate the stark contrast between self-realization of the individual in class-divided societies and in communist society. Without offering any empirical evidence, he takes for granted that the "system of communism is the riddle of history solved."[28] As a "real movement," communism, he says, will abolish the present state of things and "produce man in the entire richness of his being, the rich man profoundly endowed with all the senses."[29] In his utopian mood, Marx believes wrongly that men in communist society will radically change their nature, and in an unexplainable manner realize their potential as multifaceted creators. Professional development is alienating, narrow, and detrimental to individual fulfillment. "With a communist organisation of society," he writes, "there disappears the subordination of the artist to local and national narrowness which arises entirely from division of labour and also the subordination of the individual to some definite art, making him exclusively a painter, sculptor, etc.; the very name amply expresses the narrowness of his professional development and his dependence on division of labour. In a communist society there are no painters but only people who engage in painting among other activities."[30]

The utopian character of Marx's ideas about non-professional development in communist society is the result of his reluctance to acknowledge that even in this society men will have to do different things at different times and that in some way class distinctions are inevitable. The myth of communist non-professionalism has, in fact, been despised by communist *praxis*. Few realistically orientated modern Marxists will ever advocate a society consisting of "jacks of all trades but masters of none." On the whole, modern Marxists believe that communism can only be constructed on the basis of existing realities. Vague ideals, abstract principles, and preconceived hypotheses are usually rejected. The fact remains, however, that Marx's social theory, as expounded in *German Ideology*, is sometimes divorced from "real history and from the actual life process of existing men."[31] His ideas of non-professionalism are illusory and utopian rather than "derived from the observation of the historical development of men." In spite of what he says about the multi-sided activity of communist man, the truth is that Marx is a "practical individualist" not concerned so much with creative work of the peasant, miner, or unskilled laborer as with the mental activity of a communist élite.

In his writings Marx frequently stresses the importance of criticism for social development. "The practical communist," he thinks, must be a critic as well as a revolutionary transforming the existing world. There is nothing wrong with criticism as long as it is really free and constructive. There are many signs in Marx's writings, however, indicating his intolerance of other people's view. Today everyone knows that genuine, free criticism is non-existent in communist societies. Communist praxis has no room for Marxist critics. All those who criticize Marxist ideology are branded as "enemies of the people" or as "unsocial individuals."[32] Sociological critique constitutes a major component of Marx's philosophical outlook. Believing in the redemptive function of "radical criticism," he has mercilessly criticized all those who have opposed his views. He has critized liberals for believing that their principles could be realized in capitalist society. The liberal premise of a harmonized community of social interests is rejected. His criticizm of the "utopian" socialists is very surprising. "The founders of the socialist and communist systems, St. Simon, Fourier, Owen and others," Marx admits, "want to improve the conditions of every member of society" but their methods, in his view, are inadequate to eliminate class antagonisms and social alienation in capitalist society.[33] Marx's alternative to their "socialism" is not "administrative reform" but a sociology of conflict, revolution, and class struggle.

In opposition to the nineteenth-century sociologists, Marx expects little from persuasion and compromise and everything, as Bertrand Russell remarks, from the class war.[34] S. Simon conceived of social development as a process which, if guided by reason and with moderation, would terminate social antagonisms and lead to a perfect equilibrium. Like S. Simon, Comte also criticized the division of labor for its potentially harmful social effects; but, unlike Marx, he argued that social alienation is an inescapable part of the human condition. In harmony with other non-Marxist sociologists of the century, he believed that a "contagious altruism and social morality which directs all individual tendencies by enlightened reason"would end all forms of egoism and class conflict.[35] It is the development of benevolence in man and of the habit of "living for others" that Comte, like S. Simon and Émile Durkheim, takes as the social *telos* and standard of rational practice rather than the development of class struggle. In Comte's view, the devotion to humanity must be the guiding principle of both religious life and social morality. For Durkheim, as for Comte, the bourgeois class is essentially a stabilizing force, and the division of labor is the source of social development and solidarity.

The pathological state of modern society with its alienation indicates social disintegration. Holding that specific social phenomena can only be explained in terms of general social phenomena, Durkheim accepts the contribution of religion and morality to the solution of social pathology. The significance of religion and morality in this respect, he says, "is not to make us think, to enrich our own knowledge, but to urge us to action, to help us to live."[36] Durkheim is not interested in a class struggle against capitalism, and his proposals for a morally regulated society do not entail the use of physical force. He sees society as a moral community. Men will be able to see the importance of religion in their lives once they have substituted society for the God they worship. In sharp contrast, Marx makes no appeal to religion and morality. These, for him, are the "expression of real distress" and the source of social alienation. He believes that without the active intervention of the most alienated class and class war, the alienating capitalist state of affairs could not be abolished. This idea is emphasized particularly in *Communist Manifesto*. "The abolition of the bourgeois relations of production," according to Marx and Engels, "can be effected only by a revolution."[37]

Class antagonisms that condition and generate social alienation, in Marx's view, are based on economic exploitation. Being dominated by an inhuman force and reduced to a state of subhumanity, alienated workers can only destroy their oppressors by radical and revolutionary means. Marx rejects the social theories of Proudhon, Saint-Simon, Comte, Durkheim, and the utopian socialists because their ideas are "unscientific and anti-revolutionary." The protagonists of these theories, he argues, merely advocate the ideas of class peace and totally renounce the class struggle for revolutionary social change. They fail to see that "only a radical change in the mode of production will change the social system based on it."[38] In his criticism of the "utopian socialists" and social reformers, Marx opposes their identification of socialism with any form of utilitarianiam or ethical philanthropism. "True socialism," he indicates, must be rejected because it lacks all revolutionary enthusiasm and, preaching the universal love of mankind, it is more interested in the philanthropic bourgeois illusions than in the liberation of the oppressed classes.[39]

Social contradictions, Marx maintains, can only be resolved by social revolutions. "Hitherto," he says, "society has always developed within the framework of a contradiction—in antiquity the contradiction between free men and slaves, in the Middle Ages that between nobility and serfs, in modern times that between the bourgeoisie and the proletariat." This contradiction, he adds, explains the "abnormal, inhuman way in which the oppressed class satisfies its needs and also the narrow limits within which social intercourse and with it the whole ruling classes develop."[40] During its historical development, the bourgeoisie develops it antagonistic attitude toward the oppressed class. This antagonism gradually generates the revolutionary class that plays the decisive role in the abolition of classes and social alienation. The political economists Smith, James Mill, and Ricardo, the liberal representatives of the bourgeois production, are totally, in Marx's view, indifferent to the estrangement of the proletarians. Members of the humanitarian school are genuinely sympathetic to the suffering of the alienated workers, but in practice they are unable to alleviate their misery. The philanthropists, however, "deny the necessity of antagonism altogether and want to turn all men into bourgeois."[41] In his polemic with Proudhon, Marx, in a somewhat exaggerated manner, ridicules Proudhon's reverence for "eternal principles" and blames him for "holding things upside down like a true philosopher."[42] In a letter to P.V. Annenkov, Marx criticizes Proudhon's confused ideas about society and social relations. Proudhon mixes up ideas and things. He is "incapable of following the real movement of history and produces a phantasmagoria which," Marx adds, "presumptuously claims to be dialectical."[43]

Proudhon's socioeconomic theory envisages a society that is similar to the organization of voluntary associations. Before his quarrel with Proudhon, Marx had described his work as a "scientific manifesto of the French proletariat." In *Poverty of Philosophy*, however, Marx calls Proudhon's economic and social ideas "unscientific and anti-revolutionary," reflecting the synthesis of bourgeois thoughts and abstract ideas. Like the bourgeois economists, Proudhon, Marx argues, fails to apprehend a close correlation between definite forms of social consciousness and the economic structure of society. Men do not make several distinct histories expressed in different categories of the superstructure but only one history that of their own socioeconomic relations. This history is always conditional by the productive forces of society. "Men who produce cloth, linen and silks also produce the social relations amid which they manufacture cloth and linen."[44] Marx's conception of the relationship between productive forces and productive relations is neither always clear nor consistent. In *Poverty of Philosophy*, he emphasizes the primacy of the productive forces. "Social relations," he writes, "are closely bound up with productive forces. In acquiring new productive forces men change their mode of production; and in changing their mode of production, in changing the way of earning their living, they change all their social relations."[45] Proudhon, in Marx's view, fails to realize that "society is the product of men's reciprocal action" and that "the productive forces are the basis of all human history."[46]

In *German Ideology*, Marx advocates a similar view, indicating that "the sum of productive forces is the real basis of historical development."[47] These forces are not seen as the expression of man's essential nature, as suggested in *Manuscripts of 1844*, but rather as the exclusive determinant of the conditions of all relations between men. Having described reality as a human reality made by "real, active men conditioned by a definite development of their productive forces," Marx argues that a constructive social theory must grasp this reality not as an eternal, abstract, and ahistorical process but rather as an actual life process involving man in his dual role as producer and product.[48] He insists that the productive conditions of men taken together always constitute the economic structure of society. The economic base or substructure provides the real basis of social life. In *German Ideology* and in the Preface to *Contribution to the Critique of Political Economy*, he stresses that the mode of production of material life always conditions the general process of social, political, and spiritual life. As social producers, men enter into productive relations that correspond to a given stage in the development of productive forces. These relations are reflected in definite forms of social consciousness.

Analyzing the general development of the modes of production in the Preface to *Contribution to the Critique of Political Economy*, Marx does not clarify the relationship between productive forces and social relations. Within each mode of production, he says, the relations of production first "correspond to a definite stage of development of their productive forces" and then enter into a "contradiction" with them.[49] This could be read to mean that the productive relations contradict the forces of production only when the latter are in a state of stagnation. In *German Ideology*, it is suggested that the contradiction occurs when the productive forces turn into destructive forces. Under the system of private property, Marx writes, "the forces of production receive a one-sided development, and for the majority they become destructive forces."[50] In communist society, it is taken for granted that expansion of the productive forces will always represent the genuine flowering of man's creativity and there will be no collision or contradiction between "the productive forces and the form of intercourse."[51] On the whole, the idea of the primacy of productive forces is central in Marx's socioeconomic theory. Without a change in men's productive forces, there can be no change in "their relations of production." When the relations of production do not correspond to the forces of production, society is forced to bring about a new set of social relations. The impact of productive forces on social relations is mediated by the mode of production. Marx has never explained this mediation.

Marx has no doubt that the social relations of production always depend on the economic structure of society, which is "the real foundation" of the superstructure. Because he sometimes makes a conceptual distinction between productive forces and mode of production, he is not always certain whether change in social relations should be ascribed to productive forces or to modes of production. There are references in his writings to both of these economic factors as playing the role of social determinant. In the Preface to *Critique of Political Economy* and in *German Ideology*, he speaks of both "the mode of production conditioning the general process of social life" and "the productive forces creating the material conditions for a solution of social antagonism."[52] This duality persists even in the *Poverty of Philosophy*, in which Marx states explicitly that "a change in men's productive forces necessarily brings about a change in their relations of production," overlooking his earlier statement that the change in social relations is conditioned by the change in the mode of production.[53] On the whole, he seems to suggest that productive forces and modes of production can serve equally as an explanatory variable in the analysis of social development. Unlike Engels, he does not seem to be worried about "the possible conflict between productive forces and modes of production." However, like Engels, he maintains that "definite modes of production" are "independent of the human will" and that both productive forces and modes of production are ultimately conditioned by the economic laws of necessity.[54]

In his analysis of primitive societies in *Grundrisse* and *Capital*, Marx indicates that primitive cooperation and social unity have been the distinguishing features of these societies. Early communities in all their forms, he says in *Grundrisse*, "necessarily correspond to a development of the forces of production" that "dissolves these forms and their dissolution is itself a development of the human productive forces."[55] In *Capital* he emphasizes simplicity and nothing is said about alienation. The structure of the economic elements of ancient society, in Marx's view, remained unaffected by political trends.[56] The fact is that his ideas of primitive societies are predominantly speculative and inferential based on his general reading of social development in India.[57] In many ways, as modern social anthropologists indicate, primitive society still remains a mystery and Marx's postulates are mere assumptions of untestable events. Without clarifying the real interconnection between the economic base and the superstructure, he assumes that the emergence of social consciousness in all societies can be explained from the contradictions of material life, from the conflict between the social forces of production, and the relations of production. It is difficult to know whether the distinction between "material base and superstructure" reflects in his mind a distinction between "productive forces" and "modes of production." It is clear, however, that Marx continuously emphasizes the economic factor as the exclusive determinant of social development.

Like Marx, Engels maintains that "the economic structure of society always furnishes the real basis." It is only when starting from this real basis that "we can work out the ultimate explanation of the whole superstructure of juridical and political institutions as well as of the religious, philosophical and other ideas of a given historical period."[58] In Engels's letters to J. Bloch, C. Schmidt, and F. Mehring, written after Marx's death in 1883, he speaks of a structural interrelationship between the base and the superstructure.

"According to the materialist conception of history," he writes in the letter to Bloch, "the ultimately determining factor in history is the production and reproduction of real life. Neither Marx nor I have ever asserted more than this. If somebody twists this into saying that the economic factor is the only determining one, he transforms that proposition into a meaningless, abstract, absurd phrase. The economic situation is the basis but the various elements of the superstructure also exercise their influence on the cause of the historical struggles and in many cases determine their form. There is an interaction of all these elements in which the economic movement is finally bound to assert itself."[59] The confusion over the problem of base and superstructure, Engels maintains, results from the inability of ideologists to grasp the relationship between historical and dialectical materialism. "What these gentlemen all lack is dialectics."[60] Although the economic base is ultimately decisive in determining the course of history, the superstructure also plays a significant role in historical development.

In Engels's view, social development is only intelligible in the light of consciousness. Productive forces are not beyond consciousness, although their role in social development is "the strongest and most decisive." "Because we deny an independent historical development to the various ideological spheres," he writes to Mehring, it does not mean that "we also deny them any effect upon history."[61] The theory of dialectical materialism can only be grasped when it is applied practically. Yet, it is obvious that Engels is far from solving the question of "interaction" and feels unable to decide which way to go. Sometimes he adheres to "Marx's proof" that the final causes of all social changes can only be detected in changes in the modes of production. Sometimes he is well aware of the shallowness of Marx's proof and doubts its persuasive vigour. As a result, Engels's conception of history is confused, inconsistent, and ambivalent, and his materialist social theory remains wrapped in mystification and metaphysical abstraction. The character of superstructural elements acting as social determinants "in many cases" is left unexplained. Like Marx, he fails to realize the real significance of non-economic factors in social development and admit that they may ultimately be "the most decisive determinants" and frequently determine the mode of production itself.

Marx is sensitive to the complex interrelationships involved in social life and feels dogmatically committed to economic determinism, thus explaining all social and historical development in terms of economic determinants only. Sometimes there are hints in his social theory that social change and history could be explained in terms of human factors, including mental acitivity, but these factors have never been specified. The role of men in social change is always wrapped in mystification and abstraction. Marx's social theory is closely related to Hegel's view that the effective causes in history are impersonal forces rather than individual persons. The social movement is treated as a process of natural history governed by laws that are both independent of human will and that determine all human actions. Although man is not supposed to be a passive observer of social development, he is still "unable to choose the form of society he likes."[62] The paradox of Marx's social theory lies in the fact that men can change their mode of production but cannot choose any particular form of society. Social relations, like the form of society itself, are determined by historical necessity. This necessity is an impersonal, metaphysical force which, as in Hegel's dialectic, resists self-willed choices. Historical forces, expressing the action by which nature becomes man, are the forces behind the abolition of social alienation. It is not man but "history that is preparing the practical element for the emancipation of mankind."[63]

Marx believes men have history because they must produce their life but the way in which they produce it is always determined ultimately by their material organization rather than by their consciousness. Both the production of human life and consciousness are conditioned equally by a definite development of productive forces. Like Hegel, Marx takes for granted that the course of social and historical development is synthetic and dialectical. In Hegel's social theory, only reason, the faculty of synthesis, can apprehend the dialectical forces influencing the necessary stages of social development. Unlike Hegel, Marx maintains that the dialectic moves in the sphere of real forces and that the synthesis of opposing tendencies is independent of reason. Reason, he thinks, is not the dominating force in man: like thinking and consciousness, it is merely an abstract force that can influence man's actions only through his "social existence" and "material intercourse." The traditional materialists have erred in recognizing only those aspects of social alienation that could be defined as alien to reason. The model of rational man in abstract idealism and in abstract materialism, Marx contends, is inadequate to understand the real material forces that condition and control all social relations.

Both Marx and Engels criticize the "abstract materialists" and "utopian socialists" for failing to grasp the fundamental laws of dialectical materialism. The utopians, Engels indicates, "appeal to reason because they cannot as yet appeal to contemporary history and see the contradictions in the capitalist mode of production."[64] The mechanism for achieving the fullfilment of human aims, according to Marx, is neither the faculty of reason nor philanthropic ideals but "material force." This force is described as being practical because it plays a synthesizing role in social contradictions. Without material forces, ideas and concepts cannot transcend social alienation. Ideas, like all elements of the superstructure, are always tied up to the dominant class. "The class which is the ruling material force of society," Marx says, "is at the same time its ruling intellectual force."[65] Consequently, this class controls both the means of production and mental production. Social *praxis*, as activity by which man creates his world, is the source of ideas. Bourgeois ideas and theories, in Marx's view, are narrow and alienating. The proletariat must undertake the historically significant task of eliminating social alienation and will only accomplish this if guided by revolutionary ideas.

All previous social movements, Marx argues, have been movements of minorities or favoring the interest of minorities. Only the communist movement represents the interest of the majority. Capitalism is narrow, sectional, alienating, and class-orientated. Based on the denial of man, capitalism represents a society that generates and maintains the estrangement of man, and "when a man is confronted by himself, he is also confronted by other men."[66] In capitalist society, all men are alienated. The capitalist is alienated because his life is dominated by the greed for increasing profit. The exploited classes are the most alienated because they are deprived of "spontaneous activity" and are unable to realize their social ends. Social alienation under capitalism, Marx believes, involves the denial of man's right to create a truly humane society. Man's activity in capitalist society is neither free nor human but alienating, unnatural, and inhuman. The industrial worker in this society has "no existence as a human being but only as a worker who is free to starve to death and bury himself."[67] "The capitalist mode of production," Marx writes, "rests on the fact that the material conditions of production are in the hands of non-workers in the form of property in capital and land, while the masses are only owners of the personal condition of production, of labour power."[68] The division of labor and private property are the alienating social forces that not only prevent the dispossessed masses from identifying themselves with the products of their labor but also prevent them from having them.

The division of society into the privileged and the dispossessed, the exploiters and the exploited, Marx maintains, is the result of alienated activity. Under capitalism, man's labor becomes saleable commodity, and free, spontaneous activity becomes a forced, alienated activity. Social wealth, produced by this activity, inevitably confronts man as an alien force. As an instrument of production, capital creates a conflict between property owners and propertyless workers, between the exploiters and exploited. Conceived as an alien entity, capital, Marx says, "is the all-dominating economic power of bourgeois society."[69] Capital has split society into "hostile camps" and is responsible for social antagonisms and class wars. Social conflicts are traced back to the struggles between the existing social classes and, as Engels states, between the "fractions of classes created by economic development." Analyzing social alienation, Marx and Engels indicate in *Communist Manifesto* that "the history of all hitherto existing society is the history of class struggles."[70] In their social theory, classes are always the product of the mode of production. Although never consistently specified and defined, they are very important to Marxist ideology. It is in terms of class structure that Marx and Engels analyse capitalist socioeconomic relations and the intensifying contradications of capitalism.

In pre-capitalist societies, according to Marx and Engels, a "complicated arrangement of society into various orders, a manifold gradation of social rank" existed everywhere.[71] "The modern bourgeois society," they say in the

Communist Manifesto, "that has sprouted from the ruins of feudal society has not done away with class antagonisms. It has, in fact, created new classes, new conditions of oppressioin, new forms of struggle in place of the old ones."[72] In *Manuscripts of 1844* and *Capital*, Marx speaks of landowners, capitalists, and wage-laborers as the three great social classes.[73] These are ultimately reduced to "workers and non-workers." In *Manifesto*, the social structure is divided into "two great hostile camps, two great classes directly facing each other." What happens with the class structure of the Asiatic mode of production is a great mystery. In *Capital*, Marx speaks only of "primitive communalism" in which "each of the handicraftsmen works in accordance with traditional custom but independently and without being subject to any sort of authority."[74] There is no reference to social conflict or social aliena-tion. These, Marx believes, are the product of commodity production. It is the antagonistic relation between classes which conditions the social structure in which the producer is divorced from the means of production and thus alienated socially.

The whole process of class stratification in Marx's social analysis is linked closely with the economic process that deprives the worker of his means of production and consequently transforms him into the alienated wage-earner. "The capitalist system," he says, "presupposes a divorce between the workers and the ownership of the property through which alone their labour can be-come effective. The process which clears the way for the capitalist system is nothing but the process whereby the worker is divorced from ownership of the means of labour; a process which, on the one hand, transforms the social means of subsistence and the social means of production into capital; and, on the other, transforms the actual producers into wage workers."[75] The servi-tude of the worker expressed in his alienated social existence is the starting point of the development that has given rise both to the wage worker and to the capitalist.[76] Marx states that class distinctions and class conflicts are al-ways generated by property relations and emerge in correlation with the dif-ferences in the division of labor. The division of labor, entailing the division of man himself, implies the division between capital and labor. This division is unnatural, alienating, and inhuman. As long as commodity production exists, men cannot see themselves as natural and social individuals. The natural rela-tion of men under capitalism is an illusion.

Marx's analysis of class structures is unsatisfactory.[77] Even in alienated capitalist society, class structure is so complex that it does not appear in any definite or pure form. Transitional and intermediate social strata obscure definite class boundaries. Even if the middle and intermediate strata of soci-ety are somehow eliminated from the social net, there will still be classes of managers, businessmen, doctors, nurses, teachers, and civil servants. The bureaucracy consisting of civil servants who, according to Hegel, "work for the universal interests of society," has not been squeezed out of the commu-nist social net. Marx assumes wrongly that the class structure in capitalist society can be reduced to the bourgeoisie and the proletariat. These are not the only classes whose existence and development depend entirely on the modern mode of production. He overlooks that there are people in society who depend on this mode of production and who cannot possibly be classed either as captalists or proletarians. The criterion of working or not working cannot constitute a complete class characterisation. The amount of property owned, as Hegel indicates, is frequently a deceptive indicator of class membership.[78] The definition of classes in terms of property and non-property entails great difficulties.[79] It makes it impossible to distinguish between a small capitalist and a wage worker who owns some of the means of production and between workers and non-workers in communist society.

Like Marx, Engels also correlates class distinctions and class conflicts with private ownership. In its essence, he says in the Introduction to *Anti-Dühring*, "modern socialism is the direct product of the recognition of the class antagonism existing in modern society between proprietors and non-proprietors, between capitalists and wage-workers." For both Marx and Engels, ownership of the means of production and of labor power is the principal determinant of class. They fail to see that man can be alienated in society in which the difference in the right to property is insignificant but the difference in political power and influence is great. In communist countries in which property is "commonly owned," workers are not only alienated socially; they are alienated more than those with socio-political privileges and in political control. Marx's social theory is based on the assumption that property relations are always reflected in power relations. Capital, he says, is "the governing power over labour and its products" and the capitalist himself feels the alien power of capital.[80] Marx abhors capitalist competition.[81] Free competition brings out the inherent laws of capitalist production as external coercive laws having power over every individual capitalist. "Competition forces him continually to extend his capital for the sake of maintaining it, and he can only extend it by means of progressive accumulation."[82]

Capitalists are seen as the owners of capital who also possess political power that alienates the exploited workers. Dehumanized and alienated, these propertyless workers must emancipate themselves. "But they cannot emancipate themselves without abolishing the conditions of their own life. They cannot abolish the conditions of their own life without abolishing all the inhuman conditions of life of society which are summed up in their own situation."[83] Totally frustrated and dispossessed, the proletarians alone, Marx believes, can and must become the liberating force of society. He never explains why the proletariat is "the most alienated class of men" and why this class is the fittest liberating force of society. He is far from being empirically-orientated when he speaks of the revolutionary class as the "representative of the whole society."[84] The fact is that Marx has inherited the concept of a "universal class" from Hegel.[85] His idea of suffering as the distinguishing mark of the "redeemer of mankind" has its roots in the Judeo-Christian tradition. In the

Deutero-Isaiah's message, for example, suffering is given redemptive value. The Messiah or redeemer of the world voluntarily accepts suffering as a necessary concomitant of the task to be done in the world of alienation.[86] In Marx's view, suffering has a similar redemptive value for mankind. The suffering of the proletariat, like that described in Isaiah's "Songs of the suffering Servant," is an impressive description of vicarious sacrifice for the benefit of humanity.

The proletariat's great historical task involves, in Marx's view, the elimination of social alienation. This can be done only by consciously rejecting the established social order. Alienated workers need class consciousness, an awareness of the historical and dialectical necessity of a radical social transformation. The class struggle undertaken by the suffering workers, Marx argues, is simultaneously a struggle for the consciousness of all mankind. Becoming a revolutionary class, the proletarians cease to be the victims of "false consciousness." As an inevitable product of capitalist alienated society, they will not only sweep away the bourgeois exploiting class but also abolish all classes. "In all previous revolutions," Marx writes, "the mode of activity always remained unchanged and it was only a question of a distribution of this activity, a new distribution of labour to other persons, whilst the communist revolution is directed against the hitherto existing mode of activity, does away with labour and abolishes the rule of all classes with the classes themselves, because it is carried through by the class which no longer counts as a class in society, which is not recognised as a class and is in itself the expression of the dissolution of all classes within present society."[87] The French Revolution liberated the middle class from exploitation by the aristocracy but, Marx remarks, left it an exploiting class. This Revolution merely abolished feudal property in favor of bourgeois property. The success of the bourgeois revolution, however, has opened the way for the development of class consciousness. The proletarian class consciousness is more than "class instinct." It is, as Althusser states, the consciousness and practice that must conform to the objective reality of the proletarian class struggle. Unlike class instinct, which is emotional and subjective, proletarian class consciousness is rational, dialectical and objective.[88] As a mass, only the class-conscious proletarians can understand the revolutionary scope of Marx's social goals and fight for their realization.

Stressing that class struggle is rooted in the very existence of class societies, Marx rejects the view that he has discovered the existence of classes and the struggle between them in modern society. "No credit is due to me," he writes to Joseph Weydemeyer, "for discovering the existence of classes or the struggle between them. Long before me bourgeois historians had described the historical development of this class struggle and bourgeois economists the economic anatomy of the classes." Marx adds that he has merely "linked the existence of classes to particular historical phases in the development of production and that class struggle necessarily leads to the dictatorship of the proletariat and, ultimately, to the abolition of all classes and to a classless society."[89] Smith and Ricardo have analyzed modern society as a process involving social and economic antagonism. While they confine their analysis mainly to the antagonism between the interests of landlords and capitalists, Marx reduces this antagonism to the struggle between the alienating bourgeoisie and the alienated proletariat. In *Capital*, he writes that political economy, especially that of Smith and Ricardo, belongs to the period in which class struggle has not yet been fully developed. "The class struggle of the ancient world took the form mainly of a struggle between creditors and debtors. In the Middle Ages, the same struggle ended with the ruin of the feudal debtors who lost their political power when they lost the economic basis on which it had been upbuilt."[90] The modern class struggle is located in the contradictions between the exploiting capitalists and the exploited workers. It is with the sharpening of this struggle that social revolution, aiming at the abolition of social alienation, has become inevitable. Indicating that no class in society has "any need for general emancipation until it is forced by material necessity," Marx stresses the historical significance of the proletarian struggle against alienating forces in capitalist society. "By proclaiming the dissolution of the hitherto existing world order, the proletariat merely states the secret of its own existence, for it is in fact the dissolution of that world order. By demanding the negation of private property, the proletariat merely raises to the rank of a principle of society what society has made the principle of the proletariat, what, without its own co-operation, is already incorporated in it as the negative result of society."[91]

Marx's description of the proletariat's historical task in *Introduction to the Contribution to the Critique of Hegel's Philosophy of Right* is reminiscent of St. Paul's description of "the Second Adam." The proletariat, he says, "has done no particular wrong but wrong generally is perpetrated against it."[92] Mysteriously summing up the long role of the human race, the proletariat has been debased, dehumanised, and alienated in order to emancipate "all men from capitalist slavery." "The complete rewinning of man can only be accomplished by the complete loss of man."[93] Alienated society, in Marx's view, is a totality of isolated individuals, and the corporate element in human life involves the vicarious redemption. Bourgeois society is negatively individualistic. "Each looks to himself only and no one troubles himself about the rest." The driving force of this society is the quest for profits by the capitalist class rather than the satisfaction of human needs. Based on alienated labor, the social structure of capitalism reflects the meaninglessness of the whole social process. Because men in capitalist society seek only their particular interests, the common interest appears alien and meaningless to them. When workers cannot develop a sense of purpose that relates their physical and mental activity to the common interest and, in addition, are prevented from controlling their own life, social alienation is unavoidable.

Marx, like Aristotle, maintains that the human individual is social. "His life, even if it may not appear in the direct form of a communal life carried out together with others, is therefore an expression and confirmation of social life."[94] Because man is social by nature, he can develop his true nature only in society.[95] This development, he argues, is impossible in the social world in which there is free competition. In capitalist alienated society, man is inevitably a stranger to himself and to others. "To say that man is estranged from himself," Marx writes, "is the same thing as saying that the society of this estranged man is a caricature of his real community and that his activity appears to him as a torment, his own creation as an alien power, his wealth as poverty, the essential bond linking him with other men as an unessential bond and separation from his fellow men as his true mode of existence."[96] Under capitalism, the pursuit of riches dominates the entire social structure, and "an inhuman power" rules everything. The social world of market production is one of reification. All social organizations in capitalism are class-based. Here, Marx points out, mutual exploitation is the rule and results in poverty among the lower classes. In this situation, sympathy is shown only to the absolute losers. Even in cases of charitable deeds, sometimes charity is combined with revenge.[97]

In the introduction to *Grundrisse*, Marx criticizes "the individual and isolated hunter and fisherman, with whom Smith and Ricardo begin, and other eighteenth-century Robinsonades as being nothing but ideological projections of alienating bourgeois society." In this society of free competition, the individual is detached from his natural social bonds. The more deeply we go back into history, he adds, the more the individual appears to belong to a greater whole. In communist society, the "only society in which the genuine and free development of individuals ceases to be a mere phrase," Marx states, individual development "is determined by the connection of individuals, a connection which consists partly in the economic prerequistes and partly in the necessary solidarity of the free development of all, and, finally, in the universal character of the activity of individuals on the basis of the existing productive forces."[98] Stirner's individualism is rejected because, in Marx's view, his individual is "subordinated to division of labour which makes him one-sided, cripples and determines him."[99] As a matter of fact, Marx's own individual, although theoretically not subjected to division of labor, is also "one-sided and determined." The individual as described in his social theory acquires his social reality from the social relations into which he enters "independently of his own will."[100] Although Marx is inconsistent in this respect, he basically maintains that the development of the individual is determined by the development of all the other individuals with whom he is directly or indirectly associated.

Like Hegel, Marx argues that man's self-realization is connected closely with the structure of the society in which the individual lives. Hegel's thought is directed against the dichotomy of individualism and collectivism. Criticizing extreme Lutheran individualism, he believes that extreme individualism falsifies the real nature of man and society. Man is a social being, and he can achieve self-realization only as a member of a totality. In an ethical community, he says, the individual must conform to the universal rules. Here the "absolute will must regulate the life of individuals."[101] Marx reasons similarly when he speaks of the need of "existing men to subjugate their life to the power of the united individuals."[102] He always maintains that the main attraction of communism is its promise to facilitate the full and free realization of the individual. He fails, however, to see that this realization is impossible as long as the individual is subjugated entirely to collective actions. In his early writings he protests, in the name of human dignity, against dehumanization and depersonalization in capitalist society. He deplores the human relationships that have become impersonal, hostile, and alienated. Man as a free individual, he maintains, has vanished, and in his place capitalism has enthroned the egoistic individual. In later works, however, Marx is mostly concerned with the reality of social classes and collectivism rather than with the reality of the individual. He does not, it is true, overlook the existence of individuals as parts of a whole, but it is the whole or totality, not the individual, that possesses the ultimate reality. When he speaks of the individual as "nothing but the ensemble of the social relations," as he does in the sixth thesis on Feuerbach, he really introduces into his social theory a new abstract individual who like Feuerbach's individual, is a "veritable chimera." Marx's early humanism, as Berdyaev remarks, vanishes suddenly and passes into anti-humanism; the concrete human individual entirely disappears in the universal claim of the universal class.[103]

Marx's criticism of individualism is directed against political economy, Judaism, Christianity, "true socialism," and social Darwinism. "Society, as it appears to the political economist', he writes, 'is civil society in which every individual is a totality of needs and only exists for the other person as the other exists for him, in so far as each becomes a means for the other."[104] The economists want the alienated workers to remain in society as created by private individuals. The "true socialists" want a new society, but Marx believes their society would still be controlled by private individuals and the workers would remain alienated.[105] Distinguishing between private and social individuals, he argues that Judaism and Christianity have also failed to divorce the free development of individuals from egoistic and alienating individualism. "In its perfected practice," he writes without any sense of objectivity, "Christian egoism of heavenly bliss is necessarily transformed into the corporeal egoism of the Jew, heavenly need is turned into worldly need, subjectivism into self-interest."[106] Marx ignores the fact that the idea of a community in religious thought has been in the forefront for a long time. Defending the sanctity of the individual, Judaism and Christianity are equally concerned with society as a whole. All individuals have duties not only toward God but also toward their neighbor. This means that individuals cannot think of their own self-realization without thinking about the self-realization of others.

Because he hates religion, Marx distorts the significance of Jewish and Christian individualistic attitudes. These attitudes admittedly have not always been positive or "holy," but they certainly have not been as negative as indicated in his social theory. It is possible to argue, as many commentators do, that Marx's collectivism is a negative entity, existing only "*in abstracto*."[107] He assumes that communist man is a social individual and that all his opponents are "private or egoistic individuals." However, as non-Marxist sociologists indicate, Marx's ambitious drive for self-aggrandisement, reflected in his quarrels with the Young Hegelians, Proudhon, Lassalle, and Bakunin, does not characterize him as a social individual.[108] Both Marx and Hegel start from the premise that the essence of individual man is social and that the isolated individual is imaginary. They insist that the individual can only realize himself in a community, but their social theories are essentially hostile to the autonomy and freedom of human individuals. They fail to provide a satisfactory and realistic account of the role of the individual in society. They overlook the fact that society is the organization of individuals and that it is individuals who live and realize themselves, not the society. In serving others, human individuals serve themselves, and in serving themselves, they are serving others. In both cases they serve humanity which, as Kant remarks, must always be served and never used only as a means.

What is utopian in Marx's social theory is his ambiguous reliance on the "power of united individuals" that can only be exercised by the most alienated class of revolutionary proletarians as the "representatives of the whole of society."[109] The concept of "united individuals" has never been explained. Following Hegel's idea of universalism, Marx assumes that the totality is more real than its parts and that individuals cannot strictly be human except as members of a whole. In civil society, he states, members are private and egoistic individuals and as such they maintain social alienation. Here the whole is "under the sway of an inhuman force" and social change is strongly individualized. Confining the concept of totality to history, Marx criticizes Hegel for confirming social alienation in civil society. It is economic society, the society based on productive forces, that, in his view, is of real historical importance. As the totality in Marx's mind is the bearer of revolutionary aims, he believes the unity of parts within the whole will best be protected by the "representatives of the whole of society."

Marx's conception of the proletariat as the objective redeemer of individuals from social alienation is metaphysical nonsense. There is no empirical justification for this mystical and oracular hypothesis. He maintains wrongly that a society without private property will automatically become a society of equal opportunities, or, as he calls it, "human society or social humanity." The dialectical jump from civil society as seen through the spectacles of Hegelian idealism and "old materialism" to "human society or social humanity" is purely inferential.[110] He fails to realize that the propertyless class of revolutionary proletarians might have as many social vices and be as greedy as the alienating capitalists. Obviously Marx has idealized the revolutionary class without considering any other constructive alternative to the ruthless alienation and exploitation of men under capitalism except the inhuman dictatorship of the proletariat. By definition, any dictatorship is a tyranny that inevitably destroys all opportunity for constructive criticism and individual freedom, persecutes liberally minded individuals in all human activity, destroys the independence of scientific research, and imposes an aggressive authoritarianism without any regard for public opinion. Marx observes correctly that the mechanism of capitalist production is alienating and that in capitalist society the "worker's relation to his home is merely one of uncertainty and fear." Here, he writes, "man is regressing to the cave dwelling in an estranged, malignant form. Light and air cease to be a need for a working man."[111] The position of the working man, however, has changed considerably since Marx's time. Once the evils of unrestricted private enterprise have become clear, opinion has slowly changed, and a movement to improve the social and economic conditions of workers has slowly gained strength in public opinion and government circles. Gradually, without much violence, government regulations and social reforms in Britain and France have led to a considerable improvement in the living standards of the workers.

Analyzing the alienated society of nineteenth-century England, Marx and Engels argue that social inequalities and pauperism cannot be abolished by philanthropic theories and administrative measures, but only by radical and evolutionary means. "England, the only country where large-scale political action against pauperism can be said to have taken place," Marx writes, "explains pauperism as being caused by the bad will of the poor" rather than by the inherent contradiction in capitalist accumulation of wealth. "Regarding poverty as the fault of the poor themselves," England has tried unsuccessfully "to abolish pauperism by charity and administrative measures."[112] The phenomenon of the poor and the idle, in fact, is a necessary consequence of free competition in which the rich become richer and the poor poorer.[113] Society based on free competition, an ideal of political economy, Malthusianism, Benthamism, and social Darwinism, means "increasing misery" for the workers. The modern laborer in capitalism "becomes a pauper and pauperism develops more rapidly than population and wealth."[114]

The philanthropic intentions in the reforms of such political figures as Disraeli, Louis Bonaparte, and Bismarck "strive for a change in social conditions by means of which existing society will be made as tolerable and comfortable as possible," but they are far from desiring to revolutionize all society for the revolutionary proletarians. The reformers have no intention of destroying the system of free competition and eliminating social alienation. They merely "cherish the pious wish of abolishing the pressure of big capital on small capital, of the big bourgeois on the small bourgeois."[115] The socialistically minded bourgeois intellectuals, in fact, desire the "existing state of society minus its revolutionary elements" as embodied in the alienated and dehumanized proletariat. Only a change in the material conditions of existence and in economic relations, Marx believes, "could be of any advantage" to the workers. The pursuit of political and social reforms within the framework of capitalism is meaningless, because reforms and administrative measures here are entirely inadequate and must be ignored.[116]

The struggle for reforms in bourgeois society, Marx and Engels argue, is incompatible. with the advancement of revolutionary goals. The solution of all social and economic problems needs radical change and the complete socialization of the economic system to serve the essential needs of all society. They argue that the development of productive forces will best be promoted by the institution of a classless society. It is only here, they maintain, that the antagonism between the rich and poor, between the exploiter and exploited will be eliminated, and the "domination of the estranged thing over man" will be transcended.[117] Both Marx and Engels reproach the utopian socialists for opposing the revolutionary movement of social practice. "The rejection of the political struggle by the great utopians," Engels says, "was at the same time the rejection of the class struggle, i.e., of the only form of activity of the class whose interests they represented."[118] Engels's conception of class struggle, however, is not always clear and consistent. Arguing against social Darwinism, he uses two different and somewhat contradictory models of development in his theory of progress. One is Marx's class conflict model that reflects the divisive interests in capitalism, and the other is a mixture of conflict and harmony models, hardly different from that of "the great utopians." "The interaction of bodies in non-living nature," he writes, "includes both harmony and collisions, that of living bodies conscious and unconscious co-operation as well as conscious and unconscious struggle."[119]

Engels does not deny that history is a record of class struggle, a struggle that is the dominant theme of *Communist Manifesto*. He merely criticizes those who see "nothing but struggle" in historical development. There is a hint, however, that the pathological and alienating state of capitalist society could be remedied by evolutionary rather than revolutionary means. "It is absolutely childish," he says, "to sum up the whole manifold wealth of historical evolution and complexity in the meagre and one-sided phrase struggle for existence."[120] Carried to its logical conclusion, this means that social evils can be eradicated by legislative and non-violent methods. "The whole Darwinian theory of the struggle for existence," in Engels's view, "is simply the transference from society to organic nature of Hobbes' theory of *bellum omnium contra omnes* and of the bourgeois economic theory of competition as well as the Malthusian theory of population."[121]

Initially, Marx and Engels were pleased with Darwin's exposition of the conception of struggle. After reading *The Origin of Species*, Marx immediately "saw in it the basis for his own theory of struggle." At Marx's graveside in 1883, Engels stressed that "Marx's discovery of the law of evolution in human history is equal to Darwin's discovery of the law of evolution in natural science." However, their enthusiasm for the Darwinian theory of the struggle for existence soon evaporated. In their correspondence about "social Darwinism," they openly disclose their hostility toward Darwin and his Malthusian orientation. In his autobiography, Darwin admits that he has been influenced by Malthus's *Essay on Population* and well impressed by his argument that "the struggle for existence goes on everywhere."[122] Both Marx and Engels categorically reject social Darwinism and the application of Malthus's theory of population to human relations in society. "Darwin did not know," Engels writes, "what a bitter satire he wrote on mankind, and especially on his countryman, when he showed that free competition, the struggle for existence, which the economists celebrate as the highest historical achievement, is the normal state of the animal kingdom. Only conscious organisation of social production can lift mankind above the rest of the animal world as regards the social aspect."[123] The attempt to base the social theory on the Darwinian dogma about the struggle for existence and the Malthusian dogma about population, Marx and Engels believe, does not solve the position of alienated workers and must be abandoned.

Malthus admits that his theory of population is a profoundly pessimistic account of the poor classes in society. Unless something more radical is done to prevent the increase in birth rate, he says, society would be reduced to starvation and "the poverty and misery which prevail among the lower classes of society would be absolutely irremediable."[124] The only authors, Malthus says, who have helped him to formulate his population theory are "Hume, Wallace, Adam Smith and Dr. Price." Lately, he adds, the subject has been treated by some of the French economists, including Montesquieu. Marx, however, accuses Malthus of plagiarism, insincerity, and Protestant hypocrisy. Malthus's work on population, he says, "is nothing more than a schoolboyish, superficial and parsonic declamatory plagiarism from other writers and does not contain a single sentence thought out by himself."[125] Condorcet is the true originator of the ideas expressed in Malthus's theory of population, He believed that most major social ills could be eradicated through the spread of the ideas of the French Revolution.[126] In England, Condorcet's and Helvetius's ideals have been partly accepted by the Benthamites. Maintaining that the pursuits of private and public interests are ultimately identical, they assumed wrongly that the extension of the suffrage and political rights would automatically be followed by greater happiness by a greater number of individuals. In fact, as Marx remarks, Bentham's utilitarianism has only encouraged the thin satisfaction of a limited élite, leaving the poor even poorer.

In opposition to social Darwinism, Malthusianism, and Benthamism, Marx argues that social cooperation and common ownership are prerequisites of any effective social activity. A society in which each individual pursues his own interests without much regard for others can only be defended by *laissez faire* economists, social Darwinists, and the "reactionary conservative socialists" who fanatically believe in the "miraculous effects of their social science."[127] The real world of bourgeois or civil society is a "world of atomistic individuals inimically opposed to one another."[128] In this alienated world, "man is linked with other men only by the ties of private interest and unconscious natural necessity."[129] Criticizing civil society as conceived by Hegel and the Young Hegelians, Marx argues that this society is actually bourgeois society motivated by egoism and "practical need." The only bond that holds men together in it is "the preservation of their property and their egoistic selves."[130] The rights of men advocated by the ideological founders of civil society are valuable only for egoistic individuals. The proletarian revolution will sweep away the whole structure of civil society, and the asociability of private individuals composing it will be replaced by the sociability of the individuals of classless society. Without this revolution, Marx maintains, the "abolition of class distinctions and the abolition of the relations of production on which they rest" is impossible.[131]

The concept of civil society has been used by writers before Marx. Hobbes and Rousseau, for example, use it in their social and political theories. When Marx uses the concept of civil society in the Preface to *Critique of Political Economy*, he refers to Hegel's anatomy of it adding that this anatomy has its roots in political economy.[132] In Hegel's view, civil society considered by itself is "the battlefield" of the individual private interests of all against all and the domain in which there is also "the struggle of private interests against particular matters of common concern."[133] Civil society, therefore, must be subordinated to the state. Marx rejects Hegel's subordination of society to the state and denounces all abstract and speculative ideas about social structures. These ideas, he believes, belong to the realm of alienating mysticism and do not describe any actual human society. In opposition to civil or bourgeois society, he posits "human society."[134] Unfortunately, however, he gives little information about this human society except that it will be classless and dominated by "the power of the united individuals."[135] He assumes that after the means of production are socialized, all traces of social alienation will be swept away automatically.

What really distinguishes Marx's social theory from all other social theories is the emphasis on a classless society that will have no room for social alienation. Communist *praxis*, however, contradicts Marx's utopian goals. The old bourgeois society with its classes and class antagonisms, it is true, has disappeared from the structure of communist society, but the fact is that this new society has also "established new classes, new conditions of oppression and the new forms of struggle in place of the old ones."[136] In his *Critique of the Gotha Programme*, Marx admits that the abolition of capitalist private ownership of the means of production and the establishment of the proletarian dictatorship could not by themselves create a dealienated communist society.

Long after the establishment of the dictatorship of the proletariat, he says, communist society will remain subject to the natural laws of capitalist society and be "stamped with the birth marks of the old capitalist society from whose womb it emerges."[137] His admission of defects in communist society is realistic enough. Unfortunately, Marx's realism is annulled by his oracular statement that "in a higher phase of communist society the antithesis between mental and physical labour will vanish" and all its members will be able to live according to the principle "from each according to his ability, to each according to his needs."[138] In both *Manuscripts of 8144* and *Critique*, written in 1875, he vacillates between "thoughtless communism" and humanism or philosophical communism and is unable to specify "the necessary pattern and goal of human development" in the communal socioeconomic order.[139]

What is striking in Marx's analysis of society is his resistance to egalitarian goals. In *Critique of the Gotha Programme*, there is no reference to egalitarian treatment of human individuals. On the contrary, these individuals are seen as having different abilities and needs. If Louis Blanc's slogan used by Marx is interpreted to mean that all people's needs will be satisfied "after the enslaving subordination of the individual to the division of labour," has been eliminated, then one has to remember that Marx does not say that people's needs will be satisfied *equally*. In his analysis of alienated society, he is more interested in the abolition of classes than in the abolition of social inequalities. "One man," he writes in the *Critique*, "is superior to another physically or mentally and so supplies more labour in the same time or can labour for a longer time; and labour, to serve as a measure, must be defined by its duration or intensity, otherwise it ceases to be a standard of measurement."[140] Marx does not explain how "a quantum of labour" can be measured except that intensity and duration must be taken into consideration. These criteria are very much reminiscent of Bentham's principle of equity and his estimation of the value of pleasures in which "intensity and duration" also play a decisive role.

For the French revolutionaries, equality meant equal treatment before the law. In the light of a long reign of legal inequalities, they insisted that there should be the same law for all members of society. In England, various legal inequalities persisted until recently. One could argue, of course, that legal inequalities still exist in all capitalist countries, but these also exist in communist societies. In ancient societies, the inequalities of men were of much greater importance than their equality. The modern demand for equality is characterized by a claim to equal socioeconomic status for all men and women. "Since the French bourgeoisie, from the great revolution on, brought civil equality to the forefront," Engels indicates, the French proletariat has pressed continuously for social and economic equality.[141] Marx and Engels seem to agree with their opponents that the right to equality does not imply a right to identical treatment. In a human society based on common ownership of the means of production, Marx maintains in *Critique of the*

Gotha Programme, the distribution of the "social stock of the means of consumption" should be proportional to each worker's labor contribution. He
has never been attracted by the idea of equality. Believing in "unequal individual endowment," he indicates that the achievement of such formal equalities as equal opportunities in bourgeois society is inadequate to ameliorate
the alienated conditions of the workers.

"The demand for equality in the mouth of the proletariat," Engels writes,
"has a double meaning." First, it is the "spontaneous reaction against the
crying social inequalities" and as such "simply an expression of the revolutionary instinct." Second, this demand has arisen as a reaction against the
bourgeois demand for equality, "serving as an agitational means in order to
stir up the workers against the capitalists with the aid of the capitalists' own
assertions."[142] Although this passage is not clear, Engels evidently approves
of the proletarian demand for equality in so far as this demand leads to the
abolition of private property and social classes. "Any demand for equality
which goes beyond this, of necessity passes into absurdity."[143] The demand
for social and economic equalities in the sense of human rights and individual
liberty is a bourgeois idea for Engels and Marx. In Engels's utopian dream of
classless society, there is no reference to the realization of egalitarian goals.
Even economic equality, which can only be achieved through revolution and
dictatorship, is practically ignored. Socialism, in his view, does not entail
egalitarianism. In his examination of social alienation, Marx makes a vague
reference to the elimination of the inequality of the sexes. He seems to sym-
pathize with Saint Simon's idea of "the emancipation of women," but unfortunately makes no contribution to this relevant social problem.[144]

Essentially following Marx's and Engels's views about equality, Lenin distinguishes between formal and actual equality. "Democracy," he writes in
State and Revolution, written on the eve of the 1917 revolution, "means only
formal equality. And as soon as equality is achieved for all members of society in relation to ownership of the means of production, that is, equality of
labour and wages, humanity will inevitably be confronted with the question of
advancing further, from formal equality to actual equlaity, i.e., to the operation of the rule from each according to his ability, to each according to his
needs."[145] He accepts Marx's utopian message, but paradoxically does not
share his confidence in the certainty of the realization of revolutionary goals
even during "the second stage of communism." "By what stages, by means of
what practical measures humanity will proceed to this supreme aim," he says,
"we do not and cannot know."[146] Knowledge of the socioeconomic processes
in the first phase of communist society is much simpler, and Lenin states
confidently that here "all citizens will become employees and workers of a
single country-wide state syndicate." "All that is required," he adds, "is that
they should work equally, do their proper share of work and get equal pay."
After the revolution, however, Lenin has realized that the transition to communist society would hardly be possible without skilled administrators and

workers, and he has been forced to abandon the pre-revolutionary principle of "equal pay" altogether. Stalin has gone even farther, declaring in 1931 that "equality in wages is alien and detrimental to socialist production" and that inequality in this respect is a "fundamental socialist principle."

The cry for equal rights, like that for civil rights, is alien to Marxist sociology. In Marx's social theory, the emphasis is on the satisfaction of human needs rather than the enjoyment of equal rights. The central target of his criticism of the *Gotha Programme* is the Lassallean conception of society based on "equal rights." He believes the Lassallean draft Programme is worthless because it is ideological, petty bourgeois, anti-revolutionary, and utopian. The workers, Marx points out in *Civil War in France*, have no interests in utopias. "They know that in order to work out their own emancipation, and along with it that higher form to which present society is irresistibly tending by its own economical agencies, they will have to pass through long struggles, through a series of historic processes, transforming circumstances and men."[147] Yet paradoxically, his own ideas of communist classless society are strikingly utopian. Social alienation in communist society, although different from that in capitalist society, is still a living phenomenon, and professional division of labor and social inequalities also exist. Property ownership in practical communism is social in form, but as even some modern Marxists indicate, the actual control of the means of production and communal property is in the hands of the party bureaucrats, not the workers.[148]

Marx's social theory contains considerable elements of oracular ideology which, instead of eliminating social alienation, poses a real threat to a free and constructive development of men. In addition, his emphasis on praxis in which individuals are "subjugated to the power of the united individuals" is bound to cripple the human endeavor to construct an open society.[149] Actually, Marx is neither a liberal nor an egalitarian. Although some of his statements appear sympathetic to egalitarian demands, he tends to represent the idea of equality as an essentially bourgeois notion.[150] In *Poverty of Philosophy*, he sarcastically likens Proudhon's ideal of equality to "the mystical tendency and providential *telos*."[151] Appalled by the inhumanity of capitalist praxis, Marx claims to have discovered the law according to which the capitalist system must disintegrate and which will lead to communism. He appears not to realize that if communism is the final stage of social development, as he sometimes suggests, then the materialist dialectic must eventually logically become inactive and redundant. There us no hint in his social theory what will happen to "dialectical materialism" in the "higher phase of communist society." Actually, Marx has never produced a systematic treatment of dialectics.

Considering Marx's social theory as a whole, it is obvious that his social analysis is a mixture of polymorphous ideas that his followers do not always share. Although he criticizes the idealist view of history, he consciously or unconsciously builds his own conception of historical development on Hegelian and Christian foundations. As the French modern Marxist Garaudy indicates, Marx's idea of change is essentially a Christian concept.[152] Marx's theory of classes, based largely on his analysis of English capitalism, has been rejected by many modern sociologists and social anthropologists. His observations on pre-capitalist social formations are seen as being mainly inferential and divorced from empirical facts. Because he is preoccupied with class conflict and struggle, he has failed to tackle such important problems as public health, education, environmental pollution, population growth, and bio-technological dangers.[153] Overall, Marx has been highly sensitive to criticism, suspicious of public opinion, and scornful of individual freedom. Rejecting his view that "revolutionary force" is the only way to change human society, most modern philosophers and sociologists are confident that social and economic inequalities, including the redistribution of wealth, can be resolved peacefully without resorting to any kind of dictatorship. Experience has shown that the realization of socialist goals is possible without violence and revolution.

9
Political Alienation

The distinguishing feature of European history in the nineteenth century is the emergence of nationalism. The outburst of intense national feeling shattered Napoleon's dreams of a world-wide empire. The awakening of national feeling, the result of foreign conquest, has set in motion a force destined to change the map of Europe and to call into existence new political ideologies and groupings. Common to these groupings was the will to acquire their own independent state and to be masters in their own house. There is nothing mysterious about the drive to national sovereignty and independence. It simply indicates that this sovereignty, however limited, makes possible the fulfillment of national aims that otherwise may be suppressed and alienated. Nationalism in the nineteenth century cannot be confined to any particular class or social group; it has appealed to all classes of the oppressed nationalities. The record of the European leftist movement is one of ambivalence and ambiguity, contradiction and confusion. Although theoretically internationalist, the Jacobins fought a national war in the name of international liberation. Marx's and Engels's ideas of nationalism are also ambivalent and contradictory. Sometimes they are inclined favorably toward the achievement of independent statehood by subject peoples. Engels condemns the partition of Poland by "the Russian-Prussian-Austrian Holy Alliance," stressing that "the Polish nation is undoubtedly one of the necessary nations of the nineteenth century."[1] Sometimes they express their fear that bourgeois-orientated nationalism might provide an alternative to revolutionary socialism. The adoption of national aims free from revolutionary perspectives by the proletariat is seen as "false consciousness."

Analyzing the national German character of true socialism in *German Ideology*, Marx rejects "obstinate nationalism" as the ideology of "the bourgeoisie and their writers."[2] "National narrowness," he adds, "is everywhere repellent." A similar idea is reiterated in *Communist Manifesto*, in which the emphasis is on "the universal interdependence of nations" as opposed to "national one-sidedness and narrow-mindedness."[3] "National differences and antagonisms between peoples," Marx and Engels indicate, "are daily more and more vanishing, owing to the development of the bourgeoisie, to freedom of commerce, to the world market, to the uniformity of the mode of production and in the conditions of life corresponding thereto." They add that "the supremacy of the proletariat will cause them to vanish still faster."[4]

In spite of their primary interest in the development of proletarian internationalism and solidarity, Marx and Engels always think of the national state as
the basic unit of social, cultural, and political life. They have never wavered in
their support for the right of nations, including Poland, Italy, and Ireland, to
their national independence and statehood. "The defeat of the working class
in France and the victory of the French bourgeoisie," Marx writes, "signified
the renewed suppression of the nationalities who had responded to the crow-
ing of the Gallic cock with heroic attempts to liberate themselves. Prussian,
Austrian and English *Sbirri* once more plundered, ravished and murdered in
Poland, Italy and Ireland."[5] Both Marx and Engels accept in principle the
right of nations to self-determination, but they have denied this right to the
oppressed and alienated nations in eastern Europe. Despising the Slavs, Marx
has opposed the "national movement of certain peoples in 1848" and has
altogether ruled out Czech independence. In 1851, Engels has similarly dismissed with contempt the pretensions of the oppressed Slavs to national
independence on the ground that the German race is the best vehicle for
spreading western civilization and proletarian internationalism in the East.

Although Marx tends to favor the existence of larger national units, in *Civil
War in France* he defends the Paris Commune against the accusation that its
aims are destructive of the unity of France. "The communal constitution,"
he says, "has been mistaken for an attempt to break up into a federation of
small states, as dreamed of by Montesquieu and the Girondins, that unity
of great nations which, if originally brought about by political force, has now
become a powerful coefficient of social production."[6] The Paris Commune
was both nationalist and internationalist in its emotive appeal and political
ideology. Being international in its revolutionary implications and national
only in its immediate preoccupation, the Paris Commue of March 1871
appealed to Marx as a unique fusion of doctrinaire agitation and pragmatic
action. Confronted by the antithesis between bourgeois liberal nationalism
and proletarian revolutionary nationalism, he defends the latter. "The Commune, that sphinx so tantalising to the bourgeois mind,"he writes in the *Civil
War in France*, is "the direct antithesis" of the bourgeois empire and "the
positive form of the republic."[7] "Working men's Paris, with its Commune,
will be for ever celebrated as the glorious harbinger of a new society. Its
martyrs," he points out, "are enshrined in the great heart of the working
class. Its exterminators history has already nailed to that eternal pillory from
which all the prayers of their priests will not avail to redeem them."[8]

The Communards, who regarded themselves as Frenchmen and internationalists, attracted the sympathy and support of many revolutionaries.
Although in 1870 Marx has welcomed Prussia's victory over France, in the
following year he has enthusiastically backed the Commune against both.
Analyzing the political development in modern societies, he argues that the
"reactionary politics" of the bourgeois state has been responsible for the political alienation of the working class. In all its forms, he thinks, bourgeois

politics has always been the politics of the exploitation of one part of society by the other. The Paris Commune admittedly has its defect, but it has also indicated the passionate desire of the alienated workers to go beyond the purely economic sphere of the struggle and to fight for the conquest of political power. "Every movement in which the working class comes out as a class against the ruling classes and tries to coerce them by pressure from without," Marx writes to F. Bolte, "is a political movement."[9] He sees in the Commune a model for a new dealienating and non-exploitative political activity.

Following the abortive revolution of the French left movement, Marx could not easily ignore the relevance of political power in the class wars. In his letter to Bolte, he admits that the "working class is not yet far enough advanced in its organisation to undertake a decisive campaign against the political power of the ruling classes." The alienated workers, however, must be trained for this campaign as the "political movement of the working class has naturally as its final object the conquest of political power for itself." Socialist sectarianism is reactionary and must be rejected.[10] Profiting from the deaths of Ferdinand Lassalle and Proudhon in 1864 and 1865, Marx soon had to face a new, equally influential challenge in Bakunin, the apostle of anarchist collectivism. The controversy between Marx and Bakunin centered mainly on the question of state functions. At the fourth Congress of the First International in Bale in 1869, their differences came to a head and Bakunin with his fellow anarchists was expelled from the Marxist International. Following their expulsion, the German and English internationalists accepted Marx's ideas of the retention of the state in some form after the defeat of capitalism; the French and Italian internationalists repudiated the state altogether.

The French Revolution is generally seen as a practical, although violent, expression of the widespread desire for change toward a more equitable system of social and political life. Nowhere in Europe was the admiration for Napoleon greater than in divided Germany and, paradoxically, nowhere was the reaction against his domination more far-reaching in its political consequences. On the eve of the French Revolution in 1789, Germany was the most divided country in Europe. The only bond between the small German states, apart from their shadowy allegiance to the emperor, was the diet or assembly composed of representatives sent by princes and towns. The diet had no authority, possessing neither armed forces nor revenues. Napoleon reduced the number of small independent states to thirty-nine. The war of liberation in Germany against Napoleon was not provoked by a government interested in military expansionism; rather it was the rising of a people in arms to free itself from foreign domination. Commenting on this war, Marx praises the rule of Napoleon in the Rhenish states and condemns the admiration of the German citizens for England. "Napoleon," he says, "has rendered them the greatest services by cleaning out Germany's Augean stables and establishing civilised means of communication whereas the English only waited for the opportunity to exploit them *à tort et à travers*."[11] For a generation after the fall of Napoleon, Germany remained politically and socially stagnant. The sacrifices of the people in the course of liberation were either forgotten or ignored, and the German rulers made no attempt to satisfy their desire for unity and constitutional reforms.

At the beginning of 1848, most Germans favored political reforms and most reformers were liberals. Distrusting the willingness of the princes to grant constitutional reforms, the reformers insisted that Germany must be united on liberal lines through a parliament of the whole German nation. The triumph of the liberal constitutional party in the March revolution, however, was short-lived. Afraid of the emergence of political power of the working classes, the bourgeoisie made a tacit alliance with the king that safeguarded the interests of both parties. "After the March events of 1848," Marx writes, "the king made the concessions which the revolution compelled him to make. The crown and the people concluded a truce and the people were cheated."[12] As a result, the "first cabinet following the March revolution represented the bourgeoisie under the guise of a dictatorship of the people. The bourgeoisie betrayed the people and subjugated them to the king."[13] On 2 November 1848, the king dismissed his ministers and dispersed the parliament with the army solid behind him. In the absence of the "Assembly of old women," as Marx calls its members, Frederick William (1840–61) regained his autocratic power and again became master of the German state.

After the March revolution of 1848, the new political situation has transformed the pseudo-revolutionary orientation of the bourgeoisie into the reactionary stumbling of a senile individual "sans eyes, sans ears, sans teeth, sans everything."[14] "Without faith in itself, without faith in the people, grumbling at those above, frightened of those below, egoistical towards both and aware of its egoism, revolutionary with regard to the conservatives and conservative with regard to the revolutionaries" the German liberal bourgeoisie, Marx writes, has failed badly to eliminate political alienation "because it merely represented the spleen of an old social era and not the initiatives of a new one."[15] "The German revolution of 1848," he stresses, "is merely a parody of the French revolution of 1789."[16] Unlike the French bourgeoisie of 1789, the German bourgeoisie of 1848 "unhesitatingly betrays the peasants, its natural allies." From the very beginning, Marx indicates, the German liberal bourgeoisie of 1848 "was inclined to betray the people and to compromise with the crowned representatives of the old society, for it already belonged itself to the old society. It did not advance the interests of a new society against an old one but represented refurbished interests within an obsolete society."[17] Afraid of the proletariat and unwilling to combat political alienation, the German bourgeoisie refused to fight against the princes and shamefully compromised with the despotic monarchy. As a result, the king remained the "sole political person" and undisputed master of German politics.

It is against the background of these political developments that one must analyze Marx's ideas of political alienation and his attempt to formulate his political theory. After the defeat of the proletarian course, he moved to Cologne where in June 1848 he initiated a new left-wing journal entitled *Neue Rheinische Zeitung*. In it Marx advocates the creation of a single German democratic republic and the struggle against the "reactionary bourgeoisie" headed by the "hereditary king representing the old society within the new society."[18] Prussia, in his view, is still feudal and alienated politically. Defending proletarian internationalism and the workers' right to form their own government, he could not resist giving vent to the belief that revolutionary terrorism is the only method that can solve the political alienation of the working classes in Germany. "The royal terrorists, the terrorists by the grace of God," he says in the last but one number of the journal, "are in practice brutal, disdainful and mean, in theory cowardly, secretive and deceitful, and in both respects disreputable."[19] Because of Marx's increasing hostility toward the monarchy, the German authorities ordered him "to leave the country forthwith." He left for Paris, still expecting the imminent communist triumph. After a short stay in France, he left for London on 24 August 1849, where he continued his revolutionary activities.

Before becoming a communist by the end of 1843, Marx has hoped that the existing political system in Germany could be improved by reform. In *Rheinische Zeitung*, he defends the rational state, calling it the "great organism in which legal, moral and political freedom will find its realisation." Many of his articles have been addressed to the political authorities, emphasizing that a legal development in Germany is impossible without a development of the laws. When taking over the editorship of this daily paper in October 1842, Marx adopted a neutral position toward "socialism and communism."[20] There is no call in this short-lived paper for revolution and no expressed desire to silence differing political opinion. Marx has focused his attention on freedom of the press in response to the increasingly alienating political measures taken by Frederick William IV. Still adhering to the principles of liberal democracy, he has merely advocated the claims of freedom-loving men and women against those of the despotic German bureaucracy. Disappointed in his hopes of political reformism, he has gradually shifted his reformist position to that of proletarian internationalism and revolutionary action.

After the suppression of *Rheinische Zeitung* in 1843, Marx began writing *Critique of Hegel's Philosophy of Right*.[21] It is in this work that he expresses his early views on democracy, despotism, monarchy, bureaucracy, citizenship, constitution, law, sovereignty, alienation, and the state. The decision to write a critical commentary on Hegel's *Philosophy of Right* has been motivated by his newly formed opinion that the state is a form of alienated life and could not exist if men were not socially, economically, and politically dehumanized and alienated. Having become disillusioned with Hegel's conception of the state as the harmonizing agency, Marx is led to the conclusion that the state in its idealistic dress is simply an "abstraction" of the concrete historical processes. Hegel's treatment of political institutions, including the state, as mere predicates of the abstract Idea, Marx believes, mystifies human history and inevitably creates the conditions for political alienation. Refusing to acknowledge that the reality of the state is in its true democracy, Hegel, in Marx's view, sanctions the conditions of estrangement. In opposition to Hegel, Marx asserts that the democratic element is the distinguishing mark of "reality" in the state. "Hegel starts from the state and makes man the subjectified state; democracy starts from man and makes the state objectified man."[22] The democratic element should be that real element that "confers a rational form on the organism of the state as a whole."

Hegel distinguishes sharply between civil society and the state. Civil society is that form of political organization that follows the disruption of family. Because the association of members as self-subsistent individuals in civil society is "only abstract," no rational man can rest content with such political organization. He can only be content with the higher form of organization in the state that is "the end and actuality of the universal order and the public life."[23] It is only the state that can express the "identity of the universal will with the particular will."[24] Civil society, Hegel indicates, "may be prima facie regarded as the external state, the state based on need, the state as the Understanding envisages it." Yet, bourgeois or civil society is a manifestly evil system governed by "the law of nature." The state of nature is "a state of violence and wrong," and for this reason the idea of society based on the law of nature must be rejected.[25] The political state, according to Hegel, is "the condition in which alone right has its actuality."[26] Although a state may violate right principles and be defective in various ways, it still contains the essential moments of its existence. In *Philosophy of Right*, Hegel is concerned with the rational aspects of the political state. Admitting that the state "stands on earth and bad behaviour may disfigure it in many respects," he concentrates his analysis of the state on its "affirmative aspects."[27]

While agreeing with Hegel about some distinguishing features of bourgeois or civil society and the state, Marx argues that any assumption of their synthesis in the monarchical state is illusory and deceptive. Bourgeois society and the bourgeois state, in his view, are not what they appear to be. The political attitude of civil society in the political state constructed by Hegel is mere appearance, because the political being of civil society is an abstraction from its actual being. "The people alone is what is concrete. And it is remarkable," Marx writes, "that Hegel, who without hesitation attributes a living quality such as sovereignty to the abstraction, attributes it only with hesitation and reservations to something concrete."[28] Marx criticizes Hegel for concentrating his political analysis on the ideal development and power of the state, ignoring its real, material genesis and history. "Hegel does not develop his thinking from the object but expounds the object in accordance with a thinking that is cut and dried—already formed and fixed in the abstract sphere of logic."[29] Marx's principal complaint against Hegel's political or rational state concerns man's alienation. Political alienation, he thinks, is a consequence of the division between civil society and the state. "Hegel proceeds from the separation of the state and civil society, from particular interests and the intrinsically and explicity general; and bureaucracy itself is based on this separation." "He expounds no content for the bureaucracy but only some general features of its formal organisation." Actually, "bureaucracy as the civil society of the state confronts the state of civil society."[30]

After the separation of the state and civil society, the "citizen of the state is separated from the citizen as a member of civil society." Distinguishing between the political state in which political alienation is ubiquitous and the unpolitical material, real, or democratic state in which man is not alienated, Marx believes that the political state transforms "the real human being" into the "private egoistic individual."[31] Deserted by the political state, the individual is left to an atomistic existence in bourgeois alienated society.[32] This society, he points out, "is the realised principle of individualism." Hegel's mistake lies in his treatment of the state as the foundation of civil society rather than the other way around. "Hegel is not to be blamed for depicting the nature of the modern state as it is but for presenting that which is as the nature of the state. That the rational is actual is proved precisely in the contradiction of irrational actuality which everywhere is the contrary of what it asserts, and asserts the contrary of what it is."[33] Hegel believes the "fundamental characteristic of the state as a political entity is the substantial unity, i.e., the ideality, of its moments. In this unity the particular powers and their activities are dissolved and yet retained. They are retained, however, only in the sense that their authority is no independent one but only one of the order and breadth determined by the Idea of the whole."[34] What differentiates the state from civil society and makes it rational is that "the rational end of man is life in the state" and that without the state "the complete freedom of its members" is impossible. "The state," Hegel says, "is actual only when its members have a feeling of their own self-hood and it is stable only when public and private ends are identical."[35]

Analyzing Hegel's conception of the state, Marx insists on clarification of the state and its position in real life. For Hegel, the state is the bearer of the universal and the "march of God in the world."[36] It is actual and its actuality exists because the interest of the whole is realized in and through particular ends. "The state in its actuality is essentially an independent state, and beyond that a particular state." Because the state, in Hegel's view, is the highest and most divine of human institutions, man must venerate it as a secular deity. As an association of independent individuals, civil society is meaningful only within the state. In civil society each member is his own end, and it is only within the state that the discord of private and egoistic ends can be brought into harmony. Although in civil society "universal and particular spheres are opposed," they are bound together and harmonized within the political state. While civil society, according to Hegel, "is the battlefield of private interests," the state "acts in obedience to conscious ends of the whole" and is thus "absolutely rational."[37] The great advance of the modern state is that in it "nowadays all the citizens have one and the same end, an absolute and permanent end." Rational man living in civil society can tolerate individual antagonisms because they are tempered by the state.

Marx criticizes Hegel's political theory, arguing that it puts the cart before the horse. Instead of regarding the legal and political relations that make up the state as part of the superstructure erected on the economic base of civil society, Hegel maintains that society is a manifestation of the political state. Marx calls this a mystification. "Family and civil society," he writes, "are the premises of the state; they are the genuinely active elements, but in speculative philosophy things are inverted. Here reality is expressed not as itself but as another reality. Ordinary empirical fact has an alien spirit for its law."[38] Marx maintains that civil society and family are the driving forces in political life. In Hegel's political theory, he says, "the family and civil society appear as the dark natural ground from which the light of the state arises."[39] They are conceived as spheres of the concept of the state. "The actual idea, mind, divides itself into the two ideal spheres of its concept, family and civil society, that is, its finite phase—hence, the division of the state into family and civil society is ideal," mystical and alienating.[40] Hegel is criticized for masking the contradictions between civil society and economic life, on the one hand, and between the political state and civil society, on the other. In this way, Marx believes, Hegel maintains and justifies political alienation in civil society and the state. Hegel's description of the state as "the actuality of the ethical Idea" is illusory, far removed from the economic basis of real life. It is for this reason that he fails to realize that the political state is a sympton of alienation just as it is a mask of the lack of political freedom and individual purpose.

In his criticism of Hegel's idealism, Feuerbach argues that the essence of man is only detectable in community and that the manifestations attributed to the Idea or Absolute being are really the acts of man. Because Hegal mixes up his subjects and predicates, one must demystify them and set them right again. Like Feuerbach, Marx reproaches Hegel for starting his political analysis from the ideal instead of the real, from the idea of the state instead of the real subjects. "The idea is made the subject and the actual relation of family and civil society to the state is conceived as its internal imaginary activity."[41] In Hegel's political theory, Marx remarks sarcastically, "the idea is made the subject" and the leader of peoples and the world. "The actual becomes a phenomenon but the idea has no other content than this phenomenon."[42] Hegel ignores real political alienation and wastes his energies on eulogising the fictitious Idea that reveals itself in the world and is embodied in the political state. In Hegel, everything actual is an idea and the absolute Idea is the final end of the development of essences. His philosophical formalism and speculative inversion of historical processes is responsible for political alienation in the rational state.

Marx argues against Hegel's deification of the state and for the democratization of the political state. The idea of the real or democratic state, Marx contends, cannot be obtained from the mystification and abstraction of the political state, because this state as an external, undemocratic, and alien power dominating civil society. "Hegel is content that in the state, which he demonstrates to be the self-conscious mode of being of ethical spirit, this ethical spirit should only as such, in the sense of the general idea, be the determining factor. He does not allow society to become the actually determining factor because that requires an actual subject and he has only an abstract one—an imaginary one."[43] Hegel attempts to justify the existing reality of the political state by entirely subordinating the reality of the family and civil society to the rational, alienating state. Marx reproaches him for confusing reality and appearance. While Hegel believes that "appearance has its being in the Idea or God,"[44] Marx denies any validity to appearances in the political state. The history of the state can only be intelligible in terms of the history of real existing men. It is true, Hegel's ideas of the rational state are drawn from reality, but they are wrapped up in metaphysical clothes and drawn in illusory, mystical forms. As a result, the real alienation of man is seen merely as an alienation of self-consciousness.

In Marx's political theory, reality is essentially material and immanent in existence. The Hegelian conception of political reality as the self-projection or self-revelation of the Idea in the rational state is rejected. In *Critique*, Marx is not insisting on the abolition of the state and private property. This abolition is the theme of his later writings. The main emphasis in *Critique* is on the abolition of the non-democratic, monarchical state. It is this state that causes and maintains political alienation. He stresses the need for complete democratization of executive power at all levels. "What Hegel says about the executive does not deserve to be called a philosophical exposition."[45] Criticizing Hegel's description of the "bureaucracy as the state formalism of civil society," Marx indicates that it makes no reference to its true content. "Because the bureaucracy turns its formal objectives into its content, it comes into conflict everywhere with real objectives. It is therefore obliged to pass off the form for the content and the content for the form."[46] Hegel maintains that civil servants and members of the executive represent the "greater part of the middle class" and that "the objective factor in their appointment is the consciousness of right and knowledge."[47] In his political theory, the middle class is essential to the modern state. A state without a middle class, he thinks, "must remain on a low level." The middle class, the class of civil servants, is represented as the universal class. The task of this class, he says, "is the universal interests of the community."[48] The political power of the universal class is counterbalanced by the business class from below and the hereditary monarch from above. Marx categorically rejects Hegel's conception of the bourgeois civil service and substitutes his mystical conception of the universality of the bourgeois class by the universality of the people expressed in their role as citizens. He thinks all citizens, regardless of class, must have the same right to civil service in a democratic state. "Hegel makes citizenship, political existence and political conviction attributes of private property, instead of making private property an attribute of citizenship."[49]

Marx criticizes the existence of political state and concentrates his attack on monarchy. The monarchical state, he believes, causes and maintains political alienation. Hegel's conception of "the monarch as the true God-man, as the actual incarnation of the Idea" is mediaeval nonsense that must be demolished.[50] The monarchical power has always been the power of private property, and the "constitutional monarch expresses the idea of the constitutional state in its sharpest abstraction."[51] The true opposites in the political state are the monarch and civil society. Marx argues against the illusory political position of citizens who live in a society organized by the monarchical state, indicating that those who live in such a society are citizens only in the abstract. "That the state is a hereitary monarch, an abstract personality, means nothing but that the personality of the state is abstract or that it is the state of the abstract personality."[52]

The difference between the empirical and the metaphysical, between the democratic and the monarchical approach to political theory, in Marx's view, is revealed in the distinction between popular and monarchical sovereignty. In Hegel's theory, sovereignty is individualized in the crown, not shared with the people. For him, "the sovereignty of the people is one of the confused notions based on the wild idea of the people. Taken without its monarch and the articulation of the whole which is the indispensable and direct concomitant of monarchy, the people is a formless mass and no longer a state."[53] The people cannot be the bearers of sovereignty because they lack the unifying power of the monarchical state. Without this state, Hegel states, the people are connected only as an "aggregate, a formless mass whose commotion and activity could only be elementary, irrational, barbarous and frightful." Arguing against popular sovereignty, he states that "people as a particular section of the citizens means that section which does not know what it wills."[54] Against Hegel's conception of monarchical sovereignty, Marx advocates popular sovereignty. The idea of monarchical authority, as Hegel expounds it, is only the idea of the arbitrary and despotic will of the monarch. "Hegel defines the monarch as the personality of the state. The monarch is personified sovereignty, sovereignty incarnate, political consciousness in the flesh; in consequence, all other people are excluded from this sovereignty, from personality and from political consciousness. Hegel knows of no other content to give to this *souveraineté personne* than the I will, the element of arbitrary choice within the will."[55] Monarchical sovereignty, Marx argues, is an illusion and a symptom of political alienation.

Marx rejects Hegel's presentation of the monarch as the true God-man. "A single empirical person to the exclusion of all others" reflects the ideology of "Asiatic despotism where the political state is nothing but the personal caprice of a single individual."[56] Marx has rejected monarchism by 1842 or earlier and makes sarcastic remarks about Hegel's idea that "the concept of the monarch is not derivative but originates purely in itself." In a certain sense, he writes "every necessary being originates purely in itself—in this respect the monarch's louse is as good as the monarch."[57] If the sovereign is the actual sovereignty of the state, then the monarch could be considered as an "independent state" even without people. The sovereignty of the monarch is due to the people, not the other way around. The concept of absolute sovereignty residing in the monarch, Marx argues, is totally alien to any democratic constitution. The real obligation of obedience must be to the total interest of the people. In a truly democratic state, the legislative power is constituted by the consent of the people and is exercised for the good of all citizens. In this *Critique*, Marx, like Locke, regards the state as a means to an end that is realised only through the enrichment of human lives. Law must express the will of the people, not the will of the hereditary monarch. It is the will of the citizens, not the alien will of the bureaucracy, that is the true maker of law.

Like Rousseau, Hegel distinguishes the general will or the the will of the state from the will of the majority. The will of the state represents the true will of the individual. "If the state is confused with civil society," he says, "then the interest of the individuals is threatened and membership of the state becomes optional.[58] No rational man can be content with such political organisation. Only in the monarchical state can the individuals find the realizatioin of their will. "The objective will of the state is rationality implicit or in conception, whether it be recognised or not by individuals."[59] The government is the really living totality that preserves the state and its constitution. In the perfect form of the state, the all-sustaining and all-decreeing will representing the will of the individuals is identified with the will of "one actual decreeing individual" or monarch. For Hegel, the monarchical constitution is the constitution of developed reason. The monarch's absolute power is "grounded in the authority of God since it is in its divinity that its unconditional character is contained."[60] Marx mocks Hegel's deification of the king and rejects his idea of the "monarch as the head and representative of the executive power." Hegel "stands everything on its head" and ignores the principle that the "real bearer of the constitution is the people."[61] The democratic constitution must be built on the sovereignty of all citizens . Citizens must be able to choose rulers who are willing to observe the democratic goals of the state.

Marx is very critical of Hegel's idea that the people have no right to change the monarchical constitution on the assumption that its origin is divine. In his view, the monarchical constitution is the expression of political alienation. "In monarchy," he writes, "the whole, the people, is subsumed under one of its particular modes of being, the political constitution. In democracy the constitution itself appears only as one determination, that is, the self-determination of the people. In monarchy we have the people of the constitution; in democracy the constitution of the people."[62] Yet, Marx says nothing concrete and informative about "popular constitution" except that "democracy is the solved riddle of all constitutions."[63] He does not explain how the constitution in Marxist form of democracy is "brought back to its actual basis, the actual human being and the actual people." The assumption that the constitution must be the work of the people does not necessarily make it less dubious and mystical than in Hegel's political theory. Marx recognizes the complex problem of the constitution without contributing to its solution. He takes for granted that the popular basis of constitutional government is the answer to political alienation.

Notably, Marx's criticism of the bureaucratic state in *Critique* makes no reference to class rule. Equally significant is that his connection of the state with private property has not yet assumed ideological or proletarian interpretation. There is no advocacy for the abolition of the state. There is only a vague hint at the end of *Critique* that the state, presumably in its monarchical form, should be "dissolved."[64] On the basis of his general argument in this work, it is safe to assume that Marx wants to see the dissolution of the monarchical state in which the bureaucracy holds the state in its possession. "The bureaucracy has the state, the spiritual essence of society, in its possession, as its private property."[65] Because the bureaucracy is "the state as formalism" or "the spiritualism of the state," he argues for elimination of "state formalism." Believing that the progressive development of the bureaucracy intensifies political alienation, he reproaches Hegel for idealizing the bureaucracy and empiricizing public consciousness.[66] In the individual bureaucrat, the state objective, he says, easily turns into his private objective. "In the bureaucracy the identity of state interest and particular private aim is established in such a way that the state interest becomes a particular private aim over against other private aims."[67]

Marx criticizes the misuse of private property in the political state which, especially in primogeniture, "isolates private property from family and society and turns it into something abstractly independent." He does not say that property owners as a whole dominate the state system, but rather that the king and his state civil servants tend to own this state as their "own possession or private property." At this stage, he limits his attack on private property to the institutions of primogeniture and bureaucracy. "Primogeniture," he writes, "is merely the external appearance of the inner nature of landed property. The fact that it is inalienable cuts off its social nerves and ensures its isolation from civil society."[68] In primogeniture, private property appears as the highest synthesis of the political state and "the supreme alienation of caprice." Indeed, primogeniture is merely a particular manifestation of the relationship between private property and the monarchical state. Although Marx does not demand the general abolition of private property yet, it is possible to argue that his sarcastic remark about "the sovereign magnificence of private property, of landed property, on which so much sentimentality has been spent and so many multicoloured crocodile tears have been shed in recent times" contains the seed of his future attitude toward private property as "the necessary consequence of alienated labour."[69]

Marx's criticism of the metaphysical state dominating Hegel's political theory does not make his own theory less open to the metaphysical illusion of the society-state. Building on Hegelian foundations, he combines and confuses society and state in a single and total organization of human life. Such an organisation has no room for any separate association and no room for genuine political freedom. Like Hegel, Marx bases his political theory on the idea that the state is an organism and that its citizens can realize their political ends only when they subordinate them to the organic whole. Arguing for the organic totality of citizens in the state, Marx in fact advocates the creation of an all-inclusive and omnicompetent society-state that embraces and regulates all other associations. There is no suggestion that, in view of the many various purposes of the parts, the state should be regarded as federal. Although he abandons the Hegelian idea of a controlling system of social ethics in favor of the idea of a controlling system of social economics, he still adheres to the Platonic and Hegelian view that the whole is more important and valuable than its parts. Marx's romantic longing for a totalist unity and his dream of a relized totality are, as in Hegel's political theory of the society-state, colored by metaphysical and idealistic illusions.

Although the movement of Marx's dialectical thinking is critical, in *Critique* he fails to formulate an adequate theory of the state. As a result, his conception of the democratic or material state, like Hegel's conception of the monarchical or rational state, is a "manifest piece of mystification."[70] Sharing Hegel's idea of the state as an organism, Marx merely rejects his "proposition that this organism is the development of the idea" and that the hereditary monarch must be its head.[71] He defends "true democracy" as opposed to absolutism and insists that "the democratic element must be the actual element which gives to itself its rational form in the state organism as a whole."[72] Yet, Marx's democracy as described in *Critique* remains an enigma. Some commentators believe that his concept of true democracy in this work strongly resembles Plato's conception of the ideal state.[73] This is partly true but only because Marx, like Plato, is not a true democrat. It is perfectly correct to say, as Marx does, that "democracy is the true unity of the general and the particular," but it is not correct to say that "all forms of the state have democracy for their truth."[74] Otherwise, it would be pointless to criticize Hegel's theory of the monarchical state as being undemocratic. What connects the Marxist idea of the state in *Critique* with the Platonic rational state is the emphasis on man's rationality and real universality. Marx, it is true, does not state that "the wise shall lead and rule, and that the ignorant shall follow," but he does believe that true democracy can only exist when expressed in its rational form in the real state. Thus, his conception of true democracy is tied closely with the ideas of rationality, reality, and knowledge. The difference between Marx and Plato, however, is considerable. Plato is openly hostile toward democracy, treating it as the negation of moral government, and eulogizes aristocracy and the philosopher-king. Marx, on the other hand, detests monarchy as the expression of political estrangement and advocates true democracy, although its real characteristics are not described.

Only "true democracy," Marx insists, is compatible with social rationality. "Democracy is the genus constitution. Monarchy is one species and a poor one at that. Democracy is content and form."[75] Marx, however, does not explain the nature of political power in a democratic state and how this state can enforce its obligations on its subjects without infringing individual freedom. Like Hegel, he assumes that the will of the state is deliberate and always determined rationally. Believing that the will of the state is a particular aspect of the social whole or totality, he readily concludes that it is also identical with the will of society. Therefore, he is led to the idea of the unified society-state that is apparent in the Greek city-state and that plays an important role in Hegel's political theory. The difference between Marx and Hegel here is formal: Hegel starts from the supremacy of the state, treating it as the subject; Marx starts from the supremacy of civil society, which, in his view, is the subject. In both cases the subject is a mystical and abstract totality that is regarded as an end in itself and in which individual interests are subjugated totally to the interests of the organic all-inclusive whole. The particular appears everywhere as something general, and individuality is only a means to its generality.[76]

In *Critique of Hegel's Philosophy of Right*, Marx develops and amplifies ideas already present in the discussion of the state and civil society in Hegel's *Philosophy of Right*. He soon finds that the *Critique* lacks originality and ideological independence, qualities that "made it utterly unsuitable" for publication.[77] In subsequent works, Marx's political theory is both more original and revolutionary. He first makes his revolutionary sympathies clear in his letters to A. Ruge, published in *Deutsch-Französische Jahrbücher*. In the May 1843 letter, Marx vigorously attacks despotism and political alienation, which in that year have dominated "the philistine world" of the German monarchy. In Prussia, he says, the king is the system that creates and maintains political alienation. "He is the sole political person," and his personality determines the whole political structure of alienated society.[78] Marx is obviously disappointed that the German people are indifferent to despotism and the lack of essential freedoms. He warns them that freedom, the feeling of human dignity, has to be reawakened and that only political freedom can transform society into a community of self-fulfilling individuals. "The philistine world," he points out, "is a political world of animals, and if we have to recognise its existence, nothing remains for us but simply to agree to this *status quo*. Centuries of barbarism engendered and shaped it, and now it confronts us as a consistent system, the principle of which is the dehumanised world."[79]

Marx now is openly hostile toward the monarchy. "The monarchical principle in general is the despised, the despicable, the dehumanised man." The monarch is a despot who alienates and degrades his people. The philistine state dominated by the monarch, therefore, must be abolished.[80] In the third and last letter to Ruge, written in Kreuznach in September 1843, Marx insists on "ruthless criticism of all that exists" in the despotic monarchical state. This criticism, he tells Ruge, must be "ruthless both in the sense of not being afraid of the results it arrives at and in the sense of being just as little afraid of conflct with the powers in existence." The critic of political alienation "not only can but must deal with political problems" realistically and resolutely. "Nothing prevents us from making criticism of politics. We develop new principles for the world," he writes, "out of the world's own principles."[81] Marx concludes this letter by appealing to the reform of consciousness. "Our programme," he says, "must be reform of consciousness by analysing the mystical consciousness that is unintelligible to itself, whether it manifests itself in a religious or a political form."[82]

Marx's appeal to the reform of consciousness has been almost entirely ignored by the Young Hegelians. Initially, they held an idealist view of the state that implied that the state is what Hegel calls "the ethical universe" and the incarnation of objective morality. They followed their master in maintaining that it is only in the state that "the individual himself has objectivity, genuine individuality and an ethical life."[83] Even Feuerbach's view of the state, as expressed in *Theses*, is surprisingly close to Hegel's. "In the state," he says, "the essential goals and activities of man are realised in different classes of society but again brought to identity in the person of the head of the state. The head of the state has to represent all classes and is thus the representative of universal man." After abandoning Hegel's theory of monarchical state, Marx criticizes both Hegel and Feuerbach for their purely contemplative and reactionary theories of the political state. These theories, he states, entirely ignore the primacy of economic relations in political life and cannot be a guide to any constructive political praxis.

The ideological differences between Marx and the Young Hegelians relate to such themes as political reforms, democracy, communism, criticism, pauperism, and the state. Marx's insistence on the revolutionary solution of political alienation in the German monarchical state has been rejected categorically by Feuerbach, Bauer, and Ruge. The political difference between Marx and Ruge is analyzed in Marx's *Critical Marginal Notes on the Article by a Prussian*, published in *Vorwärts*.[84] Here Marx argues against Ruge's reformist, humanist, and non-revolutionary politics. "Socialism," he says, "cannot be realised without revolution." It cannot be brought about without "destruction and dissolution."[85] Unlike Ruge, who represents the Silesian weavers' uprising as a futile revolt of the helpless poor who have no chance of success in a politically backward Germany, Marx regards this uprising as the first significant revolt of the proletariat against the alienating bourgeoisie and the king. "In a striking, sharp, unrestrained and powerful manner," he writes, "the proletariat proclaims its opposition to the society of private property. The Silesian uprising begins precisely with what the French and English workers' uprisings end, with consciousness of the nature of the proletariat. The action itself bears the stamp of this superior character."[86] Marx emphasizes the alienating antithesis between the king and the proletariat, reasserting the view dominant in *Critique* that the bourgeois or monarchical state is "based on the contradiction between public and private life, on the contradiction between general interests and private interests."[87] The bourgeois government does not represent the people and confines itself to a formal and alienating activity. This activity intensifies political alienation and leads to the fragmentation and slavery of civil society. "This fragmentation, this baseness, this slavery of civil society," Marx says, "is the natural foundation on which the modern state rests, just as the civil society of slavery was the natural foundation on which the ancient state rested. The existence of the state and the existence of slavery are inseparable."[88]

The state, Marx argues, is the source of all social maladies. "From the political point of view, the state and the system of society are not two different things. The state is the system of society."[89] As in *Critique*, he combines and confuses state and society in a single and total organization of all human life. The idea of the unified society-state is still dominant, although the difference between the democratic road to political dealienation described in *Critique* and the revolutionary road indicated in *Critical Marginal Notes* is considerable. In *On the Jewish Question*, Marx's ideas of the state are different because here he definitely repudiates his republican views. There is a tacit assumption, for example, that formal democracy without communism as it existed in the United States is inadequate to solve human emancipation. While "the political state" is criticized on the grounds that it is "the state of independent, egoistic individuals," the democratic state is seen as a weak political organization unable to overcome political alienation. This state, like the Christian state, has no interest in abolishing religion and private property.

In his polemic against Bruno Bauer, Marx criticizes him for overlooking the conflict between the political state and civil society. Marx contends that political bourgeois state is naturally opposed to man's material life. In this state man lives a double life, a real earthly life of egoism in civil society and an illusory heavenly life of community in the political realm. Without a radical change in civil society, Marx believes, the democratic republic cannot eliminate political alienation. In the bourgeois democratic state, as in any state based on the division of labor and private property, political alienatioin is inevitable. Here, it is estrangement that matters rather than man. The only man who counts in "the perfect political state" is the king, a being specifically different from all other men.[90] In *On the Jewish Question*, Marx tends to treat the democratic state like the Christian state—as a mockery of man's political and social life. Political democracy, he says, "is Christian," because in it every man who has been corrupted by bourgeois civil society and who has been alienated "ranks as sovereign." In democracy, alienated man becomes tangible reality.[91] The democratic state in Christian cloths is "nothing more than a non-state." Marx hates religion so much that he cannot analyze any social, economic, or political category without invoking its "inverted world consciousness." As a result, Marx regards any state that tolerates the "sigh of the oppressed creature" as the "imperfect," "incomplete," "alienated," or "hypocritical" state, and one that is sustained by illusions that are symptoms of political alienation.

Political emancipation in a "hypocritical state," in Marx's view, is impossible. It needs a fundamental reconstruction of civil society. "Political emancipation," Marx insists, must "at the same time be the dissolution of the old society on which the state alienated from the people, the sovereign power, is based."[92] This seems to suggest the abolition of the state itself as part of the total reconstruction of civil society. Marx is not clear on this point, but he stresses that "only when man has recognised and organised his *forces propres* as social forces and consequently no longer separates social power from himself in the shape of political power, only then will human emancipation have been accomplished."[93] In his May 1843 letter to Ruge, he has already indicated the need to abolish "the philistine state dominated by the hereditary monarch." Now he argues that "human emancipation" will be completed only in a totally reorganized social structure and that this needs the overthrow of "the prevailing scheme of things." In *Introduction to the Critique of Hegel's Philosophy of Right*, written about six months after the *Critique*, Marx points out that it needs the "drastic dissolution of society" and the creation of a new social order in which there will be no room for "egoistic man" and private property.[94]

In the *Introduction*, Marx for the first time speaks of class polarization and of the role of the proletariat in "the general emancipation of society."[95] There is a reference to class struggle, but not in the sense in which it is described, for example, in *Communist Manifesto*. Here society is not analyzed, as in *Manifesto*, in terms of "the antagonism between the oppressing and oppressed classes" or "two great hostile camps." Instead, class struggle is seen in terms of general discontent involving the monarchy, the princes, the bourgeoisie, and the proletariat, thus echoing Hegel's description of civil society as "the battlefield of all against all." "The princes," Marx says, "are struggling against the monarchy, the bureaucrats against the nobility, and the bourgeois against all, while the proletariat is already beginning to struggle against the bourgeoisie."[96] Antagonism and class conflict are inevitable in the monarchical state. The monarchy as the expression of political alienation is still the main object of Marx's criticism. The king is seen as the big property owner, having no sympathy for the underprivileged. "By declaring the people his private property, the king simply states that the property owner is king."[97] Marx believes society needs no king, and the whole institution of monarchy is anachronistic.

In the essay *On the Jewish Question* and in *Manuscripts of 1844*, Marx explains the emergence of political alienation in terms of private property and "practical need or egoism." There is, he says, "the essential connection between estrangement and the money system."[98] In political alienation in capitalist society," money transforms the real essential powers of man into tormenting chimeras," turning "an image into reality and reality into a mere image."[99] In a parasitic state, money dominates man's whole political life. "God of the avaricious man is only an illusory bill of exchange."[100] In *Manuscripts*, Marx connects the phenomenon of alienation with the antagonism between capital and labor, emphasizing the role of private property. The emancipation of society from private property is seen as the necessary precondition of political and, consequently, human emancipation. "Because the whole of human servitude," he writes, "is involved in the relation of the worker to production, the emancipation of the workers contains universal human emancipation."[101] In this work he does not say that political emancipation is a limited form of emancipation. In the essay *On the Jewish Question*, political emancipation is seen as "the dissolution of the old society"[102] and yet, paradoxically, inadequate as an emancipatory factor. Arguing against Bauer's conception of political emancipation, Marx stresses that "political emancipation itself is not human emancipation." Having again religion in mind, he says somewhat unconvincingly and in an intolerant manner, that "the emancipation of the state from religion is not the emancipation of the real man from religion."[103]

Although Marx never explains the distinguishing features of his "real man" except to say that he is "corporeal with his feet firmly on the solid ground," he definitely has a very low opinion of man in general.[104] Like Hobbes, he thinks man is primarily an egoist, a self-interested animal always in need of a collective control. The individual in Marx's political reasoning resembles Hegel's in that he must be subjugated and forcibly immersed in the totality of individuals. Thus real man, for him, is in fact the subjugated, controlled man. Bourgeois democracy, he believes, splits every individual into egoistic man and abstract *citoyen*. Here a man is a bourgeois and a citizen or a worker and a citizen, and it is "egoistic man, not social or human individual," who is the basis of the bourgeois society and the state. This egoistic man, Marx says, is also the theoretical basis of the bourgeois conception of the natural rights of man as distinct from the rights of the citizen. In a bourgeois democratic state, every person is duplicated unnecessarily. Here, Marx argues in *On the Jewish Question*, the "rights of man, the *droits de l'homme* as distinct from the *droits du citoyen*, are nothing but the rights of a member of civil society, i.e. the rights of egoistic man, of man separated from other men and from the community."[105] Real man is recognized only in the shape of the egoistic individual who generates and maintains political alienation. "It is not man as *citoyen* but man as bourgeois that is considered to be the true man."[106]

For Hegel, right is the expression of the universal. In the moral sphere, right always means the relation of the universal to the particular. The emphasis is on the universal or whole. To have rights is to be capable of realizing the universal command consciously in an "actual ethical order." Indeed, Hegel says "the right of individuals" can only be granted and "fulfilled when they belong to an actual ethical order."[107] In this order, rights and duties are correlative; there is no right without duty. When a man has a right, he is obligated to use it for the general good. The right of life, for example, brings the obligation of treating both one's own life and that of others as sacred. Equally, the right of freedom brings with it the obligation of using one's freedom for the attainment of rational ends. There are, of course, wide disagreements about the right of property. Contrary to their general opposition to private property, Marx and Engels indicate in *Communist Manifesto* that they respect "the right of personally acquired property."[108] Yet, in *On the Jewish Question*, paradoxically enough, Marx makes sarcastic remarks about "the so-called rights of man" that he always connects with private property. The rights of man, he thinks, are valuable only for a private egoistic individual who degrades himself into a means and becomes the instrument of alien powers. They are the rights of egoistic man, separated from the community.[109]

"The political emancipators," Marx writes, "reduce citizenship and the political community to a mere means for maintaining these so-called rights of men."[110] As a result, he adds, "the *citoyen* is declared to be the servant of egoistic *homme*."[111] There is no suggestion that the defective bourgeois rights of man will be replaced by superior rights in communist society. Marx is not an admirer of human rights in any form. Indeed, he seems to suggest that the very conception of rights is bourgeois and that this conception will disappear with the elimination of bourgeois ideology. Because there will be no room for the egoistic, isolated individual in communist society, the correlative idea of man as citizen together with the illusory concept of citizens' rights will have no relevance. In bourgeois practice, Marx sees human rights as very limited and misleading. Engels concentrates his criticism on the deceptive nature of the fundamental rights of the citizen in England, claiming that these rights are not the same for the rich property-owners and the poor propertyless citizens.[112] Speaking of political rights as they existed in his time, he stresses that "the right of popular assembly and the right of association were limited and could be denied at any time by local police." Judges and executioners are synonymous. However, Marx and Engels fail to formulate any constructive theory of human rights. Hobbes and Spinoza identify right with power, and Locke identifies it with "the law of nature which stands as an eternal rule of all men." Marx and Engels, on the other hand, simply ignore the bourgeois rights to equality, liberty, and property, calling these rights illusory and antisocial and always motivated by "practical need or egoism."

"The practical application of man's right to liberty" in the bourgeois state, Marx states, "is man's right to private property." Rejecting the need for religion, he remarks sadly that in this state freedom of conscience simply means the right to practice any religion.[113] These rights, he thinks, are "the rights of separation" and "the rights of the restricted, egoistic individual" that cannot be tolerated in the communist political organization of "united individuals." No man can exist as a mere individual, independently of the totality of other individuals, although he can be conceived imaginatively as an individual. His legal existence as a free and equal citizen of a democratic state based on class division is only illusory and ideal. The bourgeois conception of "the right of man to liberty," Marx argues, "is based on the separation of man from man, not on the association of man with man."[114] The rights of man to freedom of opinion and religion are essentially political rights that can only be exercised in a community with others. In the capitalist state, in Marx's view, "man is regressing to the cave dwelling in an estranged form." Based on class division, this state is "hostile to the free development of man." He calls for the abolition of political and social conditions that give rise to the rights of "self-interest" and "self-sufficient monads."[115] Unfortunately, Marx never speaks of "equal and inalienable rights" except in derogatory terms. These rights, he says, never transcend "man as a member of civil society" and are designed to protect "private interests and private caprice."[116]

In *German Ideology* Marx merges his own theory of the bourgeois state based on "the contradiction between the particular and the common interests" with Engels's theory of the class state. The merger of these two theories, however, is merely stated but not explained. The main emphasis here is on the illusory form of common interests existing in the state based on the classes, "one of which dominates the others."[117] The modern state originates in the emergence of private property and division of labor. The division of labor, Marx argues, has led to the contradiction between the interest of the individual and the interest of the community, and this in turn to the emergence of the class power of the bourgeoisie. "Out of this very contradiction between the particular and the common interests, the common interest assumes an independent form as the state which is divorced from the real individual and collective interests, and at the same time is an illusory community. It follows from this that all struggles within the state, the struggle between democracy, aristocracy and monarchy, the struggle for the franchise, etc., are merely the illusory forms in which the real struggles of the different classes are fought out among one another."[118]

A similar blend of these two different theories of the state reappears in the same work in the section in which Marx discusses the "relation of the state and law to property."[119] Here it is suggested that the institution of the state becomes really a state when its existence is "determined by large-scale industry and universal competition or pure private property." The state as a separate entity "alongside and outside civil society" is seen as alienated political power, protecting the interests of the ruling class. "Since the state is the form in which the individuals of a ruling class assert their common interests and in which the whole civil society of an epoch is epitomised," Marx says, "it follows that all common institutions are set up with the help of the state and are given a political form."[120] In the class state, citizens have the illusion that "law is based on free will" and is neutral. Law will only appeal as legal to citizens when all share in making it. The distinguishing feature of the emergent class state is its alienating class rule. Because it is a class, the "bourgeoisie is forced to organise itself no longer locally but nationally and to give a general form to its average interests."[121] As a separate entity, the bourgeois class state is "nothing more than the form of organisation which the bourgeois are compelled to adopt, both for internal and external purposes, for the mutual guarantee of their property and interests."[122]

Building his conception of the bourgeois class state in *German Ideology* on Engels's idea of the class state, Marx fails to reconcile the contradictory theories of the state as alienated social power and as an organ of class rule. The contradiction and incompatibility between their two different approaches to the alienated bourgeois state remain unresolved.[123] Commenting on the Marxist conception of the state, Lenin overlooks the contradiction between these approaches. He praises Engels for expressing with "perfect clarity the idea of Marxism with regard to the historical role and the meaning of the state." "The state," he says, "is a product and a manifestation of the irreconcilability of class antagonisms. The state arises where, when and in so far as class antagonisms cannot objectively be reconciled."[124] Strangely enough, he attributes the conception of the class state to Marx rather than to Engels. "According to Marx," he writes, "the state is an organ of class rule, an organ for the oppression of one class by another; it is the creation of order which legalises and perpetuates this oppression by moderating the conflct between the classes."[125] This description is in harmony with the ideas expressed in *Communist Manifesto*, in which Marx and Engels speak only of the class state.

Both Marx and Engels maintain that the state as a political organization of social life has not existed from all eternity. Its origin is in the same fragmentation of socioeconomic relations that have given rise to the formation of classes. There have been societies, Engels indicates, that have managed without it and have had no notion of the state. In *Origin of the Family, Private Property and the State*, based on L. H. Morgan's *Ancient Society*, Engels argues that "the state arose from the need to keep class antagonisms in check." Its orgin must be traced to "the fight between the classes."[126] Like Marx, he believes that the modern bourgeois state is an instrument designed solely for the protection of existing property relations. It is not a natural political institution but simply the product of the class struggle. What distinguishes the class state, in Engels's opinion, is organized coercive power in the hands of "the most powerful, economically dominant class."[127] His hypothesis that there are "exceptional periods" in human history "when the warring classes are so nearly equal in forces that the state power, as apparent mediator, acquires for the moment a certain independence in relation to both," however, makes his theory of the class state untenable.[128] The basic postulate of this theory is speculative and untestable. If the state can play the role of impartial mediator and harmonize the interests of the capitalists and workers as in "the new German empire of the Bismarckian nation," then, surely, the class state could be transcended or democratized without its abolition, revolutionary violence, and the imposition of the alienating dictatorship of the proletariat. The class struggle, therefore, need not be directed against the existence of the state as such. Engels would be more consistent if he adhered to the view that the state is always an organized coercive power of the economically most powerful class rather than making "exceptions" in its mediating role.

Although Marx sometimes moves toward Engels's conception of the class state, he is more concerned with the political or monarchical state, especially in his pre-communist works, and later with the parasitic and free states than with the class state as defined by Engels. Engels describes the class state as the "organisation that bourgeois society takes on in order to support the general external conditions of the capitalist mode of production."[129] The modern state, he says, "is essentially a capitalist machine, the state of the capitalists, the ideal personification of the total national capital." The function of this class state is to maintain "by force the conditions of existence and domination of the ruling class against the subject class."[130] Marx shares Engels's conception of the class state, but he also gives more prominence to the parasitic states of oriental despotism and European absolutism than to the class despotism that has dominated human societies. Marx's hatred of alienating bureaucracy and pseudo-democracy exemplified in the German model of absolute monarchy has remained with him throughout his life. Just as the Prussian monarchical state is treated as standing above class antagonism, looking after its selfish interests, so the bourgeois state of the French post-revolutionary period is equally seen as the expression of personal rule. "Napoleon," Marx writes in *Holy Family*, "discerned the essence of the modern state; he understood that it is based on the unhampered development of bourgeois society, on the free movement of private property. He decided to recognise and protect this basis."[131]

In *Eighteenth Brumaire of Louis Bonaparte* (1852), Marx argues that "the sword that is to safeguard social power" of the bourgeois state must be out of the hands of the class itself.[132] The individual bourgeois can continue to exploit the other classes "only on condition that their class be condemned along with other classes to similar political nullity." There is a suggestion that the government of a bourgeois state need not be chosen from the bourgeois class. Yet, the Bonapartist "is not suspended in mid air. Bonaparte represents a class and the most numerous class of French society, the smallholding peasants."[133] France has escaped the despotism of a class, Marx points out, "only to fall back beneath the despotism of an individual."[134] The Bonapartist alienated state is related to "all classes, equally impotent and equally mute," but the relation involved is that of servant and master. "All classes fall on their knees before the rifle butt."[135] Marx's analysis of the Bonapartist state, like his analysis of the Prussian monarchical state, concentrates on the connection between the state and private property. Bonaparte "looks on himself as the representative of the middle class and issues decrees in this sense." Above all, Marx addds, he considers himself to be a ruler interested in "turning all the property, all the labour of France into a personal obligation to himself."[136] Just as in the Prussian parasitic state, the power of private property is the essence of the Bonapartist parasitic state. The parasitic state rests on this alienating power. By preserving the social power of the bourgeoisie, the Bonapartist state has remained "a means for the enslavement of labour by capital."[137]

The theme of the power of capital over labor in the parasitic bourgeois state is given considerable prominence in *Capital*. The concentration of capital in the hands of the owners of the means of production, Marx argues in this work, entails the progressive proletarization of the working people. As a satanic economico-political force, capitalism "can only maintain itself by sucking the blood of living labour."[138] Greed and avarice, the ruling passions of capitalism, are seen as the alien forces confronting and dominating the economically and politically weak classes. The capitalist state is parasitic and alienated, representing a despotic and alienating sphere of egoistic individuals whose only interest is the promotion of private ends. Eternalization of the alienated worker and the alienated political sphere are "an indispensable condition of capitalist production."[139] Capitalist production and political control are always despotic and aggressive. "Workers collaborating under the command of a unit of capital must have, just like an army, commissioned officers who command during the labour process in the name of capital."[140] Marx likens the capitalist behavior in the field of alienated production to a military dictatorship. "The subjection of labour to capital," he says, "is nothing more than a formal consequence of the fact that the worker is working for the capitalist instead of for himself. The command of the capitalist in the field of production has become no less indispensable than the command of the general in the battlefield."[141]

The capitalist's urge for profit and wealth, Marx maintains, is inseparable from his urge for political power and domination. In his study of the old-fashioned capitalist, Marx believes that Martin Luther has rightly indicated that "the love of power is an element in the impulse to acquire wealth."[142] What distinguishes the capitalist from the non-capitalist is the passion to dominate, enslave, and alienate other men. The capitalist state knows only privileges. Marx compares the despotic and parasitic rule of the capitalist state with the tyrannical rule of the oriental despots of antiquity. "The power that used to be concentrated in the hands of Asiatic and Egyptian kings or of Etruscan theocrats and the like," he writes, "has in modern society been transferred to the capitalists."[143] The main difference between the ancient oriental states and the modern capitalist state lies in the strength and stability of political power. Without explaining the emergence of oriental despotism, Marx assumes that the Asiatic states are distinguished by the absence of private property. The parasitic capitalist state, on the other hand, being based on the alienating system of private property and division of labor, is bound to be weaker, more ephemeral, and less stable.

Marx's hypothesis that political power in the ancient states has an essentially different quality than the capitalist parasitic state is fantastic, *a priori*, and untestable. As some modern social anthropologists rightly indicate, he falsifies and mystifies the political reality and socioeconomic perceptions of non-capitalist man. Thus he misrepresents political alienation of the Asiatic states. Marx tends to ignore this alienation, maintaining wrongly that Asiatic societies "remain untouched by the storm-clouds of the political sky."[144] He fails to realize that even under oriental despotism the bureaucracy became the ruling class, dominating and alienating others. In *Theories of Surplus Value*, he describes the pre-capitalist forms of exploitation, including slavery, as being based on "the forcible rule of one section of society over another." Yet, he is reluctant to admit that the dominant section of oriental society—the bureaucracy—represents in fact a class, confronting, dehumanizing, and alienating other members of society. The assumption that this society has been so "simple and static" that it has had few alienating effects on the political structure of the Asiatic states is very naive and purely inferential.[145]

Marx's political thought is normally directed to economic development as the primary factor in human relations. For him, economic reality is the most important locus of political relations between workers and non-workers. As the productive forces of society increase in magnitude and productive relations become those of a society divided into classes, the working classes, representing the majority, are gradually deprived of the control of their sociopolitical existence. In the parasitic capitalist state, Marx believes this loss of control becomes total. The only way out is the political struggle of the oppressed and alienated against their oppressors. Because the capitalist state merely widens the chasm between the rich and poor by preserving the egoism of capitalist society and private property, Marx argues for abolition of the modern state. This state is seen as an organ of class dictatorship in which man's real social power is alienated entirely. "The executive of the modern state," he and Engels state in *Communist Manifesto*, "is merely a committee for managing the common affairs of the bourgeoisie as a whole."[146] The state in capitalist society is always capitalist regardless of which class constitutes its government. As long as society is divided into classes, the state will inevitably remain politically alienated and class oriented. In *Critique of the Gotha Programme* (1875), Marx makes no reference to the class state. "By the word state," he says, "is meant the government machine or the state in so far as it forms a special organism separated from society through division of labour."[147] In a classless society, Marx sees no need for any state because the dichotomy of the state and society will give way to an "association of free individuals."

Abolition of the capitalist state, in Marx's and Engels's view, is impossible without the revolutionary transformation of the means of production into public ownership and without the annihilation of the alienating ruling class. "As soon as there is no longer any social class to be held in subjection" and "as soon as class rule is removed," Engels writes, "a state is no longer necessary."[148] After the socialization of the means of production, "state interference in social relations will become superfluous and then wither away of itself. The government of persons will be replaced by the administration of things. The state," he points out, "is not abolished. It withers away."[149] Because Engels does not explain his fabulous utopian picture of the classless society in which there would be no government independent and estranged from the people and no organized coercive force, it is not surprising that even his and Marx's followers have great doubt. Most of them are convinced that this theoretical nonsense can never become *praxis*. Lenin is anxious to find the way out of this obscurity but fails. Even the reversal of emphasis on Engels's phraseology does not demystify the oracular piece of mystifying ideology. Lenin distorts Engels's phraseology in this respect so much that it becomes even more obscure and mystical. Although Engels states clearly that "the state is not abolished but withers away," Lenin transforms this into a contradictory statement. Engels, according to Lenin, maintains that "the bourgeois state does not wither away but is abolished by the proletariat in the course of the revolution. What withers away after this revolution is the proletarian state or semi-state."[150]

Lenin's claim that Marx's and Engels's ideas of the abolition of the capitalist state are "entirely identical" is incorrect. While Engels speaks of "withering away," Marx generally speaks of the abolition of the state. Already in *Manuscripts of 1844*, Marx hints at the abolition of the state.[151] To avoid confusion between Marx's conception of the abolition of the state and the anarchist conception of its abolition, Lenin deliberately attributes to Marx the concept of "withering away," which in fact is Engels's expression. In his exegetical argument against the anarchists, Lenin indicates that abolition of the state is the common aim of Marx, Engels, and the anarchists. The main difference between them, he says, is the Marxist opposition to the anarchist proposition that "the workers should renounce the use of arms, organised violence, that is the state, which is to serve to crush the resistance of the bourgeoisie."[152] He admits that the "new proletarian state" is itself an instrument of class power and coercion. "The working people need the state only to suppress the resistance of the exploiters and only the proletariat can direct this suppression."[153]

In Marx's view, the abolition of private property is the most necessary negation that will follow abolition of the alienated capitalist state. Revolution is necessary because the ruling and alienating class can only be overthrown by violent means. According to Marxist ideology, only a communist revolution can break the fetters of political power held by the capitalist class. Unlike the political bourgeois revolution, the proletarian social revolution will abolish classes and the alienated state. The proletariat will use its political supremacy when the time comes, Marx and Engels state in the *Communist Manifesto*, "to wrest all capital from the bourgeoisie and centralise all instruments of production in the hands of the state, i.e., of the proletariat organised as the ruling class."[154] There is an assumption that the "future state" will ultimately wither away and that the dictatorship of the proletariat is only temporary. "Between capitalist and communist society," Marx writes in *Critique of Gotha Programme*, "lies the period of the revolutionary transformation of the one into the other. Corresponding to this is also a political transition period in which the state can be nothing but the revolutionary dictatorship of the proletariat."[155] This is far from being clear and concrete and lacks any reference to significant distinguishing mark of the proletarian state except that it is a working class tyranny. The hint that the dictatorship of the proletariat is temporary cannot convince anyone except fanatical followers of Marxist ideology. Even Bakunin expresses his abhorence, stressing that if the proletariat is to be the ruling class, then there will remain "another proletariat" subjected to the new pseudo-proletarian rule.

The dilemma of dictatorship or democracy cannot be solved by slogans and ambiguous statements. Marx and Engels have originally envisaged the eventual disappearance of the proletarian state and with it of the state as such. In communist *praxis*, however, there is no indication of its disappearance. The proletarian state in the hands of "ex-workers," as Bakunin points out, represents "not the people but themselves and possessing despotic powers, can never give way to anything but tyranny of a ruling minority." This state, like the parasitic capitalist state, "exists alongside the real life of people" and is the expression of political alienation. The idea of a temporary dictatorship to be followed by a stateless society is as utopian as the idea of the transcendence of political alienation. Marx's and Engels's promise of "an association in place of the old bourgeois society" in which "the free development of each" will result in "the free development of all" is speculative and utopian nonsense. The distinction between government and administration, first made by Saint Simon, has never been clarified in their writings. Their ambivalence in this respect has inevitably left the communist world split and confused. The anti-dictatorial currents still flow powerfully, challenging the dictatorial alienating forces that still dominate and enslave communist societies. Postulating, like Auguste Blanqui, a rule of men of learning over the ignorant masses, Bakunin criticizes Marx and Engels for imposing on the toiling people "the most distressing, offensive and despicable type of government in the world" and "consoling themselves with the thought that the proletarian dictatorship will be only temporary and of brief duration."

Many forms of alienation characterizing the capitalist state are still present in the proletarian state. The fact that the proletarian rule monopolizes all political power is hardly an advantage over bourgeois pluralism, and in some respects it is worse. As Bakunin indicates in his criticism of the proletarian state, "once the ex-workers become rulers they acquire selfish interests and treat the majority of the people as slaves." The practical result of class rule of "corrupted ex-workers," he says, is not political freedom but tyranny. Thus the capitalist state is not transcended; it is only modified into an equally bureaucratic state that allows only certain nominal and theoretical rights and freedoms. In praxis these are limited to those who agree with the dictatorial rule of the proletariat. The fact remains that Marx's and Engels's ideas of political freedom are deceptive, obscure, and inconsistent. They fail to realize that political power corrupts and that absolute power, whether in the hands of the capitalist despots or the proletarian dictators, "corrupts absolutely." Their failure to see political freedom as a positive force in history rather than as the absence of restraint has led to the creation and perpetuation of despotic and alienated regimes. Like Hegel, they maintain that freedom can only be understood when defined as the recognition of necessity. "Hegel," Engels writes, "was the first to state correctly the relation between freedom and necessity. To him, freedom is the appreciation of necessity."[156] In this sense, freedom will be realized in the higher phase of communist society. Here, "anarchy in social production will be replaced by plan-conforming, conscious organisation" and "humanity's leap from the kingdom of necessity to the kingdom of freedom" will finally take place.[157]

In practical politics, Marxist freedom, like Hegelian freedom, is nothing but compulsion. "Recognition of necessity" for the citizens of the Marxist state or society is simply obedience to authority. Here, as in Rousseau's and Hegel's political theories, there is no room for the rights and freedoms of individuals. Individual citizens attain freedom only by identifying their will with the "universal will." The collective will alone is infallible. Those who refuse to obey it "should be forced to be free" and to obey it. Political freedom as compulsion is based on the collectivist conception of the "union of freedom and necessity." Individual freedom must always be related to the needs of the social collective. Marx, however, argues that political freedom in the capitalist state "is founded on egoistic relations between man and man."[158] The bourgeoisie want political freedom for their own class and are not interested in the freedom of all classes. The capitalist state, he belives, is nothing but a disguised system of effective slavery. Men will remain unfree as long as this parasitic state exists. In *Critique of the Gotha Programme*, Marx reproaches the German Workers' Party for "treating the state as an independent entity possessing its own intellectual, political and libertarian bases instead of treating existing society as the basis of the existing state." The Lassallean and social democratic conception of the state, in his view, is ideological and anti-libertarian and must be rejected. The political demands of the authors of *Gotha Programme* are not radical enough and do not go "beyond the democratic litany familiar to all: universal suffrage, direct legislation, popular rights" and individual freedom.[159]

Marx advises the leaders of the German Workers' Party to ignore the deceptive phrases of democracy. These phrases, he says, are meaningless "in a state which is nothing but a police-guarded military despotism, embellished with parliamentary forms, alloyed with a feudal admixture, already influenced by the bourgeoisie and bureaucratically carpentered."[160] He argues that the state cannot be democratic as long as the society is divided into antagonistic classes. True democracy is possible only in a classless soceity in which there is no need for a state. Capitalism is a denial of this democracy and a negation of political freedom. As long as there is any trace of capitalist class rule, political freedom is meaningless. The capitalists are concerned only about "the freedom of trade and of exchange." This freedom, Lenin points out, "is just as utterly false, serving to mask capitalist deception, coercion and exploitation, as are the other freedoms proclaimed and implemented by the bourgeoisie, such as the freedom to work which is actually the freedom to starve."[161] To a certain extent this is true. The emphasis in the capitalist parasitic state is on "free bargaining," which always entails freedom to exploit the poor without considering the interests of the community as a whole. Marx calls the capitalist "the blood sucker of living labour."[162] The capitalist is not interested in political freedom of the working people but in his own self-expansion and in unrestrained freedom to fleece the alienated workers. Yet, Marx and Engels overlook the possibility that political freedom could be equally twisted in the communist state.

The central assumption of democratic socialism is that the state must be an association of free individuals having the same legal and economic rights and enjoying the same access to political power. Political freedom cannot be separated from economic freedom. Because individual freedom is relative to that of others, it always must be regulated. In a truly democratic state, liberty can never be the absolute liberty of each but always the qualified freedom of all. In most democratic societies, the fundamental rights and freedoms constitute the basic criteria by which citizens judge the democratic intentions of governments. Talk of "bourgeois individualists and anarchists about absolute freedom" may be, as Lenin indicates, "sheer hypocrisy," but this cannot justify the attack on such essential freedoms as the freedom of thought and freedom to resist the oppressive government. Press censorship, labor concentration camps, and authoritarian rule can only be indicative of the closed society still waiting to be liberated.[163]

The cure for political alienation is not the replacement of the democratic state, provided it allows universal suffrage, by the dictatorship of the proletariat. Marx and Engels do not recognize the possibility of a truly socialist state. It is because of their failure to realize the practical significance of democratic socialism that they argue for the abolition of the state. They overlook the fact that social, political, and economic changes can be made through parliamentary procedure without resorting to revolutionary violence. The dictatorship of the proletariat, originating from this violence, is undesirable and easily assumes the form of tyranny masquerading as the rule of free people. Lenin's advocacy of the dictatorship of a single class has inevitably led to Stalinist tyranny. This tyranny is also evident in other communist states. Actually, neither Marx nor Lenin has ever grasped the paradox of political freedom and even less realized the importance of the role of state power in the protection of human freedoms. Both Marx and Engels argue that man can only be free in a classless society in which "the public power has lost its political character."[164] They fail to realize that freedom, essential to the development of personality, is a spiritual value that can be created and maintained only by free individuals.

The road to political freedom must itself be chosen freely and the journey to it must not be undertaken with any kind of compulsion. In true democracy, citizens must have the right to decide what constitutes freedom. Marx's political theory is full of ambiguities and contradictions about political freedom. In his pre-communist days, he has defined freedom as "the essence of man" and "the most costly jewel of human nature."[165] Later, however, he speaks of freedom in terms of compulsion. Liberalism is now seen as "empty enthusiasm" and reactionary bourgeois individualism.[166] "Bourgeois freedom," he insists, "must be abolished together with the parasitic bourgeois state" and replaced by "proletarian freedom" and a non-class society knit together in the spontaneous harmony of "unforced communism." The apocalyptic vision of the replacement of "the government of men by the administration of things" is regarded by most commentators as a dream.[167] The dialectical orthodoxy on which this vision is based is so obscure that it leads inevitably to ideological controversies reminiscent of the theological wrangles over mystical and abstract points of doctrinal truths. Treating man's political life exclusively in terms of class domination, Marx has failed to produce a consistent political theory and to deal realistically with the problem of political alienation. The proletarian solution to political alienation is a pseudo-solution. "The vast political association of the whole nation" replacing the parasitic capitalist state is itself a manifestation of political alienation.

10
The Transcendence of Alienation

All theological, philosophical, and socio-psychological theories of alienation entail a concept of the transcendence of alienation. Because the idea of the negation of alienation or dealienation, like the idea of alienation, is an ambiguous concept with elusive meanings, interpretation of the transcendence of alienation depends on the theory of alienation itself. The prescriptions offered in this respect are considerably more pessimistic in non-Marxist theories than in Marxism. While the philosophical and theological theories find a partial solution to alienation in the unity with the divine forces in nature and the Freudian theory finds a limited solution in sublimation, they all give prominence to some permanent and inherent symptoms of alienation. The dominating sociological thesis is that in mass society the individual inevitably feels lost and frustrated. Being a product of specific forms of social organization, alienation is inescapable and the possibility of its transcendence is always limited. The feeling of powerlessness and meaninglessness, non-Marxist writers believe, is inherent in man's finite existence and can never be eradicated entirely.

In Marx's philosophical system, the individual feeling of powerlessness and meaninglessness, the feeling of being alienated from one's true being and from others can be transcended by eliminating the antagonisms and contradictions that engender it. Capitalism with its emphasis on egoistic needs and private profit cannot exist without exploitation, dehumanization, and alienation. All characteristics of capitalism originate in the movement of private property and exchange. Alienation, therefore, cannot be overcome until capitalism as an alien power is destroyed totally and replaced by communism, the only liberating movement of man. Lack of sympathy and affection of civilized bourgeois man for alienated and suffering human beings and humans in general is, Marx believes, the expression of the very nature of human alienation. Being an alienated man himself, without money and friends, Marx frequently gives the impression of seeing alienation in all human life. Echoing Rousseau, he sometimes blames civilization for a "bestial barbarisation" and violently attacks the egoism of civilized bourgeois society. Marx is mindful of the misery of the industrial worker and deplores the fact that he lacks "even the simplest animal cleanliness" and that the "sewage of civilisation comes to be the element of life for him. Utter, unnatural neglect, putrefied nature, comes to be his life element."[1] He is so disappointed with modern capitalist civilization that he makes it responsible for causing and maintaining all forms of alienation. In the state of nature or barbarism, "human individuals are subservient to nature" and are united by such bonds as family, tribe, and the land. In civilized bourgeois society, however, human individuals "are independent of one another and are only held together by exchange."[2]

In his analysis of alienation, Marx always denounces the institutions of private property and division of labor as the most responsible factors in the genesis of exploitation and dehumanization. These, he thinks, isolate every human individual from the community, alienate him, and inevitably lead to class antagonism. Locating the origin of alienation in the context of socioeconomic relations and concrete economic transactions, he rejects the view that alienation is either a state of mind or inherent in human nature. For him, alienation occurs when man's free activity is dominated by an alien, external, and oppressive force. All human history has been the history of alienation. The being of man and the nature of objects produced by man are alienated from the beginning. Unfortunately, Marx is vague on this point and fails to specify the location of this beginning in history. He merely links alienation with the domination of private property, arguing that it will be transcended with the transcendence of private ownership and division of labor. Without radical change in property ownership and socioeconomic relations, the transcendence of alienation is impossible.

According to Marx, the real process of production is the basis of all history. The materialist conception of history, he argues, must start from the material production of immediate life. All moments in history and all aspects of human life are the result of the movement of the economic factors involved in the development of society. Ideologies and forms of intellectual life are simply reflections of the movement of the economic base and have no independent reality in themselves. Idealist theories of historical development are rejected on the ground that they ignore or belittle the material preconditions and content without which this development would be impossible. Marx assumes wrongly that these theories alone use reified abstractions to explain this development and thus are responsible for representing particular interests as universal interests. Actually, his theory of alienation and dealienation is based on the belief that particular interests are best served within the system of "united individuals." In class societies, he thinks, the notion of genuine social harmony is a delusion. Here the protagonists of social development, in Marx's view, are not "free or social individuals" but individuals as members of social classes. Social conflict is inherent only in the class system and is incapable of being transcended within this system. There is no escape from alienation except through total transformation of socioeconomic relations. The primary antagonism in capitalist society is always between capitalists and wage earners. This antagonism can only be eliminated by socialization of the means of production.

Marx regards capitalism as an alienating and dehumanizing system that can never overcome the torments of alienation. In all its alienating forms, capitalism, he says, marks "the movement in which the general alienation appears as general appropriation and general appropriation as general alienation."[3] The existence of value "in its purity and generality" as conceived by the capitalist "presupposes a mode of production in which the individual product has ceased to exist for the producer in general and even more for the individual worker."[4] Confronted with shortcomings and contradictions, the working class will have no alternative but to transform the means of production, which in capitalist society are primarily the means of enslaving and exploiting labor, "into mere instruments of free and associated labour." "With labour emancipated, every man becomes a working man and productive labour ceases to be a class attribute."[5] As a socioeconomic phenomenon, capitalism is a unique emergence in human history, and its transcendence in communism is the end of pre-history and the beginning of new history. The distinguishing feature of communism, Marx maintains, is its capacity to overcome commodity production as expressed in capitalism and its resolution to replace it with planned production for the use and satisfaction of human needs. In planned production, human transactions will not be mediated by monetary exchanges or motivated by egoism, greed, and avarice.

Because of its own dialectical development, capitalism, Marx argues, will lead to self-destruction. When "capitalist monopoly becomes a fetter on the method of production," it will, "with the inexorability of a law of nature, beget its own negation."[6] The liberation of society and the transcendence of alienation require the overthrow of capitalism and its alien power. Under capitalism, all human relations are reduced to a "mere money relation," and all "individuals are ruled by abstractions."[7] Marx's ideas about transcendence of alienation, like his ideas about history, are based on dialectical materialism which, as Lenin states, "has fully taken over the historical traditions of eighteenth-century materialism in France and of Feuerbach in Germany—a materialism which is absolutely atheistic and positively hostile to all religion."[8] Yet, dialectical materialism is not identical with any form of "previous materialism." Marx rejects "all previous materialisms" on the ground that they fail to grasp the significance of "revolutionary or practical-critical activity."[9] Without this activity, capitalism cannot be destroyed. Because abstract or contemplative materialism is non-revolutionary and undialectical, Marx believes it can never shatter and transcend alienation. Like Hegelian idealism, undialectical materialism remains formal, regressive, and alienating. Hegel posits alienated being and introduces dialectical movement into the realm of abstraction. His negation, therefore, never negates real alienation because it remains merely a logical movement embracing ideas and concepts in thought.

Marx rejects Hegelian idealism but retains the view that reality is subject to dialectical movement. The idea that all changes in the history of the world and of man proceed by internal contradictions is common to Hegel and

Marx.[10] The main difference between them in this respect is that Hegel speaks of contradictions in a more abstract way, and Marx is more interested in the contradiction between capitalism and communism, wealth and poverty, and "existing social relations and existing productive forces." Capital itself is a contradiction.[11] The transitory nature of capitalism is a result of its contradictory character that "appears in such a way that the working individual alienates himself" and through this alienation he liberates himself, his class, and humanity. Alienation, Marx maintains, is transcended within capitalism itself. The antithetical form of capitalist production, he says, "is itself fleeting and produces the real conditions of its own suspension."[12] In opposition to Hegel, he argues that "property, capital, money, wage-labour and the like are the products of alienation and must be transcended in a practical, objective way."[13] They cannot be abolished in thought and consciousness alone.

The central idea in Marx's dialectical materialism is that theoretical criticism and practical overthrow are inseparable activities. Reality is material and contradictions exist not only in the process of thinking but also in material reality. Hegel believes reality is spiritual, but he never denies that contradiction is the essential principle of "all living things." Indeed, "the living body dies," he says, "because it is in fact a contradiction."[14] Although Marx accepts Hegel's dialectic of contradictions, he rejects his conception of the Idea or Spirit as the only reality. Hegel's idea of an "internal contradiction of self-consciousness with itself" is irrelevant to dealienation.[15] Hegel, in Marx's view, has only found the abstract, logical, and speculative expression for the movement of history that is far from being man's real history. "The entities produced in the divine dialectic are pure products of the labour of thought forever weaving in itself and never looking outward" toward material reality.[16] As a "practical materialist," Marx is enthusiastic about the materialist dialectic because it is this dialectic that not only represents all movements in history as being in the state of becoming something else, something that in the process of becoming is more perfect and more significant, but it also "furnishes an understanding of the negation" of alienation and "enables us to recognise that capitalism will inevitably break up" and be followed by communism.[17]

Marx and Engels take for granted that the development in history is dialectical and that a dialectical and materialist interpretation of history is the only real analysis of human life. They believe Hegel's dialectical method abolishes the material basis of historical movement and gives prominence to the dialectical "self-movement of the Idea." Believing, like Hegel, that the dialectic applies equally to society and nature, Engels indicates that the dialectical laws as conceived in Hegel's idealist logic are "foisted on nature and history as laws of thought" and that the universe based on these laws "has to conform to a system of thought which itself is only the product of a definite stage of evolution of human thought."[18] The idealist way of thinking, he says, "turned everything upside down and completely reversed the actual connection of things in the world."[19] The old conception of history "knew nothing of class struggles based on economic interests and equally knew nothing of economic interests."[20] It is for this reason that the idealist conception of history must be rejected, and that Hegel's dialectical method must, as Marx puts it, "be freed from the wrappings of mystification."[21]

The idealist conception of history, Marx argues, is "truly religious because it postulates religious man as the starting point of history."[22] It treats alienation as the alienation of man's self-consciousness rather than of his real life. The idealist world as seen by idealist philosophers, in Marx's opinion, is nothing more than the world of metaphysics, speculation, and abstraction. The history of man becomes "the history of the spirit which is far removed from the real man."[23] When Hegel studies the forms of man's social and economic life, he treats them only in their abstract expression. They are primarily the creatures of reason, mere alienations of pure thought. It is because of this metaphysical approach to history, that the whole history of alienation and its transcendence is merely the history of the production of abstract thought. Hegel's negation of negation, Marx believes, abolishes the concrete essence of man and transforms the false objectivity reflected in the self-knowing and self-manifesting Idea into the absolute subject.[24] Marx dissociates himself from Hegel's belief that every objectification is necessarily an instance of alienation and that alienation can only be transcended if adequately understood or known. Yet the idea of the transcendence of alienation in the sense of being adequately known is implicit in his own conception of "the negation of negation."[25]

In his examination of alienation and dealienation, Marx argues that the Absolute must be excluded from the being of both "matter and spirit" and that the materialist dialectic must start from the primacy of the concrete. By positing *a priori* objects, Hegelianism ignores the concrete and treats human history as the history of abstract man. In his view, "all history is a real part of natural history and the preparation for man to become the object of sensuous consciousness."[26] Unlike Marx, Hegel defines history as "the exhibition of Spirit," indicating that world history begins with the realization of the Idea of Spirit."[27] The whole process of history, he says, is "directed to rendering the unconscious impulse of nature a conscious one."[28] The historical process is teleological, and "Spirit displays itself in it in its most concrete reality." "God," Hegel writes, "governs the world; the actual working of his government—the carrying out of his plan—is the history of the world. This plan philosophy strives to comprehend; for only that which has been developed as the result of it, possesses *bona fide* reality. That which does not accord with it, is negative, worthless existence."[29] Marx has no room in his materialist system for any divine teleology. For him, "history is nothing but the succession of the separate generations modifying their circumstances with a completely changed activity."[30] There is no totality and no finality in the process of historical development. Sometimes Marx goes farther, saying that in history there are no ideals to be realized. "Mankind," his indicates, "always sets itself only such tasks as it can solve since closer examination will always show that the problem itself arises only when the material conditions for its solution are already present or at least in the process of formation."[31]

In Engels's view, history has its meaning and its revelation. "We lay claim to the meaning of history," he says, "but we see in history not the revelation of God but of man and only of man."[32] Marxism, he points out, has no intention whatsoever of doubting or despising the "revelation of history" for history is "all and everything to us and we hold it more highly than any other previous philosophical trend," including Christianity and Hegelianism.[33] Unlike Marx, Engels states explicitly that human history is not a meaningless and purposeless movement. Rather it is the teleological unfolding of the drama of men whose conative activity is always a striving toward an end that constitutes a value feeling. History has an immanent *telos*: it requires the emergence of the radically new elements in human development. Without these elements, which must include the change of human nature itself, there could be no materialist history at all. It is because Engels relates human ends to human values that he is able to condemn competition and "the law of the strong" and insist on the transcendence of capitalist alienation that destroys "every truly human purpose."[34] Although the conception of end is not exactly identical with the conception of value, it is, in his view, closely related to it. The end gives stimulus and direction to human endeavor while value denotes endeavor as being completed satisfactorily.

Marx resists being involved in the discussion of ethical categories, realizing that a consistent standard of values could not be secured without presupposing a central or supreme value. He prefers to speak of certain tendencies that are inherent in all periods of social development and "inevitably" lead to social changes and new social periods. Without invoking values, he believes that social newness is an intrinsic new development that occurs through the synthesis of contradictions. The synthesis of contradictions, resulting in the transcendence of alienation, is a slow process, although dialectical development may proceed by discreet jumps. Engels, like Hegel, is more interested in "discreet jumps" than in gradualism. Yet, he says "history has its own pace and, however dialectical its course may be in the last analysis, dialectics has to wait for history a fairly long time."[35] In his analysis of the transcendence of alienation, Marx vacillates between teleological and dysteleological conceptions of historical development. He rejects the mechanical point of view of "abstract materialists," and is sometimes compelled to recognize tacitly that the material elements involved in the organic process are not really external to one another but rather that they fall within a teleological system.

The impossibility of dispensing entirely with goals, aims, and ends in human history is definitely implicit in Marx's account of the transcendence of alienation. His materialist conception of history and his idea of the negation of alienation are based on the firm belief that "the social movement and the purposes of men" are guided and determined by the inexorable laws of dialectic.[36] Marx never says that these laws are fortuitous. He seems to realize that if they were, communism itself would be mere chance and thus unable to transcend the "present state of things" and capitalist alienation. Any talk about the transformation of socioeconomic evils and any vision of the "higher stage" of communist future would then be absurd and meaningless. Marx avoids being involved in metaphysical problems, and unlike the French materialists of the Age of Reason, he either ignores them or tries to explain them away by appealing to the goddess of *"praxis"* whenever it suits him. No philosopher or historian has ever denied that the originating act of the human world is a part of history. Marx, however, treats the problem of the origin of man and nature as "impossible in practice and meaningless."[37] Because this treatment lacks any concrete etiological data to support it, it must itself be meaningless. His statement that the origin of man can only be traced to nature and that human history itself is part of natural history is deliberately evasive and manifestly tortuous. He overlooks the fact that nature is blind and infinitely wasteful in the production of life and that nature alone cannot explain the "purposes of men."[38]

The fact is that all those who eliminate ends from human history and nature reintroduce them under other names. Even Darwin, who vacillates between dysteleology and teleology, is compelled to admit that "successful variations in natural selection" are indicative of progress and that progress inevitably implies a teleological striving. The self-conserving impulse that is immanent in living organisms would be meaningless unless it were purposive in some respect. Because of its theological implications, Marx avoids using the concept of teleology in his theory of alienation and dealienation. These are explained in terms of socioeconomic relations. The notion of ends and purposes immanent in nature and life is substituted by the notion of "practical aims and tendencies." Communism or the negation of negation is described as a "practical movement, pursuing practical aims by practical means."[39] Without being aware of contradiction, he sometimes speaks of "the goal of human development" and sometimes he rejects explicitly any "special goals in history."[40] These goals, he continues, are abstractions and unnecessary for explaining the history of men. Abstract goals and sacred plans are always intimately bound up, he says, "with the holy beings who pursue them." He rejects the role of non-economic factors and divine teleology in historical development and criticizes "all idealists, philosophic and religious, ancient and modern" for believing that "every movement designed to transform the world exists only in the head of some chosen being and that the fate of the world depends on whether this head is or is not mortally wounded by some realistic stone before it has had time to make its revelation."[41]

The idealist conception of history, Marx argues, is theological because it ignores the fact that "the production and reproduction of real life" are the ultimately determining factors in history. The mystifying aspect of Hegelian dialectic that conceives dialectical development as something essentially spiritual and divine must be rejected. Because Marx is ambiguous about the "active role" of consciousness and he cannot explain the existence of abstract concepts that have no direct empirical referent, Marxists, vulgar and ortho- dox alike, have been unable to agree on the ultimate determining factor in history. While accepting an "interaction between the base and the superstruc- ture," Engels reverts to emphasizing the dominant role of economic factors. His ambivalence is reflected in Plekhanov's conception of history, who at least sometimes seems more willing to allow the possibility of genuinely inde- pendent developments in the realm of ideas and concepts. Plekhanov believes that it is a mistake to reduce the materialist conception of history to "eco- nomic materialism." Paradoxically, however, he argues that the "historical factors," or what Engels calls the "various elements of the superstructure," are "mere abstractions." "When the mist surrounding them is dispelled," he writes, "it becomes clear that men do not make several histories but only one history, the history of their social relations which are determined by the state of the productive forces in each particular epoch. What is known as ide- ologies is nothing but a multiform reflection in the minds of men of this single and indivisible history."[42]

While Marx gives more prominence to the economic factor than to the dialectic in explaining socioeconomic relations and the transcendence of alienation, Engels tends to reverse their role. By relating social progress to "the meaning of history," he is convinced that the transcendence of capitalist alienation is a "process which develops in accordance with a definite dialectic- al law."[43] Modern Marxists vacillate between Marx's and Engels's positions. They generally argue that it is the point of view of totality rather than the primacy of economic factors that is central in dialectical materialism. The dialectical method, they maintain, must start from the "simplest fundamental relations" historically found in economic relations. Admittedly, economic re- lations are not the only relations detected as "moments" in complex relations of men. The character of "simple fundamental relations," however, has never been explained. Since Descartes's time, stress has been put on the need to analyze the complex metaphysical and physical structures into their simple parts. While Descartes has no difficulty in differentiating between simple and complex ideas, Marx's followers fail to clarify the difference between simple and complex relations. "The simplest fundamental relations as moments in complex relations" may have any metaphysical meaning one chooses. Some Marxists distinguish them from "practical relations," which, as Marx himself suggests, are inherent in every organized human existence. It is unclear, however, whether the "simplest fundamental relations" are inherent in anything except in economic relations. If so, the determining power of the "simplest fundamental relations" is derivatory and limited, merely reflecting economic factors involved in human development.

Engels's ambivalent position in this respect expressed in his letter to Bloch has not so far been transcended. Modern Marxists argue that "the simple relations," like moments and categories, are historically involved in "the richer and more complex determinations." What these "richer and more complex determinations" are, it is not explained. Presumably, they include the "various elements of the superstructure" that, as Engels believes, "also exercise their influence on the course of historical struggles."[44] The idea that determination is either merely economic or superstructural is dismissed by some Marxists as vulgar mechanism. Althusser speaks of Marx's new conception of the relation between determinant instances in the base-superstructure complex that constitutes the essence of any social structure. He says Marx has left us the two ends of the chain in the process of determination. In addition to the economic determinant, he also believes in the relative autonomy of the superstructure and its specific effectivity in determination.[45] Althusser obviously minimizes the differece between Marx and Engels in this respect, although he admits that Engels gives more prominence to the multiform world of the superstructures.[46]

Marx's elaboration of the economic categories and their internal connections transcends any empirical verification. The dialectical connection between productive forces and productive relations in society is explained in metaphysical terms. His idea of the transcendence of alienation in a future universal reconciliation is derived from Hegelian idealism, not from "material practice."[47] Yet, in his analysis of alienation and the possibility of its transcendence, he rejects idealism and eulogizes dialectical materialism. As a practical materialist, he argues that metaphysics is an illusory pursuit that has no relation to empirical facts. Metaphysical thought, he says, confuses the real and the abstract and conceives of the real abstractly. Whatever transcends sensuous experience is alienated and meaningless. Alienation, in his view, cannot be transcended by way of metaphysics.[48] The aim of metaphysics is to know reality as it is "in itself." The aim of dialectical materialism, on the other hand, is not merely to know reality but also to change it.[49] The historical and social process, Marx insists, must be studied empirically. Alienation is an important aspect of this process, and it can only be transcended in communism.

In spite of Marx's apparent hostility toward metaphysics, he merely substitutes his own version of materialist metaphysics for the metaphysics of idealism. His thinking and its practical consequences generally are permeated with metaphysical concepts that, needless to say, cannot be verified empirically. His own ideas of man, history, and the world are essentially Hegel's ideas.[50] Marx's thought begins from Hegel's logic and, in spite of its seeming rejection in the name of dialectical materialism, this logic has influenced his whole intellectual life. Criticizing Hegel for deploying mystical, abstract thinking in his analysis of alienation and dealienation, he never refrains from emphasizing the "positive aspects of the Hegelian dialectic within the realm of estrangement." "By grasping the positive meaning of self-referred negation,"

Marx indicates, "Hegel grasps man's self-estrangement, the alienation of man's essence."[51] His criticism of Hegel suggests that he differs from him considerably more than, in fact, he does. He accepts the Hegelian notion of *Aufhebung* or the idea of the transcendence of alienation, although he rejects Hegel's belief that this transcendence is possible merely in "pure thought." The difference between Marx and Hegel relates to the origin and nature of alienation and consequently to the nature and result of dealienation.

Arguing that Hegelianism does not provide a solution to the problem of alienation because it disregards "living men" and their socioeconomic relations, Marx categorically rejects the "esoteric history of the abstract mind," linking alienation to the mode of production. Contrary to Hegel, he maintains that living men cannot transcend their alienation by a purely cognitive act of appropriation. They must rather practically appropriate the alienated and dehumanized world of the forces of production. Hegel is criticized for maintaining the illusions of abstract alienation and for being unable to transcend the world of real alienation. "Having posited man as equivalent to self-consciousness," Marx writes, Hegel's "transcendence of alienation is nothing but an abstract, empty abolition of that empty abstraction—the negation of the negation."[52] Hegel's negation of negation, pretending to be absolutely positive, in fact ends in total abstraction and thus simply maintains the alienated process. In Marx's opinion, it is only in communism that the negation of negation will be absolutely positive. Because alienation has its source in "the movement of private property," only communism can guarantee that the system of private property is negated absolutely and positively.

The concept of *Aufhebung* in Hegel's philosophical system, as he himself states, has a "double meaning one of which is positive and the other is negative."[53] The negative meaning is denoted by such terms as abolition and negation and the positive meaning by such words as transcendence, preservation and sublation. As a matter of fact, Hegel bases his idea of *Aufhebung* on the Christian conception of the reconciliation of man to God. The idea of reconciliation underlies many of St. Paul's statements, and it is developed above all in chapters 4 and 5 in the second letter to the Corinthians.[54] Eternal life can only result from the abolition and transcendence of death. "Unless a grain of wheat falls into the earth and dies," Christ says, "it remains alone and cannot prolong its future life."[55] "Life," Hegel indicates, "is a becoming and becoming always contains Being and Nothing in such a way that these two are always changing into each other and reciprocally cancelling each other."[56] Engels gives some prominence to the Hegelian conception of the negation of negation that he, like Hegel, associates with dialectics. He believes the phenomenon of the negation of negation can be observed both in nature and human history. Because he is more interested in the dialectic of nature than in the dialectic of social development, he uses the grain of barley— unconsciously echoing Christ's notion of the grain of wheat—as the example of the law of the negation of negation in nature. "As a result of this negation of the negation," he writes, "we get not only more seeds but also qualitatively improved seeds which produce more beautiful flowers, and each repetition of this process, each fresh negation of the negation, enhances the process of perfection."[57]

In Hegelianism and Christianity, *Aufhebung* usually refers to a consecutive and higher stage in the process of development. The contradiction between life and death, being and nothing, is overcome by transcendence or supersession.[58] In applying the Hegelian law of negation to material reality, Marx and Engels take for granted that material reality develops like ideas. Hegel sees matter as essentially composite, consisting of parts that exclude each other. In seeking unity, it "exhibits itself as self-destructive." While "matter has its essence out of itself," Spirit alone is "self-contained existence (bei-sich-selbst-sein)."[59] The idea of an alien, unifying, and self-moving matter is simply a myth. Only spirit, he believes, can be truly described as autonomous, self-moved, self-determined, and self-transcending. The world is the work of the spirit, and the dialectic is the law of the movement of all things.[60] The immanent self-motion that characterizes the Idea or Spirit is the product of its inherent contradiction. All reality in the universe is interrelated, and all things, in their state of continual interaction, develop through negation. Marx accepts the Hegelian dialectic of contradictions and argues that these contradictions are primarily the property of material reality. He does not reject the existence of "intellectual contradictions," but he tends to avoid or minimize their importance. When he speaks of reality containing inherent contradictions, he usually means material contradictions in concrete reality.

The distinguishing mark of Hegel's conception of transcendence lies in its simultaneous assertion of abolition and preservation. It is these contradictory ideas that make a "unity of opposites" in any dialectical development. Marx accepts the Hegelian conception of a unity of opposites but, by secularizing it, he uses it to analyze the socioeconomic conditions of "real existing men." Binding together "denial and preservation, denial and affirmation," Hegel, Marx writes, "has locked up all fixed mental forms together in his *Logic*, laying hold of each of them first as negation—that is, as an alienation of human thought—and then as negation of the negation—that is, as a superseding of this alienation, as a real expression of human thought. But as even this still takes place within the confines of the estrangement, this negation of the negation is in part the restoring of these fixed forms in their estrangement; in part a stopping-short at the last act—the act of self-reference in alienation—as the true mode of being of these mental forms."[61] In Marx's view, idealism fails to picture the real world as the material of human labor and to describe history as the "true natural history of man."[62] Idealism conceals material needs on which human life depends and practically ignores their "real alienation." All contemplative solutions of philosophical problems, he thinks, are meaningless and illusory whenever detached from their historical conditions. Only naturalism and dialectical materialism as expressed in communism are capable of "unmasking human self-alienation in its secular form" and "of comprehending the act of world history."[63]

Marx's analysis of the transcendence of alienation, like his analysis of alienation itself, contains too many metaphysical elements and is frequently obscure and inconsistent. Realizing that his dialectical approach to history offers no objective criteria for evaluating historical development, many modern Marxists recognize that if the dialectic were the universal law of history, then the negation of communism itself must be accepted as a necessary process of historical becoming.[64] Non-orthodox Marxists are sometimes inclined to reject dialectical materialism as a whole because they believe it represents a dogmatic, metaphysical, and speculative approach to history and thus fails to contribute to the creation of critical consciousness capable of transcending the alienated process of historical development. There is an awareness among these Marxists that human history is an endless process in which there is no meaningful totality. This process is still alienated and the world, as Sartre states, "has not come to any end yet." In the light of an objective analysis of history, any historical event could be designated as a thesis, an antithesis, or a synthesis. Marx overlooks this possibility in his analysis of dealienation and concentrates his attention on communism as the only negation of contradictions in capitalism. He does not realize that there are no logical reasons against maintaining that communism is a thesis rather than a synthesis or "the negation of the negation." There are non-Marxists who regard the appearance of communism as a regressive rather than a progressive phenomenon in historical development. Communism, in their view, is not the abolition of alienation; it is its affirmation.

In Marx's and Engels's analysis of the dialectical process, communism is viewed as the real transcendence of alienation. They have no doubt that this transcendence can actually be realized here on earth. Their predictions about the future course of history, however, have been as fallible as most predictions in the realm of limited knowledge. Many commentators on Marx's predictions about historicist futurism indicate that they only have the "significance of utopias" and have nothing to do with truly scientific predictions.[65] The mysteries of historicist futurism play a significant role in his theory of alienation and dealienation. Without realizing that forecasts of the future of social trends and historical aims inevitably entail numerous speculative elements, Marx believes that his dialectical method is adequate in "discovering the rational kernel that is hidden away within the wrappings of mystification."[66] The Hegelian conception of thesis-antithesis-synthesis is rejected because he believes it ignores the social and historical world that is moved primarily by the forces of production. Marx argues that in Hegel's conception of transcendence, the highest synthesis is merely a metaphysical collection of transcended phenomena that are not relevant to the real world of alienation. As a result, Hegel's metaphysical transcendence "leaves its object intact in reality." In Hegel, the negation of the negation does not negate anything "in the real history of man," and because alienation in his system is posited only as a logical movement of the negation of the negation, it can never transcend the alienation of "man with his feet firmly on the solid ground."[67]

The future reconciliation of man within himself and the restoration of the harmonious unity within man as subject that constitute Hegel's highest synthesis become a thesis in Marx's dialectical materialism. In his philosophical system, the Hegelian conception of the triadic dialectical movement is expressed as a theory of the historical process. Each stage of human history has its own thesis and antithesis reflecting socioeconomic antagonisms among the existing classes. In Marx's materialist dialectic, the synthesis which is of great significance in the transcendence of alienation can only be achieved by a process of new socioeconomic relationships. Secularizing the Hegelian conception of *Aufhebung*, he maintains that the historical opposition between capitalist thesis and proletarian antithesis will necessarily lead to the synthesis of the new classless society in which "the class making a revolution" will play the role of "liberator" and be the only "representative of the whole of society."[68] The transcendence of the "contradiction between the productive forces and the form of social intercourse" is a relevant prerequisite for the ascendancy of a new class and the way to a better future. The future hegemony of the class "representing the whole of society," Marx contends, is guaranteed by the fact that it is the social embodiment of new productive forces. As "all collisions in history have their origin in the contradiction between the productive forces and productive relations," alienation of existing forms of human life can only be transcended by abolishing classes and class antagonism.[69]

Analyzing the tragic reality of different forms of alienation, visible at all levels of human life, Marx stresses that the products of alienation cannot be treated as "mere ideal fantasies or mere alienations of self-consciousness."[70] As a result, real and "material estrangement can never be abolished by purely inward spiritual action."[71] The idealist conception of the transcendence, he believes, is fictitious and leaves the existence of alienated men in capitalist society unchanged. To eliminate alienation, it is not enough to be merely aware of alienated products and alienated activity that are the distinguishing features of capitalism. It is essential, in Marx's view, to transform the whole ideological and practical world of capitalist society that has engendered the alienating process. This transformation must start from the transcendence of the division of labor and private property. It is by changes in material conditions that transformations in the social structure and in history are effected, not by changes in the superstructure. Elements of the superstructure are merely reflections of the "economic structure of society." Marx insists there can be no transformation of the superstructure without changes in the economic foundation.[72]

The difference between Hegel's and Marx's conceptions of the transcendence of alienation can be expressed as the difference between transcendence in thought and transcendence in action. In Marx's view, Hegel's transcendence in thought or consciousness is "nothing but an abstract, empty abolition" of real alienation.[73] The Hegelian view that "the general estrangement of the human essence and the annulment of the alienation" occur merely within the realm of self-consciousness is rejected.[74] In Hegelianism, both the history of the alienated process and the whole process of transcendence of alienation, Marx believes, are merely "thought-entities." The opposition between alienation and its transcendence is "the opposition of subject and object within thought itself, between abstract thinking and sensuous reality."[75] Contrary to Hegel, Marx argues for active rejection of the alienated process, indicating the relevance of a historical, real transcendence in the direction of a new socioeconomic reality in which man will be able to express his life in real, sensuous objects and behave as an active natural being. A valid and real transcendence of the alienated world of man can only occur within the dimensions of human history. This entails the recognition of man as a sensuous, active being and abandonment of the idea that "thought revolves solely within the orbit of thought and is devoid of everything sensuous."[76]

The novelty of Marx's conception of alienation and dealienation is the emphasis on the natural man of flesh and blood as opposed to the man of self-consciousness. His humanism demands the transcendence of all forms of alienation. Feuerbach's humanism, in his opinion, is based on a myth that "love is the true unity of God and man, of spirit and nature."[77] Actually, his humanism is even inferior to Hegel's humanism. Hegelian humanism at least starts from man's activity and is based on the dialectic of negativity as "the moving and generating principle" expressed in the self-genesis of man.[78] Not surprisingly, Marx's conception of alienation and dealienation indicated in *Manuscripts of 1844* is closer to Hegel's humanistic rationalism than to Feuerbach's naturalistic humanism. For Marx, alienation will end with the return of man to himself when "perfect naturalism" will coincide with humanism and fully developed humanism will coincide with naturalism. Looking into the future through the glasses of metaphysics, Marx, like Hegel, predicts that "perfect naturalism" will create the perfectly human individual and that by transcending the process of alienation it will preserve the entire content of man's evolution.

The theory of "fully-developed naturalism" as defined by Marx in *Manuscripts of 1844*, like his theory of dialectical materialism, can neither be proved nor disproved because it is woven into the nebulous structure of speculation and mystification. Most modern philosophers and scientists reject Marx's conception of naturalism on the ground that, as in Hegel, it is permeated with metaphysical elements. The specific metaphysical view of man and history that runs consistently through Marx's writings, they maintain, is bound to undermine the claim of his philosophical system to be a theory of world history. Marx's claim that in dialectical materialism all forms of idealism and contemplative materialism have been transformed, transcended, and reunited in a positive direction cannot be supported seriously. The Marxist belief that historical materialism is based on empirical premises rather than on dogmas is simply a myth. Exponents of historical materialism have spent much time trying to demonstrate the practical application envisaged in its fundamental goals. The fail to realize, however, that these goals are meaningless unless one assumes, as Hegel does, that history is composed of teleological moments. In true teleological becoming, Hegel indicates, there is always a single nature realizing itself and sustaining its own reality.[79] In Marx's view, the ends and goals of man always transcend his empirical existence, and the teleological view of socioeconomic reality cannot be maintained. Yet, paradoxically, his own theory of the transcendence of alienation is based on the assumption that the "tendencies which work out with an iron necessity towards an inevitable goal" are teleological.[80]

In his analysis of the transcendence of alienation, Marx vacillates between purely deterministic explanations of human history and some mystifying teleological explanations that social science can hardly support. Although, like Spinoza, he resists the view that opposes transcendence and immanence and rejects all external finality, he believes in a gradual teleological unfolding of "social laws" that negate all the negations negating "man's own being."[81] Each development in Marx's theory of historical materialism shows a tendency for its own abolition. The goal envisaged in this development would transform the relationship between the economic base and the intellectual superstructure in such a way that every alienating distinction between private and public life would be transcended and abolished. By inverting the Hegelian idealist teleology that negates the actual conditions of human life, Marx believes it is possible to transform all of history into an evolutionary process that will transcend "the last antagonistic form of the mode of production of material life" and lead to the transcendence of the alienation process itself.[82] There is no explanation why the evolution of the contradictions within the socioeconomic formations must be expressed in the "forcible overthrow of all existing social conditions" and why revolution is "the only historical way in which these contradictions can be resolved."

The fact is that Marx's theory of historical materialism is ambivalent, inconsistent, and obscure. Although he and Engels say much about the materialist conception of history, they have not formulated a clear, coherent theory of historical materialism. Whenever they deal with productive forces, social consciousness, and historical development, they easily find themselves involved in determinism. Yet, paradoxically, when they analyze some particular historical events or the communist future in which "individuals obtain their freedom in and through their association," they speak of "conscious intention" and "deliberate direction."[83] Their assertion that freedom under communism is a matter of self-determination as opposed to determination by external factors reflects their ambivalence about the role of social forces in the transcendence of alienation. The assumption that freedom in the communist future will be qualitatively different and that the economic organization of men in this society will transcend alienation is utopian nonsense. Like Hegel, Marx and Engels have never explained satisfactorily the nature and relevance of necessity that is supposedly inherent in socioeconomic development. Advocating historical materialism in opposition to idealism and "contemplative materialism," they have simply transformed the dialectic of the development of spiritual entities into the dialectic affecting the development of the means of production. The nature of a set of productive relations in a social structure is explained by the level of the development of productive forces involved. All historical struggles in human activity are seen as the expression of the "great law of motion of history" that "inevitably" leads to the transformation of the economic conditions of production and of the superstructure.[84]

Marx's conception of historical materialism, associated with the transcendence of alienation, in many respects reflects Hegel's historicist theodicy. In both Marxism and Hegelianism, a self-developing metaphysical force that forms the hidden reality behind the world of appearances controls all historical development. It is on the assumption of the existence of this self-developing force that Marx, like Hegel, confidently predicts the transcendence of alienated forms of life. Unlike Hegel, however,he lays a considerable emphasis on the revolutionary transformation of socioeconomic relations and the abolition of private property as essential measures in any successful process of dealienation. Alienation can only be abolished, he writes, "given two practical premises. In order to become an unendurable power against which men make revolution, it must have rendered the great mass of humanity propertyless. Secondly, the actual empirical existence of men in their world-historical being must be reflected in a great increase in productive power, in a high degree of its development."[85] The sum of productive forces is the real substratum of all processes of man's historical life. The capitalist form of production, responsible for all forms of alienation, is opposed diametrically to the abolition of private property and must itself be negated.

The central idea in Marx's analysis of unbearable alienation is that only a communist future will give human labor its true meaning and historical purpose. He has no doubt that after the communist revolution, the proletariat, the class alienated totally under capitalism, will definitely transcend all forms of alienation. Communist victory, Marx maintains, entails the abolition of all distorted mediations and of all illusory goals and purposes that have bedevilled the human race throughout time. After the abolition and disappearance of class antagonisms, there will be no room for the exploitation of man by man. Marx's optimism carries him as far as to suggest that in classless society work no longer will be just a way to earn a living, but will become a meaningful and joyous creative activity. Here both manual and intellectual work will cease to be a commodity. With the drastic change in socioeconomic relations, work will cease to be the principal source of wealth and exchange value will cease to be the measure of use value. Both general and collective work will have their role in production. Capitalist production based on alienation and exploitation "causes the premature exhaustion and death of labour power."[86] The alien relationship of the worker to capitalist production is a torment to him.[87] The fact that the worker is related to the product of his labor as an "alien object," means that "external labour" is a "labour of mortification."[88]

Without indicating whether theoretical presuppositions are necessary for the transcendence of alienation, Marx argues that socialization of wealth is impossible without a great increase in productive forces followed by an increase in class antagonism. The appropriation of the world by existing men is achieved by praxis, which he sees as the sole criterion of value and truth. "All social life is essentially practical. All mysteries which lead theory to mysticism find their rational solution in human practice and in the comprehension of this practice."[89] Marx assumes wrongly that he is the only thinker who insists on the unity of theory and practice, overlooking the fact that the idea of the unity of theory and practice is as old as mankind. It plays an important role in Christian soteriology. In Thomistic philosophy, theory and practice, thought and action, are not treated as opposites. Saint Thomas views immanent action as the most intense and vital form of action; and because the mind is superior to matter, it is primarily the property of the intellect. A similar idea is developed by Hegel. "The content of something thought has the form of being," he says, "but this being is something mediated, something established through our activity."[90] The theoretical is contained essentially in the practical. The theoretical and the practical are not separate because, in his view, "we cannot have a will without intelligence."[91] Like Aquinas, Hegel argues that "the practical attitude begins in thinking."[92] By positing abstract sensuousness, Marx fails to solve the dichotomy of the theoretical and practical. The conception of the unity of theory and practice is not less ambiguous and metaphysical in his system than in Hegel's. As a result, the dualism of the theoretical and the practical is never transcended. In the eighth thesis on Feuerbach, he clearly connects "human practice" with comprehension, assuming, like Hegel, that "it must begin in thinking." He merely inverts the dialectical order of consciousness and being and of theory and practice so that sensuous activity appears to be the judge of thought. Instead of being an "absolute humanism of history," total praxis, in fact, remains enmeshed in the mystifying opposition between abstract idealist and abstract materialist dichotomies of theory and practice.

Some modern Marxists believe that praxis is a norm rather than a mechanism; this does not clarify Marx's ambivalence about its role in the transcendence of alienation. To say that the distinguishing mark of Marx's praxis is not that it is action as opposed to thinking but rather action based on thinking makes, in fact, Marx's conception of praxis hardly distinguishable from Hegel's conception of "the theoretical and the practical." Marx maintains that only the reality that corresponds to the total activity of men expressed in praxis is actually true. He differs from Hegel in the belief that reality is essentially material and that praxis must be revolutionary if it is going to have any dealienating effects. Man, in his view, can be dealienated practically only by "revolutionary practice."[93] "For the practical materialist, i.e., the communist, it is a question of revolutionising the existing world, of practically coming to grips with and changing the things found in experience."[94] Ignoring the dichotomy of theory and practice in his own philosophical system, Marx argues that practical labor is the only material force capable of transcending class antagonisms and of overcoming the process of alienation itself. Theory and thought merely reflect the material base and all ideas originate from this base.[95] Theoretical products and forms of consciousness must be analyzed in terms of "material practice." There is an assumption that "material practice" and "revolutionary practice" are "identical expression,"[96] expressing the same dealienating tendency and destined to abolish capitalist alienation.

In general, Marx regards praxis as a method of reverting the "present state of things" and negating private property and division of labor that are responsible for alienation. Analyzing dealienation, he, in fact, says very little about how to eliminate alienation. "The transcendence of self-alienation," he indicates, "follows the same course as self-alienation."[97] Without explaining the characteristic features of this common course, he obviously assumes that the phenomena of alienation and pseudo-dealienation can be observed only in non-communist societies in which the history of labor and the development of productive forces are bound up with the forms of private ownership and division of labor. Although the division of labor and private property are regarded as "identical expression" in *German Ideology*, in *Manuscripts of 1844* Marx concentrates his attack on private property and insists on its abolition as a necessary prerequisite for the socialization of the means of production and the "abolition of the capitalist mode of production." He argues that the transcendence of alienation necessitates the reconversion of capital into the property of producers and the transformation of private property into social property. "It is easy to see," Marx writes, "that the entire revolutionary movement necessarily finds both its empirical and its theoretical basis in the movement of private property—in that of the economy."[98]

As "material, immediately sensuous private property is the material sensuous expression of estranged human life," Marx argues that it should be abolished and substituted by social property. "The positive transcendence of private property" is seen as "the positive transcendence of all estrangement and as the return of man to his human and social mode of existence."[99] In Marx's eschatology, the problem of dealienation is reduced to the problem of social transformation, and the problem of social transformation in the historical becoming of total humanity is reduced to the abolition of private property. Although Marx is unable to demystify the "secret" of private property and its exact role in the genesis of alienation, he still believes that the movement of private property is responsible for the exploitation and alienation of man. The resolution of the tragedy of human suffering, in his view, can have a happy ending only in communism. Communism represents the destructive force of capitalist alienated society and the termination of class exploitation. The difference between communism and class societies is that in the latter "social relationships take on an independent existence" whereas in communism social relations, according to Marx, cease to be coercive and alienating.[100] "Communism," he writes in *German Ideology*, "differs from all previous movements in that it overturns the basis of all earlier relations of production and intercourse."[101]

Presenting an idyllic picture of a communist future, Marx indicates that communism is the first and complete dealienation of mankind and that, strictly, human history will begin only with the advent of communism. Rejecting the "fantastic pictures of future society painted by utopian socialists," he maintains that only communism, as fully developed naturalism or humanism, possesses the means for overcoming the contradictions in class society. "The bourgeois society that has sprouted from the ruins of feudal society," it is stated in *Communist Manifesto*, "has not done away with class antagonisms." On the contrary, it has created "new conditions of oppression" and has intensified the process of alienation.[102] The aim of communist *praxis* is to liberate alienated man from his "hostile dwelling" and from "the sway of inhuman power."[103] The real estrangement of the life of man, Marx believes, can be overcome "solely by putting communism into operation."[104] Representing communism as the transcendence of alienation and the total revocation of self-alienation, he takes for granted that with the supercession of private property all forms of alienation will disappear. Communism is characterized in *Manuscripts of 1844* as "the negation of the negation and as the appropriation of the human essence which mediates itself with itself through the negation of private property."[105] The main defect of the social system based on the institution of private property and competition is its irrationality expressed in the "mania for possessions." This mania leads easily to "excesses, intemperance, extravagance, arrogance, morbid appetites, mutual swindling and mutual plundering." The increase in wealth is accompanied by an "extension of the realm of the alien powers which dominate and reify man."[106]

In Marx's lifetime, ideas about communism were used ambiguously by many utopian socialists who saw in communism a social movement expressing aspirations and human needs similar to those in socialism. Marx discusses some of these ideas in his analysis of social liberalism and true socialism in *German Ideology*.[107] Rejecting Stirner's "communism which begins with searchings for essence and arrives only at a philosophical category, i.e., being-for-one-another"—communism defined in terms of "equal wages," he argues that communism is a "revolutionary and highly practical movement" aimed at the abolition of private ownership and bourgeois exploitation.[108] Non-revolutionary communism, in his view, is a contradiction in terms. "The few non-revolutionary communist bourgeois who made their appearance since the time of Babeuf were a rare occurrence. The vast majority of the communists in all countries," he says, "are revolutionary. All communists in France reproach the followers of Saint-Simon and Fourier for their peaceableness and differ from the latter in abandoning all hope of an amicable settlement of private property, just as in Britain it is the same criterion which chiefly distinguishes the Chartists from the socialists."[109]

Marx's own ideas of communism are far from being clear and consistent. Like some utopian socialists, he sometimes speaks of communism in terms of socialism. After reading with some interest the writings of Proudhon, Fourier, and Sanit-Simon containing "crude communist" ideas, he has gradually come to the conclusion that their conception of communism is too dogmatic and impractical. In his letter to Ruge in 1843, Marx tells him that he is "not in favour of raising a dogmatic flag" and rejects communism as a "dogmatic abstraction." "We should try to help the dogmatists clarify their ideas." "Thus communism," he writes, "is a dogmatic abstraction and by this I do not mean some fanciful or possible communism but the real, existing communism as Cabet, Dézamy, Weitling, etc., teach and conceive it. This communism is itself separate from the humanist principle, merely a phenomenon affected by its opposite, private existence."[110] Communism, Marx points out, is not identical with the abolition of private property, and common ownership is not its only criterion. In the sense of true socialism, it cannot and must not be reduced to a simple change of the role of property or to a simple transfer of political power. Capitalism as an alienating force must be destroyed, but communism in its crude form cannot be the rational alternative system. Accepting the need for the abolition of capitalist alienation, Marx shares Ruge's ideal of socialism as expressed in humanism. Socialism as humanism is necessary for more than economic or political reasons: it is needed to terminate a system that has contradicted the elementary conditions for decent human and social life.

Before he became a communist, Marx regarded communism as an abstract doctrine far removed from the materialist and dialectical comprehension of human emancipation. His skepticism of communist ideology, frequently associated with religious hatred and political fanaticism, has been expressed strongly in an article in *Rheinische Zeitung*. Here he indicates that "communist ideas in their present form do not possess even theoretical reality" and that men "cannot desire their practical realisation" because they are vague and impractical.[111] This skepticism is reflected in *Manuscripts of 1844*, although here he seemingly adopts communism in its higher form as "the positive transcendence of private property and the complete return of man to himself as a social being."[112] Even in this work his ideal of communism is represented in terms of humanism. Without being able to decide whether communism in any form is "the goal of human development," in *Manuscripts of 1844* Marx briefly speaks of three stages of communism. It is only in the last form that communism will "solve the riddle of history" and be able to overcome human alienation.[113] The only form of communism that can be considered as a dealienating force is communism conceived as socialism and fully developed naturalism or humanism. Other forms and concepts of communism, in Marx's view, must be rejected. Because they are inconsistent and crude, they cannot build the work of social cohesion and harmony and abolish the inhuman and alien force of capitalism.

The idea that "the abolition of private property and communism are by no means identical," expressed in Marx's letter to Ruge, is reiterated vaguely in *Manuscripts of 1844*.[114] Distinguishing sharply between crude or thoughtless communism and "true communism," here Marx comes very close to arguing that communism, unlike socialism, hardly has any reality, any substance, and any constructive future. Like Moses Hess, he is well aware of the existence of raw and illiterate communism that has appealed to some figures of the French Enlightenment and to some French revolutionaries and egalitarians. This communism, based on the sense of justice and egalitarianism, is rejected in favor of German communism that Marx and Hess believe alone expresses philosophical humanism. Yet, Marx is far from being clear what this "communist humanism" should really mean. Vacillating between "true communism" and socialism, between socialism and "fully developed humanism," he continues to believe in a communist future in which there will be no room for "bourgeois private property" and no alienation. The transcendence of alienation is always linked with "true communism."[115] It is true, this transcendence, Marx indicates, remains a "distant ideal" and communism, representing dealienation, will take a prolonged course; but communism is still the only way in which human history can be made intelligible and "the only dynamic principle of the immediate future."[116] Paradoxically, however, the solution to the riddle of history does not lie in a crude, thoughtless communism that abolishes private property by merely "generalising it." The transcendence of alienation, in Marx's view, cannot and must not be confined to the purely economic or purely political sphere of human life. Therefore, he rejects crude, thoughtless communism because it represents "regression" and denies not only the essential freedoms of social and individual life but also "the entire world of culture and civilisation."[117]

In its first form, Marx writes in *Manuscripts of 1844*, communism is "only a generalisation and consummation" of private property relations. Here "the dominion of material property bulks so large that it wants to destroy everything which is not capable of being possessed by all as private property."[118] Human talents and intellectual abilities are disregarded arbitrarily, and the sole purpose of life in crude communism is reduced to "direct, physical possession."[119] This form of communism, Marx argues, is a negative phenomenon and must not be seen as a dealienating movement. It has neither knowledge nor consistent policy to be regarded seriously as a solution to socioeconomic problems. "The category of labourer is not done away with but extended to all men. The relationship of private property persists as the relationship of the community to the world of things."[120] Thoughtless communism, in Marx's mind, is so preoccupied with the concept of property that it is unable to concentrate on real socioeconomic issues. The opposition of "universal private property" to bourgeois or capitalist private property "finds expression in the bestial form of opposition to marriage which is replaced by the community of women." Here a "woman becomes a piece of communal and common property," and prostitution is a distinguishing feature of social and economic relations. By negating the dignity of man and woman and by merely universalizing private property, crude or thoughtless communism leaves the existing men and women in the same world of alienation as capitalism. The only difference between capitalism and crude communism in this respect is that in crude communism it is the community rather than the private individual, that regulates the relationship of ownership with material things. Because this type of communism is the consummation of envy, avarice, and jealousy, it is incapable of recognizing the true essence of man and real human needs. As a result, it has a very limited standard and a very limited knowledge of real human goals.[121]

Marx views thoughtless or raw communism as the universalization of capitalism and capitalist greed. The human community plays the role of "the universal capitalist" in this communism.[122] The shadow of the old alienating world lingers on in the world claiming to be liberating and dealienating. Denouncing crude communism, Marx points out that its aims are irrational and its standards lower than those in capitalism. "In negating the personality of man in every sphere, this type of communism is really nothing but the logical expression of private property."[123] Having rejected thoughtless communism, he then proceeds to give a brief but equally critical account of the second form of communism that is "political in nature—democratic or despotic."[124] Like economic or crude communism, political communism, Marx says in *Manuscripts of 1844*, is "extremely limited, incomplete and still affected by private property, i.e., by the estrangement of man." Only partially abolishing the state and demanding civil equality for all members of society, political communism cannot succeed in abolishing private property and human alienation. Because it fails to grasp the positive essence of private property, this type of communism also represents a regression and denies the personality of man in every sphere of life. Its world pretending to be new and liberating is only the sad continuation of the old world of alienation.

It is only the third form of communism which, in Marx's view expressed in *Manuscripts of 1844*, represents "the positive transcendence of private property and alienation."[125] The communism that is essentially economic "wants to destroy everything that cannot be possessed by all" and the type of communism that is essentially political is also "infected" by avarice and private property.[126] In both types of communism, alienation remains and "the riddle of history" is unsolved. All negations, suppressions, and abolitions in both types come to nothing because of the failure to posit man's natural being as the basis of social development. By themselves, these abolitions are inadequate to constitute the essence and meaning of humanistic communism that alone leads to the transcendence of alienation. Analyzing this form of communism, Marx indicates that the transcendence of alienation is neither essentially economic nor essentially political or religious; it is, he believes, essentially naturalistic and humanistic. Alienation can be overcome only by the revolutionary negation of the totality of the existing alienated world. In reality and for the communist, he says in the *German Ideology*, the main task is "to revolutionise the existing world and to change the things found in existence."[127] In true communism, the solution of philosophical, religious, and theoretical antitheses becomes possible "in a practical way." Once freed from capitalist alienated labor and servitude, man will become a truly social and practical being.

It is communism as "the genuine resolution of the conflict between man and man" and as "the positive transcendence of private property and of human estrangement" that is, in Marx's view, "the dynamic principle of the immediate future."[128] Yet, strangely enough, even this type of communism cannot be "the goal of human development."[129] This contradictory and ambivalent definition of true communism in *Manuscripts of 1844* has caused much confusion and has provoked bitter arguments among Marxists themselves. Orthodox Marxists follow Marx in believing that "communism is the necessary form of the immediate future" but are reluctant to accept his view that "communism as such is not the goal of human development." They believe that by "communism as such" Marx simply means crude or thoughtless communism, the communism advocated by Gracchus Babeuf and his followers.[130] Babeuf's emphasis is on egalitarianism. "Let there be no difference between human beings," he writes in *Manifesto of the Equals* in 1796, "but in age and sex." While it is true that Marx could not share this view, it is very difficult to believe that "by communism as such" he really has in mind only Babeuf's crude communism. Non-Marxists and some unorthodox Marxists adhere to a literal interpretation and interpret this ambiguous passage as Marx's explicit denial that communism in any form can be the goal of human development.[131] They support their interpretation by similar passages occurring in *Manuscripts of 1844* and *German Ideology*. In the latter work, Marx also states explicitly that "communism is not a state of affairs which is to be established" but only the movement that abolishes the present organization of life.[132]

Although Marx's vision of communism as the negation of alienation is far from being clear and consistent, it is impossible to deny that at least in some passages in *Manuscripts* he considers communism as a means to a higher end. The principal goal of communism, in his view, consists in the abolition of all alienated and alienating forms of human life. These are particularly prominent in capitalist society. When these forms are abolished in the process of communist dealienation, then communism itself will be transcended and abolished. If this interpretation is correct, and it is impossible to refute it without some metaphysical twisting, then communism is, like "all the rest of ideology," historical and transitory. It posits a negation as negation to negate the existing alienated world, but "communism as such" cannot be seen as a permanent goal of history or, as some may imagine, a theoretical construction of a higher moral ideal. It is merely, Marx points out in the conclusion of the account of communism in the *Manuscripts*, "the actual phase necessary for the next stage of historical development in the process of human emancipation and recovery."[133] Thus communism even in its final stage must have its own limitations and cannot be the ultimate end of historical becoming.

Politics and metaphysics are so interwoven in Marx's thought that it is not always easy to ascertain whether he is expounding a political theme in the guise of metaphysics or a metaphysical theme in the guise of politics. The fact remains that the problem of communism is a big dilemma for Marx. This dilemma results from his inability to prove that communism is not only a necessary stage in the process of human recovery but that it is also a permanent and stable state of human development. Strongly opposing ideals and principles, including communist ideals, he seems to suggest that communism is essentially a dialectical but unintelligible movement.[134] Although it is a real historical movement, its historical future cannot be guaranteed. Engels echoes this view in a letter just before his death in 1895 in which he discourages all attempts to specify the future course of communism. This task, he says, is impossible "without falling into utopianism or empty phrase-making." Unfortunately, Marx sometimes tries to envisage the communist future and, in his attempt to describe it, he fails to penetrate the mystery of this future altogether. The best he can do is to give us a very brief, vague, and utopian account of his oracular millennium. Some commentators find a parallel between Marx's conception of communist future and Christian eschatology.[135] It is ironic, they indicate, that after all his derision of religious ideas, Marx uses some aspects of Christian eschatology as a basis for his own vision of communist future.

Marx's ideas of communism as the transcendence of alienation are obscure and mystical, based mainly on doubtful and *a priori* assumptions. In spite of his occasional appeal to "empirical facts," he fails to demonstrate that the "empirical view" is "one of the most vital principles and distinguishing marks of communism."[136] It is obvious from many statements in *Manuscripts* and, indeed, in other writings, including *German Ideology*, that his vision of communist future is an object of mystical faith rather than an object of rational intuition. As in all eschatologies, the communist future is tacitly linked to goals and ideals that represent imaginary types of perfection. Marx does not claim to know a great deal about the goal of human development but he insists that any description of this goal necessitates its adequate apprehension. Although communism is not the goal of human development, it is still an aspect of this development and therefore must be considered as a cognitive act. After painful deliberation, Marx seems to be driven to the conclusion that true communism is a temporary phenomenon and an expression of philosophical comprehension. Because it is hardly a quality of any social structure, this true communism can only be regarded as the comprehension or consciousness of different qualities and heterogenous social forms appearing at relevant periods of historical development. Full communism, in Marx's view, is incomprehensible without philosophical knowledge.

In spite of Marx's conviction that neither ideas nor feelings can effectively resolve the practical problem of men, he still appeals to philosophy and metaphysics more frequently than he thinks and wishes. When he speaks of "the riddle of history of which communism knows itself to be the solution," he obviously means that full communism can only be intelligible in terms of philosophy. The intelligibility of this communism is not a matter for sense perception but rather a matter for "thinking consciousness." This is implied in the sentence following the definition of true communism as "the riddle of history." "The entire movement of history," Marx writes in *Manuscripts of 1844*, "is both its actual act of genesis and also for its thinking consciousness the comprehended and known process of its coming-to-be."[137] Here Marx's vision of the dealienated communist future postulates the existence of a chasm between the ideal and the actual, between empirical reality and human understanding. Because empirical reality is subject to instability and change, true communism seen as the transcendence of alienation can only be intelligible in terms of metaphysical knowledge. Never rejecting entirely "the outstanding features" of Hegel's transcendentalism, Marx seems to suggest that it is, in fact, theoretical knowledge rather than "communism as such" that is the consummation of the historical process as a whole. Under Hegel's influence, in the *Manuscripts of 1844* he ultimately reduces "true communism" to the category of "absolute knowledge." Although this knowledge, he surely realizes, is "beyond the sphere of actual material production," it is still significant and worth having. Without this knowledge, "the entire movement of history" sadly becomes empty and unintelligible. History, as Hegel indicates, "presents us with a rational process" that only philosophy can explain satisfactorily.[138]

The fact is that Marx's conception of dealienation is vague and inconsistent. The contradiction between a relativist solution of alienation within the realm of the material economic and social forces of man and a utopia of complete dealienation, transcending even developed forms of communism, is never overcome. Crude or thoughtless communism is regarded as a historical existent; "true communism" is tacitly assumed to be only a historical goal. Yet, without being aware of contradiction, he asserts that in both crude and political forms, "communism already knows itself to be re-integration or return of man to himself and the transcendence of human self-estrangement."[139] The emphasis on knowing hardly makes any difference between these two forms of communism and the final form that is also characterized as an expression of philosophical comprehension and consciousness.

Analyzing the process of dealienation in *Manuscripts*, Marx is aware of the gap separating crude communism as a historical existent and true communism as a historical goal. Because the gap between the real and the ideal is almost unbridgeable, he is in so much difficulty that he comes to the point of confusing historical transcendence with transcendence in thought. Marx rejects Hegel's cognitive abolition of alienation on the ground that it is "an abstract, empty abolition of that empty abstraction—the negation of the negation."[140] He also rejects "thoughtless communism" because it not only negates man's personality but it also makes alienation worse than it is in capitalism, appealing to immoral and bestialized workers who are fascinated by prostitution and plunder.[141] Yet, in spite of Marx's resistance "to arrive at communism by way of metaphysics," he fails to find any other way but the way of metaphysics that can lead him to true communism. The metaphysical dimension of his conception of the transcendence of alienation is definitely implicit in the idea of communism as the consciousness and comprehension of historical becoming.[142]

As a materialist, Marx operates with the distinction that exists in metaphysics between being and consciousness, reality and appearance. Thought and consciousness, in his view, only reflect the activity of real human beings. At the beginning of the process by which nature becomes history, human beings have "only a sheep-like or tribal consciousness."[143] Yet, it is, strangely enough, by this consciousness that the history of the world is built up and made intelligible. In spite of all dialectical interactions and syntheses, thought and materiality, consciousness and being continue to exist even when "the riddle of history" is solved in "true communism." There are no convincing arguments in Marx's conception of dealienation that these dialectical opposites will ever be overcome and that the actual abolition of real alienation will dealienate the mental and ideological forms of the superstructure. Sometimes he doubts whether the unity between thought and consciousness, on the one hand, and historical and material activity, on the other, is ever possible. Considering that existing men and women in crude communism tend to "regress to prostituted life and barbarity," it is very difficult to believe that the same tendency will not persist even in "true communism."[144]

In his vision of the communist future, Marx definitely fails to transcend the ideological world of "mental production." Praxis and the knowledge of practice, communism as the real movement and communism as the riddle of history, theory and historical existent continue to linger as two separate realms in spite of the assertions of their "dialectical unity." The duality of the empirical existence and of consciousness surely implies that the ideological world is never abolished. Although Marx claims to be a resolute opponent of dualistic systems and an advocate of materialist monism, there is clearly a tangible dualism involved in his thinking in *Manuscripts* and some other works. In his vision of true communism, he is unable to transcend the philosophical conception that opposes man's being to consciousness and reality to thought. So, theory and practice, ideas and facts remain separated and without unity. In spite of his view that every form of consciousness and every theory have hitherto been alienated, it is consciousness, theory, and knowledge that will ultimately solve the riddle of alienation. Without "mental production" and knowledge, true communism would be practically impossible and the riddle of history would thus remain unsolved for ever.[145]

Following the analysis of the transcendence of alienation in *Manuscripts of 1844*, the concept of crude communism and the concept of communism as "genuine resolution" disappear entirely from his writing, perhaps the result of Marx's inability to bridge the gap between the real and the ideal. Marx continues, of course, to analyze certain features of communism in later works, but the reference to communism as "the positive transcendence of alienation" has been dropped. In *Critique of the Gotha Programme*, written in 1875, he returns to the theme of communism without being able to avoid the same dualism that has haunted him in *Manuscripts*. In fact, the dualism detectable in *Critique* is strikingly visible as the two phases of communism are merely theoretically balanced and their interrelation is purely artificial, remote, and unintelligible. Any meaningful unity between "the first phase" and "a higher phase of communism" is entirely lacking.[146] The low phase is obviously the equivalent of crude or thoughtless communism treated in *Manuscripts*. Marx hardly adds anything new to his previous assertion that the first form of communism is only the logical expression of private property and can be characterized as rationalized capitalism. "The first phase of communism" envisaged in *Critique* is merely a copy of "the first form of communism" described in *Manuscripts* as "generalised estrangement." Like "the first form," "the first phase" of communism is full of defects that, according to Marx, "are inevitable because it follows the birth marks of the capitalist society."[147]

The first phase of communism, in Marx's view, represents the real world in which communist greed, envy, and the mania for possessions prevent any genuine attempt to transcend alienation. It is not explained how these defects disappear so quickly in "a higher phase" of communism. Marx, in fact, says very little about the distinguishing marks of this "higher phase." In one sentence he merely reiterates the dominant message of *Manuscripts* that, following the abolition of the "enslaving subordination of the individual to the division of labour," "labor will become not only a means of life but life's prime want."[148] Once "the antithesis between mental and physical labour has vanished," he says, there will be an abundant flow of material wealth and "society will finally be able to inscribe on its banners: from each according to his ability, to each according to his needs."[149] There is no reference to "communism as the positive transcendence of private property" and no allusion to the transcendence of alienation. At this stage, it is important to remember, Marx has practically abandoned the concept of alienation altogether and is concerned mainly with the "revolutionary process of transformation of society" and with the final goal of a communist economy in classless society.[150]

Marx's analysis of the transition from capitalism to communism as envisaged in *Critique* is obscure, evasive, and contradictory. While ridiculing any appeal to morality and justice as the "obsolete ideological nonsense of true socialists and reformists," he himself cannot avoid tacit appeals to morality and compare socialist and communist distribution in terms of an ideal justice rather than in terms of any demonstrable science.[151] The second phase of communism is strikingly a moral ideal, representing a future world of fulfillment and perfection. Judging from *Critique*, Marx is far from being certain that the "higher phase" will ever arrive, let alone abolish alienation. One can argue that his ultimate communist ideal as defined in this work is only an empty metaphysical ornamentation designed to compensate for the gross defects in the first phase. Marx's brief and vague reference to a higher phase could be interpreted to mean nothing more than his philosophical justification for criticizing the bestial, enslaving, and alienating forms of communism. The assumption that here he is advocating "scientific communism" is groundless and cannot be considered seriously.[152] When speaking of a higher phase, which incidentally does not exclude more phases of communism, and when describing true communism as "the positive transcendence of alienation," he is having in mind the ideal world of the historical future in which hopefully "the strife between existence and essence, between freedom and necessity will be resolved."[153] Marx rejects "immature communism" because of its myopic world outlook and its search for historical proofs merely "in the realm of the existent," and finally presents to us an ideal realm of communist future, not a scientific model that can be used in real empirical life.[154] The ideal realm is a metaphysical structure and only related abstractly to "thoughtless and defective" forms of communism.[155]

Analyzing the reality of alienation and the possibility of dealienation, Marx is confronted continuously by the dilemma of the irreconcileable opposition between "thoughtless and philosophical" forms of communism. It is true, in *German Ideology*, Marx tries to avoid making references to true communism and says nothing about communism as the transcendence of alienation. Here communism is presented as a "real movement" aiming at the abolition of the "present state of things."[156] Yet, even here some features of philosophical communism are retained, although, paradoxically, its premises are rejected. Marx's utopian description of communist future society in which "nobody will have one exclusive sphere of activity" reflects his equally utopian description of "communism as the riddle of history solved" and "communism as the positive transcendence of all estrangement" in *Manuscripts of 1844*.[157] The search for myopic goals "in the realm of the existent" is also tacitly subordinated to the search for higher philosophical goals in *German Ideology*. Although the emphasis in this work is on "actual facts," "existing practice," and "material reality," some ideas of philosophical communism still persist.

Communism as "the riddle of history solved" and as "genuine resolution" has never been rejected explicitly by Marx. He assumes tacitly that a perfect communist future may never be realized in the real world. Like Plato, he seems to realize that "philosophical communism" has "its being only in words," and "that, after all, its pattern may be laid only in heaven."[158] The abyss separating the real world of crude communism and the ideal world of philosophical communism is so great that Marx finds it necessary to transform his vision of "communism as such" into the vision of "fully-developed human-ism." Unlike communism, this humanism or naturalism presumably should become "the goal of human development." By pursuing this goal, men and women will be able to overcome alienation and its dehumanizing effects. Yet, Marx says too little about dealienation to justify any safe conclusions. Some commentators on Marx rightly indicate that his ideas of dealienation have only the significance of utopias.[159] Marxism, like any other ideology, cannot do without utopias. These utopias are the moral stimuli in the endeavor to change the existing world of alienation.

Rejecting the acquisitive model of the bourgeois economists that reduces all social goals to the accumulation of private wealth, Marx readily assumes that the abolition of market economy based on profit and avarice will neces-sarily lead to the abolition of fetishist relations and the transcendence of alienation. Capitalism is condemned because it generates production and ex-change directed to ends that are totally alien to human needs. In capitalism, work becomes exclusively a matter of physical survival rather than "life's prime want."[160] The satisfaction of egoistic needs and the motive of those who exchange their labor for alienated products must be denounced *in toto*. Attributing the alienating effects of capitalist economy to the "fetishistic char-acter of the world of commodities," Marx makes no allusion to the possibility that similar alienating effects also could be observed in communist society.[161] In *Communist Manifesto*, he and Engels indicate the appearance of inten-sified forms of alienation only in modern bourgeois societies without ever envisaging the appearance of similar phenomena in so-called classless society.[162] There is no evidence, however, that alienation will disappear after capitalism is abolished. Although modern workers are materially better off in communist societies and no longer condemned to starvation and physical exhaustion as in the last century, they are still alienated and exploited. Exploi-tation should not be conceived merely in terms of money and private profit, but also in terms of human dignity, personal freedom, and spiritual values without which the worker's reification is inevitable. Some liberally minded Marxists readily accept that the working classes in communist societies are frequently exploited and subjugated to alien powers.[163]

Although orthodox Marxists claim that the abolition of the capitalist class and the socialization of the means of production will terminate all forms of alienation, the fact is that alienation remains a dilemma that will continue to torture the minds of capitalist and communist ideologists alike. Some forms of alienation may be transcended, but it is surely illusory to believe in total dea-lienation that Marx sometimes envisages in the classless society. Any realistic appraisal of communist societies shows no evidence of any imminent change in human nature, no indication of expected equality and freedom, and, indeed, no visible sign of the transcendence of legal, philosophical, and religious realms.[164] Equally, there is no empirical evidence that the state and dictatorship of the proletariat are only temporary phenomena. The idea of the disappearance of the state, like the idea of the abolition of religion, belongs to the dream world and has nothing to do with "actual facts." It is fantasy to believe, as some of Marx's fanatical followers do, that because the ruling proletariat has "full confidence in the superiority of communist ideas," the dictatorship of the proletariat will neither interfere with personal freedoms nor suppress free ideas.[165]

The belief that the dictatorship of the proletariat is compatible with "personal freedoms and free ideas" has been rejected strongly by many genuine Marxists, including Waclaw Machalski. He and Mikhail Bakunin, the apostle of anarchist collectivism, have always believed that "the despotism of a minority" can never express the will of the people and that by definition this despotism can only intensify alienation. In Machalski's view, the workers in communist societies ruled by the dictatorship of the proletariat "will not have the privilege of having their own government even after the disappearance of the capitalists." The existence of political and economic "crude communism" in communist societies is visible proof that these societies represent a regression; thus, they cannot transcend alienation. As Marx himself indicates in *Manuscripts of 1844*, this thoughtless communism is the expression of private property and the societies based on greed and avarice, capitalist and communist alike, are necessarily involved in the process of alienation. However, Marx does not realize that alienation cannot be abolished solely by change in man's socioeconomic conditions. It can only be mitigated by man's deliberate resistance to irrational, coercive, and inhuman actions. Misled by Hegel's dialectic of "the negation of the negation" that has inspired his economic analysis of contradictions in *Capital*, Marx does not realize that alienation is a complex phenomenon that must be associated with human nature and only indirectly with "the movement of private property."[166] Any meaningful transcendence of alienation and human suffering will depend primarily on moral change within human beings themselves and on their determination to create an open society based on mutual trust and co-operation. Marx seems aware of the significance of moral change in the process of dealienation when he speaks of "fully-developed humanism," although he deliberately avoids being involved in "moral ideals and principles." It is not "communism as such," he concludes, but "fully-developed humanism" that can eliminate bestiality, prostitution, and barbarism and can promote culture and civilization.

Conclusion

The concept of alienation has a long and complex history, dating back to pre-Christian times. As used originally by theologians and philosophers, the term *alienation* denoted almost any conceivable form of malaise involving some spiritual, psychological, or mental imbalance of man. For them, alienation is rooted in human nature and thus is inherent in the finite character of human existence. Most non-Marxist writers maintain that self-alienation is an ontological fact characterizing man's limitations and the dislocation of his inner life. These are expressed in his powerlessness and helplessness, his lack of control over his own life activity, the feeling of isolation, or in the loss of personal identity, autonomy, and meaningful striving. In the Judeo-Christian tradition, alienation or estrangement is associated with the "sinfulness of the human heart" and personal antagonism to the known will of God. Following this tradition, Hegel believes that alienation is a phenomenon of consciousness, involving an inherent dissociation of man as subject and object. Self-alienation, in his view, is not simply a feeling of distance between subject and object, spirit and nature, but also man's awareness of his incapacity to achieve his spiritual goals by his own efforts. In Hegel's philosophical system, self-alienation is not an entirely negative phenomenon. Manifesting itself in nature, the Absolute somehow enriches his own being and the process of the alienated world and estranged man "implies a passing from the state of revolt and separation to that of reconciliation."[1] This is essentially a Christian idea of the estrangement of man from his divine source, resulting in redemption.

Contrary to Hegel's idealist conception of alienation as a healthy externalization of spirit, the Young Hegelians have focused their attention on negative, dehumanizing aspects of man's estrangement. Bruno Bauer and Feuerbach have blamed religion for causing and maintaining this estrangement. Rejecting Hegel's view that nature is a self-alienated form of Absolute Spirit, Feuerbach argues that man is alienated from his own being only when he creates in his mind the image of a transcendental Being and attributes to it "the essential qualities of man himself."[2] Similarly, Bauer sees in religion the objectified immaturity of man that is reflected in a tragic split in his consciousness and in a divided and confused self. While Feuerbach and Bauer analyze alienation in terms of religion or philosophy, Hess is the first Young Hegelian to treat alienation in terms of economic and social life. Like Proudhon, Hess believes that money could be as alienating and dehumanizing as belief in a supernatural Being. In the atmosphere of implicit or explicit secularization of religious and psychological ideas of alienation, it has been relatively easy for

Marx to use some of Feuerbach's ideas of religious alienation and some of
Hess's ideas of economic alienation in his own theory of the estrangement of
the laborer.

Marx's conception of alienation is a mixture of incongruous elements taken
from both idealist and materialist expositions of human misery and powerlessness. Most of his ideas about estrangement originate from Hegel's *Phenomenology of Spirit*. These ideas form the background of Marx's essentialist
theory of alienation expounded in *Manuscripts of 1844*. Although in this work
he is principally concerned with the alienation of the worker, of "real men in
their actual alienation," like Hegel, he also speaks of the estrangement of
man from his own "spiritual essence, his human being." All forms of alienation are, in fact, seen as different aspects of man's self-alienation or different
aspects of the alienation of man from his essence or nature. As in Hegel's
theory, man's history is described as a process of humanization passing
through a phase of alienation and resulting in restoration of man's true essence. This concept of alienated history and the essentialist idea of alienation
have been abandoned by Marx in his mature writings. The picture of alienated labor in *Manuscripts*, reflected in the estrangement of man from his
essential being, his life activity, and nature and society, has become a scenario
of exploitation and dehumanization described in Marx's later works.[3] Here
alienation is seen as a feature of a particular mode of production. The forms
of alienation differ from each class, but the most dehumanizing form is
located in capitalism in which the worker is treated as "the most wretched of
commodities." Thus in Marx's philosophical system alienation ends in the
diametrical inversion of its original psychological and religious meaning. The
fact that his conception of human alienation resists, as some modern Marxists indicate, psychological therapy demonstrates that he has ultimately decided to transform the idea of alienation into the more intelligible concept
of exploitation.[4]

In *Manuscripts of 1844*, Marx repudiates Hegel's identification of alienation
and objectification, indicating that objectification or object-making is not in
itself alienating. Man-made products are alien and hostile because in object-
making "the human being objectifies himself inhumanly."[5] Marx takes for
granted that only in capitalist society objectification entails alienation. Otherwise, he seems to suggest, objectification is a perfectly legitimate process
through which men externalize themselves in society and nature. Yet, Marx's
laudatory remark about Hegel's positive ideas of "the self-creation of man as
a process, of objectification as loss of the object, as alienation and transcendence of this alienation" is vague. While in *Grundrisse* he clearly rejects the
identification of objectification and alienation, in *Manuscripts of 1844* he
seems to agree with Hegel's position.[6] Many commentators, including the
existentialists, maintain that Marx has never disputed the Hegelian thesis that
man creates himself in a process of self-negation. Marx criticizes Feuerbach
for failing to conceive "the sensuous world as the total living sensuous activity

of the individuals composing it" and insists that materialism must be combined with Hegel's keen insight into the active self-making of the human race throughout history or into the self-creation of man as a process in the world of alienation. Marx believes the entire movement of history gradually leads to "the actual act of creation of communism." Being the last antagonistic form of socioeconomic evolution, capitalism is destined to beget, "with the inexorability of a law of nature, its own negation."

In his essentialist theory of alienation as expounded in *Manuscripts of 1844*, Marx regards alienation as a dislocation of man's essential nature and the loss of personal identity. In this work he is as interested in man's inner conflict as he is in the inability of man to realize himself in work. Starting with the analysis of estrangement as a psychological phenomenon, Marx then discusses the estrangement of the worker from his labor. Contrary to Hegel and Feuerbach, he argues that alienation is not a metaphysical phenomenon. The alienation of man in general, as conceived in Feuerbach's theory, is an abstraction. Equally illusory and irrelevant to Marx's theory of real alienation is Hegel's conception of the "estrangement of the real essence of man or of self-consciousness."[7] Marx, however, connects his conception of alienation with "the movement of private property," division of labor, and commodity exchange. In his view, alienation is rooted in a "concrete" relationship between man and his products, between man and society, and between man and nature. He agrees with Hegel that the creation of objects is essential to the realization of the objective forces of human nature. Marx criticizes Hegel and Feuerbach, however, for their failure to explain alienation historically. Man experiences "real alienation" in the socioeconomic context, not in abstraction. The *German Ideology* reaffirms the view, already indicated in *Manuscripts of 1844*, that transcendental concepts of alienation are incompatible with the ideas of historical materialism. This materialism is based on the belief that "there exists a materialist connection of men with one another" and that this connection "is determined by their needs and their mode of production."[8]

Generally, Marx's theory of alienation causes confusion because he never defines the term alienation itself. He merely describes the socioeconomic conditions under which men are dehumanized, exploited, and estranged. In his philosophical system, alienation is related to "real men with their feet firmly on the solid ground" and to "real existing object."[9] In alienation, the objective conditions produced by labor power dominate their producers and in the inversion process the subjects become objects and the objects become subjects, confronting them as a hostile and alien power.[10] The concept of the labor process is of primary significance to Marx's theory of alienation because it is in the light of this process that he tries to explain "the increasing value of the world of things" and "the devaluation of the world of men."[11] This inversion of values, Marx believes, is the distinguishing feature of capitalism that "dissolves the human world into a world of atomistic individuals who are inimically opposed to one another."[12] Capitalism alienates because it is based on the contradiction between "property and propertylessness." In Marx's theory of alienation, contradictions emerge when men cannot control the objective relations in their socioeconomic structure and when the reproduction of material life "appears as a process of dispossession from the standpoint of labour or as appropriation of alien labour from the standpoint of capital."[13]

Marx rejects the spiritual and psychological causes of alienation and argues that the estrangement of man is a consequence of the act of production. Unfortunately, his thought in this respect is far from being a unitary process. While in the *Manuscripts of 1844* alienation is associated with "the movement of private property," in the *German Ideology* it is connected with division of labor. The prevalent view in *Manuscripts* is that private property is "a result of estranged labor" rather than its cause. Yet, he also speaks in this work of private property as being "the cause of alienated labour." The fact is that Marx fails to demonstrate the role of private property in the genesis of alienation. In Hegel's view, reality is a logical system in which the causal relations of events and things are linked by necessity. Properly speaking, he says, there is only one cause that is identified with the Absolute or God. Representing the unity and totality of things and events, "the End, God or the Final Cause contains the effect in its own self, remaining at the end of the purely causal relation what it was in the beginning."[14] Marx rejects Hegel's transcendental causes but retains his ideas of reciprocity and necessary connections in the causal relationship between antecedents and consequents.

In Marx's causal theory of alienation, as in Hegel's, the analysis of causal relations can be intelligible only in terms of dialectical movement and necessity. In both cases, necessary connections between antecedents and consequents exist objectively in things and events. Hume's view that the relation of necessary connection between things and events is not observable in human experience and that causation is not an object of demonstrative reasoning is rejected as unwarranted skepticism. Marx, however, is unable to discover any necessary causal link between alienation and "the movement of private property," division of labor, and market exchange in his analysis of the causes of alienation. He merely assumes that there is a link between them, but he never explains their real connections. Like Hegel, he says that their relationships are "reciprocal."[15] Marx entirely ignores the relevance of internal and psychological factors in the genesis of alienation; therefore, his causal theory is unsatisfactory. Many thinkers before and after him have argued that the roots of alienation, like the roots of egoism, pride, and greed, must be sought in man himself, not in the methods of production or in private property. One can argue that all events in the universe are somehow related causally and that any event could be the effect of the multiplicity of causes. Scientists, however, want to know the immediate cause of things and events. This is not always easy, and Marx himself faces this difficulty when he analyzes the

causes of alienation. Not surprisingly, therefore, his causal theory of alienation is so obscure and inconsistent that even Marxists themselves are unable
to form a coherent and unified view and ascertain its real meaning. While
some exegetic expositors interpret Marx as saying that the causes of alienation must be sought in capitalist division of labor and market exchange, others
believe he has located its cause in the system of private property.[16]

Marx's economic theory is a synthesis of different ideas that come mainly
from classical economists, whom he reproaches for "concealing the estrangement inherent in the nature of labour" because they disregard any direct relationship between the worker and production. Emphasizing the importance of
socioeconomic relations in the genesis of alienation, he argues that the relations of production must be grounded in "the concrete," not in "empty abstractions," in concrete social and historical purposive activity, not in mere
appearances. Marx condemns the capitalist system because in it "all the
means for developing production are transformed into the means of domination and exploitation of the producer." Capitalist methods of production, in
his opinion, are so barbarous and inhumane that they "mutilate the worker
into a fragment of a human being."[17] In capitalist production, the worker
"has nothing to expect but a tanning."[18] After the worker becomes a commodity in the labor market, he is alienated, impoverished, crippled, and totally dehumanized. Although both workers and capitalists are alienated, workers are alienated to a greater extent. The capitalist or non-worker, Marx says,
is only in "a state of alienation, of estrangement."[19] As an alien force, the
worker's product cuts him off from the means of livelihood. Marx believes the
principal aim of the heartless capitalist is to use the worker's product for
profit. Contrary to the bourgeois economists, he maintains that the worker
does not receive wages that are equivalent to the labor he sells to the capitalist, and that capitalist receives a higher value than that represented in the
wages paid. In fact, he receives a "surplus value" that is created by labor and
is embodied in capitalist's profit.[20]

Marx's account of economic alienation focuses on the capitalist's "naked
self-interest" and on the movement of private property that "appears to be
the basis and cause of alienated labour." Alienation, he maintains, reaches its
peak in a developed capitalist economy. Yet, his explanation of the emergence of alienation and its development in different types of society is frequently obscure and inconsistent. His ideas of pre-capitalist structures, as
described in *Grundrisse* and *Capital*, are not based on any empirical analysis
of early types of economy and society.[21] Much of what he says about "forms
which precede capitalist production" is inferential and hypothetical. Modern
sociology and comparative anthropology reject Marx's notions of "the simplicity of the productive organism" in the ancient Indian communities and his
ideas of primitive communism. Marx believes wrongly that exchange in primitive society is fundamentally different from modern market exchange and that
primitive societies have had no knowledge of capital relations. He seems to

think that primitive man has shared communal property but has not exchanged any of his products. His antithesis between the private and the communal is exaggerated. He clearly fails to realize the complexity of rights over
property, including property in land, characteristic of primitive agricultural
communities. In spite of his romantic picture of primitive communities, Marx
says nothing about the existence or non-existence of alienation in them.

Many modern critics accuse Marx of vagueness, confusion, exaggeration,
and careless generalization, calling his "primitive communism" a myth based,
apart from some data on ancient Indian communities, on very slender ethnog-
raphic materials. Marx's economic materialism is rejected because it ignores
the role of intellectual factors in social determination. According to Marx,
productive forces are the chief determining factor in historical development.
The so-called superstructure, including religion, law, philosophy, and ideology, "must be explained from the contradictions of material life, from the
conflict between the social forces of production and the relations of
production."[22] Yet, Marx has failed to explain clearly and consistently the
nature of the dialectical connection between productive forces and productive
relations. There is no indication in his works whether social change and
social development should be attributed directly to productive forces or to
productive relations. Both Marxist and non-Marxist commentators remain
widely divided on this issue. Marx's theory that the prevailing mode of production and exchange form the basis of the superstructure and that the economic basis always determines the intellectual and ideological production is
rejected categorically by many critics as being largely speculative and hypothetical. Engels indicates his awareness of the difficulty involved and has
been forced to admit an interaction between "the basis and the various elements of the superstructure."[23]

Economic determination alone can never adequately explain the existence
of religious, philosophic, and socioeconomic forms. Marx, however, believes
that all ideas and concepts are socially and economically determined and that
"men, developing their material production, simultaneously develop, along
with their actual existence, the products of their thought."[24] Rejecting
Hegel's idea of the self as a metaphysical entity, he assumes that the self
involved in the processes of self-alienation and self-realization is essentially
the sentient self striving for the satisfaction of "natural and bodily needs." In
Manuscripts of 1844, Marx speaks of suffering as "an enjoyment of self in
man" when "apprehended humanly." What this self is, he never explains.
The fact is that in his materialist anthropology, the human self is never seen as
the indivisible subject of the processes of knowing, feeling, and willing. His
self is merely a sensuous self which, as in animals, seeks emotional satisfaction. Like Feuerbach and Comte, Marx regards humanity as one great feeling
organism constituted from the social feelings of its different members. Yet, he
does not advocate hedonism. Crude hedonism, he says, is incompatible with
man's dignity. There is a suggestion that human happiness or fulfillment must

be seen as the synthesis or harmony of pleasures rather than "the satisfaction of a single passion."[25]

The weakness of Marx's conception of self-alienation and self-realization is his belief that the essence of man is only "the ensemble of social relations." If the life of self-fulfillment is completely satisfying and the life of self-alienation is completely degrading and dehumanizing, it must be related to a personal and permanent self. Man's personality is his objectivity. Self-expression is always the expression of some permanent qualities of the self. If the self is merely "a bundle or collection of different perceptions" as Hume suggests, then Marx's reduction of the essence of man to the aggregate of social relations would be justified. In that case, his statement "I am not alone, I am another reality than the object outside me" is meaningless. Marx, unlike Bishop Berkeley, is not a solipsist; his world is essentially material. Like Berkeley, however, he seems to believe that the only experiences one can talk about intelligibly or think about are one's own, and whatever is not expressible in terms of actual or possible observations of oneself is not intelligible at all. Marx, however, believes that thought can transcend the sensible in knowing the objects, one of which is the human self.[26] How can the self that is "the ensemble of social relations" be alienated at all, and how can it realize its "essential powers" is never explained. Marx overlooks the fact that the impersonal or objective view of the mental life is self-contradictory. To phenomenalize the self and objectify the subject, as he does, inevitably leads to the negation of personal identity. Consciousness ceases to be consciousness as soon as it is divorced from the conscious subject. In the absence of a unitary, rational self, Marx has no room for moral values and objective morality. The historical appearance of dialectical materialism, he says, "has shattered the basis of all morality, whether the morality of rationalism or of hedonism."[27] Morality, according to Engels, "has always been class-related."[28] Because bourgeois morality is associated with competition and private exchange, it is categorically rejected. For Marx and Engels, morality is always relative and merely phenomenal. Men derive their ethical ideas from "the economic relations in which they carry on production and exchange."[29] Yet, they both predict the coming of a "really human morality which stands above class antagonism." Marx assumes the existence of "independent morality," the morality that "is based on the consciousness of human dignity."[30] It is on this assumption that he is able to condemns "capitalist vice and immorality."[31] Without the assumption that capitalist alienation and exploitation are intrinsically evil, he would have no ground for condemning capitalism as "an alien and inhuman force." Marx condemns morality of the oppressors, but he fails to realize that the ethics of domination is also inherent in his historicist moral theory.

Being the product of socioeconomic conditions, morality, religion, and philosophy, according to Marx, have no independent development and no history: they are determined by "a definite development of their productive forces." It is in the light of historical materialism that he analyzes all moral and religious phenomena. Hegel maintains that "Christianity is the religion of absolute freedom" and that "only a thinking being can have a religion."[32] By contrast, Marx speaks of Christianity and Judaism as the ideologies responsible for the "estrangement of man from himself and nature." Both are treated as class ideologies in which "the realisation of the human essence is only imaginary." Marx and Engels believe all religions are "a fantastic reflection of supernatural forces," "an inverted world of consciousness," and a symptom of alienation. It never occurs to them to think that man cannot live permanently on fictions and that religion reveals a vast wealth of aspiration for individual and social harmony, happiness, and progress. If the universe were entirely meaningless, then the destruction of religion would be justified. All known races have a religion, and social anthropologists now generally agree that religion is a universal phenomenon. After all, religious forces, as Durkheim rightly remarks, are human and moral forces.[33] Religion contains "eternal elements," and, he adds, it is a reality. Intellectually, man might be at home with nature because her order seems to reflect his own intelligence. Spiritually and morally, however, nature is blind, indifferent, and capricious, never answering the human spirit's questionings and cravings. In every religion, man seeks to establish a helpful relationship between himself and higher powers, and the impulse to form this relationship proceeds from a felt need.[34] The universality of a felt need is at the center of the universality of religion. Marx and Engels, of course, deny that there is such a need and that man can be satisfied by religion of any kind. They maintain that "man makes religion" and that religion always "reflects" the class interests of its adherents. Religion is false because it inculcates belief in what does not exist.[35] They suggest that some Protestant religious ideas have, in fact, promoted the class interests of the early capitalists. Religion, therefore, must be abolished, and only atheism is a natural and inseparable part of humanism or naturalism. Marx is interested mainly in the social functions of religion and says nothing about the origin and development of religious ideas. He merely assumes that religion is a social product, "the self-consciousness of man who has not yet found himself," and that it will definitely disappear in communist society. Rejecting psychology, Marx and Engels never realize that the secret of the nature and growth of religion cannot be found in the external world but only in the human soul itself. Many modern Marxists admit that Marx and Engels have misrepresented religious consciousness and that religion will persist in both class and classless society.

Man's growing capacity to generalize and abstract has been his means of attaining a rational and psychical life. Through thinking and using ideas as the instruments of his will, man has come to know himself as a self-conscious being and thus has attained the status of a voluntary agent and a morally responsible being. In his theory of philosophic alienation, Marx argues that it is not the consciousness of men that determines their social being but, on the contrary, it is their social being that determines their consciousness.[36] The social movement is treated as a process of natural history, governed by laws that are not merely "independent of the will, the consciousness and the purposes of men but, conversely, determine their will, their consciousness and their purposes."[37] Marx, however, does not explain these "laws." Although he asserts that men are not entirely passive in making their history, he still maintains that "they do not make it under circumstances chosen by themselves."[38] Both Marx and Engels are essentially against voluntarism and in favor of determinism that better suits their materialist conception of history. Embarrassed by Marx's determinism, some modern Marxists deliberately twist the meaning of his "inexorable laws" for their own purposes and prefer to speak of "tendencies." To salvage his dialectical theory of alienation, they also speak of the active and anticipatory character of consciousness, suggesting that consciousness is not merely a reflection of material life but also a constitutive element of the determining process. This, of course, is a misrepresentation of Marx's determinist conception of history.

Marx's philosophy is inspired primarily by Hegel's dialectical idealism. He agrees with Hegel that reality is a dialectical process but differs from him in holding that this process is of a material, not of a spiritual, character. Thus Marx's philosophical system is referred to as dialectical materialism. Although he has not coined the expression"dialectical materialism," his philosophic reasoning, as Plekhanov and Lenin indicate, is based on the theory that lies behind this expression.[39] In Marx's view, philosophy is "nothing else but religion rendered into thoughts and thinkingly expounded" and "speculative and mystical empiricism."[40] Therefore, it must be "condemned as another form of the estrangement of the essence of man."[41] After it has come down from "the heaven of speculation to the depth of human misery," philosophy must "unmask self-estrangement in its unholy forms."[42] The philosopher who ignores the facts of the estranged world, he says, "is himself an abstract form of estranged man." Marx sees in workers the protagonists of historical becoming despite their estrangement. Analyzing his philosophical orientation, Althusser points out that all philosophy expresses "a class position" and that Marx's philosophy is based "on a proletarian class position."[43] In Lenin's opinion, all philosophy is fundamentally political, and Marx's materialist philosophy is seen as an indispensable weapon in the class struggle of the proletariat. Positivism and scepticism are identified with "fideism."[44] Only dialectical materialism is regarded as the philosophy of action.

Marx has been called a materialist, and sometimes he speaks of himself as being one, although he prefers to be called "a practical materialist, i.e., a communist" whose mission it is "to revolutionise the existing alien world."[45] Many modern critics maintain that Marxism, strictly speaking, is not materialism at all, and that, although Marx claims it is a monist system, it is nevertheless dualistic. While believing that the essence of reality lies in matter and material production, he also speaks of something that lies "beyond the sphere of actual material production." When he wants to dissociate himself from Hegel's idealist monism and from Feuerbach's "passive materialism," he relies on abstract dichotomies between being and consciousness, the actual and the ideal, theory and practice, a historical beginning and a utopian end. The truth is that Marxism is a synthesis of the contradictory elements derived from idealist and materialist philosophies. On the whole, Marx repudiates abstract idealism and abstract materialism, disavows rationalism and empiricism, and scorns skepticism and positivism; paradoxically, however, he sometimes appeals to "empirical facts" and "materialist categories." His philosophical system is so ambiguous and ambivalent that it can hardly be characterized as a unified whole. Not surprisingly, his theory of philosophic alienation has been dismissed as "unworthy of sober attention" in the English-speaking world. Logical positivists say that Marx's philosophy does not even exist. Some sociologists and anthropologists accept Marx's materialism in a general cultural frame; others reject categorically his materialism but accept the dialectic in a Hegelian form in which ideas, not material forces, are the creative elements. There is almost a general agreement that he has not contributed to the solution of any significant philosophical problem. In spite of the claim by some orthodox Marxists, including Lenin, Marx's theory of knowledge amounts to very little. On the basis of his sporadic references to epistemological questions, he seems to be a protagonist of a common sense view according to which "things exist outside us" and are revealed to us by our senses exactly as they are. Their existence does not depend on our perception of them. Our perception and ideas, Lenin says, are the images of things, and verification of these images "is given by practice."[46] Most philosophers, however, have maintained that physical objects in the world are not "out there" in any ordinary sense, and many believe that they are in some sense dependent for their existence on the perceiving mind.

For Hegel, philosophy, including logic and ontology, is the highest form of science: it "owes its development to the empirical sciences." In return, he says, "it gives their contents what is so vital to them, the freedom of thought—gives them, in short, an *a priori* character."[47] The Absolute, which transcends the dichotomies between theoretical and practical reason, is the basis of philosophical and scientific knowledge. Actuality is knowable because it is the unity "of essence with existence or of inward with outward" and thus is experienced both as a dichotomy and as beyond the dichotomy.[48] Any attempt to postulate an unknown reality behind the known phenomenal world can easily contradict itself. Knowledge of the process of history, which is human experience, is a projected part of the totality of all existence and of all thought. Hegel believes the relationship between philosophy and science is very close. Athough he never defines his concept of science, Marx deplores the alienated relationship between science and philosophy and envisages a reciprocal intertwining of the natural sciences with "the science of man." What exactly this means, he does not explain. The fact is that his idea of the relationship between philosophy and science is so ambiguous that it has pro-voked disagreements among his own followers. Sometimes he looks to natu-ral science as "the archetype of objective truth," but at other times he looks to critical philosophy as the only human agency that can unmask the estrange-ment of man. Althusser, arguing that "Marxist science is not for everyone" but only for those interested in class struggle, defends the unity of philosophy and science as envisaged by Marx in his "science of man."[49] Most of the so-called "scientific Marxists," however, tend to treat Marxism as a new science, assuming that Marx is, above all, a scientist. They believe the task of Marxist science is to aid the workers in their struggle against capitalist exploitation. By contrast, critical Marxists emphasize Marx's conception of alienation, claiming that genuine Marxism does not consist in any specific tenet. Its distinguishing feature is dialectical materialism, and its principal task is the transcendence of alienation.

Marx's conception of one science is peculiar and certainly different from positivist science. His version of unified science has nothing in common with either that of J.S. Mill and Comte or with the later version of logical positiv-ists. On the whole, positivists repudiate Marx's scientism, indicating that his theory of scientific alienation is a mystical and unverifiable hypothesis. They view Marx's conception of "the science of man," as expounded in *Manu-scripts of 1844*, and of "the science of history," as expounded in *German Ideology*, as a mythical representation of science and a utopian ideal mas-querading as a new science. His criteria for a single science, in fact, eliminate real science without replacing it with anything comparable with natural science. Marx's and Engels's insistence that the natural scientist must be "a practical materialist," "a conscious adherent of dialectical materialism," has been rejected by most western scientists. The Marxist claim that "all bourgeois and liberal science defends wage slavery" is considered to be an indication of the transformation of science into class ideology that in "proletarian science" manifestly inhibits freedom of thought.[50] Marxist science, as Lenin and Althusser indicate, is primarily political and ideological. The alienating effects of "state-controlled science" have been demonstrated in the Lysenko's re-fusal to consider the statistical evidence for Mendelism and, indeed, in the refusal of Marxist scientists to accept Pasteur's evidence that living beings cannot be produced experimentally from dead matter. Criticizing "bourgeois science" as a form of alienation, Marx connects his science of history with in-dustry conceived as "the exoteric revelation of man's essential powers."[51] Sometimes he speaks of science as being the equivalent of techology or in-dustry. Some of his fanatical followers, including Bukharin, argue that pure science, as distinct from technology, can only exist in a class society.

The Marxist theory that all science is class science has been rejected cate-gorically by most Western non-Marxist writers and scientists. They maintain that Marxism is a system of belief which, like any narrow ideology, resists the spread of objective knowledge. Marx's "science of man" is fundamentally hostile to natural science, and is not a dealienating science. His idea of a unitary, dealienated science is linked indissolubly with the idea that the true reality of "a human natural being" is social. "The social reality of nature and human natural science or the natural science about man," he says, "are identical terms."[52] Like Aristotle, Marx maintains that man is a social being and that his life is an expression and confirmation of social life. The law of the individual life is also the law of the social life, although in a wider and different application. Full sociability of man, he thinks, is attainable only in a classless society. In capitalism, human individuality has become an article of trade and private exchange. Here men are alienated at every level of society, the proletariat suffering "a total loss of humanity." Social alienation in capitalist society is characterized by contradictions between poverty and wealth, labor and capital, suffering and enjoyment, workers and non-workers. Although the proletariat and property owners "present the same human self-estrangement, the class of the proletariat feels annihilated in estrangement; it sees in it its own powerlessness and the reality of an inhuman existence."[53] Marx condemns capitalism as a system in which men are treated as mere means in the service of things. He regards the capitalist as the most ruthless of exploiters, entirely indifferent to the misery and suffering of those living in poverty.

In capitalist society, Marx argues, "all the means for developing production are transformed into the means of domination and exploitation of the producer."[54] Here the relationship between men depends ultimately on the way things are owned and worked. Capitalist production does not simply produce man in the role of commodity; it also alienates him, mutilates him, and isolates him from society. Social alienation is the result of the tearing away from man the object of his production and of self-estrangement. If "man is estranged from the product of his labour," Marx points out, and if he is "confronted by himself, he is then confronted by the other men."[55] In his view, social relations between men in capitalist society are commercial relations. The mediating process between men engaged in private exchange, he says, is not a social or human process. The power of society that is based on private property inevitably confronts man as an external alien force. Capitalist society is described as a society of greed and egoism in which the poor man "is regressing to the cave dwelling in an estranged, malignant form."[56] Marx argues against liberal individualism and the claim of bourgeois economists that self-interest is the basis of society, stressing that self-interest is responsible for social alienation, social inequality, and class conflict. Distinguishing between civil society and human society, he believes that civil society is one of "private individuals who regard other men as a means and themselves become the tool of alien powers."[57] Civil society as such develops only with the bourgeoisie. It is, therefore, a society of class antagonism and, Marx adds, the last form of social organization in which class antagonism will take place. In it, "the so-called rights of man are the rights of egoistic man." Marx insists that emancipation from social alienation requires the total transformation of civil or bourgeois society. Because this society is based on class conflict and separates man from "his communal being" and "from other men," it must be destroyed.

"The condition for the emancipation of the working class," and thus the condition for abolishing social alienation, in Marx's view, "is the abolition of all classes."[58] Marx's ideal is a classless society that will end pre-history and the history of class struggles and initiate the true history of mankind. This ideal, as many critics indicate, is as utopian and illusory as his conception of primitive communism. Marx's assertions about the history of human society developing dialectically from primitive communism through feudalism and capitalism to proletarian communism are *a priori* and purely inferential. Without offering any empirical evidence, he takes for granted that communism is "the riddle of history solved." Only in communism, he says, will the full sociability of the human individual be realized. This, of course, is only a utopian dream. In fact, Marx's original humanism has been transformed into anti-humanism, just as his early philosophical communism has been transformed into revolutionary communism. Marx has never grasped the paradox of individual freedom. He believes wrongly that a society without private property must be a society of personal liberty. In communist practice, as we know today, there is no room for this liberty. Advocating "the principles of critical and open Marxism and humanistic and self-managing socialism," the Yugoslav *praxis* philosophers, including Marković and Stojanović, criticize the communist authorities for the lack of "intellectual freedom" without, surprisingly enough, blaming Marx. "Totalitarian practice," Stojanović indicates, is the result of "totalitarian interpretations of Marx."[59] Stojanović, however, overlooks the fact that these interpretations arise from Marx's own misconception of freedom. In *German Ideology*, Marx maintains that "personal freedom" can only be realized through the "subjugation" of all human individuals to the will of "revolutionary proletarians."[60] In *On the Jewish Question*, he links the right to liberty with egoism, self-interest, and private property.[61] Analyzing social alienation in capitalist society, Marx overlooks the possibility that the negation of capitalism may lead to the emergence of an entirely new class that is neither proletarian nor capitalist. He assumes that men in communist society will somehow radically change their nature.

The ideological movement of the nineteenth century has obviously influenced Marx's own theoretical development. His involvement in a bitter polemic against political economism, liberal individualism, "critical criticism," and "true socialism" has prevented him from seeing that the movement of private property is not the primary source of alienation. His fanatical adherence to "dialectical materialism" has led him to believe that society moves from one "inevitable" conflict to another and that communism is the "last stage of human development." He has, in fact, always looked for dialectical causes of alienation without being willing to consider any other causes. In his writings, he never stops advocating the primacy of economic factors over political organization of men. Marx believes the development of productive forces and their conflict with productive relations alone can explain social evolutions and political revolutions. On the whole, the state is seen as the indispensable "mask and weapon" protecting the economic interests of the ruling class. In his analysis of political alienation, civil or bourgois society is an aggregate of men unrelated "by any other social bonds but the naked self-interest." In capitalist socioeconomic structure, the state represents and defends the competing and egoistic interests of the rich. Like all products of human alienation, the bourgeois state is the product of man's position in bourgeois society and the guarantor of commodity production based on private exchange. As the political community of men, the bourgeois state, Marx maintains, is nothing but "a committee for managing bourgeois intertests."[62]

Marx's writings reveal his failure to formulate a consistent theory of the state. Contrary to Hegel, who advocates the necessity of the existence of the state and its superiority over civil society, Marx argues for the superiority of civil society and ultimately for total abolition of the state. The state is seen as "an abstraction and the people as the concrete." The political state, Marx believes, is an expression of human alienation *par excellence*. The bourgeois state is incapable of fulfilling its ideal of universality or its promise of political emancipation. This is, he thinks, because in the bourgeois state man does not interact freely with other men and because in his political alienation man is simply "an abstract citizen." In *Critique of Hegel's Philosophy of Right*, Marx reproaches Hegel for separating the state from civil society and for treating the state as being superior to civil society—"its immanent end."[63] Believing that the state is "mind objectified," Hegel says that "if the state is confused with civil society, then it follows that membership of the state is something optional."[64] Marx refers to Hegel's primacy of the state as "an inversion."

In his early writings, Marx advocates the existence of the democratic state. "Only democracy," he says in his *Critique of Hegel's Philosophy of Right*, "is the true unity of the general and the particular."[65] In later works, notably in *Critique of the Gotha Programme*, however, he speaks of democracy in derogatory terms and regards it as an instrument of class domination. Because "the present-day state is a fiction," he insists it must be abolished. When under communism, the state "becomes the real representative of the whole of society," then, Engels indicates, "it renders itself unnecessary" and "will be replaced by the administration of things."[66] Marx speaks similarly of the need to change "the old civil society by an association which will exclude classes and antagonism." In communist society, he says, "there will be no more political power properly called."[67] The main contribution of Marx's political analysis to political theory has been to stress that politics tends to perpetuate the power of the ruling class. It is unfortunate that he sees this tendency only in the bourgeois state, taking for granted that communism will eliminate political alienation and that "the positive transcendence of private property" will result in "the positive transcendence of all alienation." Failing to recognize the possibility of a truly socialist democratic state, he stresses the need for revolutionary action rather than reformism as the instrument for social and political change. Communism, he admits, cannot be realized without revolution and violence, and these need the backing of the proletariat. The communists, he and Engels state in *Communist Manifesto*, declare openly that alienation and oppression can be transcended "only by the forcible overthrow of all existing social conditions." Borrowing the idea of a universal class from Hegel, Marx and Engels incorrectly describe the proletarian movement as "the self-conscious movement of the immense majority." This movement can only survive when controlled by a dictatorship.

The dictatorship of the proletariat, as Marx conceives it, is a form of political transition from the "bourgeois state" to "a higher phase of communist society" or stateless communism.[68] The conception of this transition has never been defined; therefore, all serious critics view it as a purely utopian ideal. Not surprisingly, both Marxists and non-Marxists remain divided over man's final condition in Marxist eschatology. This eschatology is based on faith and speculation, not empirical facts or objective scientific observations. The fact is that Marx's conception of the final goal of human development and his philosophical premise that allows the transcendence of alienation are metaphysical and *a priori*. He fails to explain the meaning of "the return of man to his human or social existence" in any other but a mystical, *a priori* way. Few of his predictions have been realized. The ideological world has not been transcended. Men are still alienated and exploited not only in capitalist society but also in communist society. The antithesis between mental and physical labor has not been transcended. Economic inequality, mania for riches, social conflicts, suppression of freedom, and class structure still exist in both capitalist and communist societies. Marx's expectation that alienation would disappear after the transcendence of private property has not materialized.

Marx has arrived at his ideas of the transcendence of alienation metaphysically, not empirically; therefore, there is no way of proving whether these ideas are true or false. The concepts of his theory of alienation do not reflect a directly observable. The theory is criticized for its failure to explain the transcendence of alienation in realistic and historical terms rather than in terms of *"credo ut intelligam."* Marx seems to have been satisfied with theoretical solutions, letting his followers put them into *praxis*. Unfortunately, this *praxis* has many interpretations, each claiming to be the true Marxism but actually leading mostly to political monstrosities, intolerance, lust for riches and political power, alienating bureaucracy, and purges in the existing communist states. It is arguable, of course, whether Marx himself would condone these practices, but many of his statements suggest that he would. He has taught his followers to sneer at individual freedom, associating it with egoism and capitalism. Marx's view of political freedom is obscured by his ideas of "revolutionary dictatorship of the proletariat." Once dictatorial power is centralized in the hands of revolutionary leaders, they easily dismiss democracy as a "useless and harmful toy."[69] Marx's social theory may have helped "to shorten and lessen the birth pangs" of the working classes in communist societies, but it has failed to eliminate alienation and result in freedom. As a result of his abstract juxtaposition of necessity and freedom, like Hegel whom he follows in this respect, Marx has not reconciled "the realm of freedom and the realm of necessity." In practical politics, recognition of necessity for the citizens of the communist states means, in fact, blind obedience to supreme authority or "compulsory freedom."

Notes

Among the abbreviations of the titles of Marx's and Engels's writings used in this work, the most important are:

"Comments on James Mill = "Comments on James Mill's Elements of Political Economy," in *CW.*
Crit. of Pol. Econ. = *A Contribution to the Critique of Political Economy.*
CW = Marx and Engels; *Collected Works*, vol. 3.
EPM or *Manuscripts of 1844* = *Economic and Philosophical Manuscripts of 1844.*
GI = *The German Ideology.*
HF = *The Holy Family.*
Manifesto = *Manifesto of the Communist Party.*
In *On Religion* = Marx and Engels, *On Religion.*
In One Vol. = Marx and Engels; *Selected Works in One Volume.*
PP = *The Poverty of Philosophy.*

Introduction

1. See Jung, "Basic Postulates of Analytical Psychology," in *The Structure and Dynamics of the Psyche*, p. 352.
2. See Hegel, *The Phenomenology of Spirit*, section on self-alienated spirit, pp. 294–300.
3. Hegel, *Lectures on the Philosophy of Religion*, 3:1, 37.
4. See Kolakowski, *Main Currents of Marxism*, preface to vol. 1: *The Founders.*
5. Maximilien Rubel, *Rubel on Karl Marx*, ed. Joseph O'Malley and Keith Algozin (Cambridge: Cambridge University Press, 1981), p. 19.
6. Cf. J. G. Merquior, *Western Marxism* (London: Granada Publishing, 1986), p. 186.
7. See Gouldner, *The Two Marxisms*, p. 6.
8. Cf. Berdyaev, *The Beginning and the End*, p. 149.
9. German, *The Theory That Transforms the World*, p. 15.
10. Cf. Gouldner, *The Two Marxisms*, p. 59.
11. Polanyi, *Personal Knowledge*, p. 297.
12. Cf. Moore, *Marx on the Choice between Socialism and Communism* (Cambridge: Harvard University Press, 1980), p. 7.
13. Cf. *GI*, p. 65.
14. Cf. *Crit. of Pol. Econ.*, preface.
15. See Althusser, *For Marx*, pp. 239–40.
16. Ibid., pp. 167, 198.
17. See German, *The Theory That Transforms the World*, p. 62.
18. See Kant, *Critique of Pure Reason*, preface to 2nd ed., and pp. 34–35.
19. *Critique of Pure Reason*, preface to 2nd ed.
20. See *Intro. to the Crit. of Hegel's Phil.*, in *CW*, 3:175–76.
21. The Soviet Marxists seem to prefer the phrase "scientific communism" to the phrase "scientific socialism" used by Engels. See German: *The Theory that Transforms the World*, pp. 11–15.
22. Tucker, *Philosophy and Myth in Kant Marx*, p. 161.
23. Lenin, *Marx, Engels, Marxism*, p. 115.
24. Cf. Engels: *Anti-Dühring*, second preface written in 1885, after Marx's death.
25. See Lenin, *Marx, Engels, Marxism*, p. 15.

26. Although Marx's disciple, Berdyaev later became a strong Russian critic of Marxist orthodoxy and dogmatism.
27. See *Manifesto*, section II, p. 61, and section III, pp. 89–91.
28. See German: *The Theory That Transforms the World*, pp. 101–2.
29. See Polanyi, *Personal Knowledge*, p. 227; cf. Engels, *Dialectics of Nature*, p. 62, and *Anti-Dühring*, pp. 168–69.
30. See Marx, *Grundrisse*, pp. 221–224.
31. Cf. *On the Jewish Question*, in *CW*, 3:174.
32. Cf. Hegel, *Philosophy of Mind*, pp. 551, 284; Feuerbach, *Essence of Christianity* pp. 14, 63; Marx, *Intro. to the Crit. of Hegel's Phil.*, first 2 passages.
33. Cf. Kolakowski, *Main Currents of Marxism*, 1:263; Avineri, *The Social and Political Thought of Kant Marx*, introduction (Cambridge University Press), 1970; McLellan, *The Thought of Kant Marx*, pp. 69–70.

Chapter 1. Theory of Alienation

1. See "Elementary Forms of Religious Life," in *Durkheim on Religion*, p. 142.
2. Cf. Durkheim, "Religious sentiment at the present time," in *Durkheim on Religion*, p. 182.
3. Plato, *Republic*, pp. 210–12.
4. Ibid., pp. 207–9.
5. Ibid., p. 292.
6. Ibid., p. 42.
7. See Ps. 51:1–5; 14:3; Prov. 13:5–6.
8. See Matt. 7, 11; John 8:7.
9. Rom. 8:22.
10. Cf. St. Paul's epistle to the Gal. 5:20–31.
11. Gal. 2:22–23.
12. Rom. 5:12.
13. Ps. 51:3, 5.
14. Jer. 44:3.
15. Ezek. 7:10, 20.
16. Hos. 8:4.
17. Cf. Fromm, *The Sane Society*, pp. 121–22. Here idolatry and alienation are seen as synonymous terms.
18. Judg. 2:14.
19. Cf. Kierkegaard, *Purity of Heart* (New York: Harper & Brothers, 1961) p. 119.
20. Augustine, *Confessions* (Harmondsworth: Penguin Books, 1961) pp. 324, 330.
21. Cf. Dante, *Monarchy & Three Pol. Letters*. Pt. *Monarchy*, Bk. 1, chap. 8, p. 13.
22. Cf. Dante, *The Divine Comedy*, III Paradise, canto 7, p. 108.
23. Aquinas, *Selected Writings*, pp. 139–40.
24. Ibid., p. 250.
25. Ibid.
26. Ibid., p. 288.
27. Quoted by E. B. Hamley, *Voltaire*, chap. 24, p. 182. *Inter alia*, Hamley's work, contains extracts from Voltaire's *Philosophical Dictionary*. This Dictionary deals with several philosophical subjects (it is not an ordinary dictionary) and is also available in English, published in New York and London: The Century Company, 1925.
28. See Voltaire "Bien, tout est bien," in his *Philosophical Dictionary*, in E. B. Hamley: *Voltaire*, chap. 23, p. 169 (see bibliography).
29. Cf. *Intro. to the Crit. of Hegel's Phil.*, in *CW*, 3:175–76.
30. Rousseau, *Émile*, p. 22.
31. Ibid., the fifth sentence at the beginning.
32. Rousseau, *The Social Contract*, bk. 1, chap. 4.
33. Cf. Churchich, *The Ethics of Reason in the Philosophical System of D. Obradovich*, p. 19.
34. Engels, *Dialectics of Nature*, p. 24.
35. Engels, "Outlines of a Critique of Political Economy," in *EPM*, p. 177.

36. See Berdyaev, *The Beginning and the End*, pp. 63, 87.
37. Hegel, *Phenomenology*, pp. 252, 548.
38. Cf. Hegel, *Lectures on the Philosophy of Religion*, 3:1.
39. Hegel, *Phenomenology*, p. 14.
40. Ibid., p. 10.
41. Hegel, *Lectures on the Philosophy of Religion*, 3:1–2; 37; 41–42.
42. Hegel, *Phenomenology*, sec. 673, 410.
43. Ibid., sec. 490, 299.
44. Hegel, *Phenomenology*, sec. 485, p. 295.
45. Ibid., sec. 486, p. 295.
46. Ibid., sec. 778, p. 470.
47. *HF*, p. 207.
48. Feuerbach, *The Essence of Christianity*, p. xxxv.
49. Ibid., pp. 80–82.
50. *GI*, pp. 44, 46.
51. Ibid., p. 46.
52. Ibid., p. 115.
53. Ibid., pp. 488–89.
54. *EPM*, pp. 155–56.
55. Hegel, *Logic*, sec. 193, p. 256.
56. Ibid., sec. 194, p. 260.
57. *EPM*, p. 157.
58. *GI*, p. 42; cf. *Crit. of Pol. Econ.*, preface.
59. Ibid., p. 43.
60. *EPM*, p. 158.
61. Hegel, *Phenomenology*, sec. 485, p. 295.
62. Cf. Berdyaev, *The Beginning and the End*, pp. 60–63. His view that objectification has nothing to do with perception or sensation is impossible to reconcile with Marx's conception of objectification.
63. Sartre, *Existentialism and Human Emotions*, pp. 37, 50.
64. Ibid., p. 50.
65. *EPM*, p. 164.
66. Cf. Nicolaus's preface to *Grundrisse*, p. 50.
67. Ibid., p. 832.
68. Cf. Hegel, *Lectures on the Philosophy of Religion*, 3:37.
69. Cf. editor's introduction to *EPM*, Moscow ed.
70. This is discussed in some detail by Tucker, *Philosophy and Myth in Kant Marx*, pp. 165–76; see esp. pp. 175–176; 144, 218–21.
71. Althusser, *For Marx*, pp. 56, 58.
72. *EPM*, p. 170.
73. Lefebvre, *Dialectical Materialism*, p. 78.
74. Marx, *Capital* 1:53; and *EMP*, p. 103.
75. Cf. *EPM*, pp. 152, 156.
76. *GI*, pp. 98, 103, 172.
77. This is implied in St. Paul's words "The whole creation groans with pain" (Rom. 8:22). The Hegelian dialectic is not merely a dialectic of the spirit but also a dialectic of existence.
78. Sartre, *Existentialism and Human Emotions*, p. 15.
79. Cf. Popper, *Open Society and its Enemies*, 2:93.
80. Jung, "The Stage of Life," in *The Structure and Dynamics of the Psyche*, p. 388.
81. Jung, "Basic Postulates" and "The Real and the Surreal," in pp. 352, 384.
82. Jung, "Basic Postulates," in ibid., pp. 351–52.
83. Hegel, *Lectures on the Philosophy of Religion*, 3:366.
84. Cf. *GI*, pp. 45–47, and Feuerbach, *Essence of Christianity*, pp. 1–7.
85. *GI*, p. 46.
86. See Marx's letter to J. B. Schweitzer, 24 January 1865.
87. *GI*, p. 69.
88. Ibid., p. 45.
89. See "Feuerbach and End of Classical German Philosophy," in *On Religion*, p. 216.
90. Ibid., p. 211.

91. Ibid., p. 212.
92. *EPM*, p. 155.
93. Ibid., p. 157.
94. Ibid., p. 165.
95. Bell, *The End of Ideology*, pp. 365–366. This view is rejected by Mészáros in *Marx's Theory of Alienation*, pp. 228–229, in which he denies any "radical break" in Marx's development (p. 232). Bell, he says, merely borrows his ideas from Tucker.
96. Tucker, *Philosophy and Myth in Karl Marx*, p. 174.
97. For a useful, although not always coherent, discussion of this theme see ibid., pp. 165–176. Mészáros somewhat maliciously states that Tucker's work is "full" of contradictions and inconsistencies. See Mészáros, *Marx's Theory of Alienation*, p. 332.
98. Marx, *Manifesto*, p. 84.
99. *EPM*, p. 111.
100. Ibid., p. 151.
101. See Althusser, *For Marx*, p. 227.
102. *EPM*, p. 108.
103. Ibid.
104. Ibid., p. 158.
105. Ibid., pp. 74–76.
106. Ibid., p. 158.
107. "Wage Labour and Capital," *In One Vol.*, p. 80.
108. *EPM*, 106; cf. p. 158.
109. Ibid. p. 74.
110. Ibid., p. 108.
111. Ibid., p. 101.
112. Ibid., p. 74.
113. Ibid.
114. Cf. Ibid., pp. 150, 74, 156.
115. Cf. Hegel, *Logic*, sec. 81, pp. 116–17 and Marx, *Capital*, 2nd ed., preface.
116. See Col. 3:9–10 and 1 Cor. 4:16.
117. Hegel, *Lectures on the Philosophy of Religion*, 3:58, 304.
118. Hegel, *Philosophy of History*, p. 27.
119. Marx, *Capital* 1:169.
120. "Theses on Feuerbach," no. 11, in *GI*.
121. *PP*, p. 135.
122. *EPM*, p. 157.
123. Ibid., p. 105.
124. Cf. McMurtry, *The Structure of Marx's World-View*, p. 30.
125. Plekhanov, *The Development of the Monist View of History*, p. 123.
126. Ibid., p. 219.
127. Ibid., p. 217.
128. *GI*, pp. 62, 64.
129. Ibid., p. 69.
130. Cf. Althusser, *Lenin, Philosophy*, p. 22, and *For Marx*, pp. 228–29 in which the term *masses* is replaced by *productive forces and relations*. See also Tucker, *Philosophy and Myth in Karl Marx*, pp. 173, 176, and Bell, *The End of Ideology*, pp. 365–66, where the concept of classes appears.
131. *EPM*, p. 68.
132. Ibid.
133. Marx, *Grundrisse*, p. 458.
134. Ibid., p. 453.
135. *EPM*, p. 83.
136. Cf. Althusser, *For Marx*, p. 249; and Gilbert, *Marx's Politics*, p. 110.
137. *Manifesto*, p. 83.
138. Cf. *Intro. to Crit. of Hegel's Phil.*, in *CW*, 3:176.
139. Cf. *EPM*, pp. 96, 100.
140. Cf. Marx, *Capital* 1:169; and *Manifesto*, p. 48.
141. *GI*, Marx's marginal note, p. 49.

142. See Ibid., p. 42.
143. Ibid., preface, p. 29.
144. Cf. *EPM*, p. 156.
145. Kolakowski, *Main Currents of Marxism*, 1:172–73.
146. Mészáros, *Marx's Theory of Alienation*, pp. 227–32.
147. Ibid., p. 233.

Chapter 2. Causes of Alienation

1. See Hegel, *Logic*, sec. 153–56, pp. 215–19.
2. Ibid., p. 217.
3. Cf. Kant, *Critique of Pure Reason*, 2:321–22.
4. Ibid., pp. 322, 326.
5. Ibid., p. 322.
6. Descartes, "Principles of Philosophy," in *A Discourse on Method*, pp. 172, 233. God cannot be, he says, the cause of errors (p. 176).
7. *GI*, p. 419.
8. *EPM*, pp. 68–69.
9. Cf. Althusser, *Lenin and Philosopy*, pp. 163–64.
10. Cf. Althusser, *For Marx*, p. 198.
11. Cf. Fromm, *The Anatomy of Human Destructiveness*, p. 313.
12. Berdyaev believes that alienation is simply the ejection of the spiritual world into a state in which causality operates from without. See *The Beginning and the End*, p. 65.
13. Garaudy, *The Alternative Future*, p. 71.
14. Believing that the "communist conception" of human nature is based on "an untenable illusion," Freud argues that "our evils" and aggression are inherent rather than created by private property. See *Civilization, Society and Religion*, pp. 303–4, 338.
15. Cf. Fromm, *The Sane Society*, p. 28, and *Anatomy of Human Destructiveness*, pp. 619–620.
16. See Jung, "On Psychic Energy," in *The Structure and Dynamics of the Psyche*, pp. 29–30.
17. Ibid., pp. 19, 24, 27.
18. Cf. Jung, "The Soul and Death," in ibid., pp. 414–15.
19. Cf. Jung, "On the Nature of Dreams," in ibid., p. 281.
20. Cf. Jung, "Basic Postulates," in Ibid., p. 342.
21. See Jung, "General Aspects of Dream Psychology," in Ibid., pp. 279–80.
22. By using Marx's man-nature concept, Lefebvre thinks he has resolved the problem of "causal determinism" without realizing that this problem cannot be resolved in terms of necessitarian naturalism. Cf. Lefebvre, *Dialectical Materialism*, p. 144.
23. Cf. *EPM*, pp. 155, 68–69.
24. See Engels, "On the Condition of England," in *CW*, 3:460.
25. Hume, *A Treatise of Human Nature*, 1: (bk. 1, pt. 3) 89.
26. Kant, *Critique of Pure Reason*, 2:222–23.
27. Ibid., p. 326.
28. Ibid.
29. Lenin, *Materialism and Empirio-Criticism*, p. 147.
30. Ibid., p. 142. Lenin quotes a few lines from Mach's *Mechanics*.
31. Ibid., p. 145.
32. Ibid., pp. 138–39.
33. See Feuerbach, *Essence of Christianity*, p. 43.
34. Lenin, *Materialism and Empirio-Criticism*, p. 139.
35. Engels, *Dialectics of Nature*, p. 231.
36. Cf. Engels, *Anti-Dühring*, p. 249.
37. Engels, *Dialectics of Nature*, 230.
38. Ibid.
39. Engels, *Anti-Dühring*, pp. 31–32.
40. Ibid., p. 30.
41. Ibid., p. 32. Cf. Lenin, *Materialism and Empirio-Criticism*, p. 139.

42. Ibid., p. 231.
43. Hegel, *Logic*, sec. 153, p. 215.
44. Ibid., sec. 153, p. 216.
45. Ibid., sec. 156, p. 219.
46. Ibid., sec. 235, p. 291.
47. Cf. *GI*, pp. 36–37, and *Crit. of Pol. Econ.*, preface.
48. Cf. Hegel, *Logic*, sec. 204, p. 268.
49. Cf. hegel, *Logic*, sec. 142, p. 200.
50. *EPM*, p. 169.
51. Cf. *GI*, pp. 166, 188.
52. Cf. Hegel, *Logic*, sec. 205, p. 270.
53. *GI*, p. 166.
54. *EPM*, p. 161.
55. Ibid., p. 170.
56. See sec. 777, pp. 469–470.
57. *GI*, p. 43.
58. Cf. *EPM*, p. 68.
59. Cf. *GI*, p. 47.
60. Cf. Althusser, *For Marx*, p. 207.
61. See Spinoza, *Ethics*, p. 23.
62. Hegel, *Logic*, sec. 147, pp. 208–9.
63. Ibid., sec. 35, pp. 55–56.
64. Ibid., sec. 145, p. 205.
65. Cf. Sartre, *Being and Nothingness*, p. 180.
66. Cf. Althusser, *For Marx*, p. 207.
67. Cf. Hegel, *Logic*, sec. 154, p. 217.
68. Feuerbach, *The Essence of Christianity*, p. 40.
69. *GI*, p. 49.
70. Berkeley, "Principles of Human Knowledge," in *A New Theory of Vision and Other Writings*, p. 138.
71. *EPM*, p. 94.
72. *Crit. of Pol. Econ.*, p. 211.
73. *GI*, p. 42.
74. Marx, *Capital* 1:12.
75. *Crit. of Pol. Econ.*, p. 20.
76. *On the Jewish Question*, in *CW*, 3:172.
77. *EPM*, p. 68.
78. Marx, *Capital* 2:844.
79. "Condition of 18th-century England," in *CW*, 3:476.
80. Cf. *EPM*, pp. 61–62.
81. Ibid., pp. 36–37, 67; cf. Marx, *Capital* 1:10–16.
82. *EPM*, p. 80.
83. Ibid., p. 80.
84. Ibid.
85. Ibid.
86. Ibid., pp. 82, 103.
87. Ibid., p. 83.
88. Cf. "Condition of 18th-century England," in *CW*, 3:476.
89. Engels, *Dialectics of Nature*, pp. 230–32.
90. Hegel, *Logic*, sec. 156, pp. 218–19.
91. *EPM*, pp. 80–81.
92. *GI*, p. 175.
93. Hume, *A Treatise of Human Nature*, 1:163.
94. See Hegel, *Logic*, sec. 81, pp. 116, 118.
95. *EPM*, p. 103.
96. *GI*, p. 52.
97. *EPM*, pp. 127–30.
98. Cf. *GI*, pp. 52–53.
99. Ibid., p. 53.

100. Ibid., p. 50.
101. Cf. Hegel, *Logic*, sec. 115, p. 167.
102. Cf. Plamenatz, *Marx's Philosophy of Man*, p. 151.
103. Cf. *GI*, p. 53.
104. Marx, *Capital* 1:373.
105. "Marx's Comments on James Mill," in *CW*, 3:219–20.
106. Cf. Roberts and Stephenson, *Marx's Theory of Exchange*, pp. 92–93.
107. See *EPM*, p. 134.
108. Ibid., p. 135.
109. Cf. *HF*, p. 46.
110. *EPM*, p. 137.
111. Ibid., p. 129.
112. Cf. "Marx's Comments on James Mill," in *CW*, 3:228.
113. *EPM*, pp. 78, 149.
114. Ibid., p. 126.
115. Ibid., pp. 79, 83.
116. Ibid., p. 119.
117. Marx, *Grundrisse*, p. 221.
118. Ibid., p. 188.
119. Cf. Marx, *Capital* 1:85.
120. Ibid., p. 270.
121. Ibid., 1:526.
122. *EPM*, p. 140.
123. Ibid., p. 133.
124. Ibid., p. 115.
125. Hegel, *Phenomenology of Spirit*, p. 468.
126. *On the Jewish Question*, in *CW* 3:164.
127. Marx, *Grundrisse*, p. 222.
128. Cf. 1 Tim. 6:10.
129. Cf. *On the Jewish Question*, in *CW* 3:172–74.
130. Cf. "Psychological Factors Determining Human Behaviour," in *Structure and Dynamics*, p. 116.
131. Cf. Fromm, *The Anatomy of Human Destructiveness*, p. 282.
132. Cf. Mészáros, *Marx's Theory of Alienation*, p. 143.
133. Cf. Fromm, *The Anatomy of Human Destructiveness*, p. 71.
134. Cf. Spinoza, *Ethics*, pt. 3, 138.
135. See Marx, *Grundrisse*, p. 163; and *EPM*, p. 107.
136. See *GI*, p. 465.
137. Marx, *Grundrisse*, p. 222.
138. Cf. Ibid., and Spinoza, *Ethics*, pt. 3, p. 139.
139. Cf. *PP*, p. 137, and *HF*, pp. 161–62.
140. See *PP*, p. 171.
141. *GI*, pp. 41–42, 61, 166.

Chapter 3. Economic Alienation

1. Locke, *Of Civil Government*, bk. 2, sec. 40, p. 136.
2. Smith, *Wealth of Nations*, vol. 1, bk. 1, chaps. 2, 12.
3. *EPM*, p. 94.
4. *PP*, p. 115.
5. *EPM*, p. 103.
6. Marx, *Capital* 2:848.
7. "Comments on James Mill," in *CW* 3:220.
8. *EPM*, p. 103.
9. *PP*, p. 97.
10. Cf. *EPM*, p. 163.
11. See Ibid., p. 146.

12. Cf. "First Thesis on Feuerbach," in *GI*, p. 615.
13. Cf. *Crit. of Hegel's Phil*, in *CW* 3:105.
14. *EPM*, p. 152.
15. Marx, *Grundrisse*, p. 102.
16. GI, pp. 99–100.
17. Ibid., p. 99.
18. Marx, *Grundrisse*, p. 491.
19. *GI*, p. 99.
20. *EPM*, p. 115.
21. *Manifesto*, pp. 44–45.
22. Marx, *Grundrisse*, p. 266.
23. Ibid., p. 274.
24. Ibid.
25. Cf. Hegel, *Logic*, sec. 81, p. 116, and Marx, *Capital*, 2nd ed., preface.
26. Cf. Ibid., sec. 11, p. 15.
27. Cf. Ib., sec. 81, p. 118.
28. See *GI*, the second passage in the footnotes crossed out in the manuscript.
29. *EPM*, pp. 151–152.
30. *Crit. of Pol. Econ.*, p. 34.
31. *EPM*, p. 69.
32. See *Crit. of Pol. Econ.*, p. 35.
33. *EPM*, p. 25.
34. *EPM*, pp. 115–17.
35. Ibid., p. 30.
36. *EPM*, pp. 26–29.
37. Ibid., p. 67.
38. Ibid.
39. Ibid., p. 70.
40. See *CW* 3:407.
41. See *EPM*, p. 34, where Marx quotes from Buret.
42. Ibid., p. 29.
43. Ibid.
44. Ibid., p. 67.
45. Ibid., p. 69.
46. Ibid., p. 71.
47. Ibid., p. 72.
48. Ibid., pp. 70–71. Cf. Ollman's commentary in *Alienation*, p. 143.
49. Ibid., p. 71.
50. Ibid., p. 70.
51. Ibid., p. 69.
52. Ibid.
53. Ibid., p. 149.
54. See *EPM*, p. 69, where the term *congeal* is used instead of *embody*, thus making the meaning even less intelligible. Cf. Plamenatz's comment in *Marx's Philosopy of Man*, p. 118. *Congeal* appears only in the Moscow edition.
55. *EPM*, p. 70.
56. Ibid., p. 84.
57. Ibid., p. 72.
58. Ibid.
59. Ibid., p. 126.
60. Ibid., p. 22.
61. Ibid., p. 118.
62. Ibid., p. 36.
63. Ibid., p. 83.
64. Ibid., pp. 20, 24.
65. Ibid., p. 41.
66. Ibid., p. 43.
67. Ibid., p. 194
68. Ibid., p. 198.

69. Ibid., p. 119.
70. See Mat. 6:19–20.
71. Cf. Amos 2:7; 4:1; and *EPM*, p. 106.
72. *EPM*, p. 106.
73. Cf. Marx, *Grundrisse*, p. 107, and *EPM*, pp. 36, 40, 84.
74. Marx, *Grundrisse*, p. 252.
75. Marx, *Capital* 1:232.
76. Marx, *Grundrisse*, p. 257.
77. Ibid., p. 258.
78. Ibid.
79. Marx, *Grundrisse*, p. 331.
80. Ibid., p. 330.
81. Ibid., p. 172.
82. Ibid., pp. 85–86.
83. Marx, *Grundrisse*, p. 87.
84. Ibid.
85. Ibid., p. 99.
86. Ibid., pp. 99–100.
87. Marx, *Capital* 2:552.
88. Marx, *Capital* 1:460.
89. Marx, *Capital* 2:713.
90. Marx, *Capital* 1:451.
91. Ibid., p. 81.
92. Marx, *Grundrisse*, p. 308.
93. Ibid., p. 274. Marx is postulating the opposites even in exchange only to suit his dialectical purposes.
94. Marx, *Grundrisse*, p. 275.
95. Marx, *Grundrisse*, p. 307.
96. Ibid.
97. Marx, *Capital* 1:154.
98. *Capital* 1:213–14.
99. Ibid., p. 214.
100. Ibid.
101. Marx, *Capital* 2:651.
102. Marx, *Grundrisse*, p. 385.
103. Marx, *Grundrisse*, p. 762.
104. "Wage Labour and Capital," in *In One Vol.*, p. 81.
105. Marx, *Grundrisse*, pp. 326–27.
106. See "Marx's Wage Labour and Capital," in *In One Vol.*, Introduction.
107. See *Crit. of Pol. Econ.*, in *CW* p. 27; cf. Aristotle, *Politics*, chap. 9, 1257a, p. 15; and Smith, *The Wealth of Nations*, chap. 4, p. 25.
108. *Crit. of Pol. Econ.*, p. 43.
109. Ibid., p. 35.
110. Ibid., p. 42.
111. Ibid., p. 41.
112. Marx, *Grundrisse*, p. 225.
113. Ibid., p. 324.
114. Ibid.
115. See "Wage Labour and Capital," in *In One Vol.*, p. 87; Cf. Smith, *The Wealth of Nations*, ch. 7, p. 48.
116. Ibid., p. 86.
117. Marx, *Capital* 2:600.
118. "Wages, Price and Profit," in *In One Vol.*, p. 223.
119. Cf. "Wages, Price and Profit," in *In One Vol.*, p. 214.
120. Ibid., p. 211.
121. Cf. Ibid., and Marx, *Grundrisse*, p. 419.
122. Cf. "Wages, Price and Profit," in *In One Vol.*, p. 200, and *The Wealth of Nations*, 1:77.
123. See "Wage Labour and Capital," in *In One Vol.*, p. 84.
124. Cf. "Wage Labour and Capital," in *In One Vol.*, p. 77.

125. Marx, *Capital* 2:634.
126. Cf. Ibid., p. 627.
127. See Ibid., p. 619.
128. Ibid., pp. 790, 846.
129. Marx, *Capital* 1:165.
130. Marx, *Grundrisse*, p. 231.
131. Ibid., p. 240; cf. Smith, *The Wealth of Nations*, chap. 4, p. 24.
132. Marx, *Capital* 1:131.
133. See *CW* 3:172.
134. Ibid.
135. See Marx, *Capital* 1:82–83.
136. Marx, *Capital* 2:653.
137. Ibid.
138. Marx, *Capital* 1:46.
139. Ibid., p. 50.
140. Marx, *Grundrisse*, p. 239.
141. Marx, *Capital* 1:50.
142. Cf. Plamenatz, *Marx's Philosophy of Man*, p. 463.
143. Marx, *Capital* 2:846.
144. Ibid., p. 714.
145. Marx, *Capital* 2:698–708.
146. Cf. Djilas, *The Unperfect Society*, pp. 34, 138.
147. See *EPM*, p. 25.
148. Cf. Marx, *Capital* 1:232; and *EPM*, p. 119.
149. Marx, *Grundrisse*, p. 701.
150. Ibid., pp. 708–9.
151. See Marx, *Capital* 1:418ff.
152. Ibid., p. 434.
153. Cf. Marx *Capital* 1:433, 461.
154. Ibid., p. 410.
155. Cf. Sabine, *A History of Political Theory*, p. 657.
156. Cf. Croce, *Historical Materialism and the Economics of Karl Marx*, p. 65.
157. Marx, *Grundrisse*, p. 339.
158. Cf. Marcuse, *One-Dimensional Man*, p. 28.
159. Cf. Djilas, *The Unperfect Society*, p. 38, and Sartre, *The Communists and Peace*, pp. 74–85.
160. See *EPM*, pp. 29, 81.
161. See *EPM*, p. 83.

Chapter 4. Self-Alienation and Self-Realization

1. Rom. 7:15–19.
2. Cf. Churchich, *The Ethics of Reason*, p. 25.
3. *EPM*, p. 165.
4. Rom. 3:9.
5. *EPM*, p. 126.
6. Ibid., pp. 157–58.
7. Ibid., p. 72.
8. "Comments on James Mill," 3:220.
9. Ibid., p. 214.
10. Hegel, *Philosophy of Right*, p. 33.
11. Hegel, *Logic*, sec. 163, p. 227.
12. Hegel, *Philosopy of History*, p. 35.
13. Hegel, *Philosophy of Right*, sec. 132, p. 88.
14. Hegel, *Phenomenology*, pp. 111, 520.
15. Ibid., sec. 484, p. 294.
16. Hegel, *Logic*, sec. 96, p. 141.

17. Hegel, *Phenomenology*, sec. 484, p. 294.
18. Hegel, *Philosophy of Mind*, sec. 384, p. 19.
19. Hegel, *Phenomenology*, sec. 489–91, pp. 298–99.
20. Hegel, *Philosophy of Mind*, sec. 384, p. 19.
21. Hegel, *Logic*, sec. 24, p. 38.
22. Hegel, *Phenomenology*, pp. 111–13.
23. Ibid., sec. 486, pp. 295–97.
24. *EPM*, p. 153.
25. *GI*, p. 47.
26. See Feuerbach, *Essence of Christianity*, pp. 13–14.
27. *GI*, p. 47.
28. *EPM*, pp. 152–53.
29. "Theses on Feuerbach," in *GI*, no. 1.
30. *EPM*, pp. 153–56.
31. *Ibid.*, p. 72.
32. Ibid., p. 72.
33. Ibid., p. 73.
34. Ibid., p. 29.
35. "Comments on James Mill," 3:228.
36. *EPM*, p. 126.
37. Ibid., p. 35, where Marx quotes from Buret.
38. See *EPM*, p. 126.
39. See Ibid.
40. Ibid., p. 80.
41. Ibid., pp. 80, 106.
42. "Comments on James Mill," 3:217.
43. *EPM*, p. 79.
44. Ibid., p. 75.
45. Cf. Feuerbach, *Essence of Christianity*, pp. 1–3, and Hegel, *Logic*, sec. 24, pp. 37–38. See *EPM*, p. 77.
46. *EPM*, p. 74; cf. Hegel, *Logic*, sec. 24, p. 38.
47. Ibid.
48. Feuerbach, *Essence of Christianity*, p. 3.
49. *EPM*, p. 112.
50. Ibid., p. 121.
51. Marx, *Grundrisse*, p. 159.
52. *EPM*, p. 120.
53. Ibid., p. 166.
54. Ibid., p. 24.
55. Ibid., p. 73.
56. Ibid., pp. 70, 94.
57. Ibid., p. 86.
58. Ibid., pp. 73, 77.
59. Ibid., p. 86.
60. Ibid., p. 158.
61. Ibid., p. 73.
62. Ibid., p. 83.
63. See *Crit. of Pol. Econ.*, p. 192.
64. Marx, *Grundrisse*, p. 499.
65. Marx, *Capital*, 1:170.
66. *EPM*, p. 116.
67. Ibid., p. 76.
68. Marx, *Capital*, 1:170.
69. Marx, *Capital*, 3:820 (Moscow ed.)
70. Hegel, *Logic*, sec. 147, p. 209.
71. *HF*, p. 162. Ibid., p. 238.
72. *GI*, p. 87.
73. *EPM*, p. 111.

74. Ibid., p. 166.
75. Ibid., p. 108; and "Theses on Feuerbach," no. 1, in *GI*.
76. *EPM*, p. 158.
77. Ibid., p. 74.
78. Ibid., p. 76.
79. Ibid.
80. Ibid., p. 105.
81. Feuerbach, *Essence of Christianity*, p. 16.
82. Hegel, *Philosophy of History*, p. 24.
83. Ibid., p. 22.
84. *EPM*, p. 151.
85. Ibid., p. 105.
86. Ibid., p. 76.
87. Ibid., p. 76.
88. Ibid.
89. Ibid., p. 72.
90. Ibid., p. 106.
91. Ibid., p. 76.
92. Ibid., p. 112.
93. Ibid., pp. 89–90.
94. Ibid., p. 77.
95. Ibid., p. 117.
96. *On the Jewish Question*, in *CW* 3:168.
97. "Comments on James Mill," 3:226.
98. *EPM*, p. 153.
99. Ibid., pp. 106–8.
100. Ibid., p. 106.
101. Ibid., p. 89.
102. Ibid., p. 22.
103. Marx, *Capital*, 2:836.
104. "Comments on James Mill," 3:228.
105. See Hegel, *Phenomenology*, preface, pp. 11–12, 14.
106. Ibid., sec. 484–487, pp. 294–97.
107. Ibid., p. 16.
108. *EPM*, pp. 164–65.
109. See *GI*, pp. 46, 57–58.
110. Cf. Ibid., p. 280.
111. Ibid.
112. *EPM*, p. 106.
113. *GI*, p. 280; and *Crit. of Pol. Econ.*, preface.
114. *EPM*, pp. 111–12.
115. Hume, *Treatise of Human Nature*, 2:127.
116. *EPM*, p. 136.
117. *GI*, p. 153.
118. *EPM*, p. 156.
119. Ibid., pp. 152–55.
120. *GI*, p. 280.
121. *GI*, p. 280.
122. "Theses on Feuerbach," in *GI*, no. 6; and *EPM*, p. 156.
123. *EPM*, p. 157.
124. Engels, *Anti-Dühring*, p. 114.
125. *GI*, p. 264.
126. Hegel, *Logic*, sec. 60, p. 90.
127. *GI*, P. 208.
128. *EPM*, P. 114.
129. Cf. Makai, *The Dialectics of Moral Consciousness*, p. 18.
130. *HF*, p. 249. Here Marx shares Fourier's view of morality.
131. These ideas are stressed especially in *On the Jewish Question*, in *CW*.

132. *EPM*, p. 89.
133. "Comments on James Mill," 3:215.
134. Cf. Churchich, *The Ethics of Reason*, p. 208.
135. Hume, *Treatise of Human Nature*, bk. 3, pt. 1, sec. 1.
136. Engels, *Anti-Dühring*, p. 114.
137. Cf. Durkheim, *Moral Education*, in Pickering's, p. 194.
138. Engels, *Anti-Dühring*, p. 115.
139. Lenin, "Tasks of the Youth Leagues," in *Marx, Engels, Marxism*, p. 132.
140. Some of these moral ideals have been reiterated at the 21st Congress of the Communist Party of the Soviet Union.
141. Marx, *Capital*, 2:671 n2.
142. Ibid.
143. Engels, Condition of England in Eighteenth Century," in *CW* 3:486.
144. *GI*, p. 437.
145. *EPM*, p. 125.
146. Ibid., p. 121.
147. Ibid., p. 119.
148. Ibid.
149. Cf. Ibid., p. 182; and *GI*, pp. 441–42.
150. "Feuerbach and End of Classical Germ. Phil," in *On Religion*, p. 214.
151. *GI*, p. 441.
152. Ibid., p. 443.
153. *HF*, p. 249.
154. *EPM*, p. 69.
155. Cf. Makai, *The Dialectics of Moral Consciousness*, pp. 164–68, 218, in which these theories, including Ayer's "emotivism," are treated as the expression of class and bourgeois morality.
156. *EPM*, p. 15.
157. Plamenatz; *Marx's Philosophy of Man*, p. 249.
158. *GI*, p. 42.
159. *Neue Rheinische Zeitung*, p. 143.
160. Hegel, *Philosophy of Right*, p. 34.
161. Cf. Lukács, *History and Class Consciousness*, p. 199.

Chapter 5. Religious Alienation

1. Engels, *Socialism*, p. 15.
2. See extracts from Voltaire's article "Atheist" in his *Philosophical Dictionary* in E. B. Hamley: *Voltaire*, pp. 181–82.
3. Sterrett, *Studies in Hegel's Philosophy of Religion*, pp. 19, 22. Sterrett, denies that Hegel was a pantheist.
4. Cf. Hegel, *Lectures on the Philosophy of Religion*, 3:21, 176.
5. Accusing him of idealism, Engels still praises Bauer for his attempt to solve the question of the historical origin of Christianity. See "Bauer and Early Christianity," in *On Religion*, pp. 170–71.
6. Feuerbach, *Essence of Christianity*, preface.
7. "Feuerbach and End of Classical German Philosophy," in *On Religion*, p. 197.
8. Feuerbach, *Essence of Christianity*, pp. 97–98.
9. Ibid., p. 63.
10. Ibid., p. 263.
11. Ibid., p. 46.
12. Feuerbach, *Essence of Christianity*, p. 14.
13. *HF*, p. 117.
14. "Feuerbach and End of Classical German Philosophy," in *On Religion*, pp. 208, 210.
15. *GI*, p. 66.
16. Feuerbach, *Essence of Christianity*, p. 284.
17. Stirner, M., *The Ego and His Own*, translation from the German by Steven T. Byington

with an introduction by J. L. Walter (London: A. C. Fiefield, 1912), pp. 228–29. Stirner believes both Feuerbach and Marx represent the secularized theological spirit, merely substituting the sanctity of man for the sanctity of the heavenly God.
18. *GI*, p. 254.
19. Ibid., p. 35.
20. Ibid.
21. *EPM*, p. 19.
22. "Feuerbach and End of Classical German Philosophy," in *On Religion*, p. 216.
23. *HF*, p. 130.
24. *Crit. Hegel's Phil.*, in *CW* 3:175.
25. Ibid.
26. "God exists only for the man who thinks," Hegel says. See Hegel, *Lectures on the Philosophy of Religion*, 3:11.
27. *Crit. Hegel's Phil.*, in *CW* 3:182.
28. Percy Bysshe Shelley, English poet, 1792–1822.
29. *Crit. Hegel's Phil.*, in *CW* 3:176.
30. Ibid., p. 175.
31. "The personality of God is merely the projected personality of man." See Feuerbach, *Essence of Christianity*, p. 226.
32. *Crit. Hegel's Phil.*, in *CW* 3:175.
33. *EPM*, p. 164.
34. *GI*, pp. 170, 172.
35. *Crit. Hegel's Phil.*, in *CW* 3:176.
36. Hegel, *Lectures on the Philosophy of Religion*, 3:228.
37. See *GI*, p. 154. Here Marx quotes Lucrecius, whose view he obviously shares.
38. *EPM*, p. 158.
39. See Ibid., p. 103.
40. *GI*, p. 562.
41. *Crit. Hegel's Phil.*, in *CW* 3:175.
42. *EPM*, p. 114.
43. See Ibid., p. 107.
44. "Theses on Feuerbach," in *GI*, p. 4.
45. "Outlines of a Crit. of Pol Econ.," in *EPM*, p. 177.
46. *GI*, p. 101.
47. *Crit. Hegel's Phil.*, in *CW* 3:175.
48. Hegel has several different definitions of religion. In *Philosophy of Mind*, sec. 551, and *Phenomenology*, sec. 672, religion is defined as "the consciousness of absolute truth and of absolute Being."
49. Feuerbach, *Essence of Christianity*, p. 9.
50. Marx's letter to Feuerbach, 3 October 1843, in *CW* 3:351.
51. Marx, *Capital* 1:54.
52. Ibid., 1:53–54.
53. Engels, *Anti-Dühring*, p. 374.
54. Ibid., p. 375.
55. Ibid., p. 410.
56. Religious philosophers prefer the term *awe* or *the numinous* to fear, indicating the feeling of respect for the Godhead. Cf. Waterhouse, *The Philosophical Approach to Religion*, pp. 16–17.
57. Engels, *Anti-Dühring*, p. 376.
58. *Crit. Hegel's Phil.*, in *CW* 3:176.
59. Engels, *Anti-Dühring*, p. 41.
60. See *Feuerbach and End of Classical German Philosophy*, in *On Religion*, p. 212.
61. *HF*, p. 221.
62. *EPM*, p. 105.
63. See Hegel, *Logic*, sec. 221; cf. Hegel, *Lectures on the Philosophy of Religion*, 3:58–60.
64. Engels, *Dialectics of Nature*, p. 295.
65. Cf. John 12:24 and I Cor. 15.
66. Cf. Hegel, *Lectures on the Philosophy of Religion*, 3:304.
67. *HF*, p. 223.

68. Cf. *On the Jewish Question* and *Crit. of Hegel's Phil.*, in *CW* 3:174, 176.
69. See "Comments on James Mill," in *CW* 3:228.
70. Cf. Feuerbach, *The Essence of Christianity*, p. 171.
71. *On the Jewish Question*, in *CW* 3:159.
72. *GI*, p. 42.
73. See Stojanović, *Between Ideals and Reality*, p. 33, and Garaudy, *The Alternative Future. A Vision of Christian Marxism*, pp. 75–85.
74. See *Crit. of Hegel's Phil.*, in *CW* 3:175.
75. Cf. Ibid., and *GI*, p. 67.
76. Marx, *Capital* 1:53.
77. *On Religion*, p. 74.
78. Ibid.
79. Ibid.
80. Engels, *Anti-Dühring*, p. 220.
81. See Marx, *Grundrisse*, p. 232.
82. Cf. Plamenatz, *K. Marx's Philosophy of Man*, pp. 238–43.
83. See Marx's letter to Feuerbach, 11 August 1844, in *CW* 3:355.
84. See "Progress of Social Reform on the Continent," in *CW* 3:399.
85. Cf. "The Condition of England," in Ibid., pp. 447, 472.
86. Tylor's theory that the idea of God is a late conception in human history and Frazer's attempt to derive religion from magic have been refuted by modern social anthropologists. For some excellent references see Hardy, *The Biology of God*, pp. 74–85.
87. Cf. Galloway, *The Philosophy of Religion*, pp. 550–61; and Hardy, *The Biology of God*, pp. 74–87.
88. Polanyi, *Personal Knowledge*, pp. 279–84.
89. Russell, *Religion and Science*, p. 7.
90. Einstein, "Religion and Science: Irreconcilable?" *The Christian Register June* (1948): 19.
91. See Engels, *Dialectics of Nature*, pp. 254–255, 303–6; and *Anti-Dühring*, pp. 90, 442.
92. See Lenin, *On Religion*, pp. 8, 72.
93. According to *Great Soviet Encyclopedia*, Lavoisier was sentenced to death because he was a "staunch supporter of the monarchy."
94. See *Crit. of Hegel's Phil.*, in *CW* 3:176.
95. *EPM*, p. 108.
96. *GI*, p. 63.
97. Ibid., p. 253.
98. Weber, *Soteriology of the Underprivileged*, in *Selections in Translation*, p. 178.
99. There are no means of ascertaining scientifically the original belief about anything. For a good discussion on the origin and growth of religion see Galloway, *The Philosophy of Religion*, pp. 88–145.
100. For an interesting discussion on the weakness of Durkheim's *Elementary Forms of Religious Life*, see *Durkheim on Religion*, pp. 211–300.
101. See his essays "General Aspects of Dream Psychology" and "The Soul and Death," in *The Structure and Dynamics of the Psyche*, pp. 276, 408–9, respectively.
102. See *Crit. of Hegel's Phil.*, in *CW* 3:175–76; cf. *On the Jewish Question*, in ibid., p. 167.

Chapter 6. Philosophical Alienation

1. Holbach and La Mettrie stressed that only a radical break with theological "spiritism" can cure men of their illusions and prejudices. Cf. Churchich, *The Ethics of Reason*, p. 19.
2. *HF*, pp. 154–55.
3. La Mettrie, *Man a Machine*, p. 9.
4. Holbach, *The System of Nature*, p. 303.
5. *HF*, p. 158.
6. See Russell, *History of Western Philosophy*, p. 489.
7. *HF*, pp. 158–59.

8. See Hobbes, *Leviathan*, chap. 31, pp. 274–84. He was buried with Christian rites as a Christian.
9. See F. W. J. Schelling, *System of Transcendental Idealism* (1800), trans. P. Heath (Charlottesville: University Press of Virginia, 1978). See pp. 12 and 219–33. Similarities and differences between Fichte and Schelling are discussed in Vater's introduction, p. xi–xxxvi.
10. Marx's letter to Feuerbach, 3 October 1843, in *CW* 3:350.
11. "Logic coincides with metaphysics, the science of things set and held in thoughts." See Hegel, *Logic*, sec. 24, p. 36.
12. *EPM*, p. 148.
13. Hegel, *Logic*, sec. 19, p. 25.
14. Ibid., sec. 35, p. 55, sec. 96, pp. 141–42.
15. Engels, *Anti-Dühring*, p. 34.
16. Ibid., pp. 34–35.
17. Hegel, *Logic*, sec. 98, p. 144.
18. Hegel, *Philosophy of Mind*, sec. 572, p. 302; and *Logic*, sec. 1, p. 3.
19. See Hegel, *Philosophy of Right*, p. 12.
20. See Hegel, *Philosophy of Mind*, sec. 420, p. 161.
21. *GI*, p. 199.
22. *HF*, p. 238.
23. *EPM*, p. 148.
24. Hegel, *Phenomenology*, pp. 252, 295.
25. *EPM*, p. 153.
26. Ibid., p. 149.
27. *HF*, p. 238.
28. Hegel, *Phenomenology*, sec. 486, pp. 295–96.
29. *EPM*, p. 149.
30. Ibid., p. 150.
31. Ibid., p. 151.
32. Ibid., p. 156.
33. Ibid., p. 165.
34. *GI*, p. 473.
35. *Crit. of Hegel's Phil.*, in *CW* 3:176.
36. Ibid., p. 187.
37. See Althusser, *Lenin and Philosophy*, p. 105.
38. *GI*, pp. 50–51.
39. *PP*, p. 102.
40. *GI*, p. 61.
41. Engels, *Anti-Dühring*, p. 166.
42. Cf. Althusser, *Lenin and Philosophy*, pp. 9, 16; and *For Marx*, pp. 31–33.
43. *HF*, p. 26.
44. Ibid., p. 27.
45. Ibid., pp. 176–77.
46. Ibid., p. 171.
47. *GI*, p. 46.
48. *EPM*, p. 145.
49. *HF*, p. 116.
50. Ibid., p. 50.
51. "Theses on Feuerbach," no. 1, in *GI*.
52. *PP*, p. 180.
53. *EPM*, pp. 145–46.
54. "Theses on Feuerbach," no. 1, *GI*.
55. Engels, "Feuerbach and End of Classical German Philosophy," in *On Religion*, p. 197.
56. Ibid., p. 202.
57. Ibid., p. 203.
58. Ibid., p. 209.
59. See Barth's introduction to *Essence of Christianity*, XII.
60. *HF*, pp. 155–56.
61. Russell, *Problems of Philosophy*, p. 156.

62. Cf. *HF*, p. 104.
63. See Hoffman, *Marxism and the Theory of Praxis*, pp. 33–37.
64. Engels, "Feuerbach and End of Classical German Philosophy," in *On Religion*, p. 192.
65. Ibid., p. 202.
66. Ibid., p. 218.
67. Kant criticizes Leibniz for "intellectualising phenomena" and Locke for "sensualising the conceptions of the understanding." *Critique of Pure Reason*, bk. 2, p. 196.
68. Hegel, *Phenomenology*, sec. 234, p. 141.
69. "Feuerbach and End of Classical German Philosophy," in *On Religion*, p. 219.
70. See "Progress and Social Reform on the Continent," in *CW* 3:404.
71. Lenin, *Marx, Engels, Marxism*, p. 15.
72. Hegel, *Philosophy of Right*, p. 10.
73. Hegel, *Logic*, p. 21. The entire field of philosophy, he says, forms a single science, an idea that deeply impressed Marx.
74. Lenin, *Marx, Engels, Marxism*, pp. 13–14.
75. Ibid., p. 73.
76. See "Comments on James Mill," in *CW* 3:217.
77. See Marx, *Capital*, 2: preface.
78. Hegel, *Phenomenology*, p. 51.
79. See Hegel, *Philosophy of History*, pp. 9, 17; cf. Hegel, *Logic*, p. 33.
80. Lenin, *Materialism and Empirio-Criticism*, p. 309.
81. Engels, *Anti-Dühring*, p. 143.
82. See Hegel, *Philosophy of Mind*, sec. 420, pp. 161–62 and sec. 377, p. 2.
83. It is only "universal self-consciousness" that represents the "union of individuality and universality." Ibid., sec. 425, p. 167.
84. Engels, *Anti-Dühring*, p. 19.
85. "Theses on Feuerbach," in *GI*, no. 1.
86. See Ibid., no. 2.
87. See *EPM*, p. 108.
88. Ibid., p. 108.
89. Cieszkowski, *Prolegomena zur Historiosophie*, Berlin: 1838. This work is not available in English and I do *not* quote from it. Like other commentators, I merely refer to it, giving the name of the work, place and year of publication. As no commentator has given the publisher's name, one must assume that it was published privately.
90. "Feuerbach and End of Classical German Philosophy," in *On Religion*, p. 206.
91. Marx, *Grundrisse*, p. 101.
92. Cf. Hoffman, *Marxism and the Theory of Praxis*, p. 173.
93. Locke, *Essay Concerning Human Understanding*, bk. 4, chap. 2.
94. This is discussed in the second dialogue between Hylas and Philonous. See Berkeley, *New Theory of Vision and Other Writing*, pp. 241–62.
95. *GI*, p. 43.
96. *EPM*, p. 156.
97. *HF*, p. 66.
98. Ibid., p. 67.
99. Lenin, *Materialism and Empirio-Criticism*, p. 55.
100. Ibid., p. 29.
101. See *EPM*, pp. 159–60.
102. "Theses on Feuerbach," in *GI*, no. 1.
103. *EPM*, p. 76.
104. Hegel, *Phenomenology*, sec. 484, p. 294.
105. Reason, Kant says, is the faculty that furnishes us with the principles of knowledge *a priori*, See Kant, *Critique of Pure Reason*, pp. 37–38.
106. Hegel, *Logic*, sec. 10, p. 14.
107. See *GI*, p. 71.
108. *Crit. of Pol. Econ.*, p. 206.
109. Ibid.
110. Ibid., p. 207.
111. See D. D. Weiss's article in *Methodology, Metaphysics and History of Science*, ed. R. S.

Cohen and M. W. Wartofsky, (Boston: Reidel Publishing Co., 1984), following p. 331.
112. "Theses on Feuerbach," in *GI*, no. 1.
113. See Hegel, *Logic*, sec. 24, p. 41.
114. See Hegel, *Philosophy of Mind*, sec. 440, pp. 180–181.
115. Cf. C. Prokopczyk, *Truth and Reality in Marx and Hegel* (Amherst: University of Massachusetts Press, 1980) pp. 66 and 92, who treats Marx's theory of truth in terms of "correspondence."
116. *EPM*, p. 106.
117. Cf. Rose, *Hegel contra Sociology*, pp. 210, 216.

Chapter 7. Scientific Alienation

1. Life in a cellular form, according to Virchow, can only come from pre-existing life, which also has a cellular form. Growth, evolution, disease, and death are varied aspects of cellular behavior. Cf. C. P. Swanson, *The Cell* (New Jersey: Prentice-Hall 1964), pp. 5, 63.
2. Latin *scientia*, German *Wissenschaft*, and Russian *nauka*—all mean knowledge in the wider sense.
3. Cf. Popper, *Conjectures and Refutations*, P. 37.
4. See *CW* 3:143–45.
5. In *PP*, p. 183.
6. Engels, *Anti-Dühring*, p. 107.
7. Lenin, *Materialism and Empirio-Criticism*, p. 117.
8. Cf. Bronowski, *Science and Human Values*, p. 74.
9. See Lenin, *Marx, Engels, Marxism*, p. 54.
10. Scientific facts, George argues, are not independent of human beings, See George, *The Scientist in Action*, pp. 18–20. although they are impersonal in that they are independent of the judgments of any one man.
11. Marx, *Capital* 1: preface.
12. The belief that in science knowledge can be derived from observation alone is entirely false. Cf. Popper, *Conjectures and Refutations*, p. 46.
13. Engels, *Dialectics of Nature*, p. 227.
14. Ibid., p. 229.
15. Hegel, *Logic*, sec. 39, p. 64.
16. Engels, *Dialectics of Nature*, p. 227.
17. *GI*, p. 43.
18. See Feuerbach, *Essence of Christianity*, xxxiii–xxxiv, 2.
19. Quotated by G. Holton and D. Roller in *Foundations of Physical Science*, p. 230.
20. Cf. *EPM*, p. 111.
21. See "Wages, Price and Profit," in *In One Vol.*, p. 207.
22. *EPM*, p. 110.
23. *GI*, p. 482.
24. *PP*, pp. 183–84.
25. See Engels, *Anti-Dühring*, p. 390. (Old Preface).
26. See Marx's letter to Schweitzer, in *PP*, p. 182.
27. *EPM*, p. 110.
28. Cf. Graham, *Between Science and Values*, p. 22.
29. Unfortunately, modern scientists remain divided on this issue. See ibid., p. 10.
30. In his book *The Scientist in Action*, George suggests that physics in some ways is the queen of sciences.
31. Engels, *Dialectics of Nature*, p. 17.
32. Marx's letter to Schweitzer, *PP*, p. 184.
33. *EPM*, p. 110.
34. Ibid., p. 111.
35. Ibid., pp. 111–12.
36. Ibid., p. 111.
37. *GI*, p. 34n.
38. Ibid.

39. There is no agreement as to what these values should be. While Bernal, like Marx, argues for the promotion of "communist values" (see *The Social Function of Science*, pp. 408–15), George maintains that science has nothing to say about the world of values (see *The Scientist in Action*, preface, pp. 68–72).
40. See Bohr, "Light and Life," *Nature* 131 (1 April 1933).
41. Cf. Holton and Roller, *Foundations of Modern Physical Science*, pp. 132–34, 258–60.
42. Engels, *Dialectics of Nature*, p. 62.
43. Ibid., 63.
44. Marx, *Capital* 1:319.
45. Cf. Marx, *Capital* 2: preface to 1st German ed. p. 864.
46. *PP*, p. 105.
47. See Engels, *Anti-Dühring*, p. 17.
48. See Hegel, *Logic*, sec. 81, p. 116.
49. Plekhanov, *Development of Monist View of History*, pp. 74–76.
50. See Holton and Roller, *Foundations of Modern Physical Science*, p. 259. The laws of nature are seen as "descriptions," not as "prescriptions."
51. To be intelligible, Heisenberg argues, quantum mechanics required the abandonment of visualizibility in the micro-world. See Graham, *Between Science and Values*, p. 105.
52. If men knew, Laplace says, "all the forces by which nature is animated, the future, like the past, would be present to their eyes." Cf. Polanyi, *Personal Knowledge*, pp. 141–42.
53. Cf. Engels's *Socialism: Utopian and Scientific*, 1892 ed., pp. 14–15.
54. *EPM*, p. 111.This is a strange statement. All lies are *a posteriori*.
55. Ibid. Marx got the idea of "one science" from Hegel. By "a single science, however, Hegel means philosophy "viewed as a total, composed of several particular sciences." See *Logic*, p. 21.
56. To except science to be impartial in a wage-slave society, Lenin points out, is foolishly naive. In Lenin, *Three Sources and Three Component Parts of Marxism*, p. 7.
57. Cf. German, *The Theory That Transforms the World*, pp. 15–16, 49. Like Lenin, he believes that communism is a science that must be linked with proletarian politics.
58. See Engels, "Feuerbach and End of Classical German Philosophy," in *On Religion*, p. 234.
59. Engels, *Anti-Dühring*, p. 33.
60. See ibid., p. 391. Here Engels mentions Virchow's pamphlet, *Freedom of Science in the Modern State*, published in Berlin, 1877.
61. Cf. Popper, *Conjectures and Refutations*, p. 33.
62. Hegel says that Plato is "the inventor of dialectic." See Hegel, *Logic*, sec. 81, p. 117.
63. *GI*, p. 37n.
64. *EPM*, p. 102.
65. Cf. *GI*, p. 34n.
66. See Lenin, *Marx, Engels, Marxism*, p. 60.
67. Ibid., p. 54.
68. See Althusser, *For Marx*, p. 13.
69. See Althusser, *Lenin and Philosophy and Other Essays*, forward.
70. See Marx's speech at Chartist banquet, 14 April 1856.
71. Marx, *Capital* 1:393.
72. *EPM*, pp. 110–11.
73. See Marx's speech at Chartist banquet, 14 April 1856.
74. Cf. Marx, *Grundrisse*, p. 695, and *PP*, p. 117.
75. See Marx's speech at Chartist banquet, 14 April 1856.
76. See *EPM*, p. 110.
77. Marx, *Grundrisse*, pp. 70–6.
78. Marx, *Capital* 1:526.
79. Cf. *Manifesto*, pp. 53, 56.
80. Cf. L. White's article "The Historical Roots of Our Ecologic Crisis" in *Philosophy and Technology*, ed. C. Mitcham and R. Mackey 260–264.
81. See *PP*, pp. 132–33.
82. Cf. Appleton, *Science and Nation*, p. 3.
83. The pure scientist pursues knowledge for its intrinsic interest, the technologist uses knowledge for a practical end.
84. See Lenin, "The Tasks of the Youth Leagues," in *On Religion*, p. 53.

85. See Lenin, "On the Significance of Militant Materialism," ibid., p. 72.
86. See Plekhanov, *Development of Monist View of History*, pp. 218–19.
87. Marx's letter to Engels, 19 December 1860.
88. Marx, *Capital* 1:392n.
89. Engels, *Dialectics of Nature*, p. 195.
90. See Marx's letters to Engels, 18 June 1862, and 7 August 1866.
91. Engels, *Anti-Dühring*, p. 85.
92. Biologists admit that the secret of the origin of life remains a mystery. We can only specu-
    late about it and nothing else. See Rhodes, *The Evolution of Life*, pp. 88–91.
93. *EPM*, p. 112.
94. Engels, *Anti-Dühring*, p. 91.
95. Engels, *Dialectics of Nature*, p. 297. Pasteur is still regarded as a reactionary scientist in
    communist countries.
96. *Anti-Dühring*, pp. 90–91. Natural science has never claimed to have solved "with certainty"
    the origin of life, let alone the ontogenetic emergence of human intelligence. It is important
    to keep in mind that men think; acids, carbon, and its compounds do not.
97. Ibid., p. 100.
98. Ibid., p. 49. Cf. Graham, *Between Science and Values*, pp. 347–348. Some unsolved prob-
    lems involved in this explanation are discussed in non-Marxist works by S. Rose, *The Che-
    mistry of Life*, pp. 247–54, and J. M. Smith, *The Theory of Evolution*, pp. 95–96.
99. Cf. Young, *A Model of the Brain*, p. 3.
100. Engels, *Dialectics of Nature*, p. 178.
101. Marx's letter to Engels, 7 August 1866.
102. Engels, *Dialectics of Nature*, p. 43.
103. Engels, *Anti-Dühring*, p. 83; and Marx's letter to Engels, 19 August 1865.
104. Engels, *Anti-Dühring*, p. 83.
105. *Nature*, 288 (November 1980): 208, and 288 December 1980): 430.
106. *EPM,* p. 110.
107. Trofim Lysenko rejected Mendelism on the ground that "in science there is no room for
    chance."
108. After cutting off the tails of mice for many generations, Weismann found that the resulting
    progeny still had tails.
109. See Lewis's article "The Abolition of Man" in *Philosophy and Technology*, ed. C. Mitcham
    and R. Mackey, p. 146.
110. Engels, *Dialectics of Nature*, pp. 35–36.
111. Cf. *EPM*, pp. 113–114 and *Crit. of Pol. Econ.*, in *CW* preface.
112. In communist countries, the state controls all scientific research. See Kneen, *Soviet Scien-
    tists and the State*, pp. 5, 64–67.

Chapter 8. Social Alienation

1. See *Capital*, 2nd prefaee.
2. Spencer, *The Principles of Sociology*, 2:447–453.
3. Spencer, *The Man versus the State*, p. 83.
4. Ibid., p. 82.
5. Weber, "Socialism," in *Selections in Translation*, p. 261.
6. *EPM*, p. 149.
7. *GI*, p. 47.
8. *Capital*, 1st ed., preface.
9. *GI*, p. 41.
10. *Manifesto*, p. 50.
11. Marx, *Capital* 2:627.
12. *EPM*, p. 25; *Capital* 1:522.
13. Marx "Comments on James Mill," in *CW* 3:213.
14. "Comments on James Mill," 3:213.
15. Cf. Ibid., p. 217; and Smith, *Wealth of Nations*, bk. 1, chap. 4, p. 20.

16. Cf. Smith, *Theory of Moral Sentiments*, pt. 1, sec. 1, chaps. 2, 3.
17. *EPM*, p. 133.
18. "Comments on James Mill," 3:226.
19. *EPM*, p. 84.
20. Marx, *Grundrisse*, p. 831.
21. *EPM*, p. 21.
22. Marx, *Grundrisse*, p. 458.
23. Marx, *Communist Manifesto*, p. 63; cf. Marx, *Capital* 2:845.
24. *GI*, p. 52.
25. Ibid., p. 53.
26. Ibid.
27. Ibid., p. 416.
28. *EPM*, p. 102.
29. Ibid., p. 109.
30. *GI*, pp. 417–18.
31. Ibid., p. 43.
32. Cf. Djilas, *The Unperfect Society*, pp. 34–41; and Stojanovic, *Between Ideals and Reality*, pp. 111–13, 208–20.
33. Cf. *Manifesto*, pp. 89–91.
34. Russell, *History of Western Philosophy*, p. 818.
35. Comte, *Positive Philosophy*, vol. 2, bk. 6, chap. 5, pp. 289–98.
36. Durkheim, "Elementary Forms of Religious Life," in *Durkheim on Religion*, p. 145.
37. *Manifesto*, p. 88.
38. *GI*, p. 543; in Marx's article on Karl Grün.
39. Ibid., p. 483.
40. Ibid., p. 457.
41. Marx analyzes these attitudes in *PP*, pp. 114–16.
42. Ibid., p. 101.
43. Marx's letter to P. V. Annenkov, 28 December 1846, in *PP*, p. 168.
44. Marx's letter to P. V. Annenkov, in Ibid., p. 174.
45. Ibid., p. 102.
46. Marx's letter to P. V. Annenkov, in Ibid., pp. 166–67.
47. *GI*, pp. 62–63.
48. Ibid., pp. 41–42.
49. *Crit. of Pol. Econ.*, p. 21.
50. *GI*, p. 82.
51. Ibid., p. 83.
52. Cf. Ibid., pp. 42, 49, 61, 94.
53. Cf. *PP*, pp. 102, 114.
54. See Engels, *Anti-Dühring*, p. 317; cf. *GI*, p. 263.
55. Marx, *Grundrisse*, p. 496.
56. Marx, *Capital* 1:378–79.
57. Cf. Firth's article in Bloch, ed., *Marxist Analysis and Social Anthropology*, pp. 40–41.
58. Engels, *Anti-Dühring*, p. 37.
59. Engels's letter to J. Bloch, 21 September 1890.
60. Engels's letter to C. Schmidt, 27 October 1890.
61. Engels's letter to F. Mehring. 14 July 1893.
62. Marx's letter to Annenkov, in *PP*, p. 166.
63. Marx's letter to Feuerbach, in *CW* 3:355; cf. *PP*, p. 166.
64. Engels, *Anti-Dühring*, p. 315.
65. *GI*, p. 67.
66. *EPM*, p. 77.
67. Ibid., p. 85.
68. *Critique of the Gotha Programme*, in *In One Vol.*, sec. 3.
69. Marx, *Grundrisse*, p. 107.
70. *Manifesto*, p. 40.
71. Ibid., p. 41.
72. Ibid., p. 41.
73. Marx also refers to these "three great classes" in the preface to *Crit. of Pol. Econ.*

74. Marx, *Capital* 1:378.
75. Marx, *Capital* 2:791–92.
76. Ibid., p. 795.
77. For a balanced point of view, see Elster, *Making Sense of Marx*, pp. 318–97, in which Marx's criteria for class distinctions are discussed in some deail.
78. Poverty in itself, Hegel says, does not make men into a rabble. See Hegel, *Philosophy of Right*, additions 149, para. 244, p. 277.
79. Some sociologists, including Weber, postulate a link between class position and bureaucratic authority.
80. *EPM*, pp. 36–37.
81. See Marx, *Grundrisse*, pp. 650–52; and *PP*, pp. 136–38.
82. Marx, *Capital* 2:651.
83. *HF*, pp. 46–47.
84. *GI*, p. 68.
85. See Hegel, *Philosophy of Right*, sec. 303, p. 197.
86. Isa. 49:7–10; 52:13; 53:3–12.
87. *GI*, p. 60.
88. Cf. Althusser, *Lenin and Philosopy and Other Essays*, p. 16.
89. Marx's letter to J. Weydemeyer, 5 March 1852.
90. Marx, *Capital* 1:117.
91. *Crit. of Hegel's Phil.*, in *CW* 3:187.
92. Ibid., p. 186.
93. Ibid. Cf. St. Paul's Epistle to Phil. 2:6–7.
94. *EPM*, p. 105.
95. Cf. *HF*, p. 162.
96. "Comments on James Mill," in *CW* 3:217.
97. See Marx, "A Bourgeois Document," in *Neue Rheinische Zeitung* 1848–49, p. 206.
98. *GI*, p. 465.
99. Ibid., p. 462.
100. Cf. Marx's letter to Annenkov, in *PP*, p. 166.
101. Hegel, *Philosophy of Right*, sec. 145–50, pp. 105–7.
102. *GI*, pp. 89–90.
103. Cf. Berdyaev, *The Beginning and the End*, p. 32.
104. *EPM*, p. 129.
105. Cf. *PP*, p. 158.
106. *On the Jewish Question*, in *CW* 3:174.
107. *HF*, p. 51.
108. Cf. Plamenatz, *German Marxism and Russian Communism*, p. 315.
109. Cf. *GI*, p. 68.
110. "Theses on Feuerbach," no. 10, in *GI*.
111. *EPM*, pp. 117, 125.
112. "Critical Marginal Notes on the Article by a Prussian," in *CW* 3:195.
113. Marx, *Capital* 2:714–15; cf. *PP*, p. 138.
114. *Manifesto*, p. 60.
115. In the Address of the Central Committee to the Communist League, March 1850.
116. *Manifesto*, pp. 87–88.
117. Cf. "'Comments on James Mill," in *CW* 3:221.
118. "Juristic Socialism," in *On Religion*, p. 237.
119. Engels, *Dialectics of Nature*, p. 307.
120. Ibid.
121. Ibid., pp. 307–8. Engels's eulogy of Marx at his graveside in Highgate in London does not minimize Darwin's importance in biology, although he has already changed his view toward the social application of Darwin's theory of struggle for the survival of the fittest.
122. This autobiography appeared in October 1838.
123. Engels, *Dialectics of Nature*, p. 35.
124. See Malthus, *Essay on Population*, preface to 2nd ed.
125. Marx, *Capital*, 2:679–80n.
126. In *Crit. of Pol. Econ.*, Engels refers to Malthus as the originator of this doctrine. See *EPM*, p. 199.

127. *Manifesto*, p. 93.
128. *On the Jewish Question*, in *CW* 3:173.
129. *HF*, p. 140.
130. *On the Jewish Question*, in *CW* 3:164.
131. *The Class Struggles in France* 1848 to 1850, p. 123.
132. *Crit. of Pol. Econ.*, p. 20.
133. Hegel, *Philosophy of Right*, sec. 289, p. 189.
134. "Theses on Feuerbach," no. 10, in *GI*.
135. *GI*, pp. 89–90.
136. Cf. *Manifesto*, p. 41.
137. *Critique of the Gotha Programme*, in *In One Vol.*, sec. 3.
138. *Critique of the Gotha Programme*, in *In One Vol.*, sec. 3.
139. Cf. *EPM*, p. 114.
140. See *Critique of the Gotha Programme*, in *In One Vol.*, sec. 3.
141. Engels, *Anti-Dühring*, p. 128.
142. Ibid.
143. Ibid.
144. *GI*, pp. 525–26.
145. Lenin, *State and Revolution*, p. 94.
146. Ibid., p. 95.
147. See "Civil War in France," in *In One Vol.*, p. 291.
148. Cf. Stojanovic, *Between Ideas and Reality*, pp. 47–48.
149. Cf. Popper, *Open Society and its Enemies*, 2:68.
150. Cf. *GI*, p. 68.
151. *PP*, pp. 110–11.
152. See Norris, *God, Marx and the Future*, p. 91.
153. Cf. Tucker, *Philosophy and Myth in K. Marx*, p. 235.

Chapter 9. Political Alienation

1. See Marx and Engels, *Neue Rheinische Zeitung* 1848–49, p. 97.
2. *GI*, p. 497.
3. *Manifesto*, p. 47.
4. Ibid., pp. 71–72.
5. See Marx and Engels, *Neue Rheinische Zeitung* 1848–49, p. 204.
6. "Civil War in France," in *In One Vol.*, p. 289.
7. Ibid., pp. 285, 287.
8. "Civil War in France," in *In One Vol.*, p. 307.
9. Marx's letter to F. Bolte, 23 November 1871.
10. Marx's letter to F. Bolte, 23 November 1871.
11. *GI*, pp. 210–11.
12. Marx and Engels, *Neue Rheinische Zeitung* 1848–49, pp. 234–35.
13. Ibid., p. 190.
14. Ibid., 185.
15. Ibid., 184–85.
16. Ibid., 76.
17. Ibid., 184.
18. Ibid., p. 222.
19. Ibid., 254.
20. See *Crit. of Pol. Econ.*, preface.
21. *Rheinische Zeitung* ceased publication on 31 March 1843.
22. *Crit. of Hegel's Phil. of Right.*, in *CW* 3:29.
23. Hegel, *Philosophy of Right*, sec. 157, p. 110.
24. Ibid., sec. 155, p. 109.
25. Hegel, *Philosophy of Mind*, sec. 502, p. 248.
26. Ibid.
27. Ibid., p. 279.

28. *Crit. of Hegel's Phil. of Right*, in *CW* 3:28.
29. Ibid., 3:14.
30. Ibid., p. 45.
31. Ibid., p. 81.
32. Ibid., p. 79.
33. *Crit. of Hegel's Phil. of Right*, in *CW* 3:63.
34. Hegel, *Philosophy of Right*, sec. 276, p. 179.
35. Ibid., sec. 265, p. 281.
36. Ibid., p. 279.
37. Ibid., sec. 258, pp. 155–56, and sec. 289, p. 189.
38. *Crit. of Hegel's Phil. of Right*, in *CW* 3:8.
39. Ibid., p. 7.
40. Ibid., p.8.
41. Ibid.
42. Ibid., pp. 8–9.
43. Ibid., p. 122.
44. Cf. Hegel, *Logic*, sec. 131, p. 187.
45. *Crit. of Hegel's Phil. of Right*, in *CW* 3:44.
46. Ibid., pp. 45–46.
47. Hegel, *Philosophy of Right*, sec. 297, p. 193.
48. Ibid., sec. 205, p. 132.
49. *Crit. of Hegel's Phil.*, in *CW* 3:111.
50. Ibid., p. 24.
51. Ibid., p. 109.
52. Ibid., p. 108.
53. Hegel, *Philosophy of Right*, sec. 279, pp. 182–83.
54. Ibid., sec. 301, p. 196.
55. *Crit. of Hegel's Phil.*, in *CW* 3:26.
56. Ibid., pp. 26, 32.
57. *Crit. of Hegel's Phil.*, in *CW* 3:27.
58. Hegel, *Philosophy of Right*, sec. 258, p. 156.
59. Ibid., p. 157.
60. Ibid., sec. 279, p. 182.
61. *Crit. of Hegel's Phil.*, in *CW* 3:57, 87.
62. Ibid., p. 29.
63. Ibid.
64. Ibid., 3:121.
65. Ibid., p. 47.
66. Ibid., p. 61.
67. Ibid., p. 48.
68. *Crit. of Hegel's Phil.*, in *CW* 3:98.
69. Ibid., p. 99. Cf. *EPM*, p. 80. For a similar view, see Hunt, *Political Ideas of Marx and Engels*, 1:75–76.
70. *Crit. of Hegel's Phil.*, in *CW* 3:14.
71. Ibid., p. 13.
72. Ibid., p. 116.
73. See J. M. Barbalet, *Marx's Construction of Social Theory* (London: Routledge & Kegan Paul, 1983), p. 16.
74. *Crit. of Hegel's Phil.*, in *CW* 3:31.
75. Ibid., p. 29.
76. Cf. Ibid., 40.
77. See *EPM*, preface.
78. See *CW* 3:139.
79. Marx's letter to Ruge, May 1843, in 3:137.
80. Ibid., pp. 138, 141.
81. Ibid., p. 144.
82. Ibid., p. 144.
83. Hegel, *Philosophy of Right*, sec. 258, p. 156.

84. Marx, "Critical Marginal Notes" in *CW* 3. Published in August 1844.
85. Ibid., 3:206.
86. Ibid., 3:201.
87. Ibid., 3:198.
88. "Critical Marginal Notes, in *CW* 3:198.
89. Ibid., p. 197.
90. *On the Jewish Question*, in *CW* 3:158.
91. Ibid., p. 159.
92. Ibid., p. 165.
93. Ibid., 3:168.
94. *Intro. to the Crit. of Hegel's Phil. of Right*, in *CW* 3:186–87.
95. Ibid., p. 184.
96. Ibid., pp. 185–86.
97. *Intro. to the Crit. of Hegel's Phil.*, in *CW* 3:187.
98. *EPM*, p. 68.
99. Ibid., pp. 140–41.
100. *On the Jewish Question*, in *CW* 3:172.
101. *EPM*, p. 82.
102. *On the Jewish Question*, in *CW* 3:165.
103. Ibid., p. 160.
104. *EPM*, p. 155.
105. *On the Jewish Question*, in *CW* 3:162.
106. Ibid., p. 164.
107. Hegel, *Philosophy of Right*, sec. 153–55, pp. 109–10.
108. *Manifesto*, p. 63.
109. *On the Jewish Question*, in *CW* 3:162.
110. Ibid., p. 164.
111. Ibid.
112. "The Condition of Eighteenth-Century England," in *CW* 3:504–6.
113. *On the Jewish Question*, in *CW* 3:163, 161.
114. Ibid., p. 162.
115. Ibid., p. 163.
116. Ibid., p. 164.
117. *GI*, p. 52.
118. Ibid.
119. Ibid., pp. 98–101.
120. Ibid., p. 99.
121. Ibid.
122. Ibid.
123. Cf. Tucker, *Marxian Revolutionary Idea*, p. 60.
124. Lenin, *State and Revolution*, pp. 10–11.
125. Ibid., p. 11.
126. Engels, *Origin of Family, Private Property and the State*, p. 231.
127. Ibid.
128. Ibid.
129. Engels, *Anti-Dühring*, p. 330.
130. Ibid., p. 179.
131. *HF*, p. 153.
132. Marx, *Eighteenth Brumaire*, p. 55.
133. Ibid., p. 55.
134. Ibid., p. 103.
135. Ibid.
136. Ibid., p. 114; cf. *Crit. of Hegel's Phil.*, p. 109.
137. "Civil War in France," in *In One Vol.*, p. 287.
138. Marx, *Capital* 1:232.
139. Ibid., 2:627.
140. Marx, *Capital* 1:348.
141. Ibid., p. 346.

142. See Marx, *Capital* 2:651.
143. Marx, *Capital* 1:350.
144. Ibid., p. 379.
145. Ibid. See also R. Firth, "Social anthropology and Marxist views on society," in *Marxist Analysis and Social Anthropology*, ed. M. Bloch, pp. 34–36.
146. See *Manifesto*, p. 44.
147. *Critique of the Gotha Programme*, in *In One Vol.*, IV A.
148. Engels, *Anti-Dühring*, p. 333.
149. Ibid.
150. Lenin, *State and Revolution*, p. 20.
151. *EPM*, p. 101.
152. Lenin, *State and Revolution*, p. 59.
153. Ibid., p. 26.
154. *Manifesto*, p. 74.
155. *Critique of Gotha Programme*, in *In One Vol.*, IV A.
156. Engels, *Anti-Dühring*, p. 136.
157. Ibid., p. 336.
158. See *On the Jewish Question*, in *CW* 3:162.
159. *Critique of Gotha Programme*, in *In One Vol.*, p. 327 IV A.
160. Ibid., p. 328.
161. In *Marx, Engels and Lenin. On Commun. Society*, [Extracts from Their Works. Compiled by T. Borodulina, (Moscow: Progress Publisher, 1978).] p. 133.
162. Marx, *Capital* 1:232.
163. Marx, of course, had no chance to practice his political theory, but there are many hints in his later writings indicating that he is not a democrat. Hunt's exposition of Marx's democratic ideas in *The Political Ideas of Marx and Engels*, Vol. 1, can easily mislead a reader to a wrong conclusion.
164. *Manifesto*, p. 76.
165. In Marx and Engels, *Rheinische Zeitung*, 15 May 1842.
166. Cf. *GI*, p. 211.
167. In the Soviet Union, however, this vision is still credible. See German, *The Theory that Transforms the World*, p. 61. Following the withering away of the state, he says, the state will be replaced "by communist self-government." This will also lead to the withering away of legal relations. "Communist consciousness and public opinion will be the only factors regulating human behaviour."

Chapter 10. The Transcendence of Alienation

1. *EPM*, p. 117.
2. *GI*, p. 71.
3. Marx, *Grundrisse*, p. 196; cf. *EPM*, p. 83.
4. Marx, *Grundrisse*, p. 252.
5. "Civil War in France," in *In One Vol.*, p. 290.
6. Marx, *Capital* 2:846.
7. See *Manifesto*, p. 45, and *Grundrisse*, p. 164.
8. Lenin, *On Religion*, p. 18.
9. "Theses on Feuerbach," in *GI*, no. 1.
10. Cf. Hegel, *Phenomenology*, p. 99, and *Logic*, sec. 119, 172–73. See *GI*, p. 51, and *EPM*, p. 98, 84.
11. Marx, *Grundrisse*, p. 543.
12. Ibid., pp. 541–42.
13. *HF*, p. 67.
14. Hegel, *Logic*, sec. 221, p. 282; cf. *Philosophy of Mind*, sec. 426, pp. 167–68.
15. See Hegel, *Philosophy of Mind*, sec. 425, p. 166.
16. *EPM*, p. 169.
17. Marx, *Capital* 2 (preface to 2nd German ed.).

18. Engels *Dialectics of Nature*, p. 62.
19. Engels, *Anti-Dühring*, p. 35.
20. Ibid., p. 37.
21. Marx, *Capital*, preface to 2nd ed.
22. *GI*, p. 63.
23. *HF*, p. 107.
24. *EPM*, p. 165.
25. Ibid., p. 102.
26. Ibid., p. 111.
27. Hegel, *Phil. of History*, pp. 17, 25.
28. Ibid., p. 25.
29. Ibid., p. 36.
30. *GI*, p. 58.
31. *Crit. of Pol. Econ.*, p. 21.
32. "Condition of England," in *CW* 3:464.
33. Ibid., p. 463.
34. "Outlines of a Critique of Pol. Econ.," in *EPM*, pp. 197–98.
35. Engels, *Dialectics of Nature*, p. 111.
36. See *Capital*, preface to 2nd ed.
37. Cf. *EPM*, pp. 113–14.
38. See *Capital*, preface to 2nd ed.; cf. *EPM*, p. 74.
39. *GI*, pp. 231–32.
40. Cf. *EPM*, p. 114; and *GI*, p. 58.
41. *GI*, p. 561.
42. Plekhanov, *Materialist Conception of History*, p. 48.
43. Engels, *Anti-Dühring*, p. 161.
44. See Engels's letter to Bloch, September 1890.
45. Althusser, *For Marx*, p. 111.
46. Ibid., p. 112.
47. *GI*, p. 61.
48. Ibid., p. 494.
49. "Theses on Feuerbach," in *GI*, no. 11.
50. *EPM*, pp. 164–66.
51. Ibid., 164.
52. Ibid., p. 166.
53. Hegel, *Logic*, sec. 96, p. 142.
54. See esp. chap. 4, pp. 7–12 and chap. 5, pp. 18–20.
55. John 12:24.
56. Hegel, *Logic*, sec. 88, p. 133, and sec. 89, p. 134.
57. Engels, *Anti-Dühring*, p. 163.
58. Cf. St. Paul I Cor. 15:20–54.
59. Hegel, *Philosophy of History*, p. 17.
60. Hegel, *Logic*, sec. 81, p. 116.
61. *EPM*, p. 168.
62. Ibid., p. 158.
63. Ibid., p. 156.
64. German (See *The Theory that Transforms the World*, p. 101) dreams of a communist future in which even dialectical laws will qualitatively change in such a way that they will perpetuate rather than negate communist development. Endowing these laws with miraculous powers, he says that "communist being will inevitably bring forth such laws of its functioning which are unknown to the past history of mankind." This modern Soviet view is barely possible to reconcile with Marx's assertion that "communism as such" is not and cannot be "the goal of human development."
65. Cf. Kolakowski, *Toward a Marxist Humanism*, p. 186; and *Main Currents of Marxism*, 1:218–220, 223–24.
66. *Capital*, preface to 2nd ed.
67. See *EPM*, pp. 155, 161, 168.
68. *GI*, p. 68.
69. Ibid., p. 83.

70. *HF*, p. 103.
71. Ibid.
72. *Crit. of Pol. Econ.*, p. 21.
73. *EPM*, p. 166.
74. Ibid.
75. Ibid., p. 149.
76. Ibid., p. 169.
77. Cf. Feuerbach, *Essence of Christianity*, p. 48; and *GI*, p. 46.
78. *EPM*, p. 151.
79. Hegel, *Phenomenology*, sec. 256, p. 156.
80. *Capital*, preface to 1st ed.
81. *EPM*, p. 94.
82. *Crit. of Pol. Econ.*, pp. 21, 220.
83. *GI*, p. 87.
84. Cf. *Crit. of Pol. Econ.*, preface.
85. *GI*, p. 54.
86. Marx, *Capital* 1:269.
87. *EPM*, p. 79.
88. *Ibid.*, p. 72.
89. "Theses on Feuerbach," nos. 8 and 2, in *GI*.
90. Hegel, *Philosophy of Right*, p. 227.
91. Ibid.
92. Ibid., p. 226.
93. See "Theses on Feuerbach," no. 3, in *GI*.
94. *GI*, p. 44.
95. Ibid., p. 61.
96. See "Theses on Feuerbach," no. 1, in *GI*.
97. *EPM*, p. 98.
98. Ibid., p. 102.
99. Ibid., p. 103; cf. p. 107.
100. *GI*, pp. 89–90.
101. Ibid., p. 89.
102. *Manifesto*, p. 41; cf. p. 91.
103. *EPM*, pp. 125–26.
104. Ibid., p. 124.
105. Ibid., pp. 123–24.
106. See *EPM*, pp. 115–19.
107. *GI*, pp. 221–42, 484–97.
108. Ibid., pp. 231–33.
109. Ibid., p. 243.
110. Written in September 1843.
111. See *Rheinische Zeitung*, 16 October 1842.
112. *EPM*, p. 102.
113. Ibid.
114. Ibid., pp. 99, 101.
115. Ibid., pp. 101–2.
116. Ibid., p. 114.
117. Ibid., p. 100.
118. Ibid., p. 99.
119. Ibid.
120. Ibid.
121. Ibid., p. 100.
122. Ibid.
123. Ibid.
124. Ibid., p. 101.
125. Ibid., p. 102.
126. Ibid.
127. *GI*, p. 44.
128. *EPM*, p. 114.

129. Ibid.
130. Ibid., p. 114n.
131. Cf. Stojanović, *Between Ideals and Reality*, p. 22. In *Marx's Theory of Alienation*, p. 160, Mészáros takes the opposite view without giving any evidence in its support. Marxist William Ash, however, states categorically that Marx has never treated "communist society as a final stage of human development," See his *Marxist Morality* (London: Howard Baker Press, 1988), p. 138.
132. *GI*, p. 57.
133. *EPM*, p. 114.
134. See *Manifesto*, p. 62.
135. Cf. Gouldner, *The Two Marxisms*, p. 381 and R. Berki, *Insight and Vision. The Problem of Communism in Marx's Thought*, p. 33.
136. See "Prophecies of True Socialism," in *GI*, p. 566.
137. *EPM*, p. 102.
138. See Hegel, *Philosophy of History*, pp. 8–9.
139. *EPM*, pp. 101–2.
140. Ibid., p. 166.
141. Ibid., pp. 99–100.
142. Ibid., p. 102.
143. *GI*, p. 50.
144. *EPM*, pp. 99–100.
145. Ibid., p. 102.
146. See sec. 1, *Critique of the Gotha Programme*, in *In One Vol.*, pp. 320–21.
147. Ibid., p. 320.
148. Cf. *In One Vol.*, p. 320.
149. Ibid., p. 321.
150. Ibid., p. 325.
151. Ibid., pp. 318–21.
152. As a rule, orthodox Marxists speak of "scientific communism" although Marx has the ideal realm in mind.
153. *EPM*, p. 102.
154. Ibid.
155. Ibid., p. 114.
156. *GI*, p. 57.
157. See Ibid., p. 53, and *EPM*, pp. 102–3.
158. Cf. Plato, *Republic*, bk. 9, p. 295.
159. Cf. Kolakowski, *Towards a Marxist Humanism*, pp. 70–71.
160. Cf. *EPM*, pp. 115, 126; and *Critique of Gotha Programme*, in *In One Vol.*, p. 320.
161. See Marx, *Capital* 1:45–46.
162. *Manifesto*, p. 41.
163. Cf. Garaudy, *The Alternative Future*, pp. 32, 51–53; and Stojanović, *Between Ideals and Reality*, pp. 34–45.
164. Invoking Marx's utopian multi-professionalism, the Soviet Marxist S. German believes that communism is a society of equality in which everyone will have the opportunity to develop all-round, to change his activity freely, and to engage in any profession he likes. See *The Theory that Transforms the World*, p. 61.
165. Cf. Mandel, *From Class Society to Communism*, p. 148.
166. Accepting that "reason and morality do play a very considerable role in human life," the modern Marxist S. German indicates that Marxism "links man's real position in society, not with some imaginary human nature which exists outside history, but, with relations in production, the basis of social relations." See *The Theory that Transforms the World*, pp. 42, 98. This echoes Marx's negative approach to dealienation.

Conclusion

1. Hegel, *Lectures on the Philosophy of Religion*, 3:37.

2. Cf. Feuerbach, *The Essence of Christianity*, pp. 19–20.
3. The present author does not share the view of those who, like Mézáros and Kolakowski, maintain that there is no switch from the youthful humanist to the mature Marx, and that alienation and exploitation are identical processes. See Kolakowski, *Main Currents of Marxism*, 1:172–73.
4. Cf. Gilbert, *Marx's Politics*, p. 110.
5. *EPM*, p. 149.
6. Cf. Ibid., p. 151; and *Grundrisse*, PP. 831–32.
7. *EPM*, p. 153.
8. *GI*, p. 49.
9. *EPM*, p. 155.
10. Ibid., p. 70.
11. Ibid., p. 69.
12. *On the Jewish Question*, in *CW* 3:173.
13. Marx, *Grundrisse*, p. 831.
14. Cf. Hegel, *Logic*, sec. 204, pp. 267–68, and sec. 155, p. 218.
15. *EPM*, p. 80.
16. Cf. Ollman, *Alienation*, p. 160; Kolakowski, *Main Currents of Marxism*, 1:159; and E. Kamenka, *The Ethical Foundations of Marxism* (London, Boston: Routledge & Kegan Paul, 1972), p. 81.
17. Marx, *Capital* 2:713.
18. Marx, *Capital* 1:165.
19. *EPM*, p. 83.
20. Marx, *Grundrisse*, pp. 274–75, 746. See also "Wages, Price and Profit" in *In One Vol.*, pp. 209–13.
21. See Marx, *Grundrisse*, pp. 471–79; and *Capital* 1:377–79.
22. See *Crit. of Pol. Econ.*, p. 21.
23. See Engels's letters to J. Bloch, 21 September 1890, and to F. Mehring, 14 July 1893. The modern Soviet Marxist S. German merely reiterates Engels's position. The spiritual element, he says, is a necessary component of the historical process, but the interaction takes place on the basis of economic development, the root cause of all social changes. See *The Theory that Transforms the World*, p. 45.
24. See *GI*, p. 42.
25. *GI*, p. 280.
26. *EPM*, p. 157. Cf. Berkeley, "Principles of Human Knowledge" and "The Third Dialogue", in *A New Theory of Vision and Other Writings*, pp. 113–15, 266–69, respectively.
27. *GI*, p. 443.
28. Engels, *Anti-Dühring*, p. 114.
29. Ibid.
30. *HF*, p. 249. Cf. Engels, *Anti-Dühring*, p. 115.
31. Tucker maintains that Marx is a moralist rather than a scientist. Marxism, he believes, is essentially an ethical system. See *Philosophy and Myth in Karl Marx*, pp. 12–15.
32. Hegel, *Lectures on the Philosophy of Religion*, 3:366.
33. Cf. Durkheim, *On Morality and Society*, p. 192.
34. For an excellent discussion of this subject, see Galloway, *The Philosophy of Religion*, 404–49. The moral ideal, he believes, is attained in the form of a spiritual good realized in communion with the divine Source of all good (p. 437).
35. In his letters to Gorki, Lenin says that "the idea of God has always been an idea of slavery, the worst inescapable slavery."
36. *GI*, p. 42.
37. Marx, *Capital*, preface to 2nd German ed.
38. See Marx, *Eighteenth Brumaire*, p. 10.
39. Cf. Plekhanov, *Development of Monist View of History*, p. 220; and Lenin, *Materialism and Empirio-Criticism*, pp. 288–90.
40. *HF*, p. 50.
41. *EPM*, p. 145.
42. *Intro. Crit. of Hegel's Phil.*, 3:176.
43. Althusser, *Lenin and Philosophy*, p. 105.

44. Lenin, *Materialism and Empirio-Criticism*, pp. 138–39.
45. *GI*, p. 44.
46. Lenin, *Materialism and Empirio-Criticism*, p. 94.
47. Hegel, *Logic*, p. 18.
48. Ibid., p. 8; sec. 142, p. 200.
49. See Althusser, foreword to *Lenin and Philosophy*; cf. *For Marx*, pp. 13, 26–29.
50. The idea that "bourgeois and liberal science" defend "wage slavery" is prominent in Lenin's writings. See his *Three Sources and Three Component Parts of Marxism*, p. 7.
51. See *EPM*, pp. 110–11.
52. Ibid., pp. 111–12.
53. *HF*, p. 46.
54. Marx, *Capital* 2:713.
55. *EPM*, pp. 76–77.
56. Ibid., p. 125.
57. *On the Jewish Question*, in *CW* 3:154.
58. *PP*, p. 161.
59. See Stojanović, *Between Ideals and Reality*, p. 208.
60. *GI*, pp. 89–90.
61. See *On the Jewish Question*, in *CW* 3:162–63, 167.
62. See *Manifesto*, p. 44. In "Civil War in France," Marx refers to this state as "the national war engine of capital against labour." In the introduction to this work Engels likens it to "a machine for class oppression." See *In One Vol.*, pp. 286, 258, respectively.
63. See Hegel, *Philosophy of Right*, sec. 261, p. 161; cf. Marx, *Crit. of Hegel's Phil.*, pp. 5–8.
64. Hegel, *Philosophy of Right*, sec. 258, p. 156.
65. Marx, *Crit. of Hegel's Phil.*, in *CW*, p. 30.
66. Engels, *Anti-Dühring*, p. 333.
67. *PP*, p. 161.
68. Marx, *Critique of the Gotha Programme*, in *In One Vol.*, I.
69. This pattern of Marxist behavior has become common in all communist states.

Select Bibliography

The Works of Karl Marx and Frederick Engels

Marx, Karl. *Capital*, Vol. 1 and Vol. 2. London: Everyman's Library, 1951.

———. *Capital*, Vol. 3. London: Lawrence & Wishart, 1984.

———. *The Class Struggle in France 1848 to 1850*. Moscow: Progress Publishers, 1979.

———. *A Contribution to the Critique of Political Economy*. Moscow: Progress Publishers, 1981.

———. *Economic and Philosophic Manuscripts of 1844*. Moscow: Foreign Languages Publishing House, 1961.

———. *The Eighteenth Brumaire of Louis Bonaparte*. Moscow: Progress Publishers, 1977.

———. *Grundrisse*. Translated with a Foreword by Martin Nicolaus. Harmondsworth and New York: Penguin Books, 1973.

———. *The Poverty of Philosophy*. Containing Marx's letter to P. V. Annenkov. Moscow, Progress Publishers, 1976.

Engels, Frederick. *Anti-Duhring*. Moscow: Progress Publishers, 1975.

———. *Dialectics of Nature*. Moscow: Progress Publishers, 1976.

———. *The Origin of the Family*, *Private property and the State*. London: Lawrence & Wishart, 1981.

———. "Outlines of a Critique of Political Economy." In *Economic and Philosophic Manuscripts of 1844*. Moscow: 1961.

———. *Socialism: Utopian and Scientific*. Moscow: Progress Publisher, 1978.

Marx, Karl, and Engels, Frederick. *Collected Works*. Vol. 3. Moscow: Progress Publishers, 1975. Among others, this volume contains the following works: *Marx's Contribution to the Critique of Hegel's Philosophy of Right*. Letters from the *Deutsch-Französische Jahrbücher*. On the Jewish Question. Introduction to the Critique of Hegel's Philosophy of Right. Critical Marginal Notes on the Article 'The King of Prussia and Social Reform by a Prussian'. *Marx's Comments on James Mill's Elements of Political Economy*; Marx's letters to L. Feuerbach. A selection of Engels's letters and essays.

———. *The German Ideology*, Moscow: Progress Publishers, 1976. Among others, this volume contains: Marx "Critique of German Socialism." "Theses on Feuerbach." Engels, "The True Socialists."

———. *The Holy Family*. Moscow: Progress Publishers, 1980.

———. *On Religion*. Moscow: Progress Publishers, 1975.

———. *Manifesto of the Communist Party*. Moscow: Progress Publishers, 1977.

———. *Neue Rheinische Zeitung* 1848–49. Moscow: Progress Publishers, 1972.

———. *Selected Works in One Volume*. Moscow: Progress Publishers, 1980. Among others, this volume contains: Marx, "Wages, Price and Profit." Marx, "The Civil War in France." Engels, "Ludwig Feuerbach and the End of Classical German Philosophy." Engels, "Karl Marx." Marx and Engels's letters, including Marx's letter to J. Weydemeyer, L. Kugelmann, and F. Bolte. Marx, *Critique of the Gotha Programme*. Marx, "Wage Labour and Capital."

The Works of G. W. F. Hegel

Hegel, G. W. F. *Lectures on the Philosophy of Religion*. Vol. 3. Translated by E. B. Speirs and J. B. Sanderson. London: Kegan Paul, Trench, Trübner, 1985.

——. *The Phenomenology of Spirit*. Translated by A. V. Miller and Foreword by J. N. Findlay. Oxford and New York: Oxford University Press, 1979.

——. *Hegel's Logic*. Part 1. *Encyclopaedia of the Philosophical Sciences* (1830). Translated by W. Wallace and Foreword by J. N. Findlay. Oxford: Clarendon Press, 1985.

——. *The Philosophy of History*. Translated by J. Sibree. New York: Dover Publications, 1956.

——. *The Philosophy of Right*. Translated with notes by T. M. Knox. Oxford and New York: Oxford and New York: Oxford University Press, 1967.

——. *On Christianity*. Early theological writings by F. Hegel. Translated by T. M. Knox with an Introduction, and fragments by Richard Kroner. Gloucester, Mass.: Peter Smith, 1970.

——. *The Philosophy of Mind*. Part 3. *Encyclopaedia of the Philosophical Sciences* (1830). Translated by W. Wallace. Oxford: Clarendon, Press, 1985.

Other Works

Althusser, L. *For Marx*. Translated by B. Brewster. London: Verso, 1986.

——. *Lenin and Philosophy and other Essays*. London: NLB, 1971.

Appleton, E. *Science and Nation*. Edinburgh: Edinburgh University Press, 1957.

Aristotle. *The Nicomachean Ethics*. London: Everyman's Library, 1949.

——. *Politics*. London: Everyman's Library, 1952.

Axelos, K. *Alienation, Praxis and Techne in the Thought of Karl Marx*. Translated by R. Bruzina. Austin and London: University of Texas Press, 1976.

Ayer, A. J. *The Problem of Knowledge*. Harmondsworth: Penguin Books, 1956.

Bell, D. *The End of Ideology*. New York: The Free Press, 1965.

Berdyaev, N. *The Beginning and the End*. Translated from the Russian by R. M. French. London: Geoffrey Bles, 1952.

Berkeley, G. *A New Theory of Vision and Other Writings*. London: Everyman's Library, 1950.

Berki, R. N. *Insight and Vision. The Problem of Communism in Marx's Thought*. London: Dent & Sons, 1983.

Bernal, J. D. *The Social Function of Science*. London: G. Routledger & Son, 1939.

Birne, A. *An Economic History of the British Isles*. London: Methuen & Co., 1950.

Bloch, M. ed. *Marxist Analysis and Social Anthropology*. London: Tavistock Publications, 1984.

Bronowski, J. *Science and Human Values*. Harmondsworth: Penguin Books, 1964.

Churchich, N. *The Ethics of Reason in the Philosophical System of D. Obradovich*. London: Unwin Bros., 1976.

Cohen, R. S., and Wartofsky M. W., eds. *Methodology, Metaphysics and the History of Science*. Boston: Reidel Publishing Co., 1984.

Comte, A. *The Positive Philosophy*. 2 Vols. Translated by H. Martineau. London: George Bell & Sons, 1896.

Croce, B. *Historical Materialism and the Economic of Karl Marx*. Translated by C. M. Meredith. London: Frank Cass & Co., 1966.

Dante, A. *The Divine Comedy*. 3 Vols. Translated by D. L. Sayers. Harmondsworth: Penguin Books, 1959, 1960, 1962, respectively.

——. *Monarchy and Three Political Letters*. Introduction by D. Nicholl. London: Weidenfeld & Nicolson, 1954.

Descartes, R. *A Discourse on Method*. Translated by J. Veitch. London: Everyman's Library, 1953.

Djilas, M. *The Uperfect Society*. London: Methuen & Co., 1969.

Durkheim, É. *Durkheim On Religion*. Edited by W. S. F. Pickering. London: Routledge & Kegan Paul, 1975.

————. *On Morality and Society. Selected Writings*. Edited by Robert N. Bellah. Chicago and London: University of Chicago Press, 1973.

Elster, J. *Making Sense of Marx*. Cambridge & New York: Cambridge University Press, 1985.

Ewing, A. C. *The Fundamental Questions of Philosophy*. London: Routledge & Kegan Paul, 1958.

Feuerbach, L. *The Essence of Christianity*. Translated by George Eliot. New York and London: Harper & Row, 1957.

Fisher, H. A. L. *A History of Europe*. London: Arnold, 1949.

Freud, S. *Civilization, Society and Religion*. Harmondsworth: Penguin Books, 1985.

Fromm E. *The Art of Loving*. London & Boston: Unwin Paperbacks, 1985.

————. *The Anatomy of Human Destructiveness*. Harmonds worth: Penguin Books, 1984.

————. *The Sane Society*. London: Routledge & Kegan Paul, 1979.

Galloway, G. *The Philosophy of Religion*. Edinburgh: T. & T. Clark, 1948.

Garaudy, R. *The Alternative Future. A Vision of Christian Marxism*. Translated by L. Mayhew. New York: Simon & Schuster, 1974.

George, W. H. *The Scientist in Action*. London: Williams & Norgate, 1936.

German, S. *The Theory that Transforms the World*. Moscow: Novosti Publishing House, 1985.

Gilbert, A. *Marx's Politics*. New Brunswick: Rutgers University Press, 1981.

Gouldner, A. W. *The Two Marxism. Contradictions and Anomalies in the Development of Theory*. London: MacMillan Press, 1980.

Graham, L. R. *Between Science and Values*. New York: Columbia University Press, 1981.

Hamley, E. B. *Voltaire*. Edinburgh and London: William Blackwood & Sons, 1877.

Hardy, A. *The Biology of God*. London: Jonathan Cape, 1975.

Hobbes, T. *Leveiathan*. 1651 reprint. Oxford: Oxford University Press, 1952.

Hoffman, J. *Marxism and the Theory of Praxis*. London: Lawrence & Wishart, 1975.

Holbach, P. H. D. *The System of Nature or the Laws of the Moral and Physical World*. Translated from the French by S. Wilkinson. London: R. Carlile, 1834.

Holton, G., and Roller, D. H. D. *Foundations of Modern Physical Science*. Reading, Mass.: Addison-Wesley Publishers, 1965.

Hook, S. *From Hegel to Marx*. New York: Humanities Press, 1950.

————. *Towards the Understanding of Karl Marx*. London: V. Gollanz, 1933.

Hume, D. *Treatise of Human Nature*. 2 Vols. London: Everyman's Library, 1951–1952.

Hunt, R. N. *The Political Ideas of Marx and Engels. Vol. 1: Marxism and Totalitarian Democracy 1818–1850; Vol. 2.: Classical Marxism 1850–1895*. London: MacMillan Press, 1975, 1984.

Jung, C. G. *The Structure and Dynamics of the Psyche*. Translated by R. F. C. Hull. London: Routledge & Kegan, 1960.

Kant, I. *Critique of Pure Reason*. Translated by J. M. D. Meiklejohn. London: Everyman's Library, 1934.

Kierkegaard, S. *Purity of Heart*. New York: Harper & Brothers, 1961.

Kneen, P. *Soviet Scientists and the State*. London: MacMillan Press, 1984.

Kolakowski, L. *Main Currents of Marxism. Its Origins, Growth and Dissolution*. 3 Vols. Oxford: Oxford University Press, 1978.

————. *Toward a Marxist Humanism: Essays on the Left Today*. New York: Grove Press, 1968.

Korsch, K. *Marxism and Philosophy*. Translated by F. Halliday. London: NLB, 1970.

La Mettrie, J. J. *Man a Machine*. Translated from the French *L'Homme Machine*. Dublin: 1749.

Larrain, J. *Marxism and Ideology*. London: MacMillan, 1983.

Lefebvre, H. *Dialectical Materialism*. Translated from the French by J. Sturrock. London: Jonathan Cape, 1969.

Leibniz G. W. *Philosophical Writings*. London, Everyman's Library, 1956.

Lenin, V. I. *Marx, Engels, Marxism*. Moscow: Progress Publishers, 1977.

———. *Materialism and Empirio-Criticism*. Moscow: Progress Publishers, 1977.

———. *On Religion*. Moscow: Progress Publishers, 1978.

———. *The State and Revolution*. Moscow: Progress Publishers, 1977.

———. *The Three Sources and Three Components of Marxism*. Moscow: Progress Publishers, 1976.

Lichtheim, G. *The Origins of Socialism*. London: Weidenfeld and Nicolson, 1969.

Lindsay, J. *The Crisis in Marxism*. Bradford-on-Avon: Moonraker Press, 1981.

Locke, J. *An Essay Concerning Human Understanding*. London: Everyman's Library, 1948.

———. *Two Treatises of Civil Government*. London: Everyman's Library, 1953.

Lukács, G. *History and Class Consciousness*. London: Merlin Press, 1971.

McLellan, D. *The Thought of Karl Marx. An Introduction*. London: MacMillan Press, 1971.

McMurtry, J. M. *The Structure of Marx's World-View*. Princeton: Princeton University Press, 1978.

Makai, Mária. *The Dialectics of Moral Consciousness. A Contribution to the Theory of Marxist General Ethics*. Budapest: Akadémiai Kiadó, 1972.

Malthus, T. R. *An Essay on Population*. London: Everyman's Library, 1952.

Mandel, E. *From Class Society to Communism*. Translated by Louisa Sadler. London: Ink Links, 1977.

Marcuse, H. *One-Dimensional Man*. London: Ark Paperbacks, 1964.

Meikle, S. *Essentialism in the Thought of Karl Marx*. London: Duckworth, 1985.

Mészáros, I. *Marx's Theory of Alienation*. London: Merlin Press, 1982.

Mitcham, C., and Mackey, R., eds. *Philosophy and Technology*. New York: Free Press, 1972.

Norris, R. B. *God, Marx and the Future. Dialogue with Roger Garaudy*. Philadelphia: Fortress Press, 1974.

Ollman, B. *Alienation*. Cambridge: Cambridge University Press, 1976.

Plamenatz, J. *German Marxism and Russian Communism*. London: Longman's, Green & Co., 1956.

———. *Karl Marx's Philosophy of Man*. Oxford : Oxford University Press, 1975.

Plato. *The Republic*. London: Everyman's Library, 1948.

Pledge, H. T. *Science Since 1500*. London: H. M. Stationery Office, 1966.

Plekhanov, G. *The Development of the Monist View of History*. Moscow: Progress Publishers, 1972.

———. *The Materialist Conception of History*. New York: International Publishers, 1940.

Polanyi, M. *Personal Knowledge*. London & Henley: Routledge & K. Paul, 1978.

Popper, K. R. *Conjectures and Refutations: The Growth of Scientific Knowledge*. London: Routledge & Kegan Paul, 1963.

———. *The Open Society and its Enemies*. 2 Vols. London: Routledge & Kegan Paul, 1957.

Rhodes, F. H. T. *The Evolution of Life*. Harmondsworth: Penguin Books, 1965.

Roberts, P. C., and Stephenson, M. A. *Marx's Theory of Exchange, Alienation and Crisis*. Stanford: Hoover Institution Press, 1973.

Rose, G. *Hegel contra Sociology*. London: Athlone Press, 1981.

Rose, S. *The Chemistry of Life*. Harmondsworth: Penguin Books, 1966.

Rousseau, J. J. *Émile*. Translated by B. Foxley. London: Everyman's Library, 1961.

———. *The Social Contract*. An 18th-century translation with an introduction by C. Frankel. New York: Hafner Publishing Co., 1947.

Russell, B. *History of Western Philosophy*. London: Allen & Unwin, 1954.

———. *Religion and Science*. Oxford: Oxford University Press, 1974.

Sabine, G. H. *A History of Political Theory*. London: Harrap & Co., 1954.

St. Augustine. *Confessions*. Harmondsworth: Penguin Books, 1961.

St. Thomas Aquinas. *Selected Writings*. Edited by M. C. D'Arcy. London: Everyman's Library, 1964.

Sartre, J. P. *Being and Nothingness*. Translated by H. E. Barnes. London: Methuen & Co., 1984.

———. *The Communists and Peace*. Translated by Irene Clephane. London: Hamish Hamilton, 1969.

———. *Existentialism and Human Emotions*. New York: Castle, n.d.

Seth, J. *A Study of Ethical Principles*. Edinburgh and London: William Blackwood & Sons, 1905.

Smith, A. *The Wealth of Nations*. 2 Vols. London: Everyman's Library, 1950.

Smith, J. M. *The Theory of Evolution*. Harmondsworth: Penguin Books, 1966.

Spencer, H. *The Man versus the State*. Edited and introduced by D. MacRae. Harmondsworth: Penguin Books, 1969.

———. *The Principles of Sociology*. Vol. 2 New York: Appleton & Co., 1898.

Spinoza, B. *Ethics*. Translated by A. Boyle. London: Everyman's Library, 1948.

Sterrett, J. M. *Studies in Hegel's Philosophy of Religion*. London: Swan Sonnenschein & Co., 1891.

Stojanović, S. *Between Ideals and Reality*. Translated by G. S. Sher. New York: Oxford University Press, 1973.

Torrance, J. *Estrangement, Alienation and Exploitation*. London: MacMillan Press, 1977.

Tucker, R. C. *The Marxian Revolutionary Idea*. London: Allen & Unwin, 1970.

———. *Philosophy and Myth in Karl Marx*. Cambridge: Cambridge University Press, 1972.

Turner, D. *Marxism and Christianity*. Oxford: Basil Blackwell, 1983.

Waterhouse, E. S. *The Philosophical Approach to Religion*. London: Epworth Press, 1947.

Weber, M. *Selections in Translation*. Edited by W. G. Runciman and translated by E. Matthews. Cambridge: Cambridge University Press, 1978.

Weiner, R. R. *Cultural Marxism and Political Sociology*. London: Sage Publications, 1981.

Young, J. Z. *A Model of the Brain*. Oxford: Oxford University Press, 1964.

Index

361